Willie, Willie, Harry, Stee,
Harry, Dick, John, Harry three;
One-two-three Neds, Richard two,
Henrys four, five, six – then who?
Edwards four-five, Dick the bad,
Harrys twain and Ned the lad,
Mary, Bessie, James the vain,
Charlie, Charlie, James again,
William & Mary, Anna Gloria,
Four Georges, William and Victoria,
Edward, George, then Ned the eighth
quickly goes and abdicat'th,
leaving George six, then Lizzie two,
with Charlie next to see us through...
That's the way our monarchs lie
since Harold got it in the eye!
PS. Sorry, Lady Jane Grey –
you got the chop!

WILLIE, WILLIE, HARRY, STEE

ALSO BY CHARLIE HIGSON

Novels for adults
King of the Ants
Happy Now
Full Whack
Getting Rid of Mister Kitchen
Whatever Gets You Through the Night
On His Majesty's Secret Service

Young Bond novels
SilverFin
Blood Fever
Double or Die
Hurricane Gold
By Royal Command

The Enemy YA series
The Enemy
The Dead
The Fear
The Sacrifice
The Fallen
The Hunted
The End

Books for younger readers
Monstroso
Freddie and the Pig
The Gates of Death
Worst. Holiday. Ever.
Worst. Superhero. Ever.
What's That Noise?

WILLIE, WILLIE, HARRY, STEE

An Epically Short History of Our Kings and Queens

CHARLIE HIGSON

WITH ILLUSTRATIONS BY
JIM MOIR

MUDLARK

Mudlark
HarperCollins*Publishers*
1 London Bridge Street
London SE1 9GF

www.harpercollins.co.uk

HarperCollins*Publishers*
Macken House, 39/40 Mayor Street Upper
Dublin 1, D01 C9W8, Ireland

First published by Mudlark 2025

3 5 7 9 10 8 6 4 2

Text © Charlie Higson 2025
Illustrations © Jim Moir 2025
Family trees and map by Liane Payne © HarperCollins*Publishers*

Charlie Higson asserts the moral right to
be identified as the author of this work

A catalogue record of this book is
available from the British Library

HB ISBN 978-0-00-874105-1
PB ISBN 978-0-00-874106-8

Printed and bound in the UK using 100%
renewable electricity at CPI Group (UK) Ltd

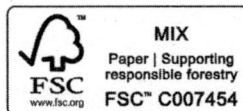

MIX
Paper | Supporting
responsible forestry
FSC
www.fsc.org
FSC™ C007454

This book contains FSC™ certified paper and other controlled
sources to ensure responsible forest management.

For more information visit: www.harpercollins.co.uk/green

For James Holland – who, by inviting me to do a couple of events at the Chalke History Festival in 2013, and by asking me back every year since, inadvertently fired up my love of history and set me on the path to writing the book that you're now holding in your hands.

And for Mark Jeeves – the excellent producer of my podcast who's had to sit and listen to me bang on about kings and queens for the last two and a half years.

CONTENTS

A NOTE ON THE ILLUSTRATIONS

I always wanted this book to have a distinctive look. I didn't want it to be a dry history text with a few slightly dull reproductions of old paintings, but who could bring it to life? Scratching my head one day, I realised that the perfect man for the job was my old friend, Jim Moir (who many of you will know as Vic Reeves, 'Britain's top light entertainer'). I first met Jim through a friend at university 45 years ago and was knocked out by his unique genius.

He was always very funny and stylish, but it was clear from the start that he was also a very talented artist, and in recent years that side of his work has really come to the fore. I was so pleased when he agreed to illustrate the book for me. It's been a real pleasure to collaborate with Jim again, having worked with him on many comedy shows during the 1990s.

Introduction

Willie, Willie, Harry, Stee,
Harry, Dick, John, Harry three,
One-two-three Neds, Richard two,
Henrys four, five, six – then who?
Edwards four-five, Dick the bad,
Harrys twain and Ned the lad,
Mary, Bessie, James the vain,
Charlie, Charlie, James again,
William & Mary, Anna Gloria,
Four Georges, William and Victoria,
Edward, George, then Ned the eighth
quickly goes and abdicat'th,
leaving George six, then Lizzie two,
with Charlie next to see us through …
That's the way our monarchs lie
since Harold got it in the eye!
P.S. Sorry, Lady Jane Grey – you got the chop!

I learned that rhyme as a small schoolboy in shorts during the 1960s. It's a way of remembering all the monarchs from William the Conqueror to Charles III in order. And I'm probably from the last generation of kids who learned the rhyme and was taught a narrative history of Britain at school.

During lockdown, to keep myself occupied, and to help me go to sleep at night, I relearned the rhyme and then set about trying to find out who all these people were and how they ended up sitting on the throne and wearing a crown. I thought their story would make for a good podcast that would serve as a narrative history of Britain. The podcast has been very popular and this book comes out of making it.

Listeners have thanked me for filling in all the bits they 'missed' at school. Truth is, they were probably never taught them.

Lessons at my prep school (yes, I was a posh little boy who went to a private school) were organised by subject and each teacher had their own room. Mr Jeffries, the geography teacher, had a room in which one whole wall was taken up by a map of the world, most of it coloured pink to represent the British Empire. Even by the 1960s, it was woefully out of date.

Mr Cooper's history room had a timeline running around the walls that told the story of Great Britain, with key dates and brightly painted pictures of important events, battles, great men and women, the birth of steam, the Second World War … You know the sort of thing.

You started at one end as an eight-year-old and worked your way around the room over the years until you were 13. From Stonehenge, you went on to Roman Britain, the Anglo-Saxons, King Alfred the Great, the Battle of Hastings, Agincourt, the Wars of the Roses, Henry VIII, Oliver Cromwell, the Great Fire of London, Bonnie Prince Charlie, Queen Victoria, the First World War … until you arrived at the present day, sometime in the mid-1960s.

It was an old-fashioned, top-down and very Anglo-centric view of history. Ordinary men and women didn't get a look in, but it gave me a solid grasp of when things happened and in what order. I hope that, for you, reading this book is going to be very much like working your way around Mr Cooper's frieze.

This book is unashamedly – indeed, *literally* – 'old school'. I'm going to be looking at the last thousand years of British history through the lens of the monarchy and trying to explain just who Willie, Willie, Harry and Stee were and how we got from them to Charlie Three. I'm neither a monarchist nor a republican – I could be persuaded either way – but I do think it's an amazing story with some extraordinary characters.

When I learned the rhyme at school, Queen Elizabeth was on the throne and who could have predicted that she was going to be our longest-lived and longest-reigning monarch? Because Elizabeth *did* rule for so long, and because she was largely uncontroversial and placid, because she just sailed through it, not ruffling any feathers –

and essentially, well, essentially not doing anything – it's given us a distorted view of the monarchy and created the impression that monarchs always *behaved themselves*, and have always gone about performing their duties in a stately and statesman-like manner. Elizabeth's reign sold us the idea that the royal family are born to serve and all they've ever cared about was the country, the welfare of its people and making sure that there's a smooth transition to the next ruler.

The rhyme 'Willie, Willie, Harry, Stee' also gives the impression that the run of monarchs is a nice, neat, orderly procession. But, actually, if you look at the line that connects King Charles III back to William the Conqueror, it's jagged and tangled, it's broken in places, and it's been hastily knotted back together here and there. Monarchs have occasionally had to be imported from other countries (Scotland, the Netherlands and Germany) in order to keep the whole thing going and they've by no means all behaved themselves. Some of them have been absolute stinkers.

There has been much controversy recently, with certain types bemoaning the behaviour of present-day royals such as Prince Harry, the Duke of Sussex, claiming he's been disgraceful and has undermined the dignity of the monarchy. *Has he no respect? Has he no idea of history? Can the royal family ever recover?*

Ha! Compared to some of the things that members of the royal family have done in the past (particularly younger brothers of kings), Harry's behaviour has been so mild and uncontroversial it's hardly worth mentioning. The history of the monarchy is a story of fratricide, patricide, uxoricide (look it up) and nephewcide (is that a word?), kings have been, variously, kicked off the throne, starved to death, beheaded and despatched with a red-hot poker up the fundament. It's an alarming, violent and often sordid tale, and thus a very interesting and entertaining one.

I have to stress that I'm not a historian, I'm a storyteller. There is no fresh research in this book; I haven't gone back to original sources, I haven't physically trudged up and down the country visiting castles and palaces and the sites of bloody battles. But I've been lucky enough on my podcast to talk to people who *have* done all those things – proper historians – and what I want to do in this book is weave everything I've learned about the British royal family and the history of the last 1,000 years into a grand narrative.

Well, I say British, but using these terms is quite tricky. Do I refer to this as British history? Or English history? Or should it be 'The History of the United Kingdom of Great Britain and Northern Ireland'? That's a bit unwieldy, and also misleading because this is fundamentally a history of England, but – after Queen Elizabeth I, from King James onwards – our monarchs have technically ruled England, Wales, Scotland and (at least part of) Ireland. So we can't refer to them as English monarchs. But this is the story as seen through English eyes – the view from London, if you like – and I'm going to risk upsetting a lot of people by, for the most part, referring to these kings and queens as the English, or the British, monarchs.

But what do we even mean by 'English' anyway? Very little is known about pre-Roman Britain. The British Isles had originally been connected to the rest of mainland Europe by a low-lying, marshy strip of land called Doggerland (no sniggering at the back). Europe at that time was occupied by many different tribes who shared a common group of languages, Celtic, but not necessarily a common culture. When rising sea levels cut Britain off from the rest of Europe, its people became more isolated, although they continued to trade far and wide. The Pretaniki, or Bretaniki, as they were known in the classical world, unfortunately left no written records so we know very little about them. When coins started coming out of Britain, the Romans reckoned the British were advanced enough to be taxed, and the emperor Claudius, mocked by his fellow Romans for his disabilities, decided to show the world how macho he was by invading strategically worthless Britain in AD 43.

The Romans ruled Britain for the next 400 years, by which time the empire was riven by civil wars as rivals sought to become emperor. This internal weakness was exploited by rival groups like the Vandals, the Visigoths and the Huns, who began to encroach on the empire. Rome needed the legions stationed in Britain and withdrew them, leaving the country undefended. England was now wide open and began to be attacked by the Scots (confusingly from Ireland) and the Picts (from Scotland).

Groups of Germanic tribes from northern Europe, principally the Angles, the Saxons and the Jutes, who lived up near Denmark and shared a common culture with the Norse people, now started to arrive in Britain in great numbers. Some were invited over as mercenaries to defend England against the northern 'barbarians', and some came peacefully as settlers in search of fertile land, since nomadic tribes from the east were forcing the Germanic tribes westwards into ever smaller territories. Others came as raiders themselves and took land by force. By the time of King Alfred the Great, 400 years after the Romans had left Britain, England had become an Anglo-Saxon country, with the native British culture surviving mainly in the west – in Cornwall, Wales and Cumbria. As is often the case when a powerful and determined coloniser arrives, Saxon culture had become dominant across the rest of England. But during the 800s, raids by the Vikings were threatening to change all that. Vikings not only attacked, but they also began to settle, to such an extent that they ended up ruling the north of England, with their capital at York, while also having a strong presence in East Anglia.

Alfred used the threat of the pagan Vikings to unite the Saxon peoples with a shared Anglo-Christian culture and language. He was a writer and translator, using his own language, Old English (as it's called now), and he commissioned the writing of the *Anglo-Saxon Chronicle*, which not only collated known history, but acted as a year-by-year journal of current events. Started in around 890, the chronicle only stopped being updated in 1154. It can be a bit patchy, but has been an invaluable research tool for historians ever since.

Under Alfred, the disparate Anglo-Saxon peoples of Britain started to think of themselves for the first time as a single country under a single ruler. Alfred's 'us and them' tactic against the Vikings wasn't entirely successful, however. For the next 150 years, the Saxons and the Vikings vied for overall control of England. In 1013, King Æthelred, doomed to be known ever after as Æthelred the Unready, lost his kingdom to the Vikings and fled to Normandy (an originally Viking – or Norse – settlement in northwest France), the homeland of his wife, Emma. For a while, England was ruled by the Viking King Canute, but his sons lacked both his qualities of leadership and, crucially, sons of their own. Ultimately, Æthelred's eldest surviving son, Edward, was invited back from Normandy to rule England. Edward's mother, Emma, was Norman and he'd spent nearly all of his life in Normandy. He was more Norman than English, but he proved to be a respected, popular and pious king, earning himself the Marvel superhero-style sobriquet – 'The Confessor'. Edward was officially made a revered English saint in 1161, the only one of our monarchs to be so honoured. And, let's face it, that's never going to happen again.

By now, the 'English' were a mixture of British, Roman, German and Norse, and they were about to get a large injection of French, because Edward the Confessor made a terrible mistake, the worst mistake a monarch can make – one that always leads to trouble, unrest and, in most cases, civil war. The saintly Edward died without producing a direct heir and the story of England took an unexpected twist.

Now the throne of England was up for grabs and several contenders were sharpening their swords, getting ready to contest it. The year of 1066 was to become known as The Year of Three Kings.

So, settle down in a comfy chair, or plump up your pillows, or adjust the volume on your headphones, or whatever, and let me tell you the story of what happened next …

SAXON AND NORMAN KINGS

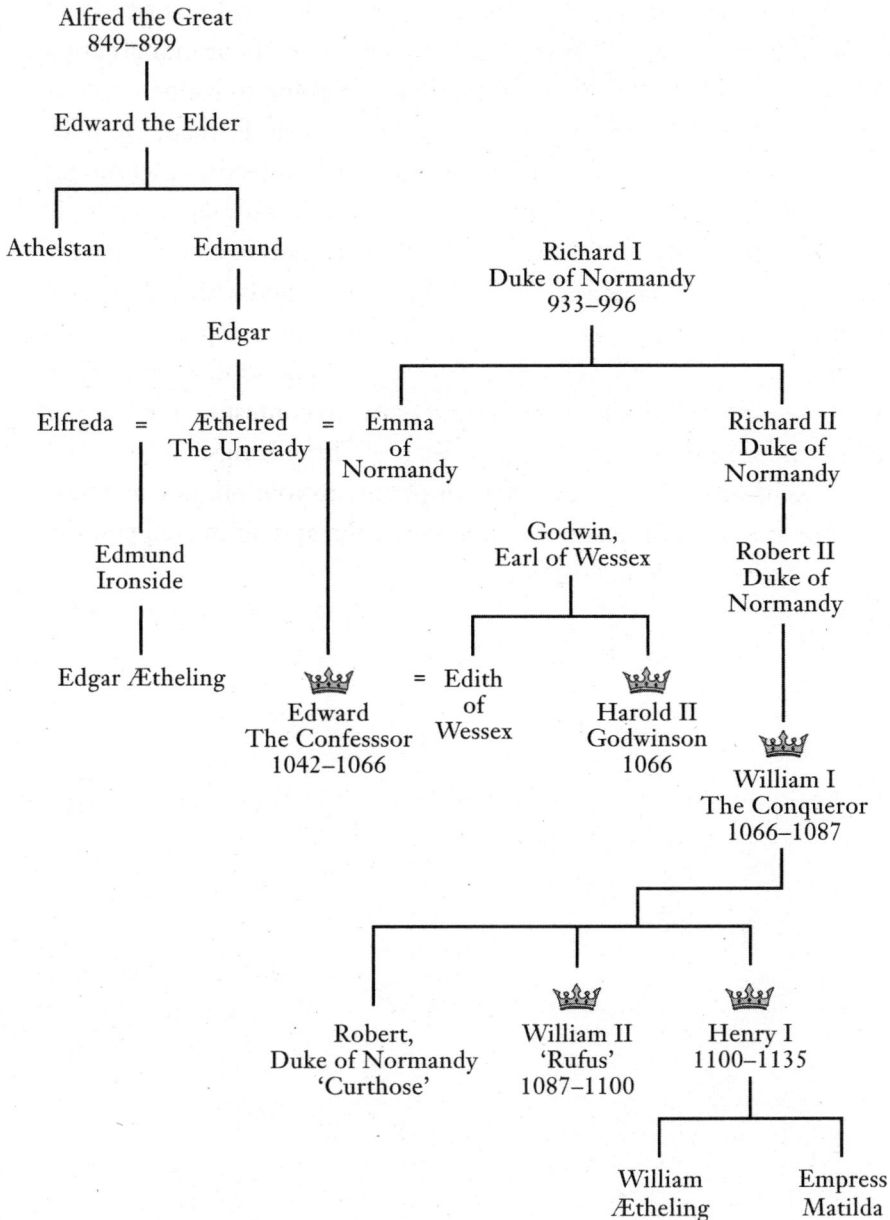

Alfred the Great
849–899

Edward the Elder

Athelstan

Edmund

Edgar

Richard I
Duke of Normandy
933–996

Elfreda = Æthelred = Emma
The Unready   of
              Normandy

Richard II
Duke of
Normandy

Edmund
Ironside

Godwin,
Earl of Wessex

Robert II
Duke of
Normandy

Edgar Ætheling

Edward
The Confesssor
1042–1066

= Edith
  of
  Wessex

Harold II
Godwinson
1066

William I
The Conqueror
1066–1087

Robert,
Duke of Normandy
'Curthose'

William II
'Rufus'
1087–1100

Henry I
1100–1135

William
Ætheling

Empress
Matilda

1
WILLIE

WILLIAM I – *c*.1028–1087
William the Conqueror/William the Bastard/Duke of Normandy
Reigned 1066–1087
Lived for 59 years. Ruled for 21 years.
Died of an exploding stomach.
Remembered for: conquering England.

William was known in his time as William the Bastard because, well, he was illegitimate. And he was a bit of a bastard.*

He was a hard man. The *Anglo-Saxon Chronicle* even describes him as that, but it's not necessarily meant to be a slight. You had to be hard to take control and keep it. All the successful Norman rulers were hard, but William was the hardest. He was a soldier through and through, happiest when he was in the saddle campaigning. He'd grown up fighting, came to prominence by invading England in his late thirties and carried on fighting until he died.

Despite his achievements, not a great deal was recorded first-hand about William the man. All we really know is that he had a harsh, guttural voice, was powerfully built and became a bit of a lump in later life. There were no accurate portraits made of him. His crudely stitched face on the Bayeux Tapestry is the closest we can get to a likeness. We can't even try to reconstruct him from his bones. His grave was ransacked by French protestants in the 16th century and finally destroyed in the French Revolution as the new regime tried to obliterate all traces of their despised monarchy. All that's left of William is his thigh bone – his femur – from which we can deduce that he was about five foot seven tall.

* I know I'm not supposed to use bastard as a pejorative term these days, but, come on …

Even the details and dates of his early life are vague. He was born sometime around 1028 in Normandy where his father, Duke Robert, was the ruler. Robert never married William's mother, a commoner called Herleva, but he still appointed their son as his successor.

Duke Robert died when William was still a child, which meant that Normandy descended into chaos as rival lords fought for dominance. Some saw the young William as vulnerable and easily got rid of, believing he had no firm hold on the dukedom, particularly as he was illegitimate.

Others fought to claim William as their own so that they could rule with him as a puppet. He spent his early years being passed from stronghold to stronghold and often having to hide from his enemies. If we think of this as a game of chess, William was something of a pawn in these power struggles, but if he could stay alive and not be captured, he would reach the other end of the board and end up as king.

As he got older, he grew into a tough soldier. He had no choice. It was fight or die. Not only was he battling to keep control of his dukedom and stop local rivals from usurping him, but he also had to contend with the rulers of the surrounding territories, who had eyes on the prize of Normandy. Early on, William found an ally in the king of France, Henry I, but when the young duke started to beat his enemies, Henry worried that he was getting too powerful and turned against him. But William no longer needed Henry. By 1063, he was in complete control of Normandy and nobody dared confront him. You'd think he might want to settle down, put his feet up and have some peace and quiet, but when his cousin, Edward the Confessor, died childless over in England, William saw the opportunity for a massive land grab. He now claimed that Edward the Confessor had promised him the throne in 1051, while he was exiled in Normandy.

There were three other claimants to the English throne. The only surviving member of the Saxon royal family (the House of Wessex) was Edward the Confessor's great nephew, Edgar Ætheling (Ætheling being an old Anglo-Saxon word for a princeling). The Saxon ruling council, the Witan, rejected Edgar as Edward's successor, as he was only about 14 at the time, commanded little respect and was way too young to lead an army. With William making warlike noises across the

Channel, England needed a strongman in charge. The strongest man in England was Harold Godwinson, Edward's brother-in-law.

Harold's father, Godwin, a wealthy and powerful bully boy, had forced King Edward to marry his daughter, Edith, thus uniting the two families. When Edward died, Harold was at his bedside and claimed that the king had whispered into his ear that he wanted Harold to succeed him. And if anyone had a problem with that, they could take it up with Harold's personal army – the biggest in England.

Harold was a popular choice with the people of England. Unfortunately, his brother, Tostig, was also a hard man and, having fallen out with Harold, he thought he might have a go at taking at least a chunk of England for himself. So he dashed off to Norway to suggest a scheme to King Harald Hardrada – the hardest of them all (the nickname, Hardrada, basically means 'Hard Nut').

The treacherous Tostig made Hard-Nut an offer: bring an army to England, defeat Harold and we'll split the country in two. Tostig could rule in the north and Hardrada could rule in the south. Harald Hard-Nut had some initial doubts about the scheme, but he was an adventurer and thought, what the hell, he might as well try to restore Viking rule to England.

In Normandy, William pushed his claim further, saying that while a guest at his court, Harold had sworn over some holy relics that he accepted William's claim to the English throne. Harold said that he'd been tricked and didn't know that there were holy relics hidden under a table and, anyway, it never happened in the first place.

It was a mess. The idea that the bona fide English king, Harold, was usurped by William is not really the whole truth. When it came down to it, Harold (who was half-Viking, via his mother) had no more right to the throne than William. It has to be said that of the four contenders, Edgar Ætheling was the one with the strongest claim and Harold's was possibly the weakest. His only connection to the royal family was that his sister had married Edward. But, hold on a minute. What am I saying? Does a monarch have every right to rule as long as they're born into it? Is that really the best way to decide who's going to govern a country? 'Oh, my dad was king, therefore I'm going to succeed him, even though I'm a halfwit. Get used to it.'

Nobody had a 100 per cent solid claim to the throne, so it was going to come down to whoever fought hardest for it. Even in the 11th century, however, there were rules. You couldn't just go around invading Christian countries and replacing Christian kings willy-nilly. William was cunning, though. Of all the contenders for the English throne, he was the only one who thought to go to the pope and get his blessing. The pope's support meant being accepted by the whole of Christendom. The last thing William wanted was for every other country in Europe to turn on him if he was successful in taking the throne.

Putting together an army and an invasion fleet costs a colossal amount of money, however. So William turned to his right-hand man – his half-brother, Odo, the wealthy and powerful Bishop of Bayeux. Back then, bishops were like the chess pieces; they fought alongside the knights and kings. Odo saw the chance of becoming even more wealthy and powerful, so, like a present-day capitalist investor, he helped finance the building of William's fleet.

The conditions for crossing the channel were terrible, however. It's a fairly narrow stretch of water, but it can be hard going. You're reliant on the winds being in the right direction, and if there are storms, it's too risky to set sail.

Harold had time to put together his own army and settled in to wait for William to arrive, but, as the days turned into weeks, it seemed as if he wasn't going to come. Then Harold heard that his brother, Tostig, gambling that Harold wouldn't abandon the south, had landed in the northeast with a Viking army led by Harald Hard-Nut. They defeated the local earls, Morcar and Edwin, at the Battle of Fulford and marched to York, declaring themselves kings of the north.

But Harold marched his army towards York, covering some 185 miles in only four days. He took Tostig and Harald Hard-Nut completely by surprise and, at the Battle of Stamford Bridge, destroyed their army and killed them both.

At which point the weather in the Channel improved and William finally set sail.

If Harold hadn't had to take his army north to deal with Tostig and Harald Hard-Nut, things would have gone very differently for

William. He would have had a much tougher time landing his men and horses with Harold's army harrying him from the shoreline and the cliffs. As it was, William's army was ashore and ready to fight by the time Harold's exhausted and depleted army arrived near Hastings at a place called Battle. I mean, what are the chances of that? OK, yeah. It was only renamed Battle afterwards. Obviously.

Harold had the higher ground and fortified his position with a shield wall – ranks of warriors lined up behind overlapping shields. The Normans' preferred style of fighting was to rely on heavy cavalry charges, and the shield wall, bristling with spears, was extremely difficult for a cavalry charge to break.

Even though the Saxons weren't used to fighting against mounted knights in chainmail, they held on to the upper ground for most of the day. It was a terrible slog, bloody and merciless, and it could have gone either way. In the end, to break the stalemate, William moved his archers forward and they shot arrows onto the heads of the Saxons behind their shield wall, until they were so worn down and reduced in numbers that William could go in for the kill. A series of cavalry charges at last broke through and the Normans set about slaughtering the Saxons.

William instructed a gang of his best knights to go after Harold. If the king was removed from the battlefield, it would be the end of the fighting. People used to believe that Harold was killed by an arrow in the eye. There's a figure in the Bayeux Tapestry clutching at an arrow embedded in his face, but it's ambiguous whether this figure is supposed to be Harold. Plus, the tapestry has been altered over the years; originally, this Saxon warrior was throwing a spear, not pulling an arrow from his eye. So it may be that this was retrospectively changed to fit the myth that Harold had been killed by an arrow, rather than the more sordid reality that he'd been butchered by a hit squad.

William's men cut Harold down, stripped him naked, hacked at his body and castrated him. William was furious when he found out what they'd done. While he'd sent these men to kill his rival, he hadn't meant them to humiliate and mutilate Harold in this way. He wanted to look like a legitimate, Christian ruler come to take his rightful place on the throne, not a murderous thug.

Legend says that Harold's body could only be identified by his wife,* Edith Swan Neck, who searched the battlefield until she found his remains. You can imagine the ghastly scene when a soldier holds up Harold's wedding tackle and asks, 'Do you recognise your husband, ma'am?'

Immediately after the winning the battle, William secured Dover, Canterbury and Winchester and then marched to London, where, on Christmas Day 1066, he became the third king to rule in the Year of Three Kings. In a final irony for the English, the ceremony was held in the just-finished Westminster Abbey, which was all Edward the Confessor's work and had been intended to be his greatest glory. But he died before it was completed, so the first monarch to be crowned there was the foreign upstart, William the Bastard. The Saxon line of monarchs was terminated and a new royal line was founded, which is why our rhyme starts with 'Willie'. Every other monarch in this book was crowned in Westminster Abbey, apart from Edward V, Lady Jane Grey and Edward VIII, who never had coronations.

Edward the Confessor had set up a royal palace next to the cathedral, well outside the walls of the crowded City of London, where the great church of Saint Paul's was located – the East Minster. The new abbey therefore became the West Minster and gave its name to the area. The royal Palace of Westminster was eventually to become the seat of the English parliament.

William demanded all the important Saxon lords attend the ceremony and, to make sure there wasn't any trouble, he surrounded the abbey with Norman soldiers. He needed his coronation to be legitimised and ordered the Saxons to swear loyalty to him. As he was anointed with holy oil, they all dutifully yelled their support, but when the soldiers outside heard all the noise, they mistook it for a riot and went on the rampage, looting, setting fire to nearby houses and attacking the locals. The ceremony carried on inside, surrounded by noise and chaos, with William on his throne, growling, 'Get on with it. It's nothing. Just ignore it.'

---

* It's complicated. Harold had another, official, wife. Edith Swan Neck was his common-law wife.

This was not a great start for William's reign – and was a dark portent of things to come. Over the next few years, he systematically dismantled the old English ruling class, disinheriting the Anglo-Saxon lords and giving their lands to his cronies. He also put Normans in charge of the churches, appointing them as bishops and archbishops. This was a gradual process. William needed to appear to be the rightful king of England, not a bloody freebooter holding his throne by force, but he was facing threats from all sides. The Welsh and the Scots, as ever, exploited the disruptions in England, while in France the rival dukedoms and the French king were horrified that William might become the most powerful ruler in Europe. William was also increasingly at war with three of his sons – Robert, William and Henry – who were all eager to grab what land they could for themselves.

There was some initial resistance in England, famously in East Anglia where the legendary proto-Robin Hood figure/freedom fighter Hereward the Wake fought against the Norman incomers.* But every time there was an uprising, William used it as an excuse to confiscate more Saxon lands and wipe out more of the old ruling elite. One of the ways he stamped his authority on the land was by building castles (another piece on our medieval chess board).

The British had built hill forts, surrounded by ditches and fences, but the Normans built more substantial motte-and-bailey castles. Any sign of trouble and the army would go in, violently suppress the locals, demolish half of their buildings and use the rubble to pile up a great mound, the motte, on which they built a wooden keep, finishing it off with a walled courtyard, the bailey. If the threat persisted, they'd replace the wooden fort with a stone castle and upgrade wooden fences to stone walls.

Many castles became enduring stone structures, which are now seen as romantic ruins, the relics of a colourful and chivalrous past. At the time, though, they represented brutal authoritarian rule. The most

---

* Not to be confused with Hereward the Woke, who sent lots of petitions to King William about the correct use of pronouns, diversity in the Norman army and the effect that setting fire to villages had on global warming.

famous castle William built is the White Tower, which stands to this day as a royal palace in the Tower of London and plays a big part in this story.

The north of England, the old Norse lands, almost saw itself as a separate nation and, ever since the invasion, there had been fighting over who was going to be Earl of Northumbria – essentially the ruler of the north. William had tried installing both Saxons and Vikings as earls, but they'd all killed each other. When Edgar Ætheling, the surviving Saxon contender for the throne, got involved in 1068, William ran out of patience and took an army north. The rebels did a runner and William put his own man in charge, a Norman called Robert de Comines. He didn't last long. When he rode into Durham that same year, the locals set upon him and his men, slaughtering them. This sparked a series of uprisings all around the country. William doggedly put out fires, but the Saxons in York were emboldened and Edgar Ætheling saw an opportunity to take his rightful place as king. He raised local support and invited King Sweyn of Denmark to come and help him. They took control of York and Edgar claimed to be the lord of the north.

William was having none of it. He stormed back to York and, again, nobody would face up to him and local resistance melted away. He paid the Vikings to go home. Edgar fled to Scotland, where he was taken in by Malcolm III. This was Malcolm from Shakespeare's *Macbeth* and, over the following years, he and Edgar mounted several unsuccessful invasions.

William had had enough. If he couldn't defeat the rebels in battle, he would remove the threat of an uprising in the north once and for all with a scorched earth policy. He replaced all the local Saxon lords with Normans and set about obliterating villages, destroying farms, burning crops, looting, raping and slaughtering. This campaign – known as the Harrying of the North – led to a massive famine, during which people ate dogs, cats, rats and each other. The famine caused up to 100,000 deaths and the population of the north of England wouldn't return to pre-Norman levels for hundreds of years.

William had sent a clear and stark message to the English: 'Don't try to stand up to me or I will destroy you.' After that, nobody dared confront him in England (apart from a minor rebellion in 1075). But what *was* England? What exactly had William conquered? To effectively govern and extract revenues, he needed to keep track of what his new Norman landlords owned, so he organised a survey which became an invaluable record of England at the time. In 1085, he sent clerics and clerks around the country to visit every landowner and record the details of their holdings. The English nicknamed the result the Domesday Book, partly because the work recorded the unalterable facts, like those recorded in heaven at the Last Judgement, and partly because it felt like the end of the world had already come. In terms of who owned the land and ran the country, this spelled the end of Saxon England.

That William commissioned the survey when he did shows that, as far as he was concerned, Norman rule in England was established and settled, and things weren't going to change. This meant he could return to Normandy and carry on campaigning there against his unruly sons, his pesky neighbours and the king of France. While attacking the town of Mantes, however, his horse stumbled and he was thrown forward. The Normans had high pommels on the front and the back of their saddles so that they were very firmly seated when using a lance. The pommel dug into William's belly and ruptured his intestines.

William was mortally wounded and he knew it. He called his men to his bedside and they discussed who should succeed him. The problem was that William didn't really like any of his sons. He had very little respect for them, but there was a strict rule in Normandy that the succession should pass to the eldest son. Even though he'd basically been at war with his eldest boy, Robert, he had to give him something – and decided on Normandy. He made his second son, William Rufus, king of England. To his third son, Henry, he gave a lump sum of money and wished him luck. None of the great conqueror's family were with him at his deathbed. As soon as he'd heard he was going to get England, William Rufus had hurried over there and was poised to take control, and Robert and Henry wanted nothing to do with their father. William's powerful cronies were also leaking away and taking sides, shoring up their positions. William was no more use

WILLIAM I
TAKES A
TUMBLE

to anyone, and when he died – in Rouen, five weeks after the accident – he died alone. He'd been totally abandoned and his servants ransacked his possessions. So much for being king. What had it all been for?

William was taken to an abbey in Caen to be buried, but there wasn't a coffin big enough, so his bloated body, which was already decomposing and filling with gases from his ruptured guts, was squashed into a box too small for him. As they tried to stuff him into a makeshift tomb in the floor of the cathedral, his stomach exploded, filling the cathedral with a foul stench.

So that was the sordid end of King William. He ruled England for 21 years and died from an exploding stomach.

2
WILLIE (AGAIN)

WILLIAM II – c.1057–1100
William Rufus
Reigned 1087–1100
Lived for 43 years. Ruled for 13 years.
Shot to death with an arrow while hunting.
Remembered for: being shot to death with an arrow while
hunting, and not much else.

Let's face it, some of our monarchs are better known than others. Most people probably know something about William the Conqueror, Richard the Lionheart, Wicked King John, Henry V, Richard III and Henry VIII, but William II would likely draw a blank. He did nothing particularly memorable and didn't reign for very long. The best we can say about him is that he at least managed to hold on to everything his father had won.

William the Conqueror had at least nine children (we're not sure of the exact number), four of whom were sons. We know less about his daughters, because women at the time were only considered important if they married some influential foreign dignitary, or entered a religious order; otherwise, they tended not to be recorded in history.

As we've seen, William the Conqueror didn't think much of his sons, as is evidenced by his nicknames for them. He called his eldest boy Robert Curthose. Curt is the French 'court', or short, and hose were what medieval men wore instead of trousers (somewhere between leg warmers and stockings). They were tied to your belt and you covered your parts with a separate sort of nappy arrangement and then wore a long tunic over the top. So, 'Curthose' roughly translates as 'Shortpants'.

Yes, Robert was mocked for being a bit of a short arse and it stuck. William's second son was Richard. You can forget him, though. Not long after the Norman invasion, Richard was out hunting in one of his father's new forests (imaginatively named the New Forest) when his head came into contact with a low-hanging branch and he was removed from history.

The Conqueror's next son was called William. Nicknamed Rufus, or Red, to differentiate him from his dad, he possibly had reddish hair or a ruddy complexion (he was certainly fond of his food and drink).

William's last boy was called Henry and nobody bothered to give him a derogatory nickname because, as a younger son, he wasn't expected to be a major player. He might as well have been a girl.

After the invasion of 1066, the history of the next few years was very heavily influenced by infighting between these three men and their father. As we will see, through the course of this book, sibling rivalry has played a big role in the history of our monarchy. It still does. Siblings are always jostling for the love and attention of their parents and for status. And when there are vast royal estates at stake, the rivalry can get pretty intense. It didn't help that in the Conqueror's family there wasn't a great deal of love and respect coming down from Dad. Mum – Matilda of Flanders – was a different proposition. She always supported her eldest son, Little Bobby Shortpants, sometimes behind William's back, which led to massive family fallouts over the years.

The problems between the brothers can be traced back to an incident that happened in 1077, little more than a decade after the Norman invasion. The three boys were in Normandy, trying to help their dad by fending off incursions from neighbouring dukedoms. Little Bobby Shortpants was downstairs having a serious, grown-up conversation with his retinue about the situation, while, upstairs on the balcony, William Rufus and Henry were playing dice and getting pissed. Game over, they decided to play a prank on Bobby Shortpants and emptied their piss pot over the balustrade onto his head.

They thought this was enormously funny. Shortpants didn't. He went crying to his father, who just laughed at him. 'Good prank!' And, when the Conqueror refused to punish his two younger boys, Shortpants flounced off, taking his men with him. In a fit of pique, he tried, unsuccessfully, to seize the nearby castle of Rouen, but when William came after them, Robert fled to Flanders from where he declared war on his father (with the secret support of his mother). In a battle a couple of years later, Shortpants actually got into hand-to-hand combat with his father without realising who he was. He was on the point of smashing his head in when William cried out from inside his helmet and Robert recognised his voice. Shortpants spared him, but probably regretted it ever after; the two of them never really made it up. At the end, when William was dying, he knew he had to give Robert something meaningful because of the laws of primogeniture, which was why he gave him Normandy. Was the petulant Shortpants happy? 'No! I wanted England! You promised!'

Owning land gave you wealth, influence and power. If, when you died, you carved up your land between all your offspring, that power base would be broken up. The concept of primogeniture – the eldest son inheriting everything – was introduced to hold big estates (and kingdoms) together. Wealth and power could be passed down the generations in a solid chunk. This meant that if you weren't the first-born son, you could easily end up with nothing. This is why many younger sons went into the church; bishops and archbishops had land and thus wealth of their own.

So, Shortpants was fobbed off with Normandy, while England went to William Rufus. Henry got a pittance, just some money to buy a small piece of land of his own. By giving Shortpants Normandy, William had effectively divided his kingdom in two. This wasn't a smart move. As soon as William Rufus was crowned as William II – surprise, surprise – Shortpants immediately started plotting against him.

The Norman lords, most of whom held land in both England and Normandy, had to decide who they were going to back: the king of England, William Rufus, or the Duke of Normandy, Robert Shortpants. Pick the right man and you'd end up being given more lands by the victor. Pick the wrong man and it'd be over for you.

Rufus had more support in England, from the Anglo-Norman colo-nisers, who wanted to hang on to their new land. But Shortpants had more support in Normandy, where local lords who'd missed the boat by not going to England with the Conqueror saw the chance to gain new lands.

The Conqueror's half-brother, the wealthy and powerful Bishop Odo, sided with Robert Shortpants. They raised an army and Odo travelled to England to confront William. Robert's fatal problem was that he was not a great military commander, nor a very inspiring leader. He was actually a bit of a coward and the decision not to lead the army himself was a major miscalculation. It made him look weak. The lords were looking for the strongest man to get behind and it didn't look like being Shortpants.

William Rufus managed to bribe some of Robert's supporters, offering them what they wanted: good lands in England. He also managed to persuade the people of England that he would make a better king than his older brother. He assured them that he had their best interests at heart and promised them, Donald Trump-style, 'the best law that had ever been in this land'. They fell for it and, with their help, Rufus defeated Odo before taking his own army over to Normandy where he battered the useless Shortpants into submission, forcing him to promise not to challenge him again. Fat chance.

While William Rufus was trying to deal with all his problems, King Malcolm III of Scotland, sensing disunity across the border, tried to take lands in the north of England. Unlike Shortpants, however, Rufus took after his father and was a tough and efficient soldier. He went to war with Malcolm, who was killed at the Battle of Alnwick in 1093, and gained himself a period of relative peace and stability in England. This kept his lords happy (apart from the Earl of Northumbria who had a go at a rebellion in 1095). All monarchs want absolute power, but they soon realise that they can only rule by mutual consent. If you can keep the country secure and ensure the prosperity of your lords, then they'll accept you. Upset the system and you could be deposed.

All of William Rufus's campaigning was expensive, however. We think of medieval kings as not having to worry about money, but everything they did had to be paid for and his need for cash led to him falling out with the church. Rufus wasn't a religious man and saw the church mainly as a useful source of revenue. When several bishops died, including the Archbishop of Canterbury, he never quite got round to replacing them so that he could keep their incomes for himself. In the end, he gave in to pressure and at least appointed a new archbishop, Anselm, but the two of them immediately fell out. Throughout the medieval period, there were tensions between the archbishops of Canterbury, who were head of the English church, and the kings, who were head of the English state. The understanding was that the church ruled over people's souls and the king ruled over their bodies. William and Anselm argued furiously because they both thought the other wanted to encroach on their territory. Anselm declared that William wasn't fit to be king, then lost his nerve, fled the country and went crawling to the pope.

Because history was written by priests and monks, William got a lousy press and Anselm's judgement of him as a shit king was handed down to posterity. William was accused of being a lazy, greedy, self-indulgent drunk who wore clothes that were too fancy, didn't look after his people and was, to top it all, both a womaniser and a sodomite.

William never replaced Anselm, which gave him the archbishop's income, but he did very much need to get the pope onside, because ultimately the pope had authority over everyone. So Rufus did what his father had done before him and tried to get the pope's blessing. It helped that at the time, due to complicated politics and infighting in Europe, there were actually two popes. There was the official pope, Urban II, and there was a rival 'antipope', Clement III, who were competing with each other for legitimacy.

Europe's rulers were busy picking sides and it was very much a case of 'you scratch my back, I'll scratch yours'. Rulers would approach their chosen pope and offer their support, in return for which they would receive his blessing. Rufus picked Urban II, who declared him the legitimate ruler in England and instructed the clergy and his many rivals to leave him in peace.

Pope Urban needed a big PR coup to consolidate his position, so he announced that he was going to send a Christian army into the

Holy Land. For centuries, Jerusalem had been under Muslim control, but pilgrims had still been allowed to visit. In recent years, however, rival Islamic groups – the Turkish Seljuks and the Egyptian Fatimids – had been fighting for control. These groups had also been expanding their dominance and threatening Christian Byzantium.

Because of these developments, it was increasingly difficult for Christian pilgrims to travel to Jerusalem and there were reports of religious persecution. Urban had found his cause: 'We're going to free the Holy Lands from these oppressors in a great crusade and make Jerusalem Christian again.' His hope was that the various European rulers would stop fighting each other and unite against a common enemy, allowing him to claim undying glory and reverence as the pope who freed the Holy Land from 'the heathens'. As it turned out, he didn't live long enough to hear the news that the 'Franks' (as the crusaders were generically known) had seized back control of Jerusalem and established the Crusader states in the Middle East.

There was a rush to get on board and Rufus probably couldn't believe his luck when Robert Shortpants signed up for the expedition and persuaded Bishop Odo to go with him to hold his hand. Taking an army to the crusades was eye-wateringly expensive, though. So Robert made peace with Rufus – 'Give me enough money and I'll get out of your hair. And Normandy is yours 'til I get back.' And off he went to Jerusalem. The great Odo, like so many other crusaders, died before he even got there, but Robert, for the only time in his life, displayed some military skill on the campaign and was among the crusaders who captured Jerusalem in 1099.

With Shortpants off his back, William Rufus was able to get on with doing what he enjoyed most: feasting and hunting and buggery. He'd already built himself a gigantic feasting hall at his Palace of Westminster. Westminster Hall is one of the few parts of the Palace of Westminster that survived a devastating fire in the 19th century and is now part of the Houses of Parliament.

Hunting was the main pastime of the aristocracy and William I had enclosed a vast amount of common land for his own use, denying access to the locals. One day, William Rufus set off to the New Forest with his younger brother, Henry, and his favourite archer, Walter Tyrrell, one of the greatest bowmen in the country. Did Rufus ever consider that hunting was a rather dangerous sport? After all, his older brother Richard had been killed in a hunting accident in this very forest, as had his nephew, another Richard (an illegitimate son of Robert Curthose), just a year ago. Again – *in this very forest* …

But they were having a lovely time when – SCHWIIIP! AAARGH! Oh, no there's been a terrible accident! William's been hit by an arrow. Shot by Walter Tyrrell, of all people, such an experienced archer, too. Who could have seen that coming? Well, Henry, perhaps? What did he do? He left his big brother's body lying there in the dirt and rode as fast as he could to Winchester, site of the royal treasury. And once he'd got hold of all the money, he declared himself king. And nobody batted an eyelid.

The spare had taken the throne.

3
HARRY

HENRY I – 1068–1135
Henry Beauclerc
Reigned 1100–1135
Lived for 67 years. Ruled for 35 years.
Died from an exploding stomach.
Remembered for: losing his son and heir in a boating accident
and eating a fatal 'surfeit of lampreys'.

We'll never know whether William Rufus's death while out hunting on 2 August 1100 was an accident or a planned assassination by his little brother, Henry. But, whatever the case, Henry was an opportunist who, throughout his reign, showed himself to be ruthless, strong-willed and tough. You didn't mess with Henry. Of the three brothers – Robert, William and Henry – he was the one most like his father, the Conqueror. He knew Rufus was unpopular with the church, the people and the lords, and, seeing his brother struck down by an arrow, didn't waste any time feeling sorry for him.

One of the things Henry had learned from his father was this: if you're in charge of the money, you're in charge of the country. So he rushed to secure the treasury at Winchester with indecent haste and had himself crowned at Westminster Abbey three days later, which gave him just enough time to put together a coronation charter known as the Charter of Liberties. It was in many ways a forerunner of Magna Carta and set out the laws that a king must be bound by. As well as promising to treat the church better than his irreligious brother, he was also sucking up to the lords who had felt badly treated by the high-handed Rufus. Of course, once Henry made the proclamation, he pretty much ignored it, as did pretty much every subsequent monarch for the next 200 years.

Henry had never expected to inherit anything and when Robert Shortpants returned from the First Crusade, he found Rufus dead and Henry sitting on the throne. Robert was furious; he declared himself the rightful king of England, raised an army in Normandy and brought it over the Channel. But Robert was barely known in England, whereas Henry had been born there and had made himself popular with his Charter of Liberties. Shortpants couldn't gather together enough support for his cause and was seen as a useless military commander. In the end, he had to humiliatingly back down and renounce his claim to the throne.

But he wouldn't let it lie and spent the next few years plotting against Henry, drinking heavily, hanging with harlots and generally neglecting his duties in Normandy, until eventually Henry said, 'OK, enough is enough', took his own army over to Normandy, attacked Robert and easily defeated him at the Battle of Tinchebray in 1106.

Henry must have been tempted to have Robert executed and put out of the way for good, but there was a code of chivalry and it was considered particularly bad form to execute a member of a royal family. It would have brought down the wrath of the pope and the other European monarchs on him. So Henry spared Robert, locking him up instead. In some ways, perhaps poor Robert might have preferred to have been executed because he spent the rest of his life in various prisons, bemoaning his fate and wishing he was old enough to die. He lingered on into his eighties and eventually died in Cardiff Castle. Apparently, he spent his last few months trying to learn Welsh, which, as any Englishman can tell you, is completely impossible. So that was the sad, and sadly mundane, end of Little Bobby Shortpants.

Henry spent the first years of his reign shoring up his kingdom, using a successful combination of politics and force. He had to keep on top of the native English, as well as the newly installed Anglo-Norman lords, who were all jostling for power and status. To the west there were also the Welsh, who were not at all keen on English interference. William Rufus had tried to subjugate them and largely failed, partly because the Welsh had a secret weapon, the longbow, which was as tall as a man and required immense upper body strength even just to pull the bowstring back. So Henry stuck to a policy of containment, setting up his most powerful knights, who became known as the Marcher Lords, along the border to create a buffer zone.

Meanwhile, to the north, the Scottish were always a threat. Whenever there was any unrest in England, they'd take the opportunity to invade. So Henry used the tried and trusted tactic of the political marriage. He married Matilda of Scotland, daughter of Shakespeare's King Malcolm III.

———— • ◆ • ————

Unfortunately, the Middle Ages are complicated by the fact that everybody has the same name. Henry's mother was called Matilda (of Flanders). He then married another Matilda (she'd actually been christened Edith, but changed her name to Matilda to fit in) and, just to make my life more difficult, he called his daughter Matilda as well. His daughter, Empress Matilda, went to war with her cousin, King Stephen, who was married to a woman called … Matilda. So, we have three queens of England called Matilda, plus one would-be-queen, Empress Matilda. If you think that's complicated, wait until we get to the War of the Roses where we have to contend with seven Edwards, six Richards, four Johns, four Henrys and three Edmunds …

———— • ◆ • ————

This created a strong alliance with the Scottish – it also played well with the English. Via her mother, Matilda was Saxon royalty, an actual descendant of Alfred the Great. So, Henry was saying to the English, 'I am one of you'.

The Vikings remained a constant threat. If Henry looked weak, they might well come over in force and try to reclaim the throne. And there were the endless territorial conflicts in France, where the powerful dukedoms – like Aquitaine, Brittany, Anjou, Maine and Blois – were always on the lookout for any opportunities to exploit. And the French king, Louis the Fat, supported William Clito, the son of Robert

Shortpants, to be Duke of Normandy. In 1119, however, Henry shut them all up when he annihilated a French army at the Battle of Brémule and secured Normandy.

Compared to the party animal that was William Rufus, Henry was sober and respected, and a successful warrior king to boot. He went to great lengths to make England secure and stable, and to keep the English onside. To this end, he reinstated some old Saxon legal and governmental practices. Henry was interested in money and knew that if there's peace and order, more wealth is generated and it's easier to tax it.

One of the ways he kept on top of all this was by using an innovation that came from the Arabs, the abacus. A very useful tool for keeping on top of finances, Henry created his own version. He had a large table covered by a checked cloth, resembling a chessboard. When landowners, or their representatives, came in to pay their taxes, the money would be represented by counters of different value, which were moved around the board from row to row. That way, the chancellor of the exchequer, as the man in charge of the Treasury came to be known, could easily calculate what was coming in, what was going out and what was owed. This is why we talk about 'cashing cheques' (well, we don't any more. Young people won't know what I'm talking about. Except, I suppose it lingers on, in the form of the paycheck). It all goes back to Henry's chequered tablecloth. As I say, he loved money. He was the last English monarch for several hundred years who died without being in debt.

I don't want to give the impression that all Henry cared about was campaigning and money, though. He also loved sex. He had at least nine illegitimate sons and 15 illegitimate daughters. This wasn't seen as an anything scandalous. Kings were expected to have as many children as they could, with whoever they could get their hands on. It was a sign of their virility and these illegitimate children weren't hidden away (Henry's father William I had been illegitimate, after all). The extra-marital children were given land, titles and positions of power at court. The common practice was to stick 'Fitz' onto the front of a father's name to create a new surname. So, through history, there were many FitzWilliams, FitzHenrys and endless FitzRoys who had almost the same status as a monarch's legitimate sons, apart from one thing: the law stated that none of them were allowed to become king.

Henry was something of a lad, but he seemed to have no sense of humour. A young courtier once made up a ditty about his shenanigans and ended up being sentenced to blinding and castration. To avoid his terrifying fate, the poor guy managed to kill himself by banging his head against his cell wall on the night before his punishment.

Henry did produce two legitimate children, William and Matilda. He married Matilda off to King Henry V of Germany, who went on to become the Holy Roman Emperor, which made her an empress. Don't forget her, because she's going to come back into our story in a big way.

Henry's sole legitimate son was known as William Ætheling (or Adelin). Again, we can see Henry playing the English card there, using the old Anglo-Saxon word for a princeling, saying, 'Look, William is one of you, he will be a properly English king.'

By 1120, Henry had everything under control. William Ætheling was his golden boy – handsome and charismatic, with his own entourage of young noblemen and women. The royal family would spend half their time in Normandy and half in England, travelling backwards and forwards across the Channel using fast knarr ships, adapted from Viking merchant vessels, as a sort of ferry service.

A ship's captain called Stephen FitzAirard had brought William the Conqueror across the channel in 1066 on his ship the *Mora* and William had kept him on as his personal captain for the rest of his life, the equivalent of a modern private chauffeur. In 1120, FitzAirard's son, Thomas FitzStephen had recently refitted the pride of his fleet. The *White Ship* was fast and state-of-the-art, the equivalent of a Russian oligarch's super-yacht. And as Henry was preparing to travel back to England with his court from the port of Barfleur, FitzStephen approached the king and said it would be a huge honour if Henry would sail over on his boat. The *White Ship*, however, wasn't ready to sail and Henry suggested FitzStephen took William Ætheling and his friends while he himself went on ahead.

Henry was in a hurry and knew that the *White Ship* would be something of a party boat. Ætheling and his friends, who had been drinking in Barfleur, were already rolling barrels of wine onto it. Among the group was Henry's nephew Stephen of Blois, who ducked out at the last minute as he was suffering a bout of drunken diarrhoea.

It was a still night and, as Henry sailed across the Channel, he could hear shouts and happy shrieks of laughter from the young people aboard the *White Ship*. Sadly, however, what he was actually hearing were screams and calls for help because Thomas FitzStephen, as drunk as his passengers, had steered the vessel into a rock just outside Barfleur's harbour.

It was cold, it was dark and the passengers, none of whom could swim, were wearing heavy robes. There had been 300 people on board. There was only one survivor: a local butcher who had jumped onto the ship just before it sailed to try to retrieve some unpaid debts was pulled from the sea the following morning. He told how, at one point, FitzStephen had surfaced, grabbed hold of a piece of wreckage and called out, 'What's happened to the Ætheling?'. When he was told that William was lost, FitzStephen let go of the wreckage and said, 'In that case, I shall go down too,' knowing that if he survived, he'd be horribly tortured and executed.

Nobody had the guts to tell King Henry what had happened. They knew how devastated he would be. He got all the way back to London without hearing any news of the disaster and two days passed before his terrified retainers forced a small boy into his rooms to tell him.

Henry was utterly broken. He never recovered, and never managed to produce another legitimate male heir, despite marrying a younger woman after his first wife, Matilda, died.

King Henry's only remaining legitimate heir was his daughter, the Empress Matilda, but he knew that many people would hate the idea of having a woman as their ruler, so, he called all his lords to his court, including his nephew, 'Shitpants' Stephen of Blois, and got them to swear that they would accept Matilda as their queen. Four years later, just to make sure, he got them to do it all over again.

When Matilda's husband, the Holy Roman Emperor, died, King Henry ordered her to marry Geoffrey, Duke of Anjou, one of his powerful Norman neighbours. He hoped that Matilda and Geoffrey would help to protect Normandy's borders, but this was a pretty dysfunctional family. William the Conqueror had fought with his sons, his sons had fought with each other and now Henry fought with the next generation. Matilda and Geoffrey argued with him over how much land and power he was prepared to offer them, and Henry feared that Geoffrey might get too high and mighty and try to take everything. There being no family therapy at the time, the argument was settled in the medieval way. They went to war with each other.

So while Henry was insisting that Matilda would rule England when he died, he was simultaneously leading an army against her and her husband. He was now in his sixties, frail and riddled with health problems. His physicians told him to be careful what he ate and to steer clear of his favourite dish, rich and oily – and quite frankly disgusting – parasitic, eel-like creatures called lampreys, which used to be considered a great delicacy.

Henry was campaigning in Normandy, when he stopped at a castle where the cook served him up a platter of lampreys, knowing how much he liked them. Henry knew he shouldn't eat them but couldn't resist. A week later he was dead.

Before he died, though, he summoned his lords to his deathbed to swear one last time that they would support Matilda. But Matilda wasn't there, and neither was Stephen of Blois. So what happened next? Well, the fact that this book's called *Willie, Willie, Harry, Stee*, not *Willie, Willie, Harry, Matilda*, gives you a big clue. For now, I'll just say that several English kings in the Middle Ages died from diarrhoea, but Stephen is the only one whose life was saved by a bout of it.

4
STEE

KING STEPHEN – 1096–1154
Stephen of Blois
Reigned 1135–1154
Lived for 58 years. Ruled for 18 years.
Died of an exploding stomach.
Remembered for: The Anarchy – usurping the throne and
causing a 20-year civil war with his cousin Matilda.

England had got so close to being peaceful and prosperous after the upheavals of the Norman invasion, with a strong, clear line of succession that would have guaranteed stability. And then one unexpected, random event happened. When the heir to the throne, William Ætheling, died in a shipwreck, the whole ship of state was wrecked and English history sank into a maelstrom of violence and anarchy. Thank you, God.

King Henry, a serial shagger, had screwed up. He wasn't able to produce another legitimate male heir. He did have a healthy, living, son in the shape of Robert FitzRoy, 1st Earl of Gloucester. But, as his surname suggests, Robert was illegitimate, and nobody, from the pope down, would ever have accepted him as king.

So Henry had had no choice but to appoint his daughter, Matilda, as his successor. She actually had everything you wanted in a monarch: she was tough, smart and, as the wife of the Holy Roman Emperor, Henry V, had been closely involved in the running of a royal court. She'd even ruled parts of the empire in her husband's place while he was campaigning. She was perfect in every respect.

Except for the fact that she was a woman.

———————— • ◆ • ————————

The Holy Roman Empire was a peculiar anomaly in Europe. When the Roman Empire split into two during the first half of the millennium, the eastern, Christian half, based in Constantinople (Byzantium), became the dominant twin. The western empire withered until the mighty Frankish King Charlemagne, with the pope's blessing, revived the title of Western Roman Emperor in 800. Originally centred around France, the seat of power migrated to Germany and the empire became a powerful confederation of central European states. The post of Holy Roman Emperor was an elected one, but usually went to a German king. The empire lasted until 1806 when it was dismantled during the Napoleonic wars. The Russian title, Czar, and the Roman title, Kaiser, are both derived from Caesar and are call-backs to Roman times and the days of empire.

———————— • ◆ • ————————

Henry V of Germany had been much older than Matilda, and we've seen how, when he died, Matilda's father married her off to a new husband, Geoffrey, the heir to Anjou, a major duchy to the south of Normandy. At the time of their marriage, Geoffrey was only 14 and Matilda, at 25, was 11 years older than him and had already achieved much. When King Henry I had arranged the marriage to Geoffrey of Anjou, he must have thought, 'OK, Matilda's going to go along with what I say, and Geoffrey's just a boy, so he'll be easy to push around. I'll give them a couple of castles, just enough to keep them occupied and to warn off any land-grabbing neighbours until I shuffle off this mortal coil.'

But, as we've seen, Matilda and Geoffrey were not satisfied with this arrangement and begged the king to give them real power and to let them properly defend Normandy. But Henry became paranoid that Geoffrey and the Angevins would try to take over Normandy for themselves, so he refused their request. At this point, there was a rebel-

NORMAN AND PLANTAGENET KINGS

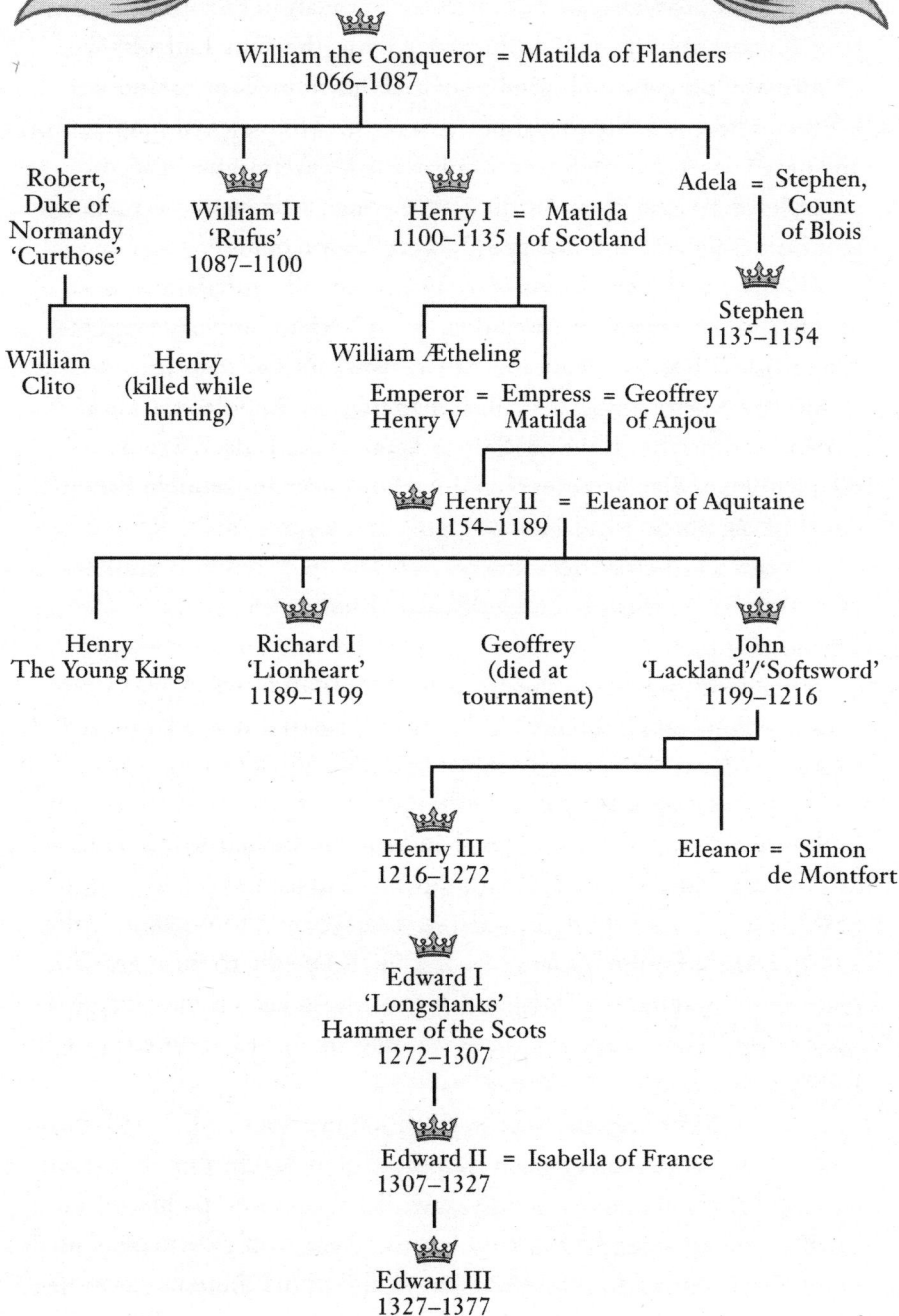

William the Conqueror = Matilda of Flanders
1066–1087

Robert,
Duke of
Normandy
'Curthose'

William II
'Rufus'
1087–1100

Henry I = Matilda
1100–1135 of Scotland

Adela = Stephen,
Count
of Blois

Stephen
1135–1154

William
Clito

Henry
(killed while
hunting)

William Ætheling

Emperor = Empress = Geoffrey
Henry V   Matilda   of Anjou

Henry II = Eleanor of Aquitaine
1154–1189

Henry
The Young King

Richard I
'Lionheart'
1189–1199

Geoffrey
(died at
tournament)

John
'Lackland'/'Softsword'
1199–1216

Henry III
1216–1272

Eleanor = Simon
de Montfort

Edward I
'Longshanks'
Hammer of the Scots
1272–1307

Edward II = Isabella of France
1307–1327

Edward III
1327–1377

lion as some of the Norman lords, sensing a weakness, turned on Henry. Geoffrey and Matilda sided with the rebels against him. Everything that he'd feared was coming true.

And then Henry stuffed his face with lampreys and dropped dead before anything was resolved. Matilda wasn't at his bedside, which didn't help her cause. Henry had got his lords to swear allegiance to her, but whereas in life everybody had been absolutely terrified of him and never dared question him, as soon as he was dead, he might as well never have existed. As far as they were concerned, his lords reckoned that both England and Normandy were up for grabs.

The man who acted first was Stephen of Blois, Matilda's cousin. Stephen was a grandson of William the Conqueror, via his daughter, Adela. Blois was another one of the rival French counties on the borders of Normandy, and William had married Adela to the man who would become the count of Blois to keep him onside. The count had died while Stephen was young and the boy had been brought up at the court of his uncle, King Henry. Henry had even considered Stephen as his successor before deciding on Matilda, so he did have something of a claim to the throne. And he'd made himself very popular. He was affable and clubbable, as happy sitting chatting and eating with his servants as he was with the lords and ladies. He was very good at backslapping and glad-handing, and had the support of a large part of the Anglo-Norman nobility, unlike Empress Matilda, who was pretty much unknown in England.

Stephen was also wealthy, which helped. He had a great deal of land in England and France, especially after he married Matilda, Countess of Boulogne. Crucially, Stephen's brother, Henry … (Oh, bloody hell, another Matilda, and, now, another Henry. We'll call this one *Henri*. As I mentioned before, these names are confusing. At least Stephen's easy to remember; he's the only Stephen in this story and the only English king to have that name.)

Henri was Bishop of Winchester, making him one of the most powerful figures in the English church, which gave Stephen the confidence to think he might get away with a throne-grab. Matilda and Geoffrey were stuck in France with their supporters, who included Henry I's illegitimate son, Robert FitzRoy, Earl of Gloucester. Stephen was better placed. He was just across the Channel in Boulogne, so he rushed over to England and headed for Winchester. Growing up at his uncle Henry's court, he'd learned much about politics and power, and would have been very familiar with the story of how, after William Rufus's suspicious death in the 'hunting accident', Uncle Henry's first action had been to hurry to Winchester to secure the Treasury.

Stephen copied this tactic. He took charge of the Treasury and, with the help of his brother, Bishop Henri, got himself crowned before anyone could object. You couldn't have a coronation in Westminster Abbey unless the people of London accepted you. Without their support you were stuffed, but, as we've seen, Stephen was very popular. And he offered the promise of stability. The last thing anyone wanted was a war over the succession. Or a woman on the throne.

Stephen was the epitome of the mediocre male who gets promoted over the head of a better qualified woman because his face fits and he was in the right boys' club. Once you were crowned and anointed by God, then, regardless of who you were before, that's it – you're king. Everybody seemed happy with Stephen, except for one person: his cousin, the now 33-year-old Empress Matilda, backed up by her husband, Geoffrey, who was now 22. Matilda persuaded her half-brother, Robert FitzRoy, to mount a rebellion against Stephen in England in 1138, while she stayed in Normandy to consolidate her position there and use it as her power base, which meant that she remained relatively unknown in England.

Robert's rebellion went well to start with. He gained useful support in the southwest but was unable to win a decisive victory against Stephen and a stalemate ensued. Stephen had been sitting on the throne for nearly four years before Matilda felt confident enough to cross the Channel in 1139 with a small company of knights, intending to join up with Robert. But it was a miscalculation. She was not made welcome and ended up being captured and imprisoned in Arundel Castle in Sussex. This could have been the end of it, if Stephen hadn't done something quite extraordinary. He agreed to a truce and let Matilda go.

Why? Was he feeling chivalrous? Did he think she wasn't that important and that Robert was his main threat? Was it that she was his cousin, and a lady, and he didn't want to harm her? Or was he just too soft, too kind-hearted? The traditional take on Stephen and Matilda is that Stephen was too nice, and Matilda wasn't nice enough. For whatever reason, Stephen allowed Matilda to travel safely to the southwest, where she joined Robert.

What happens next is 20 years of bloody civil war; 20 years of the country being torn apart. One of the reasons the war went on for so long was that the two sides were too evenly matched and neither could persuade enough barons to join their cause and tip the balance in their favour. In the Middle Ages, commanders tried to avoid risky, and costly, pitched battles, preferring to take shelter in their castles, so it became a grinding war of attrition.

The Victorians aptly named this period The Anarchy. It was a miserable time for the English people whose land was being fought over. Crops would be burnt, villages destroyed and people either slaughtered or ravaged by famine. A civil war is perhaps the nastiest of all types of warfare and the lords used the chaos and confusion to settle old scores and attack their neighbours. They could also profit from selling their support to either Matilda or Stephen and would constantly switch sides depending on which way the wind was blowing.

The misery was vividly described in a famous passage in the *Anglo-Saxon Chronicle* that describes a time of lawlessness, violence and torture: 'I neither can, nor may I, tell all the wounds and all the pains which they inflicted on wretched men in this land … every man robbed another who could … and they said openly that Christ slept and his Saints.'

There was an explosion of castle building. Before the advent of siege machinery, castles were pretty much impregnable. The best an attacking force could hope for would be to starve out the occupants. Castles pinned down besieging armies, who were left vulnerable to attack by a relief force – which is exactly what happened a couple of years after Stephen let Matilda go. His army was besieging Lincoln Castle when the empress's army, led by Robert of Gloucester, arrived and attacked him. Stephen was captured by Robert and incarcerated in Bristol Castle.

This was Matilda's big chance. First, she hurried to Winchester – following the tried-and-tested route of securing the Treasury – only to discover that it was empty. Stephen had spent all the money pursuing the war and all that was left was his crown. That was enough for Matilda, though, and she started negotiating with Stephen's brother, Henri, Bishop of Winchester, to be crowned. She made promises to enrich the church and, feeling that Stephen's cause was now hopeless, Henri switched sides. Stephen had made himself unpopular with the church, getting rid of senior churchmen and confiscating their lands to give to his supporters. So Henri was not best pleased with him.

Matilda was declared 'Lady of England and Normandy', but she couldn't call herself queen until she had an official coronation at Westminster Abbey. However, when she got to London, she was greeted by a hostile mob. The city was still loyal to Stephen and saw Matilda as a foreigner. She'd also committed the cardinal sin of behaving like a man. It was fine for a medieval queen to lead an army or govern a country, if it was on behalf of her husband, the king, but to do it for yourself was just not ladylike.

Matilda's portrayal by historians is interesting. She was a very rich and powerful woman, 11 years older than her husband, and, even today, she's criticised in the same way as many powerful women, whether they're politicians, executives or in the media. They're portrayed as being too unwilling to make compromises, too abrasive, too pushy. Characteristics that are applauded in a man are seen as negatives in a woman and make her 'hard to get along with'. As an anonymous 12th-century historian put it in his *Deeds of King Stephen*, Matilda 'put on an extremely arrogant demeanour, instead of the modest gait and bearing proper to the gentle sex'.

In the end, poor Empress Matilda was chased out of town by King Stephen's wife, Queen Matilda, who was leading his army while he was locked up. Of course, Queen Matilda was never accused of being too warlike and unladylike because she was acting on behalf of her husband and was therefore still subject to male authority.

Bishop Henri quickly switched his support back to Stephen. Empress Matilda advanced on Winchester with her army to try to get him to change his mind and, in the confusion, Queen Matilda's forces captured Robert of Gloucester. So, we have another stalemate. Two 'queens' still on the board (Matilda and Matilda), but two 'kings' in check (Robert and Stephen). Once again, the bishop is brought into play. Henri negotiates an exchange of prisoners. Stephen is swapped for Robert and everything is back to square one.

Depressingly, the war resumes. And not long after the release of Stephen, Empress Matilda is nearly captured herself when she's surrounded in Oxford Castle by Stephen's army in 1142. The story goes that, just before Christmas, she managed to slip away with her household in the dead of night. Dressed all in white, they escaped unseen across the frozen river and into the snowy countryside. These fanciful extra details are no doubt apocryphal, but Matilda's escape has become one of those great romantic legends from English history.

So what's been going on over the Channel all this time? Remember Empress Matilda's husband, Geoffrey of Anjou? Well, he's now a grown man and has taken control of Normandy and Anjou, trying to secure them against Stephen's supporters in France. He's also been bringing up his son by Matilda, annoyingly another Henry, who had been born in 1133. The boy had been only two when Henry I died and the war started, but, because it had dragged on for so long, he was now old enough to join the fighting himself. Actually, he wasn't *quite* old enough. In 1147, when he made his first attempt to help his mother, he was only 14. He hired some mercenaries and invaded England, but it all went horribly wrong. He had neither the backing of the Anglo-Norman lords, nor enough money to pay his troops, who took him hostage. His mother, who hadn't asked for his support, was mightily pissed off with him and Stephen seemed to treat it as all a bit of a joke. He paid off Henry's men and sent the boy back to France.

Stephen obviously didn't feel seriously threatened. The war was fizzling out, with many of the lords wanting it over, and that same year, 1147, Robert of Gloucester died. Matilda then followed her son back to France and concentrated her efforts there, helping to make sure that at least Anjou and Normandy stayed in their hands.

By this time, Stephen and Matilda were no longer thinking about securing the English throne for themselves, but for the next generation. Matilda had Henry and Stephen had his own son, Eustace. For

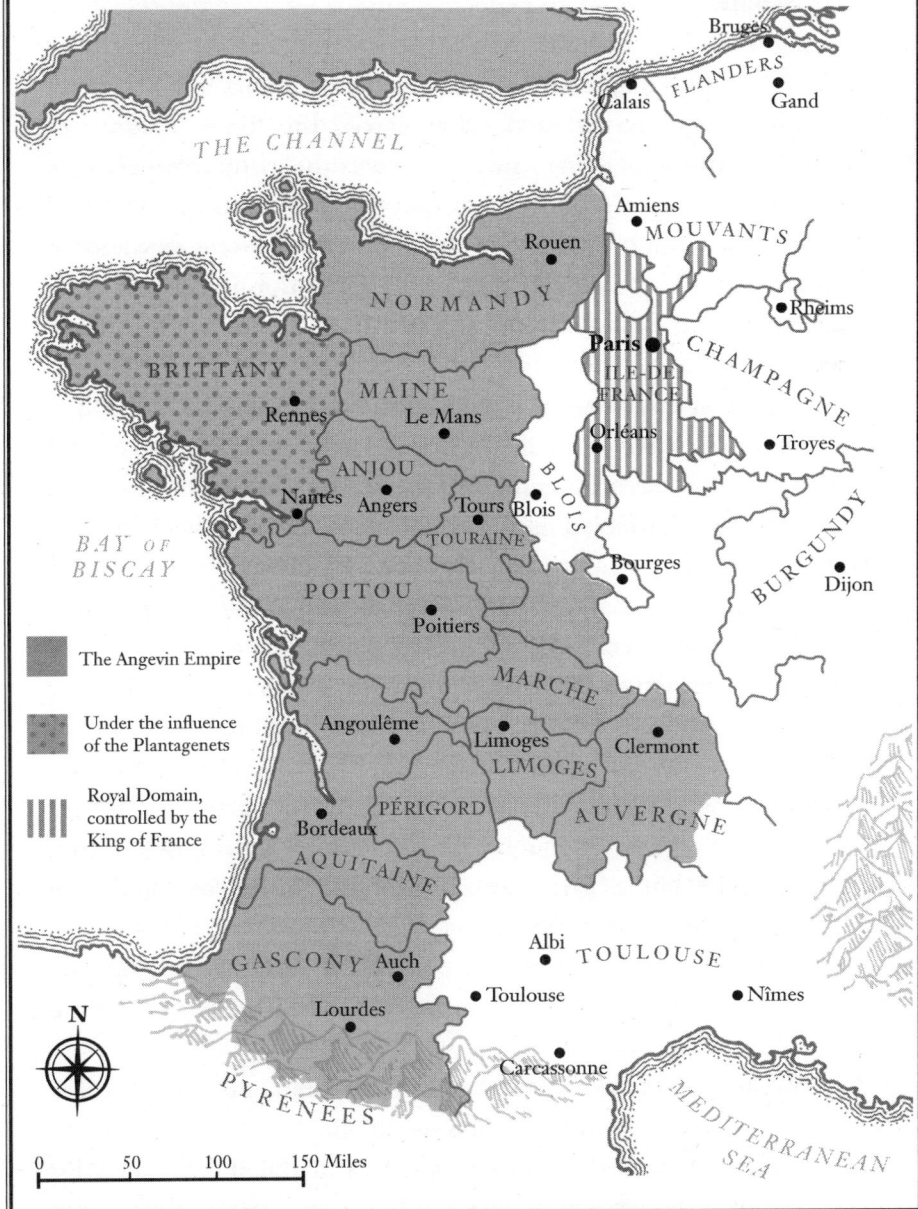

FRANCE AT THE HEIGHT OF THE ANGEVIN EMPIRE – 1180

THE CHANNEL

Bruges

FLANDERS

Calais

Gand

Amiens

MOUVANTS

Rouen

Rheims

NORMANDY

Paris

CHAMPAGNE

ILE-DE-FRANCE

BRITTANY

MAINE

Rennes

Le Mans

Orléans

Troyes

ANJOU

BLOIS

Nantes

Angers

Tours

Blois

BURGUNDY

BAY OF BISCAY

TOURAINE

Bourges

Dijon

POITOU

Poitiers

MARCHE

The Angevin Empire

Angoulême

Limoges

Clermont

Under the influence of the Plantagenets

LIMOGES

Royal Domain, controlled by the King of France

PÉRIGORD

AUVERGNE

Bordeaux

AQUITAINE

Albi

TOULOUSE

GASCONY

Auch

Lourdes

Toulouse

Nîmes

N

Carcassonne

MEDITERRANEAN SEA

PYRÉNÉES

0   50   100   150 Miles

the next few years, young Henry earned his chops in Normandy, fending off the French king, Louis, who supported Stephen and Eustace. Henry gradually gained the upper hand and became an experienced and adept soldier who could command an army – and thus command respect. In 1153, he felt the time was right to once again take an army over to England and to do it right this time.

As it turned out, the war didn't fully reignite. There were some skirmishes, but no major battles, and eventually Henry and Stephen's armies lined up against each other across the River Thames at Wallingford in the pouring rain. There was the awful prospect of a final, apocalyptic battle, but nobody had the stomach for it. This had gone on for too long. Even if one side did win the battle, it would be at a huge cost and it wouldn't necessarily settle things. So, just as he had done before, Bishop Henri stepped in and negotiated a peace treaty.

It was agreed that Stephen would be allowed to stay on the throne until his death, when it would be handed over to Henry. Why did Stephen agree to this arrangement? One reason was that his own son, Eustace, had recently died (and was not much missed – he'd been an erratic and violent young man who enjoyed going round burning crops, killing peasants and plundering churches). Another reason was that the Anglo-Norman lords were turning against him now that they had a viable alternative. While they'd hated the idea of being ruled by a woman, things were different now. It would be Empress Matilda's son Henry who sat on the throne, not her.

Within a year, Stephen was dead, which was very handy for Henry and Matilda. Perhaps too handy? There were no accusations of foul play at the time, but, as Henry was now on the throne, he could have easily quashed any nasty rumours.

Stephen might well have been poisoned but, officially, he died of a stomach illness. Another exploding stomach. The runs got him in the end.

So, Stephen's gone, not the greatest of our kings, and poor Matilda would never get to sit on the throne – but she did at least live to see her son, Henry, crowned. And every single monarch in the rest of this book, is a direct descendant of hers. So, in the end, she was the winner.

5

ᚼARRY

HENRY II – 1133–1189
Henry Curtmantle
Reigned 1154–1189
Lived for 56 years. Ruled for 35 years.
Died of an exploding stomach.
Remembered for: the killing of Thomas a Becket.

Henry was viewed with suspicion at first. He was an outsider, an Angevin ('from Anjou'), his style of dress was considered weird, scruffy and foreign, and led to his nickname Curtmantle ('short cloak'). But he turned out to be just what England needed: a dynamic, warrior king. In fact, he spent so much time in the saddle that he became bandy-legged. Stocky and fiery, with an insane temper and an energy that his courtiers struggled to keep up with, Henry was also well read and ferociously intelligent. He loved a good argument.

During his reign, he expanded the Anglo-Norman empire to the largest it would ever be, but he trod a depressingly familiar path to the previous Norman kings, having to deal with endless disputes, not only with the Scots, the Welsh, the Irish, the church and his neighbours in France, but also with his own family. We've seen the arc before: youthful success, a consolidation of power in manhood and then a sad decline into ill-health and familial infighting. What a family to fall out with, though. His wife was the formidable Eleanor of Aquitaine and two of his sons were Richard the Lionheart and Wicked King John.

The emblem of his father, Geoffrey, Count of Anjou, was a sprig of broom, a tough plant with vivid yellow flowers. In Latin, broom is called *planta genista* and this seems to be the origin of the family name. They were known at the time as the Angevins and later as the Plantagenets.

When Henry came to the throne at the age of 21 in 1154, he was the first Plantagenet king of England after the run of Normans. He'd been a boy when the civil war had broken out and now, 20 years later, he was the winner. When I think of my youngest boy, Sidney, he's a couple of years older than 21 now, but I still wouldn't trust him to run the country. He can't even do his own laundry.

Henry had married Eleanor of Aquitaine before he came to the throne, when he was 19 and she was 30. His mother, the Empress Matilda, had also been 11 years older than her husband when she'd married him, so there was evidently no shame in marrying a much older woman – particularly when she came with a chunk of land. In Eleanor's case, this was the duchy of Aquitaine, a huge region in south-west France.

Eleanor had already been married to the French king, Louis VII, and they'd had two daughters together, but, after 15 years of marriage (she'd married him when she was 15), Eleanor had produced no sons. Both of them wanted out and they got the marriage annulled on the grounds of consanguinity.*

Keen to produce a son and heir, Louis was happy with the separation, but he was furious when Eleanor almost immediately remarried – to one of Louis' biggest rivals, Henry Plantagenet† – only eight weeks later. Eleanor had sent a personal invitation to Henry telling him he could do a lot worse than marry her. And she was right. When Henry became king of England a couple of years later, his combined lands made him one of the most powerful men in Europe, with an empire that stretched from the border of Scotland all the way down to the Pyrenees. He eventually controlled the whole of the left-hand side of France, a bigger area than was ruled over by the French king.

England was in tatters after 20 years of The Anarchy. The wealth generated by the ever-growing Angevin Empire helped Henry to shore up the finances and gave him the bedrock he needed to restore

* Consanguinity is when a husband and wife are too closely related and was often used as a handy get-out clause for aristos in the days before divorce was permitted.
† He wasn't officially called Plantagenet until much later, but I'll use that name to keep things clear.

order and put in place a system of sound governance. Luckily, he was good at being a king. He was a warrior, but he also made an effort to behave decently towards the English. He brought in a fairer legal system that benefitted the ordinary people. He settled the ongoing problems with Scotland, pushed further into Wales, and fortified his castles there. He also built new castles in England and France, but he came unstuck when he tried to reform the church.

Henry wanted the church to be governed by the same laws as everyone else in the country, so that if a member of the clergy committed a secular crime, they would be tried in the same regional courts as any other Englishman. The church refused any changes and insisted that the clergy would only ever be under their own jurisdiction. This problem of self-discipline persists to this day, as demonstrated by the scandals in the Catholic Church where priests' wrongdoings – such as child abuse – are dealt with internally and brushed under the carpet.

Henry badly wanted more control over the church and saw a solution when the post of Archbishop of Canterbury became free. His lord chancellor was a smart, ambitious and energetic man from a humble background called Thomas Becket (the 'a' was added in the 16th century). Because Becket had come from a relatively poor background, he liked making and spending money and showing off his wealth. He and Henry were men about town, competing over who had the latest, most expensive and fashionable clothing, and there was a lot of 'roistering', which I believe is the correct term for medieval laddish behaviour. They loved drinking, feasting, hunting, womanising and generally having a good time. So Henry thought Becket would be the perfect crony to have in his pocket as the new archbishop. Becket begged him not to give him the job, fearing it would ruin their friendship, but Henry insisted. And as soon as Becket took up the position, something unexpected happened. He found God. He suddenly became the most pious man in the country and sided with the church against the king. Henry was furious. Instead of Becket being his closest ally, he became his biggest opponent.

Becket was a vain and ambitious man who knew he was never going to become number one; Henry had that sewn up. But if he could maintain the church's independence from the monarchy and rule over all Englishmen's souls, it would make him almost an equal to Henry. And while he had to stop wearing his smart, bling outfits, he could still wear his archbishop's robes and fancy hat – his mitre – which made him taller than the king. Every time Henry tried to impose any changes on the church, Becket opposed him. He managed to antagonise everyone – including many of his fellow bishops – with his high-handed attitude and, in 1164, fled to France in self-imposed exile. He stayed there for six years, excommunicating people left, right and centre, and generally making a nuisance of himself.

Henry was forced by the pope to allow Becket back to Canterbury in 1170, but the dispute dragged on until Henry blurted out 'Who will rid me of this turbulent priest?'. Well, he never actually said those exact words. Henry had got drunk while campaigning in France and gone into a furious, gammon-faced rant about Becket – this lowly clerk whom he'd raised up and who was now trying to lord it over him. Four of his knights hurried off, crossed the Channel and rode to Canterbury Cathedral, where they burst in on Becket while he was at his prayers and tried to arrest him. Becket refused to leave the cathedral. They gave him to time to rethink, went away, and when they came back later on, there he was, still praying.

Was this an act of vanity? A deliberate way to bring about his own martyrdom? Or did he just think that they wouldn't dare harm the Archbishop of Canterbury? The fact that we're still discussing this incident today – and it is such a key moment in British history – tells us what a massive transgression their attack was.

Anyway, there was an argument and one of the knights twatted Becket round the head with his sword, slicing off the top of his skull, splattering brains and blood all over the floor. Another knight took a swipe and his sword rebounded, hitting one of the monks who was protecting the archbishop. It was a chaotic and ugly bloodbath, and Becket was slaughtered.

The knights panicked – *Had they gone too far? Maybe this wasn't what Henry had in mind* – and rushed off to hide out up in the north of England. Tellingly, they were never punished. Did Henry fear that a trial might expose his part in the outrage? Or was a big part of him grateful that Becket had been got rid of? Because when old friends fall out, it's far worse than a dispute between people who don't really know each other.

That might have been the end of Becket's time in the spotlight of history were it not for the fact that, when the monks stripped his dead body for burial, they apparently found that he was wearing a hairshirt under his robes. Heavy-duty Christians liked to wear undergarments made of woven goats' hair or horsehair to show just how pious they were. These shirts were horribly scratchy and uncomfortable, and, in Becket's case, crawling with maggots and lice. Becket was sending the message that, although he was a great man, he was nowhere near as great as God. He was just a humble sinner who would make his skin red raw – although I can't find anything in the New Testament that says Jesus wants us all to be miserable and itchy.

But everyone fell to their knees – Becket was a *really* holy guy – and cried out for him to be sanctified. This put Henry in a very awkward position, worried his subjects might turn on him. He was a good politician, though, and figured that if he became the chief advocate for making Becket a saint, it'd paint him in a good light and reflect well on the country to have such a major holy icon. Becket's death could become a useful bit of propaganda and even bring in some money from tourism. Once Becket was sanctified, Henry thought it prudent to do a bit of PR. He made a pilgrimage to the cathedral, walking the last part on his knees while stripped of his royal robes, and when he went inside, he knelt to pay penance at Becket's shrine while monks whipped him. It paid off. Henry was largely forgiven and Canterbury became a major destination for European pilgrims, as immortalised in Chaucer's *Canterbury Tales*.

Henry may have got away with it, but he still had to deal with problems within his own family. He had five sons. The eldest to survive childhood was, confusingly, also called Henry, and ended up being called 'Henry the Young King' because Henry II had him crowned while he was still alive. This was against church rules, so Henry had it done while Becket was in France. This had prompted the pope to order Henry to bring Becket back to England and had led to their final falling-out.

But Young Henry kept his position as 'Junior King'. The title was honorary. He was just a teenager at the time and didn't hold any real power. Giving him castles and land now would make him a potential threat. It meant, though, that if anything happened to Henry II, there would be no dispute about his successor.

Henry The Young King was only 15 when he was crowned, but he was already a veteran in the marriage game as he'd married the daughter of the king of France when he was five and she was only three – another example of King Henry II's astute political nous. He reckoned that if the English royal family was tied to the French royal family, it might bring an end to the constant territorial fighting in France. Needless to say, it didn't – partly because when young Henry was crowned Junior King, his French wife was not officially made queen. King Henry II forbade it, fearing that if his son died and his daughter-in-law was technically queen, she would have a claim to the throne. So all Henry's big plans to smooth things out with France backfired on him and his relationship with the French worsened.

Henry II and Eleanor had three other surviving sons – Richard, Geoffrey and John, who would each inherit parts of the Angevin Empire when Henry died. As the eldest, Henry the Young King would get England and Normandy, Richard would get Aquitaine, Geoffrey would get Brittany, and John … well, John would get nothing, earning him the nickname, 'John Lackland'. Feeling sorry for him, King Henry said he could be lord of Ireland. Henry had started the process of English colonisation in 1169. At the time, the country was ruled by a load of warring minor kings so there was little unity. Through a policy of divide and conquer, Henry was able to consolidate his position there and eventually hand John extensive estates.

All of Henry's boys were ambitious, particularly Henry the Young King, who soon started complaining that he had no actual land to gain an income from. Henry II told his son to be patient, but the boy wasn't having it and rose up against his father in 1173, 19 years into Henry's reign.

The big sport of the aristocracy was the tournament and the Young King was a renowned jouster, a playboy prince, famous in all the great jousting tournaments of France. He was described as being tall,

HENRY II ON HIS PILGRAMAGE

handsome, athletic and empty-headed. He was a superstar, a David Beckham figure, much-loved and able to command a great deal of support, including that of his mother, Eleanor of Aquitaine. By this time, she and King Henry II were no longer close. Henry was absent a great deal of the time and had a string of mistresses. Eleanor was looking to the future and sided with her son against her ageing husband in what became known as the Great Rebellion. It didn't go well for Eleanor. King Henry defeated his son's army and locked up his wife. Eleanor was to spend the next 16 years imprisoned in various English castles, only let out for special occasions, like Christmas, and she and Henry maintained an intense love/hate relationship.

Henry the Young King was just given a slap on the wrist, but his younger brother, Richard, sensing that his father was losing his grip, started cosying up to King Philip II of France. The two of them began plotting against King Henry, planning to get him out of the way and put Richard in charge of Normandy. And then, in 1182, nearly 10 years after the Great Rebellion, there was a second revolt, in which Henry the Young King tried one last time to take on his father.

Conditions in medieval military camps were appalling, with men packed together in filth and squalor. Many more soldiers died from dysentery, 'the bloody flux', than died in combat, and disease is no respecter of title. During the campaign, Henry the Young King came to a soldier's end: he shat himself to death.

Three years later, in 1186, 27-year-old Prince Geoffrey, was show-ing off at a tournament in Paris when he fell off his horse, which then trampled him to death. Geoffrey and King Philip were very close; the French king was so upset that he tried to climb into Geoffrey's coffin with him at his funeral – 'Take me too! I can't bear to let you go.' Which I think says quite a lot about their relationship.

Geoffrey's wife was pregnant at the time and gave birth to a son, Arthur, a few months later. Keep him in mind, he becomes important in the next chapter.

Meanwhile, the war dragged on as poor old King Henry was forced to fight against his own family as well as the king of France. It's no surprise he developed an ulcer. He tried to battle on through it, but, in the end, it burst and he died in 1189 at the age of 56.

Henry had understood that, to be a successful king, you had to balance success on the battlefield with good governance at home. Sadly, his successor, Richard the Lionheart, was only interested in the fighting bit.

6
DICK

RICHARD I – 1157–1199
Richard the Lionheart
Reigned 1189–1199
Lived for 42 years. Ruled for 10 years.
Died of gangrene.
Remembered for: being a Crusader king while wearing
the cross of St George.

There's only one statue of a monarch directly outside the Houses of Parliament, King Richard I, sitting astride a charger, one hand outstretched towards the heavens, gripping a mighty broadsword. When I was growing up in the 1960s, Richard the Lionheart was one of those stand-out kings we all knew about. He was our courageous, crusader king, with three lions on his shield and the cross of St George on his tabard.* He was the personification of England and empire, the hero king of the Robin Hood stories.

But Richard is one of those monarchs whose reputation has sunk during my lifetime. 'He only spent six months in England during his whole reign!' 'He didn't even speak English.' 'The Robin Hood stories were written 200 years after he died.' 'The crusaders were a bunch of violent, uncivilised thugs!' 'He bled England dry, raising taxes to support his military campaigns.' 'He was having an affair with the King of France.' And so on.

---

* Apparently, Richard had nothing to do with St George. He wore a white cross while crusading (not a red one) and his association with the saint was tacked onto his legend by the Tudors. It was Edward I who actually adopted St George as his patron saint, an idea that was cemented by Edward III who wanted a warrior saint's banner to march behind. Henry V ultimately made George a popular *national* patron saint.

You have to see these monarchs in their historical context. And, in terms of what was expected of a king during the medieval era, Richard was a huge success. He won battles; he fought the infidels; he knocked the French about; he brought glory to England. Eight hundred-odd years later, we can't berate Richard the Lionheart for not behaving like a modern, tofu-munching, latte-sipping liberal democrat.

It has to be said, however, that although Richard was born and mostly grew up in England, once he came to the throne, his attention was increasingly drawn overseas. In the end, his impact on England didn't go much beyond raising taxes and inspiring the nation with his exploits in the Holy Land.

He was tall, handsome and athletic, with red/gold hair and something fiery and demonic about him. His family, the Angevins, were supposedly descended from a legendary female demon, Melusine – half woman, half serpent – who had given them 'infernal blood'.

As we've seen, the last years of King Henry II's reign were marred by bad relationships with his sons, who were impatient for him to die so that they could come into their own. Richard couldn't wait – he wanted power, wealth and status NOW – and tried to depose his father. Not only was he at war with Henry when he died, but to make matters worse, Richard had allied with Henry's great enemy, King Philip II of France of all people.

We saw how Richard's younger brother, Jousting Geoffrey, was a *very dear friend* of Philip and there's been much speculation about whether Richard may also have been in love with Philip. They were certainly close when Richard was younger and there were a couple of occasions when they spent the night in bed together, but this was very much a political act, a symbolic gesture, meant to demonstrate their friendship and alliance. At the time, there was no hint that this might be anything sexual. Plus, the room was no doubt full of attendants.

The first thing Richard did when his father died was to release his mother, Eleanor of Aquitaine, from her long imprisonment. She was at Westminster Abbey when he was crowned. Everything that Richard did was touched by violence and his coronation was no exception. Christians were banned from lending money with interest – usury –

and when William the Conqueror had needed a system of borrowing to effectively govern the country and mount military campaigns, he'd invited Jewish merchants and bankers over to England after 1066. By Richard's time, there were several Jewish communities around the country. But Jews were banned from royal occasions and, when a group of them tried to attend his coronation to congratulate him, Richard's men attacked them. This led to rumours that Richard had ordered all Jews to be killed and there were anti-Jewish riots all over the country. There was an infamous massacre in York, where the Jews took refuge in the castle. Surrounded by a violent mob, they ended up taking their own lives rather than be massacred by the locals.

To his credit, Richard put the revolts down and condemned them. He needed the Jews to help finance his military campaigns, after all. It has to be said that this antisemitism had been partly provoked by a growing antipathy within Christianity towards other faiths, which had been ignited by the Crusades.

Richard was 31 at the time of his coronation in 1189 and impatient to *do* something. He immediately set about raising money to fund taking an army to the Holy Land on what was to be the Third Crusade. He needed a vast sum and introduced the 'Saladin tithe' – basically a 10 per cent property tax. He also sold off anything he could – parcels of land, aristocratic titles – and later said, 'I would have sold London if I could find a buyer.'

————————— • ◆ • —————————

After the First Crusade, the Christians had created Crusader states all the way along the Mediterranean coast between Egypt and present-day Turkey. By Richard's time, they'd become independent kingdoms, each with their own ruler. The locals were understandably never very happy with this state of affairs and, in 1144, a Sunni leader called Zengi had attacked and captured the most northerly of the states – Edessa. This led to the Second Crusade, when two Western armies failed to get back what had been lost. In the chaos and confusion that followed, a new Kurdish Muslim leader emerged – Saladin. He'd already conquered Egypt and Syria, and now he took on the Christians. In 1187, he captured Jerusalem, prompting a third crusade two years later.

———————•◆•———————

Richard was worried about what might happen in England while he was away. He didn't fully trust his younger brother John not to seize power, so he bribed him with gifts of lands and titles, which came with conditions. Before setting off, Richard left a couple of lords in charge and made Prince John swear to stay in France for at least three years and not meddle with affairs in England. However, when Richard announced that he was appointing his four-year-old nephew, Prince Arthur (the son of Jousting George), as his successor, John was livid. He had coveted the role and broke his promise to Richard. He soon returned to England where he started to undermine and sabotage the lords, eventually manoeuvring himself into pole position.

The crusader army was under the joint leadership of Richard, Philip II of France and Frederick Barbarossa, the king of Germany (and Holy Roman Emperor). Barbarossa had once been a mighty, all-conquering warrior, but was now nearly 70 and well past his prime. He brought his army by land, down though Eastern Europe and into Turkey, where he fell off his horse crossing a river, wearing heavy armour, and drowned. Most of his army returned home; those who were left eventually came under the leadership of Leopold of Austria, a nobleman of lower status who commanded little respect from Richard and Philip.

When he was a boy, Richard had been betrothed to King Philip's half sister, Alice – another doomed attempt by Henry II to create a meaningful and peaceful alliance with the French. But now the Lionheart announced that he was breaking off his engagement to Alice and was going to marry a Spanish princess, Berengaria of Navarre. This, naturally, pissed off Philip.

Richard married Berengaria in Cyprus, which he'd taken by force from the local ruler after an argument, and then took her crusading for their honeymoon. They never had any children. They never had much of a chance. They were separated on the way back from the Crusades and never saw each other again.

The first thing Richard and Philip did when they arrived in the Holy Land was to join the Siege of Acre, which had been captured by Saladin's troops. Acre had been designated the capital of the Kingdom of Jerusalem after the city of Jerusalem had fallen to Saladin. But there was sickness in the Crusader camp and both Richard and Philip were affected. Richard was struck down by a scurvy-like illness called arnaldia. Nobody today is quite sure what arnaldia was and whether there's any modern equivalent. It caused fever, hair loss, loosening of the teeth and fingernails, ulcers and blistering of the skin. It was very debilitating, although Richard did find the strength to pick men off the battlements of Acre with a crossbow while lying on a stretcher.

Despite all this, the Crusaders broke the siege and took Acre's defenders prisoner. Riven by rivalries, the Crusaders were always falling out with each other and when the jumped-up tea boy, Leopold of Austria, tried to hang his own banners alongside those of Richard and Philip on the walls of Acre, the two kings were furious. They pulled down Leopold's banners and chucked them in the moat. Leopold stormed off home in a huff, taking the remnants of the German army with him.

Philip left not long after; he'd grown (literally) sick and tired of Richard and the whole crusading thing. Richard was now isolated and in sole charge. Needing to move on and unable to take nearly 3,000 prisoners with him (after their ransom payment had failed to materialise), he executed the lot of them. This was not unprecedented, militarily speaking, and, although barbaric, it was the only option Richard had. It didn't go down very well with the locals, however, or with Richard's fellow Christian companions, who didn't consider what he'd done to be exactly chivalrous.

Richard's campaigning was largely successful after that. He secured several other cities and states up the coast, although he was never able to take back Jerusalem. It's hard to imagine what it must have been like for these soldiers from Western Europe, weighed down by chainmail, carrying heavy weapons and shields, fighting in the heat of the Middle East, but, somehow, they did. In the end, though, neither side was able to secure a decisive victory. Richard needed to get home and sort out the mess that his brother John was making and he knew that even if he could take Jerusalem, he wouldn't be able to hold it for long. So, he came to an agreement with Saladin at the Treaty of Jaffa that left Saladin in control of the city as long as he allowed Christian pilgrims and merchants to once again be free to come and go.

The whole area had been a mess since the wars between the Seljuks and the Abbasids that had drawn in the Byzantines and then the Crusaders. The Crusaders had made matters a lot worse, but, compared to the later Mongol invasion, their incursions and interference were considerably less violent and destructive.

Richard shored up the defences of the Crusader states and set off home. He was still unwell and everything was against him. The weather was stormy. He lost ships at sea. Men deserted. By the time he was shipwrecked on the northern Adriatic coast this once almighty crusader, this great king, the leader of a 50,000-strong army, was down to an entourage of only a handful of men. He'd pissed off so many rulers and lost so many friends on the crusade that he couldn't trust anyone and he now had to take the dangerous mainland route home through enemy territory. He and his men disguised themselves as templars and set off. Trying to cross Austria, Richard was captured by

RICHARD I AND HIS LION PUNCH-UP

the gleeful Leopold, the man he'd insulted and belittled outside the walls of Acre. Leopold couldn't believe his luck. He locked Richard up and began negotiations to see what profit he could make out of his captive. In the end, he sold Richard on to another of his enemies, the new Holy Roman Emperor, Heinrich VI, who demanded literally a king's ransom for his release.

He sent a bill to Richard's brother, Prince John, for 100,000 pounds of silver, roughly three times the annual royal income in England, and substantially more than Richard had raised to finance his crusade with his 'Saladin tithe'. Now, only three years later, the English nobility were being asked to cough up all over again. Poor old John got a bad reputation for relentlessly squeezing taxes out of the English people, but it was all to raise money to save his stupid, bloody brother.

Richard was to spend over a year in captivity and various romantic myths grew up around his time in chains. One was that Emperor Heinrich tried to bump Richard off by putting a lion in his cell, but Richard thrust his hand down the lion's throat and tore out its heart. His hand was protected by a wrapping of silk scarves given to him by Heinrich's daughter who had inevitably fallen in love with him.

The truth is more mundane. Back in England, little brother John was dragging his feet. He quite liked running the country and, for the first time in his life, he had proper power, wealth and status. He even plotted with Philip of France to send money to Emperor Heinrich – not to free Richard, but to keep him locked up. John had been busy forging his own relationship with Philip, by trading chunks of Richard's empire in France with him, and would have been very happy never to see Richard again. But, even locked up, Richard still had influence. Despite not having been in his kingdom for years, his reputation was so great that his people were prepared to pay to have him back.

Fearing the wrath of Richard's supporters John caved in, leaving it up to his mother, Eleanor of Aquitaine to scrape the money together for the ransom. Philip sent John a message: 'Look to yourself – the devil is loose!' The full fury of the Angevin demon was coming home. John hid from his brother in France and, luckily for him, Eleanor pleaded on his behalf and Richard was lenient. But he had to spend the rest of his reign clawing back the French territories that John had ceded to Philip. He won a major battle against the French at Fréteval in 1194 and, four years later, at the Battle of Gisors, Richard took as his motto '*Dieu et mon Droit*' – '*God and my Right*', still used by the monarchy today. Richard was saying that the only power higher than him in France was God, not Philip.

It turned out Richard was going to meet that higher power sooner than he expected. The story goes that, in 1199, having slaughtered many of the local population, he was besieging Châlus-Chabrol, an insignificant little castle in the Limousin, when a young lad whose family had been killed by the English shot Richard in the shoulder with his crossbow from the castle walls. The wound became gangrenous and Richard was soon on his way out.

Eleanor rushed to be by his side and he died in her arms, but not before summoning the young crossbowman, Pierre. 'This is war,' he told the lad. 'You did what you had to do. Your family had been killed. My dying wish is to pardon you. You will not be punished for what you've done.'

This was seen as a fine, chivalrous act by Richard. Although, as soon as Richard was dead, his men got hold of Pierre, flayed him alive and hanged him. And so it was that 'the Lion by the Ant was slain'.

Richard had requested that his entrails should be buried where he died, in Châlus, and then – in a twist on the old song 'I Left My Heart In San Francisco' – his heart was taken to be buried in Rouen, the capital of Normandy, and his body was buried at his father's feet at Fontevraud Abbey in Anjou. And England, where he'd been king? What was buried there? Not a thing. He evidently did not give a toss about England. You'd think he might have spared a toe, an eyebrow, a bollock – something, *anything* – to be buried in Westminster Abbey.

All he left England was a huge tax bill, a self-aggrandising motto, and his royal 'Three Lions' crest.

7

JOHN

KING JOHN – *c*.1166–1216
John Lackland/John Softsword
Reigned 1199–1216
Lived for 50 years. Ruled (officially) for 17 years.
Died of an exploding stomach.
Remembered for: pissing everybody off and being forced
to sign Magna Carta.

John is another king who the average punter might know something about and could probably dredge up at least one of these four facts about him.

1. He's the chief villain in the Robin Hood stories.
2. He was the brother of Richard the Lionheart.
3. He was fond of heavy taxation.
4. He signed Magna Carta.

So, what else can I tell you about him? Well, he was about five foot five, stocky, with dark red hair. He liked expensive clothes and jewellery. Like most of the Angevins, he had an insane temper and a restless energy. He was always on the move, never staying long in one place, travelling nearly every day throughout his reign, with his own furniture, as well as panes of glass to fit in draughty castle windows, and even a dressing gown. His barons and bishops lived in dread of John turning up at their castle with his entourage, often made up of hundreds of people. He was the guest from hell. He would try to sleep with your wife and/or daughter, eat all your food, drink all your wine, extract money from you and then threaten to have you thrown in jail.

He could be genial and witty, but was quite unstable, often behaving like a petulant child and stamping his little feet: 'I'm the king! I should be allowed to do whatever I want!' This meant that he fell out with just about everybody he ever had any dealings with. In short, he was a ghastly man and a terrible king.

As we've seen, though, John never expected to *be* king. When he was growing up, he was fourth in line to the throne with three strapping elder brothers ahead of him. He was a very junior member of the royal family, with no lucrative estates and no great castles, which meant he had considerably less power and wealth than the average, high-ranking baron. He was the classic spare prick at a wedding.

We've seen how his father, King Henry II, wanted to help John and made him lord of Ireland. Prince John was only 19 when he crossed the Irish Sea in 1185 with a small force, but initially he had some military success and declared that he would become king of Ireland. The pope was having none of it, however; John would have to make do with the lowlier title of lord of Ireland. Neither the original Irish nor the recent Anglo-Norman colonisers were keen on English inter-ference and John failed to win them over. He turned out to be a hopeless diplomat with a genius for making enemies. He threw his weight around, took the piss out of the Irish lords for being provincial and having unfashionable beards, and was soon chased back to England. It was to be 25 years before he returned to Ireland, in 1210, this time with a little more success.

So, let's look at those four key facts about John.

HE'S THE CHIEF VILLAIN
IN ROBIN HOOD

Robin Hood stories only really started to appear about 200 years after John's death. Robin is obviously fictional and John didn't feature in many of the original stories. He was, however, the perfect baddie. At the heart of the stories is the conflict between the stout Saxon yeomen of England and the despised, arrogant, poncy French elite. It's telling that Robin and his merry men hide out in Sherwood Forest. The newly enclosed royal forests were as hated as the royals. There's a clause in Magna Carta that orders all the forests created during John's reign to be given back to the people.

HE WAS THE BROTHER OF
RICHARD THE LIONHEART

Apart from his disastrous foray into Ireland, John's teenage years were taken up with family in-fighting in France. He and his brothers – Henry the Young King, Richard and Geoffrey – were constantly ganging up to fight, either against each other, or against their father. But, one by one, they fell away. Henry the Young King died from dysentery while campaigning against his father and Geoffrey managed to get himself trampled to death by his own horse in a jousting tournament. By the time Henry II died, John found himself unexpectedly second in line to the throne behind Richard. Or was he? There was the small complication of Geoffrey's son, Arthur.

We've seen how, after Richard went off crusading, he was barely seen in England again, but that he appointed Arthur as his successor. John plotted his own advancement as soon as Richard boarded his ship and ended up running things while Richard was away. John relied on the support and experience of his mother, Eleanor, who commanded the respect in England that he lacked. (Eleanor eventually died in 1204, 15 years after Richard went on the First Crusade, at the age of 82, which left John devastated.)

We saw in the previous chapter how King Philip of France returned early from the Crusades, furious at Richard's high-handed behaviour. There was another reason for his early return, however. With Richard busy crusading, his lands in France were vulnerable. The ever-untrustworthy, ever-scheming John travelled to Paris to pay homage to Philip and the two of them set about plotting to divide up Richard's lands between them. We've seen how, when Richard came roaring home, Eleanor begged him to forgive his little brother, and Richard conceded that, although John was 27, he was 'a child who has had evil counsellors'. Five years later, the Lionheart was dead and John was ready to officially take the throne.

If only Prince Arthur wasn't standing in his way. It was now up to the lords to decide. John had age and experience on his side. After all, he'd been the acting CEO while Richard was absent. Arthur had the backing of the pope and the king of France, but was still very young. Luckily for John, enough English barons thought that if they put a 12-year-old boy on the throne, the country would descend into chaos and civil war. And so, in 1199, John was crowned king of England. Which did not go well.

HE WAS FOND OF HEAVY TAXATION

John must have hoped that, on the back of their earlier plotting, he and King Philip of France would be friends for life, but that was a huge miscalculation. Philip knew that John was not a great warrior king in the mould of his brother. He was no great military tactician and he had a terrible habit of falling out with his allies.

Under the pretence of trying to put the rightful heir – Arthur – on the English throne, Philip attacked John's holdings in France, dismantling the Angevin Empire that John's father had so tirelessly built. Eventually, even Normandy fell to Philip. To lose Normandy was a disaster for John that destroyed his reputation and utterly changed the politics of Europe, as France became by far the most dominant power.

John was, at least, a trier. He was forever raising taxes to pay for armies in England and France as he attempted a fight back. He had precious few victories, but one thing went his way. In 1202, his barons captured the 15-year-old Arthur, who ended up imprisoned in a castle in Rouen, from which he never emerged. The belief was that John had ordered him killed in one of his rages or, in some versions of the story, had actually killed the teenager himself. In Shakespeare's play, *King John*, while heroically trying to escape, Arthur jumps from the castle walls to his death.

If he'd won some big battles and had a brilliant military career, like Richard, things might have gone differently for John, but he was a loser and the barons grew increasingly fed up with the constant drain on their resources. He also leaned very heavily on the Jews, forcing them to pay him so much in taxes that they had to call in debts early, which further infuriated the barons. If a lord couldn't pay up, they'd lose their estates to the lenders. But, as the Jews weren't allowed to own land, and John basically owned the Jews, the forfeited estates went to the king.

John was ruining the economy and wound up offending everyone, even the pope. He got into an almighty row with Innocent III after he rejected his choice for the next Archbishop of Canterbury. This was a classic example of a monarch resenting the influence of the church and the argument led to Innocent slapping an interdict on England in 1208 that banned anyone from attending religious services. Churches were closed. The bells were silenced. There were no sermons, no weddings, no funerals, no burials in churchyards – dead bodies were thrown into ditches. John stubbornly refused to budge even when the pope excommunicated him, condemning his immortal soul to an eternity of suffering. But after six years of this John had had enough. He effectively bribed the pope to lift his restrictions and un-excommunicate him, but he knew he was never going to win in France and would have to accept the loss of his territories, so he made peace with Philip and swallowed his punitive terms.

All that money wasted, all those men killed, for nothing. John had earned himself a new nickname. No longer John Lackland, he was now John Softsword. And if that sounds like a double entendre, it's supposed to. Richard was the model medieval king, proudly holding his sword aloft, rigid and hard, while the image of Softsword says it all about John.

He'd lost all respect and, in 1215, a group of barons marched on London, styling themselves the 'Army of God'. On 15 June they demanded that John meet them beside the Thames, near Windsor Castle, at a marshy site called Runnymede. John would have to agree to their demands or they'd get rid of him.

HE SIGNED MAGNA CARTA*

Magna Carta (the 'Big Charter') is a very misunderstood document that's become something of a totem – used and misused over the years and made to stand for whatever you want it to stand for. In fact, it was only law for a few weeks and many of the clauses in it were dumped.

The first part of the charter guarantees the freedom of the church, and after that it's basically a contract between the king and his lords, outlining what he's allowed to do and what they're allowed to do. The charter spelled out that the king only ruled by the consent of the lords who were to set up a committee of 25 barons to act as a sort of proto-parliament. In the end, this part never really happened as nobody could agree on who the 25 would be. The ordinary people of England don't really get a look in – other than saying that they had the right to fair trial.

A lot of the charter is very specific to the time it was drawn up. There's stuff about making peace with the Welsh and the Scots, and there are a few dodgy clauses about the status of foreigners, Jews and women (their testimony in court is worth less than men's), which might come as a surprise to anyone who thinks the charter's all about liberty and human rights and the birth of democracy.

There were some practical clauses to do with regulating fish traps on the Medway and the Thames. Weights and measures were standardised. The law of the land was clarified and local courts were to be set up around the country. There would also be a regular parliament in a set location.

The main thing was that, after it was signed, everything was sorted out once and for all and there were never again any bad kings. *Yeah, right.* In actual fact, neither side intended to stick to any of what they signed up to. It simply bought everyone a little time to muster their forces. No sooner had he put his seal to the charter than John went running off to the pope and bribed him to say that Magna Carta was 'shameful, demeaning, illegal and unjust'. By the end of the year, a bloody civil war had broken out, dubbed the First Barons' War. The

---

* He didn't actually sign it – just attached his royal seal.

KING JOHN LOSES HIS JEWELS IN THE WASH

barons even invited the heir to the French throne, Louis, to bring an army over and become a replacement king. John trudged up and down the country trying to drum up support: 'I'm the king – don't give power to this elite.'

At one point, while on another weary forced march, he got trapped by rising waters in a tidal inlet between East Anglia and the Midlands called The Wash. His baggage train got sucked under and he lost most of his possessions, including the crown jewels, which was pretty symbolic. Not long afterwards, he contracted dysentery and was taken to Newark Castle, where somebody had the bright idea of feeding him peaches as a cure. (Reader, if you ever get dysentery, don't stuff your face with peaches. It only makes things worse.) John is sometimes described as dying of a surfeit of peaches.

Matthew Paris, the Benedictine monk historian, wrote 'Foul as it is, hell itself is made fouler by the presence of John.' So, that gives you some idea of what the English people thought of him.

John is one of only four British monarchs who don't have a regnal number (the other three being Stephen, Anne and Victoria). No future king ever wanted to be named after such a stinker.

8

ḢARRY 3

HENRY III – 1207–1272
Henry of Winchester
Reigned 1216–1272
Lived for 65 years. Ruled for 56 years.
Died of an exploding brain (a series of strokes).
Remembered for: signing an updated Magna Carta and going to
war with Simon de Montfort, the 'father of parliament'.

Nobody remembers Henry III. He was like a lesser-known sequel to his father, John. He made the same mistakes, he wasn't a great military leader, he lost even more French territories, alienated his barons and ended up at war with them.

But perhaps Henry III shouldn't be written off as a nonentity. With 56 years on the throne, he was our longest-reigning monarch until George III, 500 years later, so he must have done something right. Even if it was more by accident than design. On the one hand, he was an uncomplicated, straight-down-the-line kind of guy, and on the other, he was gullible, easily led and too willing to listen to the first piece of advice he heard, no matter who it was coming from. He couldn't tell what was a sensible policy and what was a terrible one. When his barons eventually turned on him, they claimed they simply wanted to force him to ask them for their advice before flying off on one of his stupid, expensive undertakings.

Henry should also get credit for helping to forge an English identity. Realising that France was gone and that he would only ever rule over England, he decided to concentrate on becoming accepted as an *English* king and promoted the idea that England was more important than France. He reached back into the pre-Norman past to dredge up Edward the Confessor, the great Saxon king, adopting him as his patron saint and promoting the cult around him. He built a shrine to Edward in Westminster Abbey (the cathedral that Edward had commissioned) and named his eldest son after him.

Using a Saxon name for a Norman/Plantagenet prince was a radical break from tradition. The previous kings all had their roots in France and stuck to French names. The English were the conquered race, second class. If you wanted any status at court, you needed a name like Richard, William (Guillaume) or Stephen (Étienne). But Henry (Henri) wanted to say to his English subjects that he was one of them: an Englishman. It was all he had going for him.

England had very nearly become a French vassal state towards the end of John's reign. From 1216 to 1217, we technically had a French king on the throne, Prince Louis, son of King Philip. He was never actually crowned, though, and the pope didn't recognise him as monarch. In fact, he excommunicated him. It would set a very bad precedent for a Christian king to depose another Christian king.

As it was, John died soon after Louis was proclaimed king, at which point the English barons asked themselves whether they really wanted a Frenchman on the throne. The rightful heir, Henry, was nine years old and the barons reckoned they could keep him as a puppet and run England exactly as they wanted. So, the focus of the war changed from attacking John's supporters to attacking Louis's French army. Louis quite fancied being king of England, but, after he lost a couple of battles, he got the message and accepted a big bribe to go back home to France.

Prince Henry was affirmed as king, but a council of 13 barons and clergymen ruled on his behalf. The man in charge, and Henry's chief guardian, was William Marshall. Marshall was the model of a romantic, chivalrous, medieval knight. He was present at the signing of Magna Carta and served five kings in his long life. He protected Henry and helped bring much-needed peace and unity to the country. The other barons on the council were a pretty rackety bunch, untrustworthy and unreliable, who had been forever switching sides for their own personal gain during the civil wars.

Under Marshall's guidance, the first few years of Henry's reign went smoothly. Magna Carta was dusted off a couple of times, updated and reaffirmed, but as Henry got into his teenage years, he became more independent and started to assert his own authority. He massively resented what the barons had done to his father, but made the mistake of thinking that as he'd been accepted as king, it gave him the mandate to do whatever he wanted. He started to lord it over the barons and take on highfalutin royal airs, including the belief that he had the ability to heal the sick with his touch.

Henry enjoyed the trappings of royalty, his crown and his expensive robes, the pomp, the ceremony and the rituals of the court life. He also put on a big outward display of piety, with a lot of theatrical kneeling and praying. Basically, he enjoyed the performative side of being king but wasn't so keen on the boring bits, all the actual ruling stuff, and hated having to deal with either the people or his barons.

He did make some home improvements, though. He was very keen on architecture. As well as building the new shrine to Edward the Confessor in Westminster Abbey, he expanded and updated the Tower of London to make it more comfortable and secure as a royal palace. He also established a royal zoo there. He'd been gifted many exotic animals by foreign rulers, including a camel, an elephant and a polar bear that caught fish in the Thames.

Henry married relatively late in life, in 1236. It's a bit of an understatement to say that there was an age gap between him and his bride, Eleanor of Provence. He was 28 and she was 12. Make of that what you will. Henry, having lost most of his remaining lands in France, needed a good political marriage. Eleanor may have been young, but she was French, and marrying her allied Henry with a large power bloc in southern France. It turned out to be more than just a good political marriage, though. Henry grew to genuinely love Eleanor and she proved to be much tougher and more determined than him. She also gave him five children. Her first child, the future King Edward I, was born when she was only 15.

Henry much preferred spending time with his wife than doing the traditional kingly stuff – campaigning, leading armies, hitting people with a sword. There's a story that an assassin came to his chambers to kill him but couldn't find him. It turned out he was in Eleanor's chambers, 'enjoying her company'. So, he was saved by the simple act of shagging his wife.

Henry didn't spend all his time canoodling with Eleanor. He twice tried to get back what had been lost in France. In 1228, he made an alliance with the dukes of Normandy and Poitou to regain his Angevin lands, but he dithered about in England and his lords weren't keen on the expense. By the time he'd scraped the money together and turned up for the fight with a small army, he was two years late. The opportunity had passed and he came home looking pretty foolish.

His next attempt came over 10 years later. This time, he jumped the gun and arrived too early, going off half-cocked, underfunded and under-supported in France. The considerably wealthier French king, Louis IX, gave a sneery French 'puh' and Henry chickened out. He tried to make a deal with Louis almost as soon as he'd landed, but the French gave him another 'puh' and Henry ended up sloping back to England with his tail between his legs. Again.

The knock-on effect of these pathetic campaigns was that Louis felt emboldened to take over more French territories and he successfully attacked the lands held by Henry's in-laws – Provence and Savoy. Suddenly, a whole load of Eleanor's dispossessed relatives started tipping up in England. Henry welcomed them and made them his new favourites at court, handing them favours – land he'd confiscated from his other barons and fancy titles. This went down with his English barons about as well as a cup of cold frogspawn.

Desperate to impress his barons, become a player on the world stage and keep the support of his subjects, Henry came up with a scheme to make his son, Edmund Crouchback, king of Sicily (the island was a useful staging post for Crusaders). But when he asked for money from his barons, they point-blank refused. Henry had to extort the money from the church instead. In the end, though, Henry never actually sent an army and wasted all the money on trying to bribe the pope and various foreign heads of state to get Edmund put in place.

With nothing to show for his Sicilian designs, Henry announced that he was going on a crusade, which was a sure-fire way of gaining respect. It was also a great way to fill his empty coffers. But, having raised the funds through hefty taxation, somehow Henry never actually got round to setting off. Did he ever intend to? Or was it, more likely, a cynical money-raising scheme? After all, Henry was never the crusading type.

Of course, all his dodgy dealings had the opposite effect to what he'd intended. People liked and respected him even less now. And then, in 1257, the harvest failed, plunging England into famine. Tensions in court between the Nouveau French and the old-school English contingent broke out into fighting. The Anglos said that unless Henry sorted out the Frogs, there'd be trouble. Fearing that he might be deposed, Henry agreed to sign what was essentially a new Magna Carta, a contract between the king and his barons known as the Provisions of Oxford.

This new charter established a regular parliament (from the French word, *parler*, meaning 'to talk'), sitting three times a year, and introduced the idea that not only the nobility should have a voice. Representatives of the common people (mayors, merchants, guild members etc.) were for the first time allowed to attend sessions.

Henry also agreed to be governed by a council of 24 barons and church leaders. Almost as soon as he'd signed up to all this, however, he went crawling to the pope to try to get himself off the hook, just like his father before him. The result? A Second Barons War.

The leader of the rebellion was a man called Simon de Montfort. Even though he had the very English title 'Earl of Leicester', de Montfort was a powerful French crusader lord. Tough, stern and unyielding – and anti-monarchy/pro-parliament – he was very much a proto-Oliver Cromwell figure. De Montfort was married to Henry's sister (another Eleanor, I'm afraid), but the two men had never got on. De Montfort had been one of the king's miltary commanders in France, where he'd become disgusted by Henry's behaviour, accusing him of being a coward and a fool.

It was de Montfort who forced Henry to sign the Provisions of Oxford, which is why he's called the 'father of parliament'. It would be wrong to think that de Montfort's parliament would be recognisable to us today, however. There was still very limited representation and its main role was to organise taxation. Simon de Montfort has gone down in history as a great parliamentarian, but he was an appalling man who did some awful things, particularly to the Jews.

Ever since William the Conqueror had brought Jews over to England to set up a money-lending system, they'd been pretty much forbidden to do any other kind of work. They couldn't own land but could be farmers, and they couldn't join any of the merchant or artisan guilds, because you had to swear a Christian oath to do so. There were more restrictions on them. By Henry's time they weren't allowed to mix with Christians or intermarry and they had to sew identifying badges onto their clothing and stay in their own areas. This made Christians suspicious of them – 'Oh the Jews, they stick to themselves. They've got no interest in us. They just want to take all our money. They're all rich bankers. They're real money grabbers, aren't they?'

As a further insult, the Jews were also *owned* by the king, listed among his goods and chattels, so, they had absolutely no independence at all. Whenever hefty royal taxes were introduced, the barons would borrow money from the Jews and they resented paying the interest. So they were forever trying to get the king to wipe the slate clean and clear their debts. This was one of the main reasons de Montfort created his new model of parliament: to sort out what he saw as the Jewish problem. He'd already expelled the Jews from his Earldom of Leicester in 1231, 'for the good of my soul and for the souls of my ancestors and successors'. This is what crusading did to you. Following in his zealous father's footsteps, de Montfort had been a major player in the Albigensian crusade against 'heretics' in southern France, and he brought all his crusading zeal to the new Baron's War. He had early success when he captured both Henry and his eldest son, Edward, at the Battle of Lewes and imprisoned them. In a further echo of Cromwell, the fundamentalist Earl of Leicester set himself up as the ruler of England, which meant he was able to fulfil all his wishes, including wiping all the Jewish debt. He figured that the best way to do this was to essentially slaughter the Jews and destroy all their records. He and his sons organised several massacres and forced the captive Henry into passing various new anti-Semitic laws.

But de Montfort's rule didn't last long because Henry had a secret weapon. His son, Prince Edward, was a very different man to his father. A tough, macho warrior, he escaped captivity, rallied an army and took on de Montfort at the Battle of Evesham. De Montfort had done

something radical that didn't go in his favour. True to his beliefs, he'd raised an army of commoners, which meant that he was no longer subject to the rules of chivalry. At the time, it wasn't done to kill noblemen or royalty in battles. You tried to capture them and then issue a ransom for a hefty sum. You were free to hack down the ordinary foot soldiers, though, of course.

De Montfort had lost the support of many barons, who were fed up with his puritanical, overbearing manner and his promotion of the ordinary people, and were leaning heavily towards Henry. Before the battle, de Montfort, knowing he was outnumbered and had little chance of winning, said to his men, 'God have mercy on our souls, for our bodies are theirs.'

By breaking the rules of chivalry, de Montfort had made himself fair game, so Edward sent a hit squad to find and kill him. The earl's prediction was correct – he was cut down on the battlefield and his body was dismembered and mutilated. The chronicle at the time put it well, he 'was severed from his body'.

One of the king's supporters, Roger, 1st Baron Mortimer, sent de Montfort's head in a box as a gift to his wife, Maud, with his testicles hanging on either side of his nose. If any of you guys reading this are stuck for a birthday present for your wife, why not simply cut off the head of your rival and give it to her with his testicles dangling off his hooter? I think she'd really love that.

So that was the end of de Montfort and, soon after, the Second Barons' War. Henry wasn't able to properly relish his victory, because he died five years later, probably of a stroke. He was in his sixties and, because he'd been so young when he'd come to the throne, he'd had an unusually long reign. He was succeeded by his mighty, warrior son, Edward, who was about as much of a contrast to Henry as you could imagine.

9
1–2–3 NEDS (#1)

EDWARD I – 1239–1307
Edward Longshanks, the Hammer of the Scots
Reigned 1272–1307
Lived for 68 years. Ruled for 35 years.
Died of an exploding stomach.
Remembered for: hammering the Scots and expelling the Jews.

'Edwardus Magnus' was undeniably a great king who did a great deal to restore pride, order and stability to England and to establish a working parliament. But he was also a 'terrible king' – *Magnus Terribilis*, as he was recorded in the histories. This is 'terrible' in the original sense, in that he inspired awe and terror in friend and foe alike.

The fact that Edward I was the first king since 1066 to have a pre-Norman, 'English' name marks a shift away from French dominance to a monarchy that's more recognisably homegrown. Our kings were starting to think of themselves as fully English (Edward was recorded as speaking the language on the Crusades) and while he inevitably had to deal with the usual problems in France, his attention became increasingly focused on what was going on at home. His dream was to unite Ireland, Wales and Scotland under English rule.

Today, his colonial ambitions and achievements are seen as 'bad things'. At the time, they were viewed (by the English, at least) as 'good things'. After the disappointments of the hapless Henry III, Edward was just what the English wanted – another Richard the Lionheart, a warrior, a crusader, the hammer of his enemies. Like his great-uncle Richard, Edward was tall, standing at about six foot two, which earned him the nickname Edward Longshanks. His long arms meant he could outreach his enemies in battle and smite them silly with his mighty broadsword.

He had a slightly drooping eyelid, which he inherited from his father, and a bit of a lisp as well, but woe betide anyone who tried to mock him. In true Plantagenet style, he had a furious temper and terrified many who came into contact with him (a bishop is said to have dropped dead from fear in his presence).

Henry III had given Edward control of Ireland long before he became king. He also put him in charge of Gascony in southern France, which was just about all that was left of the once-mighty Angevin Empire, and, in order to strengthen his position, arranged a political marriage between Edward and Eleanor of Castile. (Yes, another bloody Eleanor, I'm afraid.)

Castile was a powerful kingdom in northern Spain just over the Pyrenees from Gascony. The marriage to Eleanor was designed to neutralise any cross-border threat and send a message to the French not to interfere. Eleanor was the half-sister of the king of Castile, Alfonso X. At the time of their marriage, Edward was 15 and his bride was 13. Edward and his father did have one thing in common. They both loved their wives and stayed faithful. Neither of them had the usual string of mistresses. They also both had a lot of children. Edward and Eleanor had at least 14.

When King Henry went to war against the rebel barons under Simon de Montfort, after he'd been forced to sign up to the Provisions of Oxford, Prince Edward showed a strong independent streak. He flip-flopped between supporting his father and supporting the English rebels under de Montfort. Henry even feared at one point that Edward might mount a coup against him, but, in the end, Edward declared for Henry. He was one of the commanders of his father's army when it went up against de Montfort at the Battle of Lewes. As we saw, this didn't go well – both Edward and his father were taken captive.

But de Montfort couldn't hold Edward for long. The story goes that while the prince was being held in Hereford Castle, the castellan took delivery of some fine war horses. Knowing how much Edward loved a war horse, the castellan asked him if he'd like to try one. Edward put the horse through its paces, charging about and pulling up the reins to do skid stops, like a teenager showing off on a motorbike. Having ridden the first horse into the ground, Edward went on to check out the rest of them, exhausting each one in turn. Finally, he jumped into the saddle of the last horse and rode off over the hill into the sunset. His guards couldn't chase him because all the other horses were completely knackered. The story is at best embellished, at worst fake news, but Edward *did* escape captivity and there's a poetical truth to this folk tale. It shows what sort of a man Edward was – and how he was perceived.

Once free, Edward led the counterattack against de Montfort and, as soon as he'd secured a victory, he paused just long enough to make sure that his father was safe before doing what every Christian knight was expected to do: he went on a crusade.

We're now up to the Ninth Crusade. Repeated attempts by Christian forces to regain Jerusalem had failed and this latest attempt would turn out to be no different. Edward was there just long enough to prove himself to be a good military leader and campaigner, before having to hurry back when Gascony was threatened by the French king, who was called either Louis or Philip. (I could look this up, but for 200 years, all of the French kings were called either Louis or Philip, and it makes no difference to our story what his name was.)

Eleanor of Castile travelled with her husband on his crusade and was with him when he narrowly survived an attempt on his life by a member of the professional order of assassins known as the Hashashin. Edward fought off his assailant and killed him, but was wounded by the assassin's poisoned blade and was ill for a long while afterwards. There's an apocryphal story that Eleanor sucked out the poison and saved his life, which I guess is another poetic truth showing how devoted they were to each other.

On his way back from the crusade, Edward heard that his father had died, but he didn't exactly rush home. He first visited Gascony to shore up his defences, before travelling up through France, where he joined in a tournament and tried to settle his relationship with Louis/Philip. It would be two years before he finally got to London in 1274, where he was crowned at the age of 35.

The English people readily accepted Edward. He was the type of tough, no-nonsense warrior knight they admired. They may not have liked him very much, but they certainly respected him. Edward was relatively mature when he came to the throne, with a wealth of experience to draw on, and he set about trying to be the conscientious ruler the country needed. He stabilised the finances. He agreed to various charters that properly defined the monarch's powers. He brought in new laws, agreed to regular parliaments and accepted that taxes couldn't be raised without the full consent of his barons.

But there are always problems. Edward's started in Wales. Ever since William the Conqueror's time, the English had been making regular incursions to subdue the locals and assert their dominance, and the Welsh would regularly rise up against them. Edward put down an uprising in 1276 and then, in 1282, a much more serious rebellion prompted him to try to properly conquer Wales once and for all. He comprehensively defeated the Welsh in a series of campaigns and built a network of immense, heavily fortified castles, such as Beaumaris, Caernarfon and Harlech. These are some of the biggest and most beautiful castles in the world and are today visited as romantic ruins, but they're symbols of colonial oppression. This was Edward's stone boot coming down on the necks of the Welsh. To further cement his overlordship of Wales, Edward introduced the tradition of naming his heir 'Prince of Wales' – the supreme ruler of the country. It's a practice that has controversially endured to the present day.

As well as building castles, Edward built new towns, and enlarged others, like Aberystwyth, so that he could fill them with English colonists. Despite all this, Wales has never lost its strong national identity, language and culture.

Scotland was Edward's next target. The death in 1286 of the Scottish king, Alexander III, without a male heir led to a succession crisis, with 13 claimants to the throne. They were eventually whittled down to two main contenders: John Balliol and Robert Bruce (grandfather of Robert the Bruce). Edward backed Balliol and had him installed as king in 1292.

But these were difficult times for Edward. His beloved wife Eleanor died in the Midlands in 1290, after 36 years of marriage. Edward was absolutely devastated and led her funeral cortege down to London. He later erected a stone cross everywhere they stopped for the night, 12 in all. There are three Eleanor crosses still standing and they've left their mark in some English place names, such as Waltham Cross and Charing Cross in London, where a Victorian version of a cross stands just outside the station entrance. Most people walk past it and barely notice it's there.

The response to Eleanor's death shows Edward's human side, but, unfortunately, 1290 was also the year in which he did something that became a permanent stain on his character and reputation. We've looked at how badly the Jews were treated in England and how they were the property of the kings, who'd been squeezing as much money out of them as they could. They'd now been squeezed so hard that there wasn't much more juice left and the barons were still complaining about their debts. To raise money for his campaigns in Scotland and France, and to keep his barons on side, Edward confiscated the Jewish population's property and money and expelled them from England. The Jews wouldn't return for nearly 400 years, when Cromwell allowed them back in 1656.

Over in France, either Louis or Philip was still trying to take control of Gascony and Edward needed to put together an army to hold him off. He set about raising taxes for his campaign and told the Scots to contribute. This did not go down at all well north of the border.

John Balliol was Edward's puppet and, while he was grudgingly compliant, the Scottish lords weren't. They resented Edward's interference and when he demanded that the Scots join him in his French campaign, they refused and instead formed an alliance with France. The two countries were united by their mutual antagonism towards England, and this new arrangement became known as 'the Auld Alliance'. Pissed off by their deal with the French, and vowing to sort the Scots out for good, Edward led an army north in 1296 and crushed them at Berwick-upon-Tweed. He then grabbed their sacred stone of destiny – the symbol of the Scottish monarchy, the Stone of Scone – and took it back to London.

The English only fairly recently gave the Stone of Scone back to the Scots. It's currently kept in Perth, but it's been an integral part of the English coronation ceremony since Edward built it into his throne – King Edward's Chair – in Westminster Abbey. All subsequent monarchs have symbolically sat on the Scottish stone to be crowned. In the lead-up to the coronation of King Charles III in 2023, there was a lot of very delicate diplomacy around allowing the stone to be brought back down to London for the ceremony, which annoyed a great many Scots.

Edward then deposed John Balliol, locked him up in the Tower of London and declared himself king of Scotland. His first hammer blows had been struck, but he never managed to fully drive the nails home. His harsh, heavy-handed treatment of the locals fuelled a growing resistance movement and soon there was another war. One of the rebel leaders was the famous William Wallace. Mel Gibson portrayed Wallace in *Braveheart* as a half-naked, kilt-wearing wild man covered in woad, but he was actually a Scottish nobleman, who would have been indistinguishable from any minor English baron.

Wallace had some initial success against Edward and defeated his army at the Battle of Stirling Bridge in 1297 by kettling the English soldiers on the bridge. But his triumph was short-lived. Edward had greater resources and defeated the Scots at the Battle of Falkirk, forcing Wallace to go on the run. The Scots bowed to Edward and Wallace was frozen out by his countrymen, who eventually betrayed him to the English. He was taken to London in 1305, where he was hung, drawn and quartered, a grisly punishment reserved for traitors which involved hanging someone until they were almost dead, then cutting them down, opening them up and drawing out their intestines while they were still alive, before burning them (and often their private parts) before the victim's eyes. Finally, their bodies were chopped into four parts to be displayed on spikes in different locations around the king-dom, to discourage others.

The Scots gradually regrouped around Robert the Bruce, who was a better politician than Wallace. In 1306 he killed his rival to the Scottish throne and declared himself king, at which point Edward had to pull together another army and march north to try to reassert his authority. But he was by now in his late sixties, and no longer the virile warrior he'd once been. On the way up to Scotland, he came down with dysentery and died.

It was a damp squib of an ending for Edward. He never had his final decisive battle against the Scots and had failed to conquer them. On his deathbed, he reaffirmed his only surviving son, another Edward, as his successor. From Henry III to Henry IV, England went through a cycle of bad king/good king/bad king/good king/bad king/good king. By the standards of the time, Edward II was a 'bad' king, but he was a lot more interesting than that, as we shall see.

10

1–2–3 NEDS (#2)

EDWARD II – 1284–1327
Edward of Caernarfon
Reigned 1307–1327
Lived for 43 years. Ruled for 20 years.
Murdered.
Remembered for: favouring the handsome Piers Gaveston,
losing control and being murdered.

People tend to know about Edward II because he died a very colourful death (for 'colourful' read 'horrific'). Yes, Edward was the king who was reputedly dispatched to the afterlife by having a red-hot skewer thrust where the sun doesn't shine. It was a rotten end to a rotten reign.

You might think that, as the youngest of Edward I and Eleanor of Castille's 14 (possibly 16) children, Edward never expected to become king at all, but as we saw with John, elder brothers could quite easily drop off the line of succession. And, sadly, most of Edward I and Eleanor's children died young, including all the boys apart from Edward. If Edward's older brother hadn't died, we could have ended up with a King Alphonso, which is quite hard to imagine (Eleanor was Spanish and named the boy after her half-brother). Although, of course, if he had become king, Alphonso would be just another familiar, boring, English name, like Victoria or Albert, both of which, in their day, had sounded weird and foreign.

But Edward's older brothers, John, Henry and Alphonso, died before he was born and we ended up with another bloody Edward. There's a famous – but once again, apocryphal – story about his birth. We've seen how Longshanks hammered the Welsh before he got round to the Scots, and built a ring of oppressive castles to keep them in line. Prince Edward was born in one of those castles – Caernarfon. The story goes that his father displayed the newborn baby from the battlements to the Welsh people, saying 'Here you are! This is what you wanted. A Prince of Wales born in Wales who can't speak a word of English. Ho, ho, ho.'

According to the legend, the Welsh thought this was a most amusing jest and took both Edwards to their hearts. But the castle wasn't completed when Edward was born, most of the Welsh didn't much care for him and he didn't become Prince of Wales until he was a teenager. The story was made up in the 16th century.

Edward had a pretty miserable childhood. He was lonely and neglected. His parents left him to be brought up by others, his mother died when he was six, and his sisters were married off young. Against all the odds, he survived, though, and grew up to be tall, muscular, athletic and a fine horseman. He never joined in the royal sport of jousting, however, which was held against him. He was always being accused of not being manly enough, a coward, but his father didn't allow him to joust. As we've seen, it was a suicidally dangerous sport and Prince Edward was the king's last surviving male heir.

Edward was apparently very witty, with a marvellous sense of humour, and he loved simple, peasant pursuits, like ditch digging, blacksmithing, building walls, swimming and rowing. None of these were considered suitable for a member of the royal family. A prince was supposed to be rowed by someone else, but Edward, although he dressed expensively and enjoyed the theatricality of being a monarch, wasn't interested in royal pastimes. He liked to hang out with ordinary working men and was much happier chatting to his servants and his grooms, ploughmen, farmers and ordinary soldiers than the stuffy nobility at court. In many ways, he was like our modern monarchs, who go out of their way to appear normal. The thing is, though, people don't want 'normal' monarchs. If they're just like us, what's the point of them? And back in the 14th century, people *really* didn't want an ordinary king. They wanted another Edward I.

Prince Edward had inherited *some* of his father's characteristics, such as the vicious Plantagenet temper. He could be cruel, petty and vindictive, as well as passionate and loyal. His Achilles heel was an obsession with favourites, the two most prominent of which were Piers Gaveston and Hugh Despenser. It was his devotion to these two young courtiers that was to define his reign and lead to his downfall.

He was made Prince of Wales when he was 16, in 1301, and acted as regent in England while his father was away campaigning in Flanders in 1298. While he was still an adolescent, the prince also gained some first-hand military experience, helping his father on various campaigns.

England was in danger of becoming a backwater, ignored by the rest of Europe, so, in an attempt to keep the family plugged in to the dynamic French scene, Longshanks betrothed Prince Edward to Princess Isabella, daughter of King Philip IV of France, in 1303. Like almost everything else in Prince Edward's life, that didn't go well, either. Up until now, Longshanks had approved of his son, but he started to get annoyed by his extravagant lifestyle and teenage ways. The two argued over money, but it was when Piers Gaveston entered the prince's life that relations between father and son really broke down.

Gaveston's father was a lowly French knight from Gascony who'd been in the service of Longshanks. His son, Piers, joined him in the royal household in 1300 and Prince Edward's life was never the same again. In full Mills & Boon, cheesy, royal romance style, a contemporary chronicler wrote: 'Upon looking on him, the son of the king immediately felt such love for him that he entered into a covenant of constancy and bound himself with him before all other mortals with a bond of indissoluble love, firmly drawn up and fastened with a knot.'

Piers and Prince Edward were knighted alongside each other by King Edward I in 1306 at a lavish, mock-Arthurian ceremony called the Feast of the Swans and, after that, the two were inseparable. There's always been a huge amount of speculation about their relationship. We can never know the truth, but the modern consensus is that they were gay, because the modern consensus is that *everybody* is gay. But Edward and Piers lived in a very different time when close bonding between men was considered the norm and there was no concept of homosexuality. As far as anyone was concerned, the world was full of straight men, some of whom indulged in the sinful practice of sodomy.

EDWARD II WITH HIS B.F. PIERS GAVESTON

Both Gaveston and Edward were married – in fact, Gaveston married Edward's niece, Margaret de Clare – and they both had children. Of course, being married and having children is no proof that a man isn't gay, but Gaveston did conform to some gay stereotypes. He dressed flamboyantly, he had a sharp and waspish tongue and he openly expressed his love for young Edward, but he was also something of a tough guy and very fond of jousting. He loved nothing more than humiliating the stuffy old barons at court who disapproved of him by defeating them in tournaments.

The big problem with Gaveston was that he wasn't part of the posh, venerable Anglo-French nobility who'd been established in England for 250 years. He was an outsider, not on their level. So, later on, when Prince Edward became king, promoted Gaveston to positions of power and authority, and made him his chief advisor, the barons seethed with jealous resentment.

Prince Edward's other problem was that his father, Edward I, had no respect for him. Compared to the macho king, the Prince of Wales was a sensitive soul. Not long after he was knighted, the young man had his first big falling-out with his father when he asked him to give some of the royal estates in France to Gaveston. It would be an understatement to say that this didn't go as well as the prince had hoped. The king, whose temper was legendary, flew into a terrible rage, screaming and frothing at the mouth. He tore out clumps of his son's hair and promptly exiled Gaveston.

This was to be the first of several exiles for Gaveston, and each time young Edward managed to get him back. Death played a hand in Gaveston's return from his first banishment. King Edward I died on his way to invade Scotland and, when Prince Edward took over as king, the first thing he did was recall Gaveston from France, marry him off to his niece, Margaret, and make him Earl of Cornwall, gifting him a hefty and valuable estate that should really have gone to one of the old guard. He even made him regent of England to rule in his place while he popped over to France to marry Isabella in 1308. Everything he did confirmed the worst fears of the establishment. If only Edward had studied history and seen what happened to kings who didn't keep the aristocracy onside …

Later, Isabella was to become known as the She Wolf of France, largely because, as we shall see, she turned against her husband. She's often portrayed as a femme fatale figure, the original evil scheming queen, beautiful and cruel, which is unfair. Few noblemen at the time respected Edward II, but they all believed that a wife should remain faithful, loyal and subservient. Isabella was only 12 when she married Edward, who was in his early twenties, and there's no suggestion that they might have been in love. It would have been a few years before they actually slept with each other and Isabella had her first child in 1312, when she was 16 (yes, another Edward, who would go on to become Edward III).

Edward didn't get on with Isabella's father, King Philip, who was highly suspicious of Edward and his cloddish English ways. Things got worse at Edward and Isabella's joint coronation ceremony. She had come over with her French entourage and they were furious at the way she was treated. As the new queen, Isabella should have been the centre of attention, but Piers Gaveston stole the show and took pride of place. Dressed in sumptuous purple and gold robes, he led the procession through Westminster Abbey, carrying the crown. And then, at the feast afterwards, Edward spent all his time talking to Piers and ignoring Isabella. You can't really blame Edward. He and Piers were two guys in their twenties and Isabella was a 12-year-old girl. What was Edward going to talk to her about? Embroidery and kittens?

Partly due to sneery French reports, word got around that Gaveston was the man in charge of England. Neither he nor Edward realised that they were dancing on very thin ice. Gaveston took great pleasure in mocking the barons and giving them crude, insulting nicknames. He called the earl of Lincoln 'Burst Belly', the earl of Pembroke was Joseph the Jew and the earl of Lancaster was the Fiddler. When Gaveston dubbed one of the most powerful barons, Guy de Beauchamp, the 10th Earl of Warwick, 'The Black Dog of Arden', Warwick warned him, 'Don't forget that dogs can bite'. Gaveston just laughed at him.

The next few years of Edward's reign followed a regular pattern. Gaveston would push his luck, the barons would get angry and, to save his crown, Edward would agree to Gaveston being exiled. Then Edward would decide he couldn't live without Piers and would agree to all the barons' demands if they'd let him come back. Edward would then immediately forget all his promises and the cycle would start all over again. The king never quite took the process seriously. When Gaveston was exiled to Ireland, for instance, Edward promoted him to lord lieutenant of Ireland. As it turned out, Gaveston was actually a much better ruler than Edward and he ran Ireland rather well.

Heavy taxation and a lack of success in dealing with the Scots added to Edward's unpopularity. A group of discontented barons and clergy, led by Lancaster the Fiddler and Warwick the Black Dog, imposed so many regulations (ordinances) on the king that they became known as the Lords Ordainers. Following an expensive and futile expedition into Scotland, in which the canny Robert the Bruce refused to engage with Edward, he agreed to the Ordainers' demands. It wasn't enough, though; the rebellious barons wanted Gaveston gone.

Realising they were in danger, Edward, Isabella and Gaveston fled London and headed north. They got split up on the way, whereupon Gaveston abandoned Isabella, along with most of the crown jewels, and was soon afterwards captured in Scarborough by the Earl of Pembroke. Pembroke vowed to protect Gaveston under the rules of chivalry. When his back was turned, however, Warwick, the Black Dog, kidnapped Gaveston and delivered his long-threatened bite. He cut Gaveston's head off and left his body lying in a muddy field.

Edward was devastated, while Pembroke was furious with Warwick, who started to lose support. This meant that Pembroke was able to arrange a peace between Edward and the Ordainers and a full-scale civil war was averted. Edward once again agreed to whatever the barons wanted, as long as they'd support him in another face-saving invasion of Scotland.

This time, Robert the Bruce stood up to fight Edward, at Bannockburn. The English troops got hemmed in and bottled up, their archers were misplaced and the Scottish pikemen easily fended off their cavalry. Edward fought hard and bravely, but in the end had to be dragged off the battlefield by Pembroke to protect him from the rampaging Scots. It was a disaster and gave the Ordainers the excuse they needed to finally take full control. Lancaster and Warwick had avoided joining Edward and thus sidestepped the Scottish debacle.

Now Lancaster was pushed forward to run the country. He passed various ordinances, charters and treaties, but he was no better at governing than Edward. Things were made even worse when there was a Europe-wide famine following crop failures in 1314, followed by seven years of bad weather. Harvests were washed out and the English economy, which had been thriving due to the lucrative wool trade, was ruined. Edward can't be blamed for bad weather, but it was as much of a factor in the unpopularity of his reign as was defeat at Bannockburn.

Edward tried to help his people. He brought in new laws to stop people from hoarding grain, but, like everything else he did, it was fairly ineffective. To top it all off, Robert the Bruce invaded northern England. This was absolutely not the time for Edward to choose a new favourite at court, and Hugh Despenser the Younger was an even worse choice than Gaveston. The Despensers were Marcher Lords, powerful barons who defended the border territory between England and Wales, and who had been at the heart of the royal court since Edward I's time, but Hugh Despenser the Younger and his father, the Elder Despenser, were nasty pieces of work. Cruel, ruthless and ambitious, they latched onto Edward, who fell for Hugh the Younger. Between them, they started confiscating lands and dividing them up between the Despensers and their cronies. It wasn't long before war broke out between Edward's faction and enemies of the Despensers, led by a rival Marcher Lord, Roger Mortimer (later to become the 1st earl of March. He was also grandson of the Roger Mortimer who'd gifted de Montfort's bollocks to his wife).

To start with, Edward was pretty successful. He captured Mortimer, locked him in the Tower and managed to beat the rebel army at the Battle of Boroughbridge, during which he captured Lancaster. The Fiddler was tried in a kangaroo court, found guilty of treason and beheaded. Until now, the barons – particularly those with royal blood – had been largely immune from prosecution. The worst they could fear was exile. This was different. Lancaster wasn't allowed to say anything at his trial, which set a bad precedent. The rule of law was breaking down and many aristocrats were to be executed without fair trial.

With England in chaos, King Charles IV of France took the opportunity to invade Gascony. Edward sent Isabella to Paris to try to make peace terms with her brother, the king, taking their eldest son, the young Prince Edward, with her. While she was there, she started an affair with her husband's enemy, Roger Mortimer, who'd escaped from the Tower and fled to France. The two of them began plotting against the king, with the aim of deposing him and putting Isabella's son on the throne.

In 1326, Isabella invaded England with Mortimer. King Edward made a run for it with his few remaining supporters, including the two Despensers. Trying to get to Ireland via Wales they were all captured. Hugh the Elder was very quickly hanged and, just to make sure of it, also beheaded and his body cut up and fed to the dogs. His enemies wanted to make a bigger deal of Hugh the Younger's end, though. He was found guilty of treason at a summary trial in Hereford and sentenced to be hung, drawn and quartered. He was stripped naked and Biblical verses were written on his skin before he was dragged by four horses across the city to the walls of his own castle where he was subjected to his grisly punishment. For good measure, he had his genitals sliced off as well.

It didn't pay to be one of King Edward's favourites. And, in the end, it didn't pay to be King Edward. Isabella and Mortimer forced him to abdicate and he ended up in Berkeley Castle in Gloucestershire. Following attempts to free him, he 'mysteriously' died in September 1327. Not a mark was found on his body, so it looked like he hadn't been murdered, but the story soon started to circulate about a trumpet being forced into his arse, though which a skewer (possibly heated) was slid inside him, so it wouldn't leave any marks, but would still turn him into a human kebab.

Who knows if the best-known fact about Edward II is actually true? At a time when sodomy was a sin, there's a suspicion that some pious monk made up what they felt was a fitting death for this wicked loser.

Poor Edward. Of all the medieval monarchs, he's probably the one you'd most enjoy going down the pub with. He liked entertainment, he liked minstrels, he liked people who made him laugh. And he had a remarkable lack of concern for social hierarchy. He just didn't know how to be a king.

11

1–2–3 NEDS (#3)

EDWARD III – 1312–1377
Edward of Windsor
Reigned 1327–1377
Lived for 64 years. Ruled for 50 years.
Died of an exploding brain.
Remembered for: dealing with the Black Death,
starting the Hundred Years' War and a spectacular
victory at the Battle of Crécy.

Many monarchs feared that their sons would grow too powerful and try to replace them while they were still alive. In Edward II's case, it actually happened. He was betrayed, dethroned and kebabbed by his own son, Prince Edward. Actually, Prince Edward was only 14 when his father was murdered, so the blame must be placed at his wife's bedroom door. Isabella, daughter of the French king, obviously intended to reign alongside her lover, Roger Mortimer, Earl of March, expecting Young Edward III to do as he was told as their puppet king. But people don't stay children for ever. They grow up and develop minds of their own. It wouldn't take long for Edward to take control – of both his life and his kingdom.

Edward III restored England's pride and steered the country through some very challenging times without ever being seriously challenged by either the ordinary people or the barons. It was under him that the country had its first parliament held in English, in 1362. English was spoken at court and used in official documents, and Edward cemented the idea of England being important in itself, not just as an Anglo-Norman territory. It suited him to push the idea of a threatened English nationhood as a way of establishing himself firmly on the throne and squeezing the maximum amount of money out of his people. He played the nationalism and patriotism card and spread the idea that the country had to pull together against a common enemy: the French.

As a way of rewarding his close supporters, he created a new super-elite, the Premier League of nobility – dukes, who were one notch above earls. He also created the Knights of the Garter, another elite of 24 extra-special knights who he could both reward and use for his own protection.

Culture flourished under Edward III. Several important medieval writers came into their own during his reign, such as William Langland, the author of the narrative poem 'Piers Plowman', and Geoffrey Chaucer, the author of *The Canterbury Tales*, who worked in Edward's Court.

But all that is yet to come. First, he had to deal with Roger Mortimer. Once Edward had been crowned, Mortimer, like so many power-hungry lords, started feathering his own nest, taking titles and land for himself and becoming fabulously wealthy. He justified it by saying he was strengthening his position as ruler, but that only worked while Edward was young. The boy quickly grew to resent Mortimer, who foolishly tried to keep him in his place, lording it over him in parliament and at court.

Things took a turn for the worse for Mortimer when the Scots, smelling weakness in England, did what they always did – they invaded and plundered the north of England. The two countries had technically been at war since Edward I's time, with the English insisting they had overlordship of Scotland and the Scots begging to differ.

At huge cost, Mortimer put together an army, which included a large contingent of expensive mercenaries, and rode north with Edward. But the smaller Scots army refused to engage and, after some ineffective manoeuvring, Mortimer and Edward's army sloped off back south while the Scottish army romped home with its plunder intact. Edward felt humiliated and was forced to sign a treaty with the Scots that confirmed their independence and handed many English estates over to them.

In 1328, Edward married the young Philippa of Hainault. Hainault was a strategically important territory in what is now Belgium. Back then, this area of northern France, Holland and Belgium was known as Flanders. Philippa proved to be more than just a good political choice for queen, she was a good match for Edward, she became his close adviser and even ruled as regent during the times when he was away at war.

She also gave him a fine strapping son, who would go on to be hailed as one of England's greatest knights, confusingly also called Edward. This is the fourth bloody Edward we've had to deal with in this part of the story, but, luckily, he was given a useful nickname: the Black Prince (nobody's quite sure why, but he may have first been called that by the French, who didn't like his habit of killing them in great numbers on the battlefield). If Mortimer had been hoping to take over as monarch, the arrival of a solid heir to the throne made it much harder for him. By 1330, Edward had had enough of his overly ambitious earl and decided to do something about him. During a council in Nottingham, while Mortimer was staying at Nottingham Castle with Isabella, Edward made his move. He sneaked a party of soldiers into the castle via a secret tunnel, overpowered Mortimer's guard and arrested him. Edward's mother pleaded with him: 'Bel filz, bel filz! Ayez pitié de gentil Mortimer!' ('Fair son, fair son, have pity on gentle Mortimer'). But Edward had no pity for his mother's lover. Mortimer was taken to the Tower of London, tried without being allowed to speak and hanged at Tyburn, allowing Edward to take over his vast estates. He did take pity on his mother, however. He put all the blame on Mortimer and, after a short period of luxury confinement, Isabella was free to go about her life – away from the court – and lived comfortably into her sixties.

Edward was now firmly in charge, but a group of English and Scottish lords who'd lost land in the earlier peace accord and went by the name of 'The Disinherited', funded a private military campaign to try to win everything back. Edward tacitly supported them and The Disinherited, by skilfully deploying their longbowmen, beat the much larger army of the Scottish king, David, at the Battle of Dupplin Moor in 1332. They then installed the son of the previous English puppet king, John Balliol, on the Scottish throne. I wish I could say the new king was called Angus, or Hamish, or Big Tam, or Spud, but, no, he was another sodding Edward. Edward Balliol. This led to a Second War of Independence. Just like the first, there was a long period of inconclusive back and forth between the English and the Scots, who were fighting to get their own king, David (son of Robert the Bruce), back on the throne. The war dragged on sporadically until 1337, when Philip VI of France appropriated Gascony, King Edward's last holding on the continent.

If Edward had agreed to pay homage to Philip and accept his overall sovereignty, he could have kept his lands. Instead, he made a quick truce with the Scots, declared himself the rightful king of France – via his mother – and invaded. And that, ladies and gentlemen, is how the Hundred Years' War started.

To raise the funds to pay for his French expedition, Edward whipped the English people up into an anti-French frenzy: 'They want to control us, they want to control trade, they want to destroy the English language …' These were all the same dog whistles that were blown during the Brexit vote in 2016, with France replaced by the EU.

To start with, not much happened. There were some skirmishes and a naval battle, but the war was still costing a lot of money and parliament wasn't supportive. So Edward kicked out a lot of older barons from court and replaced them with younger, more bellicose men. But he knew that, to keep everyone onside, he needed a great victory, so in 1346 he took an army of 15,000 troops into France and started marauding through the countryside, trying to provoke the French into battle. They eventually confronted the English, at a place called Crécy in northern France. Edward used tactics the English army had learned in their Scottish wars, relying on longbowmen. These great bows required huge strength to draw and years of training. Edward banned a lot of sports to ensure that the young men of England, instead of playing football, cricket or hockey, practised archery. The Welsh had taught the English about the longbow and there were a lot of Welsh archers in the army.

In contrast, the French didn't allow their peasants to do any kind of military training in case they rose up against their masters. So you had a poorly trained French army of foot soldiers, bolstered by a mercenary force of Genoese crossbowmen, supporting the mounted knights, the crème de la crème of the French aristocracy – who didn't rate the English at all. These knights trained in formal tournaments and jousts, and weren't prepared for a new down-and-dirty style of warfare. The French army was bombarded with arrows before they got anywhere near the English, who also used cannons for the first time in a pitched battle. First, the French foot soldiers, and then the knights, were slaughtered. It wasn't done to kill aristocrats – you were supposed to capture them – but Edward wasn't playing by the rules. This was Total War. He gained a bad reputation for his unchivalrous tactics, but after his spectacular victory at Crécy, he pressed on. King David of Scotland, honouring the Auld Alliance, rashly decided to use this opportunity to

EDWARD III AT CRECY

invade England, despite his treaty with Edward. The English were in a fighting mood and David was defeated and captured at the Battle of Neville's Cross on the outskirts of Durham.

Now that Edward didn't have to keep troops in England to counter the Scottish threat, he was able to bring an extra army over to France, swelling his numbers to somewhere in the region of 35,000 men. He set his sights on the port of Calais. If he captured the town, it would give him a much-needed toehold in France and make it easier to get ships, troops and supplies across the English Channel. The siege of Calais lasted a year, with Edward setting up court outside the walls. Two great romantic tales from English history came out of the siege. One was that while the English knights and the ladies were dancing at a ball, a young lady who Edward had his eyes on, Joan of Kent, had an embarrassing mishap. One of her stocking garters slipped down around her ankle. To prevent her from becoming a laughing stock, Edward gallantly stepped forward, took the garter and tied it around his own knee, saying 'Honi soit qui mal y pense' ('Shame on him who thinks badly of this'). Edward had been telling everyone he was going to found a new Arthurian Round Table of knights, but, following his tactics at the Battle of Crécy, any pretence that he was honouring chivalric traditions had gone right out of the window – so he set up the 'Order of the Garter' instead. But the part about Joan of Kent is sadly a myth. There are no contemporary references to the incident and ladies didn't wear stockings at the time. The garter depicted on the coat of arms of the order is more likely based on a strap for fastening armour, and the phrase 'Shame on him who thinks badly of this' was actually coined by Edward about his invasion of France.

The other reported incident at the siege of Calais *did* actually happen. The starving inhabitants sent a letter to the king of France asking for help. 'We've eaten our horses, our dogs, our cats, our rats. If you don't come soon, we shall have to start eating each other.' But the demoralised French king, following the defeat at Crécy, was very wary of taking on the English, who had proved themselves to be brutally effective, and refused to help.

Edward said he'd spare the citizens of Calais if they sent out their six top representatives to be executed in their place. Six emaciated local burghers came out, chained together. When she saw them, Queen Philippa, who was pregnant at the time and feeling a bit emotional, begged Edward to spare these brave men. And Edward did, whereupon the town surrendered. Edward expelled most of the population and replaced them with English people from across the Channel, the same tactic his grandfather, King Edward I, had used in Wales.

The English would hold Calais for the next 200 years, making it a crucial staging post in France. Edward returned to England in triumph in 1347 and there were huge celebrations. He had done what a king was supposed to do. He'd defeated his enemies in battle – both the Scots and the French. There were feasts and tournaments and celebrations. England was in a very good place. Edward had plundered a lot of wealth, the wool trade was roaring, but later that same year, a trading ship put in at the port of Melcombe (now part of Weymouth) in Dorset, with an unexpected cargo: a bacterium called *Yersinia pestis*.

There were merchants from all over southern England in Melcombe, a major trading town, and when they left, they took the bacteria with them. By autumn, it had reached London, and by the summer of the following year, only 500 days later, it had infected every part of the country. At the time, the disease was known as the Great Mortality, or simply The Pestilence. The proper term is bubonic plague, because the bacteria multiply in the lymph nodes, under the armpits and in the groin, which swell like onions and push up under the skin; the medieval term for these lumps was buboes. When the bacteria erupt from the lymph nodes, they spread through the body, causing organ collapse and rupturing blood vessels, so that the infected areas turn black, hence the plague's other name: the Black Death. By the time the plague died down in December 1350, up to half the population of England had been wiped out.

While the rich were able to isolate in their manor houses and thus avoid being cooped up in crowded conditions like the poor, they were not immune to the disease, for which there was no cure. The plague had spread right through Europe before anyone knew what was happening. In 1348, Edward's daughter, Joan, was on her way to Spain to marry Prince Pedro, the son of the Spanish king, when she caught it in France. One by one, her party started to die. Joan was among the last to go. In a letter to Pedro's father, Edward expressed his deep sorrow.

In the end, the plague burned itself out (although it was to return sporadically over the next few years). Society could have completely collapsed, that it didn't was partly down to Edward. As a strong, respected and level-headed ruler, he held things together, and even introduced a form of lockdown. But there was a big knock-on effect. The available workforce had suddenly halved and the marriage market was similarly disrupted. This meant that there were big changes to both workers' and women's rights. For the first time, ordinary men and women had a say in how they were treated. The barons needed workers to bring the harvest in, but if they didn't have enough men on their own land, they were forced to hire them from elsewhere. Labourers could now offer their services to whoever paid the most.

Naturally, the lords resented having to pay more and be at the mercy of peasants. So, in 1349, they passed The Ordinance of Labourers and, in 1351, the Statute of Labourers, which were designed to control wages. But you can't legislate against the law of supply and demand, so these measures were doomed to failure. All they really did was stoke up resentment from the peasant class towards the ruling class and eventually make the House of Commons more powerful.

The economy recovered enough for Edward to resume his war against France, but as he was now in his forties, he increasingly left the military side of things to his son, Edward the Black Prince. The prince was a mighty and popular warrior who first led part of King Edward's army at Crécy before using similar tactics at the Battle of Poitiers in 1356. The French didn't seem to have learned their lesson and, once again, the English army cut down their knights. They even captured the French king, John, who was taken back to England, where he eventually died in captivity, having failed to raise enough ransom.

With the French army beaten once again and the Black Prince rampaging around the countryside, the French agreed to Edward's terms, which is what Edward had hoped for all along. He can't ever have seriously expected to become king of France; what he really wanted was the previously English-held territories back again. He couldn't get all he wanted, however, and, in his later years, as his health declined, the French managed to claw back everything they'd given to him. When Edward died of a stroke in 1377, all that was left were Calais, Brest, Bordeaux and Bayonne.

Edward's position towards the end had been weakened when his champion and heir, the Black Prince, died of dysentery in 1376. Everyone had expected Edward to nominate as his successor his oldest surviving son, the very capable John of Gaunt, but he'd insisted on following the laws of primogeniture to the letter and declared that his grandson, Richard (son of the Black Prince), should be king. In doing this, Edward unwittingly sowed the seeds for a devastating conflict that was to erupt during the next century as different branches of his family went to war over a disputed line of succession. As Duke of Lancaster, John of Gaunt was head of the Lancastrian branch of the family. His younger brother, Edmund, Duke of York, was head of the Yorkist branch of the family. These two lines would eventually try to wipe each other out in what became known as the Wars of the Roses.

12

ℛICHARD 2

RICHARD II – 1367–1400
Reigned 1377–1399
Lived for 33 years. Ruled for 22 years.
Died of starvation.
Remembered for: standing up to the Peasants' Revolt
and falling out with his cousin.

Everything that Edward III had achieved – beating the French (not once but twice), sorting out the problems with Scotland, shoring up the economy, steering England through the Black Death – were all for nothing, because his grandson, Richard II, was completely bloody useless. His main problem was that because he seriously believed that he was divinely appointed he thought he could do whatever he wanted. He never grasped that a monarch only ever rules by the consent of his people.

Vain and narcissistic, he was the first monarch to have his portrait painted from life. The most famous painting of him, in Westminster Abbey, plastered in red and gold, shows him sitting on the throne in all his glory, wearing a gorgeous crown. With his big, pale face, he manages to look both conceited and angelic.

Richard really felt that he was the king that England had been waiting for, but, like his great grandfather, Edward II, he wouldn't listen and thought he knew best. He chose the wrong advisers and tried to curb the powers of the barons with predictable results. He believed that he was so majestic, nobody should ever question him, but his rule was to end in ignominy, defeat and incarceration, from which he never emerged.

His problems began when he was born in Aquitaine on the Feast of the Epiphany in 1367. The story was told that there were three kings present at his birth – the king of Spain, the king of Navarre and the king of Portugal – who all gave him precious gifts. The parallels with a certain Jesus H. Christ are obvious. Well, they were obvious to Richard, who grew up believing he was The Special One.

His father was the national hero, the Black Prince, and his mother was Joan of Kent, the woman around whom the legend of the dropped garter grew. King Edward III had had his eye on her, and maybe more than just his eye. Aristos sometimes passed their discarded mistresses on to their sons to marry.

When Richard was born, he had several illustrious, grown-up uncles, including John of Gaunt, Duke of Lancaster, Edmund, later Duke of York, and Thomas, the future Duke of Gloucester, all of whom would have made better kings than the moon-faced idiot. But Edward III's insistence on strict primogeniture meant that Richard became his successor, despite being only 10 at the time.

The most prominent of his uncles was John of Gaunt. At the time, noblemen were referred to either by where they were born or what their principal titles were. Hence the endless earls of Leicester, dukes of York, Somersets, Norfolks and Essexes that make studying history, or reading Shakespeare, so confusing. Gaunt is an Anglicised version of Ghent, in the Low Countries, where Uncle John was born.

John of Gaunt had been running the country towards the end of Edward III's reign, which meant that Richard grew up believing that his uncle wanted to be king in his place. He never openly challenged Richard, however. As the wealthiest man in England after the king, Gaunt was extremely unpopular and perhaps knew he would have no support, and so accepted that the crown had skipped a generation.

We've seen how the Black Death led to social unrest and a desire by the ordinary people to get a better deal in life, and while King Edward III had still been alive, the lords had made a concerted effort to clean up the out-of-touch royal court in 1377. Corrupt barons had been removed and reforms put in place to help the general population in a sitting of parliament called The Good Parliament. Gaunt wasn't happy with these changes and, not long after the reforms were made, in 1377, he got rid of them all in a session dubbed The Bad Parliament, which reinstated the corrupt noblemen and brought in the first poll tax to pay for the ongoing war with the French, who were now making attacks on the south coast. This was a new type of taxation. Before this, only the wealthy landowners paid tax; under the new system, everyone over the age of 14 was required to pay a groat per head, whatever their status. Suddenly, the population of England appeared to shrink, as thousands of people avoided having their names on the register. Unsurprisingly, the poll tax was virulently unpopular, just as it was when Maggie Thatcher tried to reintroduce it in the 1980s. Both times it led to riots.

Another knock-on effect of the Black Death was that a huge amount of land and property had become available very cheaply because the owners had died. A whole new class of people were buying up this land and becoming property owners. This was the birth of the bourgeoisie, who were hacked off when they found that they were now expected to pay tax.

People were becoming increasingly resentful of their overlords and since the Black Death, they'd also started to question the power and the wealth of the church. Well-to-do priests had not only failed to save anybody during the plague, they'd also died in great numbers, just like everybody else. Could it be that they were actually no closer to God than the average serf? A philosopher called John Wycliff preached that people should find their own path to God, without the help of priests, and denounced the worldliness of the organised church. His prayer-muttering followers became known as Lollards ('lollard' being a medieval word for a mumbler).

The uneasy mood in the country was the background to Richard's accession. But, to start with, it wasn't really the 10-year-old king's problem. A council of appointed nobles was set up to run the country for him (unpopular with both the lords and commons, and Gaunt was excluded). The council tried to mould Richard into the type of monarch they wanted, but failed. Richard grew up to love art and culture and had no real interest in warfare. Left to him, the Hundred Years' War would have been a lot shorter, and he wasn't really interested in hammering the Scots. He just wanted to parade around his palace in fine robes and a crown, trilling 'Look at me, I am the king.'

Under the ruling council, parliaments kept raising the hated poll tax to finance the war and eventually the people snapped. There was rioting in Essex and Kent, and a popular movement formed that become known as the Peasants' Revolt. They weren't exactly peasants. They were the new class of middle-class yeomen. Their main leaders were John Ball, Jack Straw and Wat Tyler, three names that still resonate today. They joined together and converged on London. As so often happened in history (and still happens today), many of the 'ordinary people' believed that the monarch was on their side and could do no wrong. Royal mistakes were always the fault of their corrupt advisers. And so their rallying cry was, 'For King Richard and the True Commons'.

John Ball was a Lollard preacher and when the Kent contingent of the 'peasant' army stopped at the edge of London, he gave a sermon about how God hadn't created rich and poor, master and servant, lord and serf, and how feudalism wasn't the natural order of things: 'When Adam delved and Eve span, who was then a gentleman?'

When the peasant armies arrived in London, the locals rose up in sympathy and went on the rampage. John of Gaunt's Savoy Palace on the Thames was burnt down (luckily for him, he was away at the time) and the 14-year-old King Richard was bundled into the Tower of London along with his treasurer, the Archbishop of Canterbury and the Lord Mayor of London. The main group of rebels gathered in Mile End and demanded to speak to the king. Nobody knew what to do – except Richard, who believed his own PR. He had God on his side! The next day, he rode out to meet the rebels, which was either a very courageous or a very foolish thing to do. It might have been the end of the monarchy, but the peasants fell for it. Richard was their friend. He'd listen to them.

Their demands were simple: equality for everyone, except Richard. He could stay as king, but there would be no more villeins or serfs, lords and dukes and earls, and church money would be confiscated and distributed among 'the people of the parish'. While Richard was talking to the rebels, another group attacked the Tower of London and got inside, where they killed the Archbishop of Canterbury, the treasurer and others. Meanwhile, Richard agreed to all of the rebels' demands, offering them 'all that he could fairly grant'. This diffused the situation. The peasants stopped the looting and pillaging and murdering, and the next day, Richard met with the rebels' leader, Wat Tyler, in Smithfield to discuss terms in more detail. Tyler greeted Richard as his brother and took his hand, saying 'We shall be good companions'. It's a bit murky exactly what happened next, but it seems that the powers that be had by now gathered their forces and were ready to take on the peasants. Tyler was provoked to violence by the lord mayor who then fought back, badly wounding the rebel leader.

At this point, the rebels could have attacked Richard, who was just sitting there on his horse. But Richard was a king, their friend. He raised his hand and said, 'I am your captain. Follow me.' And he led the silly sods away to safety so that there would be no major battle in London.

Soon afterwards, the London militia arrived, the lord mayor dispersed the crowds and that was that. The rebels went back to where they'd come from, trusting their good pal, the king, to give them everything they'd asked for. And what did he give them? *Nothing*. He had no intention of making everybody equal. What a ridiculous concept.

The lord mayor dragged Wat Tyler out of the hospital where he'd been taken and cut his head off. Many of the other leaders were rounded up and killed, while the rest of them were given hefty fines. Richard gratefully received the extra money and sent a small force to wipe out the last of the rebels in a battle at Billericay in Essex.

That might have been the end of the Peasants' Revolt, but a political movement had been born that would gradually lead to increased rights and better conditions for working people.

For Richard, it was the high point of his reign. He was now considered a 'man'. He had won his spurs by dealing with the rebellion, so it was decided that he should get himself a wife. He married Anne of Bohemia, daughter of the Holy Roman Emperor, a potential ally against the French.

Like many of these royal marriages to foreign princesses, the union was not desperately popular in England. Anne brought over courtiers from Flanders, who got up the noses of the old guard. They didn't like

these foreign elites lording it over them. Sadly, for Richard and Anne (and, in many ways, sadly for the course of English history too), the marriage was childless and Anne went on to die of the plague 12 years later. Richard was so upset that he burned down the palace where she died.

Richard felt able to take control of his own court and reformed his royal council, getting rid of any men connected to his father and grandfather, and bringing in new blood. But, wouldn't you know it, he started to nurture favourites (stop me if you've heard this one before). He was particularly fond of two men who were viewed with suspicion for different reasons. Michael de la Pole, a merchant's son who became Richard's government fixer, was resented as a jumped-up social climber. Robert de Vere, the young Earl of Oxford, was accused of being a new Piers Gaveston. Richard, however, wouldn't hear a word against de Vere and made him Duke of Ireland.

Gaunt still had influence at court and urged Richard to properly engage in the war against the French. Richard dithered, organising a few half-hearted raids while secretly trying to make peace. Disgusted, Gaunt gave up on Richard and stomped off to Spain with a small army to pursue his own ends. He'd married into the Castilian royal family and had claims on the throne. He was ultimately unsuccessful, but was away from England for some time. However, his brothers, Edmund, Duke of York, and Thomas, Duke of Gloucester, were still prominent at court. We've had the Good Parliament and the Bad Parliament, and now we had the Wonderful Parliament, where the lords and Richard's uncles tried to force King Richard to dismiss his new inner circle. Richard famously snapped at them, 'I will not dismiss as much as a scullion from my kitchen at Parliament's request.'

He heeded the warning not to be another Edward II, though, and end up with a poker up his arse, so gave in, dismissing favourites like de la Pole and de Vere. But he'd had a quiet word with de Vere and now sent him north to Chester to recruit a private army. Once ready, de Vere marched towards London. Richard's lords had made so many appeals to him to behave himself they were calling themselves the Lords Appellant. The Appellants now sent their own army to stop de Vere and defeated him. He fled abroad and the Lords Appellant capitalised on their advantage. In 1388 they sat down for The Merciless Parliament.*

The Merciless Parliament came down hard on Richard, either executing or exiling most of his inner household and favourite knights. To keep his crown, Richard, still only 21, had to agree to all of parliament's demands.

So Richard now made a fresh start and worked tirelessly for the well-being and profit of his people. My arse. He never learned. People reported him just sitting on his throne for hours at a time in all his royal regalia, staring into space, being king.

He did at least make peace with France. It was supposed to last 28 years and saved him a lot of money, and the next few years were relatively settled and prosperous as a result. You'd think it would have made people happy. It didn't. They hated the French. To cement the peace, Richard married Isabella of Valois, the six-year-old daughter of Charles VI of France, who went down about as well as his previous wife. She was *French*, after all.

Richard couldn't help himself and started to gather more sycophantic young men around him, derisively known as the Duketti – the little lords – and in 1397, he proved right the old adage that 'revenge is a dish best served cold', when he mounted his own palace coup against the Lords Appellant who had executed his friends. He arrested two earls and one duke, his uncle, Thomas, Duke of Gloucester. He executed one of the earls and banished the other to the Isle of Man for life, but what to do with Thomas? It was a step too far to execute a member of the royal family. So, instead, Richard sent Uncle Tom to Calais and had him secretly suffocated.

Richard's bold moves were partly made possible by the return of John of Gaunt from his failed campaigns in Spain, seeking the king's favour. He even led some of the trials himself. Emboldened, Richard went full despot, ruling without parliament. The final part of his reign became known as Richard's Tyranny.

The king was very relieved when John of Gaunt died in 1399 and was no longer a potential threat to his sovereignty. Gaunt did have a

* I love these names. Today we have to make do with The Crap Parliament.

son, Henry Bolingbroke, but he'd been exiled following a squabble at court, so Richard thought he was safe. Now he made possibly his worst mistake. He confiscated Gaunt's lands, which should have gone to Bolingbroke, and took them for himself. This put Henry in a desperate position and with nothing to lose. While Richard was off campaigning in Ireland, Henry landed a small force in Yorkshire with the aim of trying to win back his inheritance. As he marched south, however, he was given an enthusiastic welcome and started to gather support. When he got to London, he found the Palace of Westminster empty and undefended. Richard had left his surviving uncle, Edmund, the Duke of York, in charge while he was away and uncle Edmund, like everyone else, was utterly fed up with Richard's behaviour.

When Richard came back from Ireland, he found that he'd lost all his support. A rather pathetic figure, he was arrested and Henry claimed his throne. Some people were saying that Richard had graciously agreed to step down; others said that he was absolutely bloody furious and smashing his head against the wall. Henry knew that, as long as Richard was alive, his grip on the throne would be slippery and, following an attempt to free the imprisoned ex-king, Richard conveniently died. Rumours soon spread that he'd been starved to death.

Richard had loved the *idea* of being king. And was good at the bits that involved sitting down wearing a crown. He even introduced the new term 'Your Majesty', as an advance on 'Royal Highness'. But his downfall was a fatal inability to read the room and he ended up being deposed by his cousin.

13

HENRYS 4, 5, 6 (#1)

HENRY IV – 1367–1413
Henry Bolingbroke
Reigned 1399–1413
Lived for 46 years. Ruled for 14 years.
Died from … Leprosy? Syphilis? Kidney failure?
Nobody really knows.
Remembered for: deposing Richard II.

Henry IV's place in history was overshadowed by the colourful misadventures of Richard II and the heroic exploits of his son, Henry V. Despite having two Shakespeare plays written about him, he feels like a background figure in his own story. However, he was a survivor who spent his whole reign fighting off challenges to his sovereignty, dodging at least 10 assassination attempts, dealing with invasions from Scotland, a war with the Welsh, the ongoing problems in France and a really nasty skin complaint. He was quite a guy when he was young – tough, athletic, a champion jouster – but he had a long and pitiful decline. Against all the odds, however, he managed to pass his stolen throne on to his son.

He was born at Bolingbroke Castle in 1367; his mother, Blanche of Lancaster, died of the plague (or possibly in childbirth) only a year later. His father, John of Gaunt, then married Constance of Castile and took on a young woman called Catherine Swynford as a governess. As so often seems to happen in posh households, he had an affair with Catherine, the equivalent of shagging the nanny. Gaunt and Catherine had four illegitimate children together. When this all became too scandalous, Catherine had to leave the household for a while. However, when Gaunt's second wife Constance died, Catherine returned and he married her. He then persuaded the pope to legitimise the children they'd already had together and this branch of his family became known as the Beauforts.

Henry Bolingbroke grew up alongside his step-siblings and was very close to them. Another of his playmates was his cousin, the future King Richard II, and, in 1377, when they were both 10, they were knighted together before being admitted to King Edward III's new Order of the Garter.

Within a few years, it had all changed. Henry was one of the Lords Appellant who rose against Richard. When Richard's favourite, Robert de Vere, brought his private army down from Chester to take on the Appellants, Henry was leading the force that stopped them at Radcot Bridge, west of Oxford. He was the hero of the day, winning fame and honour, but fell out with the other lords after the Merciless Parliament. He thought they'd gone too far in executing so many of Richard's supporters.

When Henry's father, Gaunt, returned from Castile, Henry seemed to lose interest in politics and went back to what he most loved doing: jousting. He also – surprise, surprise – wanted to go on a crusade like every other nobleman. But, because of the war with France, King Charles VI wouldn't allow him passage through France, so he diverted north and got involved in a minor crusade in Lithuania. The Crusades weren't always directed at the Holy Land. They were designed to pester anyone who was considered not Christian enough. Lithuania was sold as the last pagan country in Europe and a group of Christian special forces troops known as the Teutonic Knights were busy attacking Vilnius, so Henry joined them in 1390. The following year, he was able to push on east and travelled down through eastern Europe to the Holy Land. It was a pilgrimage rather than a crusade, but it was still good PR for Henry, and the loyal men who joined him on his adventures became the nucleus of his retinue for the rest of his life.

Once back in England, Henry got into an argument with Thomas Mowbray, the Duke of Norfolk, who'd been one of Richard's favourites before becoming a Lord Appellant. To tell you the truth, I'm not exactly sure what this argument was about, and accounts vary. It's all a bit confused, but it seemed to have involved Henry and Mowbray simultaneously accusing each other of being traitors.

HENRY IV CHAMPION
JOUSTER

To settle the argument, King Richard organised a trial by combat. This was to be the event of the year, like Royal Ascot. The high and mighty, as well as common spectators, gathered in anticipation of the deadly tournament. Henry was waiting, ready for the big fight, in the fancy new armour he'd had made in Milan, when, right at the last minute, Richard called it off, saying he wanted no more bloodshed and exiled both combatants. This seems like a flimsy excuse; perhaps this way he could get rid of two potentially troublesome young men, rather than being stuck with one dead nobleman and one entitled winner. While Henry was safely out of the country, Richard kept his son (the future Henry V) hostage.

We saw in the last chapter how, not long after Henry was exiled, John of Gaunt died and how, foolishly, Richard didn't allow Henry to inherit his father's wealth and lands, including the duchy of Lancaster. He confiscated the lot and kept it for himself. With nothing to lose, Henry brought a small group of soldiers back to England and his support snowballed to such an extent that he was able to dethrone Richard and take his place.

Henry was the first king of England to speak English at his coronation, where he made an address to the people, saying, basically, 'I am one of you. I am a proper English king'. After the ceremony, he went back to speaking French, which was still the language of the court, but he'd made his point. Very quickly after his coronation, he invested Prince Hal as Prince of Wales to cement the boy's position as heir to the throne.

The start of Henry's reign was pretty shaky. As long as Richard was alive, there would always be the threat that he might be reinstated by zealous followers. And it wasn't just the lords Henry had to fear. He'd lived through the Peasants' Revolt, so he knew that if he didn't keep the people happy, they might rise against him. It was therefore no surprise when Richard was found dead in his cell. Almost immediately, though, stories started to circulate that he'd escaped and was still alive. To quash the rumours, Henry had Richard's body displayed in St Paul's Cathedral – 'Look, here he is, dead as a doornail. He's not coming back. Forget about him.' People could clearly see that there were no marks on Richard's body. He was a little thin, maybe, but he definitely hadn't been stabbed. This tactic didn't work for Henry, however. For the rest of his reign, there were rebellions in Richard's name, claiming they were either bringing the rightful king back or that they were deposing a king who had no right to be there.

Henry hoped to maintain peaceful relations with his neighbours, but King Robert III of Scotland refused to accept him as the rightful king and used it as an excuse to start raiding northern England. Henry led an army up to Scotland as a show of strength but returned to England before any actual fighting broke out and never went back.

The Welsh also figured that Henry's throne was sitting on shifting sands and they rose up under the leadership of the mighty Owain Glyndwr, who declared himself Prince of Wales and said that the English no longer had any authority in his country. The English had long ago established buffer zones between Wales and Scotland known as the Marches, protected by castles and overseen by powerful local barons – the Marcher Lords. In the west, protecting the Welsh borders, were the Mortimers, the earls of March. Two Mortimers have already featured in our story, both called Roger. It seems there was a law that you always had to have a Roger Mortimer present at every major historical event.

Henry had to perform a tricky balancing act when it came to the Mortimers. He couldn't risk upsetting them because they were holding back the Welsh and sending troops to fight Glyndwr, but, at the same time, he couldn't allow them to become too powerful – particularly as one member of the family was technically the rightful heir to the throne. Edmund Mortimer was the great-great-grandson of Edward III (via Edward's second son, Lionel of Antwerp), and the childless Richard II had designated him as his heir before being deposed by Henry. Edmund's claim led to countless rebellions and plots against Henry – and was one of the factors that led to the Wars of the Roses.

The most powerful Marcher families in the north were the Percys and the Nevilles. The Percys were earls of Northumberland. London is a long way from Northumberland, and north and south had never got on. The south, and London, were seen as where the poncy south-

DESCENDANTS OF EDWARD III

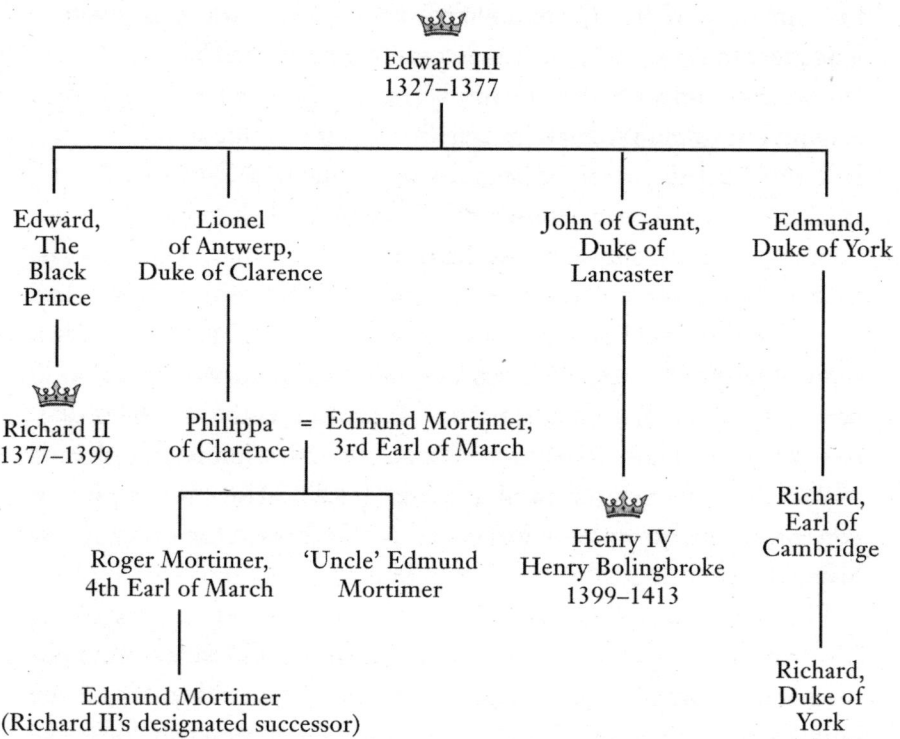

Edward III
1327–1377

Edward,
The
Black
Prince

Lionel
of Antwerp,
Duke of Clarence

John of Gaunt,
Duke of
Lancaster

Edmund,
Duke of York

Richard II
1377–1399

Philippa
of Clarence
=
Edmund Mortimer,
3rd Earl of March

Henry IV
Henry Bolingbroke
1399–1413

Richard,
Earl of
Cambridge

Roger Mortimer,
4th Earl of March

'Uncle' Edmund
Mortimer

Richard,
Duke of
York

Edmund Mortimer
(Richard II's designated successor)

ern elite hung out, while the northerners saw themselves as the proper lords of England.

Chief lord of the north was Henry Percy, 1st Earl of Northumberland, who had a dashing son, also called Henry. Don't worry, though, Henry junior had a nickname, thank God – 'Hotspur' – so called because of his hot-headedness and eagerness to charge into battle. He was a national hero, although he wasn't as young as he was portrayed in Shakespeare's *Henry IV*. He was actually three years older than Henry IV, and 20 years older than Henry V and was in his late thirties at this point of our story. (While we're on it, *The Hotspur* comic and Tottenham Hotspur football club were both named after him.)

The Percys may have considered themselves lords of the north, but their neighbours, the Nevilles, had other ideas. Inevitably, the two families hated each other. At the start of Henry's reign, the Percys were firmly on his side. They'd supported him against Richard and were still supporting him now that he was king. But, nervous of their growing power, Henry started favouring the Nevilles, giving them lands and powers that the Percys believed should have gone to them.

In 1402, the Scots raided England again. They got as far as Newcastle, ravaging Northumberland in the process, but on their way back with their loot, they were ambushed by Hotspur at Homildon Hill. Back in Edward II's day, the Scots had had great success against the English by forming up into schiltrons, huge blocks of men bristling with spears and pikes. This was the ideal defence against a cavalry or infantry attack, but the English had perfected the use of archery and a schiltron was now simply a great big sitting target for longbowmen. Percy and his army absolutely destroyed the Scots, many of whose leaders were killed or captured. With the glint of gold in his eye, Hotspur rubbed his hands together and started to organise their ransom.

But King Henry wouldn't let him do it. He was worried that these Scottish leaders would simply return to Scotland, put another army together and come back. Hotspur was livid. This went against every convention of warfare. He'd won this battle for Henry who was now disrespecting him and he stood to lose a great deal of money. So he said 'Sod you' and simply let all his hostages go. Henry's plan had completely backfired. Many of these freed Scottish leaders pledged to support Hotspur, who they saw as a potential ally against King Henry.

Meanwhile, Owain Glyndwr's rebellion in Wales was going gangbusters. The Mortimers were fighting back, but one of them was captured at the Battle of Bryn Glas, which led to another ransom wrangle. Remember Edmund Mortimer, heir presumptive to the throne? Well, this is his uncle and, you guessed it, he's also called Edmund. Let's just call him Uncle Ed.

In a variation of what had happened with Hotspur's Scottish hostages, Henry now refused to pay the ransom to get Uncle Ed back. He was suspicious that the whole thing was a set-up and that Uncle Ed wanted to go over to Glyndwr's side, join forces with him and push his nephew's claim to the throne. Henry's scheming backfired here as well. Whatever his intentions were before, Uncle Ed now started plotting with Glyndwr.

Henry's treatment of Uncle Ed was the final excuse the Percys needed to denounce the king. They accused him of usurping the throne and killing King Richard, then raised an army and marched south. They met King Henry's army at the bloody Battle of Shrewsbury in 1403, the carnage made all the worse by the fact that both sides had a large contingent of longbowmen. Countless men were struck by arrows long before they could get anywhere near the enemy, including the commander of King Henry's left wing – his 16-year-old son, Prince Hal. Hal was hit in the right cheek by an arrow, and, not wanting to appear a wimp and demoralise his troops, he snapped off the shaft and carried on fighting, with the arrowhead embedded in the back of his skull.

It looked like Hotspur was going to win the battle and defeat Henry's army, but then he was hit by an arrow as well. The great Hotspur wasn't as lucky as Prince Hal. He dropped dead, his army fell apart and King Henry won the day.

Hotspur's father, the elder Henry Percy, then joined forces with Uncle Ed Mortimer and Glyndwr. Together they cooked up the idea of the 'Tripartite Indenture'. It sounds like a complicated dental procedure, but it was basically just a plan to defeat King Henry and divide his kingdom into three. Percy would rule in the north, Glyndwr in

Wales and the west, and Mortimer would get southern England. It was a great plan, but it relied on one key thing: they first had to defeat Henry.

They recruited a senior churchman to give their plan legitimacy; Richard le Scrope, the Archbishop of York, was put in command of a new army. Henry sent Ralph Neville, the Earl of Westmorland and Henry Percy's main rival in the north, to deal with them. Neville was clever. He didn't engage Scrope in battle but sat down with him to parlay, saying he totally understood the archbishop's concerns and sympathised with him. He agreed to all the rebels' demands and would pardon them for the uprising if Scrope disbanded his army.

Scrope shook hands on the deal and let his army go, at which point Neville gave a big Simpsons 'Ha-ha' and arrested the archbishop and his allies. King Henry moved quickly and had Scrope beheaded. Bad move. Very bad move. You really shouldn't go around beheading archbishops.

According to the chroniclers of the time (who, of course, were all either biased monks or priests), King Henry was instantly struck down with leprosy. Now, you can believe that this was God's work or you can believe that this was simply church propaganda. We do know, however, that around this time, Henry developed a terrible skin disease.

Nobody really knows what afflicted Henry. His symptoms don't look like leprosy and it's impossible to diagnose someone 600 years after the event, particularly as human diseases change with time. Whatever it was, Henry's skin complaint came and went over the following years, and wasn't the only undiagnosable disease he was struck down by. He probably had heart troubles that left him unable to walk on occasions. One of the problems we're certain he suffered from was a prolapsed rectum, but one of the court surgeons did at least manage to fix that. Henry himself believed that this was all divine punishment for executing an archbishop.

He pushed through it, though (the leprosy, not his prolapsed rectum), and after he'd put down the tripartite rebellion, he started to make plans to properly go on a crusade to atone for his sins – although, in the end, he was never well enough to actually go. He also brought in a new law, making heresy a capital offence, with a fun new punish-

THE STAKE

ment: burning at the stake. This was mainly an attempt to suck up to the clergy by keeping down the radical Lollards, who threatened the wealth and power of the church.

The last few years of Henry's reign were pretty miserable. He was so enfeebled that Prince Hal took over running things. The problems in Wales went away when Owain Glyndwr disappeared in 1412 and the now-leaderless Welsh rebellion fizzled out. This was to be the last significant Welsh uprising against English rule. No one quite knows what happened to Glyndwr; he walked out of history and into myth, becoming a kind of legendary Arthurian figure who will one day return and lead the Welsh to independence.

A story started doing the rounds that one night, towards the end, Prince Hal visited the ailing Henry in his bedchamber and, thinking he was dead, tried on his crown. But suddenly Henry woke up. Seeing Hal parading around with his crown on, he asked him what he thought he was doing. To which Prince Hal replied with words to the effect of 'Bugger me, I thought you were dead. As heir to the throne, I just took what was mine.' Henry supposedly replied 'What right could you have to the crown? When I have none.'

14

Henrys 4, 5, 6 (#2)

HENRY V – 1386–1422

Henry of Monmouth/Prince Hal

Reigned 1413–1422

Lived for 36 years. Ruled for nine years.

Died from an exploding stomach.

Remembered for: pudding-bowl haircut; the Battle of Agincourt;

'Once more unto the breach, dear friends, once more … We

happy few, we band of brothers … Cry "God for Harry, England,

and Saint George!"'etc, etc, etc.

Henry V only ruled for nine years, but in that time, he made his mark on history and became central to the idea of plucky little England standing up to the might of arrogant, foreign aggressors – in his case, the French. Shakespeare played a big part in creating that image when he wrote *The Life of Henry the Fifth*. The play is propaganda, written in Queen Elizabeth I's time, when the overbearing foreign superpower was Spain and it's wheeled out whenever the English need a pep talk.

During the Second World War, Henry became a potent symbol of England holding out against the might of Hitler's Germany when Churchill's Ministry of Information commissioned Sir Laurence Olivier to make his film of *Henry V*; the parallels with what was going on in Europe were obvious. This was a rallying cry. Don't give up! A tiny, beleaguered army could defeat a much larger, more formidable and better-equipped enemy. You can see the storms of flying arrows as representing the fighter planes of the RAF. The play trumpets English notions of nationalism, patriotism and the glory of war, and our views of it (and of Henry V) change as our views of those concepts change. During the Second World War, Henry was presented as a valiant hero, but modern productions of the play tend to present him as a psychopathic villain – cold, violent, warlike and jingoistic. The reality probably lies somewhere in between the two poles. In his day, he was well liked because he did what a king was supposed to do – he was tough and he enjoyed nothing more than smiting foreigners. At well over six foot, he stood alongside the great warrior kings, Richard I and Edward I.

He didn't ignore domestic affairs altogether, though. He had a strong sense of justice and was hot on organisation, order and discipline. He wanted an efficient government. He wanted the finances to be properly controlled. He also understood the importance of ceremony, ritual, propaganda and showmanship. OK, so he needed all this mainly so he could promote and finance the war against France, but it nevertheless meant that England was well run; there are certain benefits to having a king who is organised, unemotional, ruthless, disciplined and anal. Henry also avoided the political infighting and rivalry at court that had marred the reigns of so many of his predecessors. He had no outright favourites, yet kept a core of loyal advisers close to him, many of whom had fought alongside him in his various campaigns.

He carried this approach through to how he ran his campaigns in France. It was important to him, as the leader of the army, that it was well-run, well-supplied and well-equipped, because he knew that soldiers would fight better if they were properly looked after.

Henry was no numbskull, brute soldier. He went to Oxford University, where he was very interested in the arts and music. He was a cultured man and very pious, which meant that the histories were very much on his side. He also continued his father's promotion of the English language and the concept of Englishness. He read and wrote in English, and had many books translated into his people's tongue.

Henry was born in Monmouth Castle in southeast Wales and was very involved in his father's military campaigns. He led English troops against the great Welsh hero, Owain Glyndwr, when he was only 15. He also served under Henry Percy – Hotspur – who became a friend and mentor. When Hotspur turned against King Henry IV, he and young Prince Hal ended up on opposing sides, and Hal was still only 16 when he led some of his father's army against Hotspur at the Battle of Shrewsbury. As we've seen, they were both struck by arrows and only Hal survived, even though he ended up with an arrow embedded in his face. It had gone in just next to his nose, passed through his nasal cavity and lodged in the back of his skull. Even though it must have been unimaginably painful and debilitating, Henry carried on fighting and became a symbol of defiance, strength and bravery, whereas Hotspur just became a symbol of, well, being dead, I suppose.

Various surgeons tried unsuccessfully to remove the arrowhead and then, rather like in a Hollywood caper movie, they decided that the only man for the job was the ex-royal physician John Bradmore, who was in prison for counterfeiting coins. He was very quickly given a royal pardon, sprung from his cell and summoned back to court, where he invented his own device to get this lump of metal out of the prince's skull.

Over the course of several days, Bradmore drove cloth-covered wooden wedges smeared with antiseptic honey into the wound to open it. Various opioids were used as a basic anaesthetic, as well as strong drink, but still, the pain must have been excruciating. Once the wedges were in deep enough, Bradmore prised them apart so that he could get to the arrowhead and then screwed his special device into the socket. Finally, with a fair amount of brute force, he dislodged the arrowhead and pulled it out. Then he washed the wound with wine to disinfect it and sewed it up. Henry must have been one tough bugger. He was badly scarred and, if you look at portraits of him, they are nearly always in profile – on his good side – which wasn't the convention at the time.*

In his later years, when King Henry IV became increasingly infirm, the prince tried to help him, but the king, fearing Hal's ambition, pushed him away. Hal was kept at arm's length and not allowed to have anything to do with royal affairs. He resented this, but as Henry IV got even more feeble, he relented, needing his son at his side. By the time of the king's death, Hal was already running the country, so it was a smooth transition when he came to the throne.

To start with, Henry V's reign continued to be dull and stable, for which, if you were the average merchant or yeoman trying to go about

---

* The portrait details have been disputed, but let's not spoil a good story.

HENRY V AND HIS SPECIAL FACE ARROW TOOL

your daily business, you would have been very grateful. Henry worked hard to repair relationships with the lords who'd rebelled against his father, and he brought the powerful Percy family back in from the cold and restored most of their estates in the north.

The really fun stuff was going on in France, mainly because the French king, Charles VI, had gone completely bonkers. He was officially known as Charles the Beloved, but everyone just called him Charles the Mad. He'd become manic and paranoid, exacerbated by an assassination attempt on one of his friends at court. He was leading a small military force to Brittany to punish the suspect when a page dropped a lance, hitting a soldier's helmet with a mighty clang. King Charles began screaming – 'They're on to us, quick, fight back!' – and started attacking his own men, killing several of them before he was restrained. After that, his condition worsened and there were periods when he couldn't remember who he was nor recognise his wife. He told his servants, 'Whoever that woman was, can you make sure she doesn't get back in here?'

Charles ran around the palace howling like a wolf, claimed he was Saint George and believed that he was made of glass – and, unless he was very careful, he'd shatter. Sometimes his servants would wall him up in his rooms for a bit of peace and quiet. And to stop him from shattering, I suppose.

The state of the king led, inevitably, to a three-way dynastic feud at the French court between members of his extended family. The seeds of the conflict had been sown by the king's cousin, John the Fearless, Duke of Burgundy; his feckless younger brother, Louis, Duke of Orleans (leader of the Armagnac faction); and his ambitious wife, Queen Isabeau, who was promoting her son, the dauphin.* I wouldn't try to remember those names, though, because they'd all been killing each other and by this time the country had slid into a civil war known as the Armagnac–Burgundian War (which you can remember as brandy vs wine), which was the French equivalent of the Wars of the

---

* The heir to the French throne was always known as the dauphin. You might childishly think, *Ho ho, sounds a bit like 'dolphin'*. That's because dauphin *is* the French word for dolphin. The royal heir's coat of arms had two dolphins on it.

Roses with rival branches of the same extended family at each other's throats.

This was all going on when Henry became king of England in 1413. With France destabilised, he saw the opportunity to restate his family's claim to the French throne (through Edward III's royal French mother, Isabella). And he started planning for war, making advances to the Burgundians, who he thought would make useful allies against the dauphin. Burgundy had originally been a duchy in northeast France but, through a complicated series of marriages and alliances, had ended up controlling a significant part of Flanders. The Low Countries was the major textile manufacturing area that relied on English wool, so the Burgundians had good reason for making an English alliance. Unfortunately, the Duke of Burgundy, John the Fearless, was a slippery customer and assured both the dauphin and Henry that he was on their side.

Before Henry left for France, though, he had to deal with some challenges at home. The first was a Lollard uprising led by an old friend of his, Sir John Oldcastle – the model for Falstaff in Shakespeare's plays. The Lollards wanted reform of what they saw as a corrupt and venal church. The second rebellion, known as the Southampton Plot, was led by a group of lords loyal to Edmund Mortimer, the young man descended from Edward III who'd been chosen by Richard II as his successor.

Henry dealt with both rebellions in typically ruthless and efficient fashion. The Lollards were hanged or burned for heresy, while the ringleaders of the Southampton Plot were beheaded. He didn't punish Edmund Mortimer himself, though, as the young man had had nothing to do with the plot and had warned Henry of the conspiracy in his name. There were suspicions that the plot was backed by the French and, before Henry left England, he sent an ultimatum to the dauphin: he would withdraw his claim to the throne if he was given back all the lands that the English had lost in France.

The dauphin derisively sent him some tennis balls instead. 'For Henry and his lords to play with and some soft pillows to sleep on, to help him grow to manly strength.' Henry didn't find this joke very funny and set sail with a significant force of 700 ships carrying some

12,000 fighting men, including 500 Welsh bowmen. His undertaking had been partly funded by loans from several wealthy grandees, including the famous mayor of London, Dick Whittington of pantomime fame.

Henry landed at Harfleur, a fortified port at the mouth of the River Seine. Needing a secure place to land more troops and supplies, Henry laid siege to the port, convinced it would only last a couple of days. He'd brought 12 huge cannons with him and, when he started pounding the walls of the town, the story goes that he sent a message to the dauphin saying that 'the tennis balls had changed into hard and great gunstones for him to play with'.

Henry also undermined the walls with tunnels packed with gunpowder. Even so, it still took him a month to get Harfleur to surrender, by which time his army had been ravaged by dysentery. He was advised to return to England, but he wasn't finished. He set off through France with his greatly reduced force, following the same route that Edward III had taken to the Battle of Crécy. He was heading for English-held Calais and soon discovered that a much larger French army was following him. He got as far as the River Somme before they caught up with him. This was, of course, the same landscape where the ghastly trench warfare of the First World War was later fought. It was mostly wide, open and flat – perfect for a pitched battle. Henry was trapped on a stretch of land hemmed in by dense woodland on both sides and was vastly outnumbered by the French who were confident of the superiority of their elite fighting force, their aristocratic knights.

On the night before the battle, the French knights were feasting and singing, laying wagers on how many English noblemen they would kill or capture. There was complete silence in the English camp. Henry's demoralised men were sleeping out in the open and getting rained on. As depicted in Shakespeare's *Henry V*, the king went among them, encouraging them, building up their hopes, trying to instil a sense of patriotism in them. In the morning, the battlefield was completely waterlogged and very muddy, but the French still thought that all they had to do was send in wave after wave of cavalry and ride over the English. Their horses weren't able to get up much speed, though, as they floundered in the mud. Most of their knights dismounted and tried to get to the English on foot, but the English bowmen, the largest part of Henry's army, relentlessly fired white-tipped arrows at the French that fell like snow. The heavily armoured French were bogged down, climbing over each other, desperate to avoid the iron hail. When the English archers ran out of arrows, they attacked with short swords and knives, killing any Frenchmen they could get to.

Henry's tactics on the battlefield were seen by the French as brutal and unchivalrous, and he now did something else that appalled them. His wagon train, parked behind his army, was attacked and looted from the rear by local villagers. This unnerved Henry and, when there were reports of a counterattack by a fresh French army, he over-reacted. By then, he'd captured a fair number of French knights, who were being held behind the lines. Henry couldn't spare too many of his men to guard the captives and had them killed. It turned out the counterattack was a false rumour and, after the battle, the victorious Henry was enemy number one in France.

Henry sailed home from Calais to great celebrations but soon returned to France for two more years of campaigning before forcing the French to negotiate with him. The subsequent Treaty of Troyes confirmed him as the rightful heir to the French throne, which would technically place all the English lands lost in France back under his control, and, when mad King Charles died, the crown would be his. To cement the deal, Henry married Charles's daughter, Catherine of Valois. Leaving his younger brother, Thomas, Duke of Clarence, in charge, Henry took his new bride back to England, where she was given a lavish coronation. *Job done*, Henry thought.

But it's not as simple as that. It never is.

Nobody in France had any intention of sticking to the Treaty of Troyes and war soon broke out again. Thomas, Duke of Clarence, was killed and Henry realised the only way he could hang on to power in France was to physically be there, so he went back over with another army and resumed his campaigning.

While Henry was fighting in France, Catherine gave birth to a little boy, also called Henry. Sadly, Henry V was never to see his son. He was struck down by a soldier's disease, possibly dysentery (certainly a loss of bodily fluids, a 'bloody flux'), and he died a long, slow and painful death. He was only 36.

Henry V never got to sit on the French throne. Mad King Charles VI outlived him by a few weeks. But, when Henry died, his little baby was proclaimed Henry VI, King of England and, when Charles VI popped his clogs six weeks later, the boy also became king of France. And, *quelle surprise*, that didn't go well at all.

15

HENRYS 4, 5, 6 (#3)

HENRY VI – 1421–1471
Reigned 1422–1461; 1470–1471
King of France (sort of) 1422–1453
Lived for 49 years. Ruled for 40 years (in two stints).
Died of a broken heart (actually, he was probably murdered).
Remembered for: being away with the fairies and inadvertently
starting the Wars of the Roses.

This part of the 'Willie, Willie' rhyme runs 'Henrys four, five, six, then who ...?' *Then who?* indeed, because we've come to that tricky part of English history where the crown ends up being tossed around like a Frisbee. Yes, it's the Wars of the Roses, which is a rather romantic and gallant-sounding name for a brutal civil war that grew out of a family squabble (between the House of York and the House of Lancaster). The war ultimately led to the end of the Plantagenet dynasty that had ruled for 300 years and England moving from the medieval into the Tudor period.

The Wars of the Roses ran from 1455 until 1487, through the reigns of five kings – Henry VI, Edward IV, Edward V, Richard III and Henry VII. And, to complicate matters, Henry VI and Edward IV both had the dubious honour of ruling England twice. It wasn't 30 years of constant warfare, though, with knights in shining armour knocking the crap out of each other on a daily basis. Across those 30 years, there were only a few months of actual fighting and fewer than 20 battles (although a considerable amount of time *was* spent besieging castles). Before we open that can of worms, though, let's just run through a few facts about Henry VI.

He was born in Windsor in 1421 and came to the throne when he was only nine months old, making him England's youngest-ever reigning monarch. He was also the only English monarch to rule France – from 1422 until 1453. Henry's hold on the French throne was extremely tenuous, however, and his hold on the English throne was only *slightly* less so. As it says in the Bible, 'Woe to thee, O land, when thy king is a child'. A heavy crown can very easily slip off the tiny head of an infant, particularly if your family is considered by many to have stolen it. From the off, if Henry VI showed any weakness, the throne would be disputed again. Which is exactly what happened.

There were four main fault lines that led to civil war.

1. Henry was a child when he was crowned, which meant that powerful factions in the court vied with each other to control him.
2. Henry inherited a war with France, which he and the Lancastrian branch of his family wanted to get out of – causing much resentment among the more war-like Yorkist faction at court.
3. Henry also inherited huge war debts from his father, with the English economy being further battered by a famine and a shortage of silver.
4. Henry went bonkers.

His mental health was probably the biggest factor in his dethronement. He gradually began to suffer spells of mania, grandiosity and paranoia, followed by plunges into deep depression. These are all symptoms of bipolar disorder, or possibly catatonic schizophrenia, but it's impossible to diagnose Henry all these centuries later. At the time, his problem was called a 'frenzy' or simply 'madness'. There's speculation that he inherited his condition from his grandfather, Charles the Mad of France (the one who thought he was made of glass), and his descent into catatonia in the 1450s was the final catalyst for the challenge to his rule.

Even without the mental illness, however, Henry VI just wasn't cut out to be a medieval king. His father, Henry V, has gone down in history as a great warrior and a strong leader – tough, ruthless, disciplined, cold and psychopathically charismatic. His son was the complete opposite. Henry VI was a pacifist – timid, shy, passive, well-intentioned, well-dressed, pious, disorganised and, when he wasn't in one of his frenzies, compassionate and generous. Perhaps *too* generous. In later life, he got into financial troubles by being overly extravagant towards members of his family and his supporters, rewarding them with money and lands that he could ill afford.

Henry never really got the whole king thing. The business of ruling didn't interest him. He was much more interested in peripheral things, in fun things. He founded Eton College, where he built a beautiful chapel. He also founded King's College in Cambridge and built a very similar chapel there. He mainly just wanted to be nice to everyone and have a nice time, which his people resented. Kings weren't supposed to be nice. In many ways, he was quite childlike (even more so when he began to lose his marbles) and could perhaps best be described as 'simple' with all the positive and negative connotations of the word. His sensibilities might feel quite modern, but for the Middle Ages, he was a disaster. His reign is a good example of what happens when a king goes wrong and when the bond of consent between him and his people is broken.

On one level, the Wars of the Roses can be explained very simply: they were a dynastic struggle between two branches of the same family – a bit like if Prince Andrew's grandchildren went to war with King Charles's grandchildren, with a surprise attack from Prince Edward's family thrown in at the last minute.

But as soon as you start to dig a little deeper, you sink into a pit full of worms, the facts muddied by a mixture of propaganda and fake history. Even the term 'Wars of the Roses' is a nonsense. Walter Scott came up with the name in one of his historical novels, based on the apocryphal scene in Shakespeare's *Henry VI, Part 1* in which rival lords pick red or white roses to declare which side they're on. The Yorkists did sometimes use a white rose as a badge, but for the most part the various lords identified themselves and their troops on the battlefield with a bewildering array of emblems – sun, star, boar, dragon, falcon … It would have been much easier if each side *had* identified themselves with different-coloured roses, because there was so much confusion that groups of men on the same side, not recognising their emblems, sometimes attacked each other.

Often in history there's a problem when a monarch only produces a single son and heir. If they die, it leads to chaos. But in the case of the Wars of the Roses, the problem stemmed from King Edward III having *too many* sons. When Henry Bolingbroke disrupted the line of succession by deposing Richard II, it threw everything up into the air and the descendants of Edward's various sons ended up going to war against each other. As I say, this wouldn't have happened if Henry VI had been a strong and popular king like his father, but once he lost his grip, chaos ensued.

The family tree opposite might help make sense of it.

It was Richard, the 3rd Duke of York (not to be confused with King Richard III*) who mounted the challenge to Henry VI, claiming to have a better right to the throne than Henry because, through a classic bit of royal in-breeding, both his mother and his father were descended from Edward III (as you can see in the family tree). What's more, his mother, Anne Mortimer, was descended from Lionel, Duke of Clarence, the *older* brother of John of Gaunt, so, technically, his line had precedent over that of King Henry's (although it was via the female line of the family).

What initially caused Henry's unpopularity was his handling of the war with France. His side of the family, the Lancastrian faction, wanted to withdraw English armies from France and seek peace. The Yorkist-led faction was appalled at Henry's unpatriotic lack of warlike spirit. He was, at heart, a pacifist – and he was also desperately short of funds. His father, Henry V, had left him a massive bill for the war and to continue fighting would mean raising ever larger taxes. To make things worse, there was a famine in England caused by crop failure and compounded by a major economic disaster unfolding on the continent. Basically, Europe was running out of silver, so it was getting harder and harder to mint coins, causing trade to dry up and the economy to nosedive. The Black Death had drastically reduced mining,

---

* As I mentioned before, one of the things that makes the Wars of the Roses so hard to follow is the similarity of all the names. In some ways, it would be easier to just say that everybody had the same name, they all married each other and they all killed each other.

THE WARS OF THE ROSES

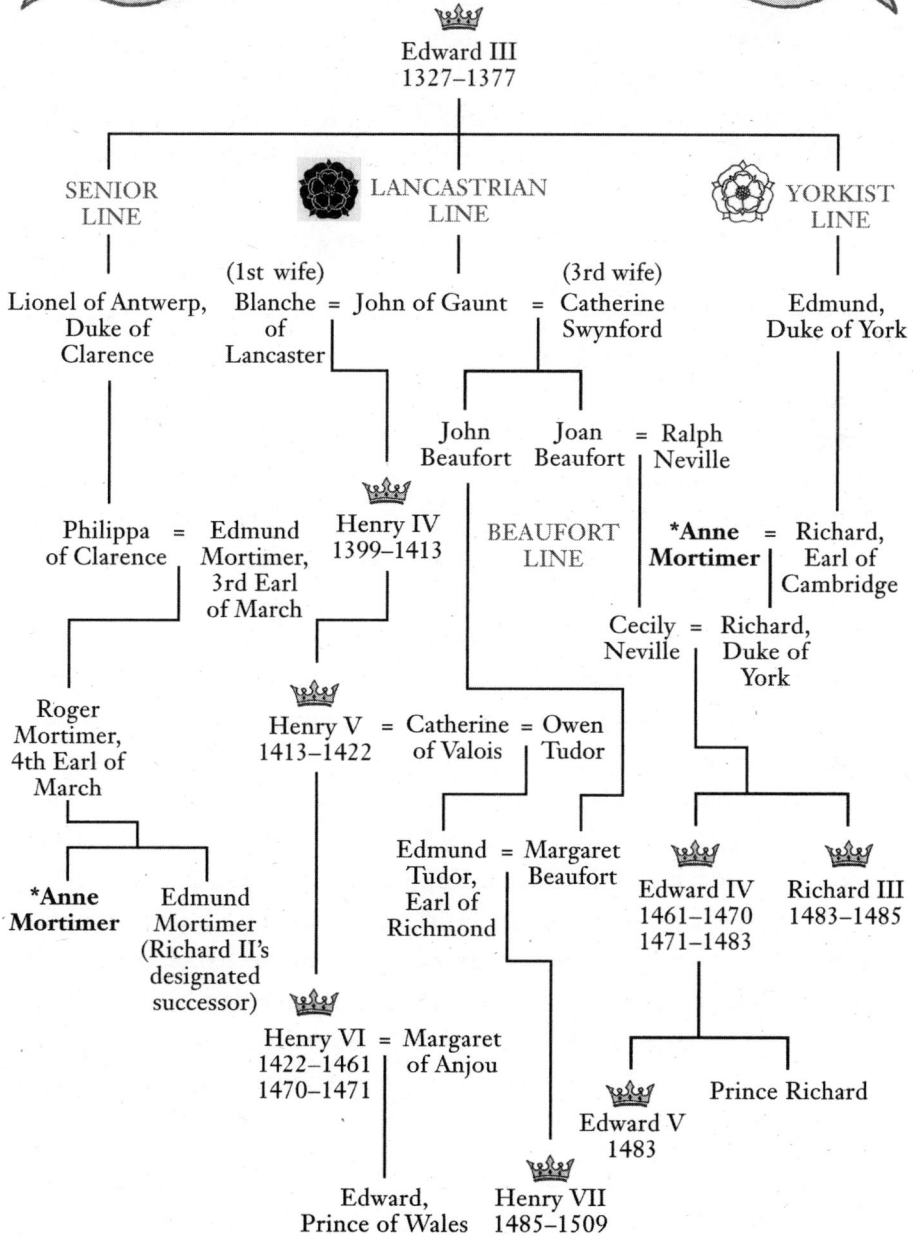

Edward III
1327–1377

SENIOR
LINE

LANCASTRIAN
LINE

YORKIST
LINE

Lionel of Antwerp,
Duke of
Clarence

(1st wife)
Blanche = John of Gaunt = Catherine
of   Swynford
Lancaster

(3rd wife)

Edmund,
Duke of York

John
Beaufort

Joan = Ralph
Beaufort   Neville

Philippa = Edmund
of Clarence   Mortimer,
3rd Earl
of March

Henry IV
1399–1413

BEAUFORT
LINE

*Anne = Richard,
Mortimer   Earl of
Cambridge

Cecily = Richard,
Neville   Duke of
York

Roger
Mortimer,
4th Earl of
March

Henry V
1413–1422

= Catherine = Owen
of Valois   Tudor

*Anne   Edmund
Mortimer   Mortimer
(Richard II's
designated
successor)

Edmund = Margaret
Tudor,   Beaufort
Earl of
Richmond

Edward IV
1461–1470
1471–1483

Richard III
1483–1485

Henry VI
1422–1461
1470–1471

= Margaret
of Anjou

Edward V
1483

Prince Richard

Edward,
Prince of Wales

Henry VII
1485–1509

*Appears twice

while old-fashioned mining practices meant that many mines had been shut down as unworkable. Trade had also opened up to the east, all the way to China. This was something of one-way trade, so a substantial amount of coinage was leaving the west and migrating eastwards.

The Europe-wide economic slump known as the Bullion Famine was one of the main driving forces behind the exploration of the Americas. Europeans needed to find a fresh source of silver (and gold started to be used as a workaround). It also meant a push down into Africa to take resources from there.

Back at home, the key members of Henry's court were Humphrey, Duke of Gloucester, John of Lancaster and Henry Beaufort, the Bishop of Winchester. Humphrey and John were uncles (they were brothers of Henry V, but I couldn't fit them onto the family tree) and Henry Beaufort was a great-uncle.* These three grandees had been running the country while Henry was a child, which meant running the war as well. For a while after Henry V's death, things had gone well for the English in France, largely down to the efforts of his loyal and capable brother, John of Lancaster, the Duke of Bedford, but then, in 1429, when Henry VI was only seven years old, something happened that completely altered the course of the war. A 17-year-old girl, Joan of Arc, arrived at the court of the disinherited dauphin, in Chinon, with a message from God. Joan (technically Jeanne or Jehanne) was nothing – a peasant from Domrémy in northeast France who claimed she'd been having visions and had been visited by various saints and the Archangel Michael, who all told her that France would only be saved if the dauphin was crowned king of France.

Joan must have been a hell of a young woman because, amazingly, the dauphin took her seriously, gave her some troops to command and sent her off to where the English army was besieging Orléans. She defeated the English, lifted the siege, imprisoned several high-ranking English noblemen and miraculously tipped things in favour of the

---

* The Beauforts were the branch of John of Gaunt's family who were descended from his mistress, Catherine Swynford, whom he later married. Originally illegitimate, Gaunt persuaded the pope to legitimise them and they took the name Beaufort. They were very close to the Lancastrians and were key supporters of Henry. Like Henry V's brothers, I couldn't fit all of them onto the family tree.

French. Joan became a talismanic figurehead, with her own suit of armour, horse crest and banner, and she went on to lead the French army to further victories. She didn't win the war outright – it was to rumble on for another 20 years after her death – but, from this point, things mostly went the French way.

Joan of Arc did get the dauphin crowned king of France; not in Paris, but in Rheims, where he became Charles VII. So, now, France had two kings – one English, one French. We've seen how the dukes of Burgundy had been trying to take control in France and had allied with the English against the dauphin, and not long after his coronation, they captured Joan and sold her to the English, who got a partisan bishop, Pierre Cauchon, to try her as a heretic. A mere three years after she'd arrived on the scene, and still only 19, she was burned at the stake in Rouen in May 1431. Even at the time, though, the English realised they'd done a terrible thing by killing this extraordinary young woman. And Joan, like Obi-Wan Kenobi (if you strike her down, she will come back more powerful than ever), became a great martyr, the symbol of France and of French resistance. This all worked out very well for the dauphin, because she'd already started to become a bit of an irritant and too big for her iron-clad boots. She was more use to him dead.

With the dauphin proclaimed king in Rheims, the English nobility thought they'd better get young Henry to Paris to have him properly crowned. They hurried over to France, but got caught up in the war and Henry was stuck in Rouen for a year before he made it to the capital. Once there, his cobbled-together coronation was a shambles. He was crowned by great-uncle Henry Beaufort, who was now a cardinal, at Notre Dame. Arguments broke out with the French clergy who thought the English were being too English about it, while the English thought the French were being too French. To make things worse, a group of locals tried to get in, shouting words to the effect of 'Not my king!'.

Henry was quickly taken back to England, never to return. The Burgundians gave up on the English and signed a truce with the dauphin, accepting him as their *real* king. Cardinal Beaufort and another aristocrat, William de la Pole, the Earl of Suffolk, wanted to call it a day. The war seemed pointless and doomed to failure. Henry's uncle, John of Lancaster, who had held things together, died in 1435 while negotiating a treaty with the French. And Henry's remaining uncle, Humphrey, Duke of Gloucester, and his cousin, Richard, Duke of York, were furious about the way things were now being run. As far as they were concerned, William de la Pole and the Beauforts were incompetent, trying to cover their arses by stopping the war because they didn't know how to win it. As leader of the armies in France, Richard of York felt he was being given no support at all.

The one idea that everyone agreed on was that Henry should be married to a French royal to make his position in France more secure. The French didn't want to give him an actual, direct, royal princess, however, so Henry had to settle for Margaret of Anjou, a niece of Charles VII's wife, Marie. As it turned out, Margaret was to play a huge part in Henry's rule. We've seen before how weak kings are often kept in power by strong queens; we'll see how later on, when Henry's mental health incapacitated him, Margaret led his armies in the civil war.

The marriage was brokered by the Duke of Suffolk, William de la Pole, who Margaret became very fond of and upon whom she was to rely heavily when she got to England. To sweeten the deal for the French and secure a truce, William secretly agreed to give them the English-held county of Maine. He kept quiet about this dirty deal because he knew it wouldn't go down well with his compatriots. When it all came out, he was accused of plotting against England.

As long as Henry didn't have any sons, the next in line to the throne was his uncle Humphrey. Henry was becoming increasingly paranoid and grew suspicious of Humphrey, making wild accusations against him and his family that included charges of witchcraft and treason. In the end, Humphrey was arrested, but died before he came to trial. There were inevitably rumours that Margaret had had him poisoned. It's highly unlikely that she had anything to do with Humphrey's death, but she and Henry did begin stuffing the royal court with allies and cronies, which always leads to trouble. Chief among their supporters were the de la Poles and the Beauforts – not just Cardinal Henry, but a younger favourite, Edmund Beaufort, whom they made Duke of Somerset.

With Humphrey dead, Henry's biggest threat was now Richard, Duke of York, who'd moved up the order of succession to become next in line to the throne. To get him out of the way, Henry used the old tactic of sending a rival off to Ireland and putting him in charge there. Richard was none too happy about this, particularly as his command in France was handed over to Edmund Beaufort, who was completely useless. Like most of Henry's plans, his attempt to neutralise the Duke of York backfired, however, and Richard was able to build a power base, and a private army, in Ireland.

For now, though, with Richard sidelined, Edmund Beaufort came into his own. He'd already had an affair with Henry's mother, Catherine of Valois, the widow of Henry V, and was now rumoured to be having an affair with Henry's wife, Margaret of Anjou. Many powerful women in history have been accused of being sexually voracious – it's a way of undermining them. And, if they make alliances with powerful men, it stands to reason that they must be shagging. Poor Margaret was never really accepted in England. She was capable enough to rule in her husband's place but, as a Frenchwoman, she was never trusted. She was becoming framed by her enemies as an evil, hard-nosed, French bitch.

Everything Henry or Margaret now did made them more unpopular and it didn't help that Henry was showing signs of mental instability. The people, unable to vent their anger on the king himself, turned on his closest associate, William de la Pole. A mob came for him and, despite Henry and Margaret's efforts to protect him, he was forced to flee London and take a boat to France. But he was captured in the Channel, given a mock trial and his headless body was found on the beach at Dover.

Edmund Beaufort was losing very badly in France. He had no navy to speak of any more and the French were able to raid along the English south coast unopposed, causing the cloth trade with Flanders to dry up and deepening Henry's economic woes. Unpaid troops were returning home, angry and bitter and willing to sell their services to the highest bidder. With strong echoes of the Peasants' Revolt, a soldier called Jack Cade raised an army of discontents and marched on London, saying he wanted to get rid of the awful advisers around the king and calling for the return of Richard of York from Ireland.

Henry didn't know how to handle Jack Cade and it was left to the people of London to sort him out. They put together their own army and killed him. Seeing the disorder in England, Richard of York returned in 1450 to try to sort things out. There was eventually a stand-off with Margaret, who was desperately trying to prop up her husband's regime. Just like Cade, Richard claimed he wasn't trying to depose the king, but merely wanted to get rid of his bad advisers, particularly Edmund Beaufort.

An agreement was reached. Richard swore allegiance to Henry in return for being made protector of the realm while Henry got his act together. In 1453, it was announced that Queen Margaret was pregnant. The king didn't have much time to appreciate that he was going to be a father because affairs in France took a turn for the worse and, in July, there was a final, decisive battle in the Hundred Years' War, at Castillon, where the English were utterly demolished. This was the end of English hopes in France and Henry promptly had a full mental breakdown, sinking into catatonia.

Richard of York saw his opportunity to properly take power and the lords began picking sides. One of the reasons the ensuing civil war was so destructive was that old family rivalries bubbled to the surface and erupted into violence as scores were settled. When a petty argument between the two big families in the north, the Percys and the Nevilles, escalated into armed conflict, they both offered to support either Henry or Richard if they agreed to help their cause.

Henry's Lancastrian power base was in the north so, when the Percys sided with him, it gave him a substantial northern stronghold. Richard was already married to a prominent member of the Neville family, Cecily. So the Nevilles were natural allies for him, although his family estates were actually in the Welsh Marches. Richard was a southerner who was well-liked in London so, in some ways, the Wars of the Roses were fought between the north of England and the south.

Richard also made a firm friendship with Cecily's nephew, Richard Neville, the Earl of Warwick (I'm really sorry that there are so many Richards on the Yorkist side. To keep things clear, let's call this one Warwick). York had firm support now, but he knew that if Margaret gave birth to a son, he would no longer be next in line to the throne. And that's exactly what happened. Margaret named her newborn boy Edward. Henry was still catatonic, recognising nobody, not even his wife, and had no idea that she'd had a baby, which fuelled the gossip around court (perhaps the real father was Edmund Beaufort, Duke of Somerset?). When Henry suddenly emerged from his fog of befuddle-ment at Christmas 1454, he was amazed and delighted to find he had a son. He thought it was a miracle and had no memory of being the father. You can imagine how this set tongues flapping.

So Richard of York's plans were knocked back. Henry was in charge again and, fearing the support for Richard and the Nevilles in London, called a Great Council in Leicester, closer to his northern stronghold, to which Richard was not invited.

Both sides were equally suspicious of each other and, having scraped together armies, they met at St Albans. Everybody assumed that this would merely be a civilised diplomatic discussion between the two factions, but Richard had other ideas and went on the attack. And so it was that the Wars of the Roses finally kicked off, at the 1st Battle of St Albans, in 1455.

Normally, battles – such as the Battle of Hastings or the Battle of Agincourt – are so named because they were fought *near* those places. But the 1st Battle of St Albans was basically a street brawl in the town itself. Henry was camped in the centre with his personal guard, but Richard got hemmed in before he could get to him. It looked like he might be captured or killed. Meanwhile, however, Warwick had taken his troops around the outskirts of the town and entered through the back streets. He took Henry completely by surprise, overpowered his guard and declared himself the winner.

Probably fewer than 300 men were killed, but several of them were aristocrats loyal to Henry. This had been York and Warwick's plan from the start: to take their rivals out and remove them from history. Among the casualties were Edmund Beaufort, Duke of Somerset, and a senior member of the Percy family (Henry, a son of the legendary Harry Hotspur).

King Henry himself was wounded by an arrow, but not seriously. York and Warwick could have slaughtered him there and then; instead, they knelt before him and Richard declared that they had no fight with him. They simply wanted to get rid of the bad men around him. Henry was still their king – as long as he accepted Richard of York back in a significant position at court. Henry agreed and came up with a soppy idea to make everybody happy and stop all this silly arguing. He would host a great festival in London, called Loveday,* where all the warring parties would come together and make friends with each other.

Amazingly, Loveday actually happened, on 25 March 1458. A procession set off from Westminster and made its way to St Paul's Cathedral, with all the rivals holding hands. Queen Margaret was forced to hold hands with Richard of York, her greatest enemy. Also involved were the sons of the lords who'd been butchered in St Albans. They had no intention of giving up their feud, however, and vowed to take revenge on Richard and Warwick as soon as bloody Loveday was over. Nobody trusted that it would go off peacefully. The Lord Mayor armed 5,000 men just in case, and Warwick brought along his own private army of 600 men. In the end, there was no fighting and the event led to 18 months of uneasy truce, giving the various factions time to build up their strength.

To get Warwick out of the way, Henry and Margaret effectively exiled him to Calais (he'd been appointed Captain of Calais by Richard). This wasn't a great idea, as he used it as a power base to build his own navy and recruit a bigger army. He also freed up trade across the Channel by stopping the French from raiding the south coast and seeing off pirate ships, which made him very popular among the merchants and businessmen in London.

When he was ready, Warwick invaded England and joined forces with Richard. But when half his army deserted, and the rest surrendered to the Lancastrian army at Ludford Bridge in Shropshire, Richard and Warwick fled – York back to Ireland and Warwick back to Calais. Margaret was now leading the Lancastrian army, as King Henry was in no fit state to do it himself. He spent most of his time in a tent, mumbling and twittering to himself.

Margaret thought she had the upper hand now, but as she was preparing a fleet to attack Warwick in Calais, he struck first and captured all her ships. In no time at all, Warwick was back on English soil and heading for London where he was sure of support and where

---

* It sounds like a modern music festival.

Margaret was unpopular. With York stuck in Ireland, Warwick joined up with Richard's son, Edward, and marched to the capital where he was indeed made welcome. Deciding to press his advantage, he pushed on north and confronted Margaret's army at Northampton, where he ordered his troops to go for her noblemen and kill as many as possible.

At the Battle of Northampton, it was Margaret's army that disintegrated. A large number of her men defected to Warwick's side and the defeated queen went on the run with her son, Edward. Margaret and the prince, who was only six at the time, found refuge in Scotland, but they hadn't managed to take King Henry with them. He'd been left sitting in Northampton trilling, 'Tra-la-a, hello clouds, hello sky. Oh, what a pretty battle. I wonder who's going to win. I hope it's the goodies!' But for him, the baddies won. I mean, you can't really say who the goodies and baddies were in this nasty war, but Warwick captured Henry and locked him up.

The ambitious Warwick had separated Henry from his wife and his supporters and had London in his pocket. He was in all probability eyeing up the post of regent when Richard of York turned up from Ireland with an army of his own, saying, 'OK guys, here I am! How about you all declare that I am king? King Richard the third!' His arrival was met with a deathly silence. Neither Warwick nor the other lords wanted Richard to be king. Somewhat put out, he grumpily agreed to being simply the protector of the realm again.

Margaret, meanwhile, had been busy putting together an army with the Scottish royal family and now she marched south. Richard strapped on his armour and confidently rode north to meet her, his son Edmund at his side, the wind in his hair and a big grin on his face. This was his chance of ultimate victory! But, at the Battle at Wakefield, something happened that really wasn't supposed to. Richard and his son were killed and suddenly written out of our story. Richard of York never did become king. The closest he got was lord protector.* Luckily for

---

* He's now chiefly known as a way of remembering the colours of the rainbow in order – **R**ichard **O**f **Y**ork **G**ave **B**attle **I**n **V**ain (red, orange, yellow, green, blue, indigo, violet).

Warwick, he hadn't been at the battle, but his father and brother had. His brother was killed in the fighting and his father was captured and executed. His head was then hung over one of the gates of York alongside those of Richard and Richard's son, Edmund. Richard's head was given a paper crown. A sign read, 'Let York overlook the town of York'. And Margaret left a space on the walls for Warwick's head.

Filled with a fresh hope and feeling that the tide of war had turned in her favour, the queen pressed on south and defeated Warwick at a second Battle of St Albans. Once again, he was forced to flee, leaving Margaret able to liberate Henry, who'd been brought along to the battle. He was found sitting under a tree singing songs. Margaret's family was reunited and she was back in power but, when she got to London, the people slammed the gates and locked her out. As far as they were concerned, there was a barbaric army of northerners outside their walls who they couldn't understand and who would most probably run riot in their city. The queen backed off and retreated north, allowing Warwick to take control of London – and thus Westminster and the country. He knew, however, that he didn't have any rightful claim to the throne. But if you can't be king, you *can* be a kingmaker.

Richard of York's oldest son was still alive – the Edward of York who'd fought alongside Warwick at the Battle of Northampton. The 18-year-old Edward had two things going for him: he was in London and he had royal blood. So Warwick earned the title he's been known by ever since – Kingmaker – as he proclaimed the teenager, King Edward IV of England ...

16

THEN WHO?
EDWARDS 4–5 (#1)

EDWARD IV – 1442–1483
Reigned 1461–1470; 1471–1483
Lived for 40 years. Ruled for 21 years
(across two different stints).
Died from overdoing it.
Remembered for: usurping Henry VI's throne; marrying
Elizabeth Woodville; ruling twice.

Edward was only 18 when he first came to the throne. He'd already led armies into battle and lost his father and brother at the Battle of Wakefield. We're so used to seeing medieval kings depicted as middle-aged men with beards that it's a shock when you realise how many of them were teenagers when they were crowned, not to mention how much they'd already done by the time they came to the throne.

Edward was very much the image of a sexy, virile, young monarch: tall, at six foot three, and handsome. But he did do a bit of a Henry VIII and get badly out of shape as he got older. Like Henry, he was also a worldly man, a keen womaniser who enjoyed self-indulgence and all the good things in life. Not at all pious or stuffy, he was interested in how the world worked. He liked making money and keeping hold of it, and consequently was involved in several trading ventures, exporting wool and tin, and importing wine, paper, sugar and oranges – anything that was hard to get hold of in England. Some people have characterised Edward as England's first businessman monarch who understood the value of corporate hospitality. He was a back-slapper and a hand-shaker, telling dirty jokes to amuse the men around him with the equivalent of a pint in his hand. He made sure he knew the names of everyone he had dealings with and what exactly they did, from baron to servant, and was forever laying on hunting and feasting for those noblemen, merchants and businessmen in London whom he wanted to keep onside.

The one person Edward wasn't able to stay on good terms with was Richard Neville – Warwick the Kingmaker – and this was to upset both their plans. To start with, though, the new king offered peace and stability after a long civil war and allowed the lords and the business-men of London to get on with making money, which is one of the reasons he was able to hold on to his throne. He was the first king in more than 150 years who didn't die in debt.

It wasn't all plain sailing for Edward, though. Warwick the Kingmaker may have put him on the throne, but King Henry VI was still at large and Queen Margaret remained a formidable force in the north. There were now two kings in England at the same time and, unless Warwick could win a decisive victory, nothing would be settled. Two days after Edward's coronation, the Kingmaker led an army north, financed by the wealthy merchants of the City of London.

Warwick decisively won the subsequent Battle of Towton in Yorkshire, but the cost was appalling, with no mercy given on either side. This apocalyptic battle has the dubious fame of being the blood-iest ever fought on British soil. The two armies hammered away at each other for 10 hours in the snow and it was said that the local rivers ran red for days. There were about two and a half million people living in England at the time and it's thought that 20,000 men, around 1 per cent of the population, were hacked to death that day, lords and common foot soldiers alike.

Warwick's army had the wind behind it, blowing snow and arrows into the faces of the Lancastrian archers whose own arrows fell short and, as a result, their army was smashed to pieces. The only thing that didn't go Warwick's way was that Henry VI and his son, Prince Edward, escaped. There were still two kings in England.

In London, Edward declared that he was going to be merciful towards Henry's supporters. This was easy enough to do because Warwick's policy of slaughtering any high-born opposition meant there were very few adult Lancastrian noblemen left alive. Henry was skulking around

WARWICK THE KINGMAKER

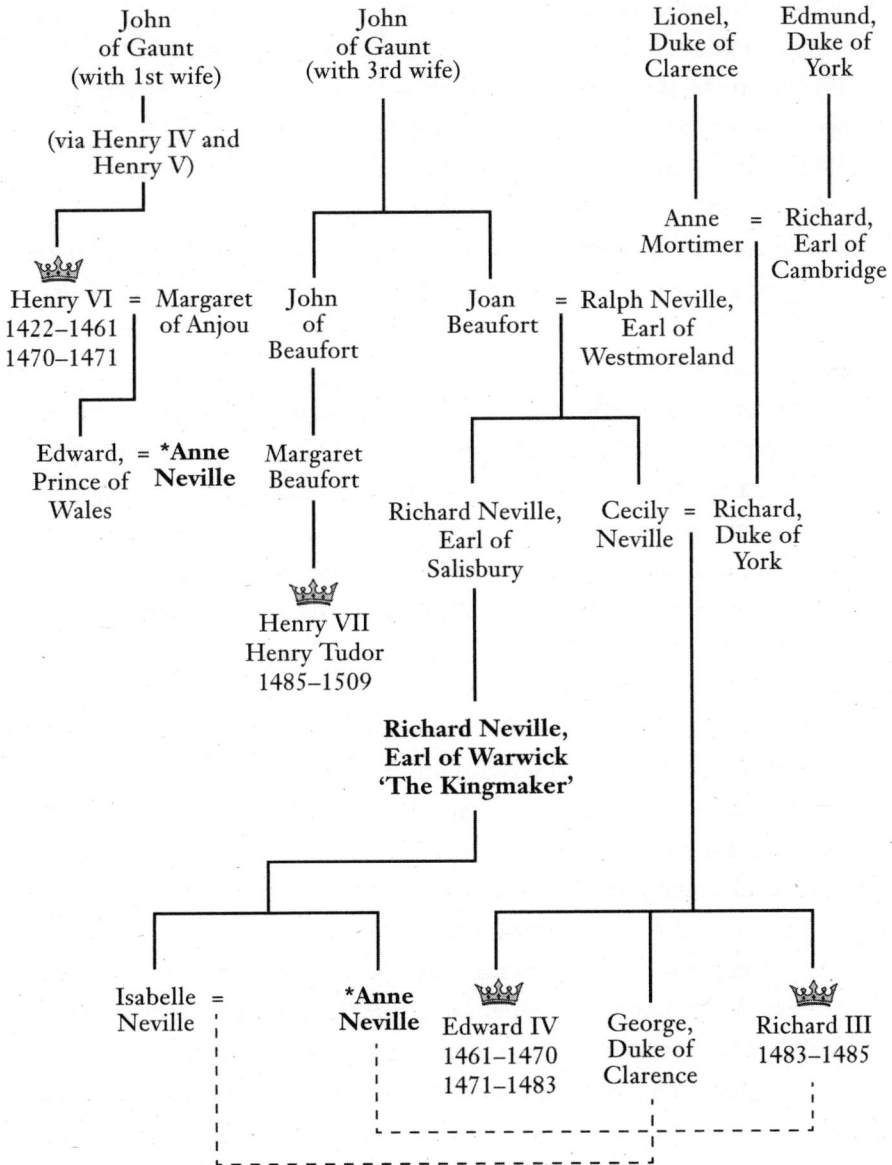

John of Gaunt (with 1st wife)

(via Henry IV and Henry V)

John of Gaunt (with 3rd wife)

Lionel, Duke of Clarence

Edmund, Duke of York

Anne Mortimer = Richard, Earl of Cambridge

♛ Henry VI 1422–1461 1470–1471 = Margaret of Anjou

John of Beaufort

Joan Beaufort = Ralph Neville, Earl of Westmoreland

Edward, Prince of Wales = *Anne Neville

Margaret Beaufort

Richard Neville, Earl of Salisbury

Cecily = Richard, Neville Duke of York

♛ Henry VII Henry Tudor 1485–1509

Richard Neville, Earl of Warwick 'The Kingmaker'

Isabelle = Neville

*Anne Neville

♛ Edward IV 1461–1470 1471–1483

George, Duke of Clarence

♛ Richard III 1483–1485

*Appears twice

in the north, but everyone wanted this disruptive war to be over and he was eventually betrayed by one of his old supporters and handed over to Edward, who paraded him through the streets of London with his feet tied to the stirrups of his horse. Poor, doolally Henry was incarcerated in the Tower, where he remained for the next five years.

There was no point in executing Henry as long as his son, Edward, Prince of Wales, was still alive. Kill Henry and you simply made the Prince of Wales king, and he wasn't your prisoner; he was still out there with Margaret. No, Henry was most useful as a hostage.

The parallel struggle in France between the French king and the slippery dukes of Burgundy wasn't over. Edward IV knew that if he got involved and picked a side, it would send a message that England had sorted out its internal problems and was ready to engage with the wider world again. However, he leant towards England's old allies, the Burgundians, while Warwick favoured the French king. Warwick felt that he was the real power in England and expected Edward to do as he was told. So he ignored him and started negotiating a treaty with King Louis XI, as well as a good political marriage for Edward to a French princess.

Edward resented Warwick behaving as if he was ruling the country and felt the need to exert his authority. In no particular order, he married his youngest sister to the Duke of Burgundy; forbade Warwick from marrying off his own daughter to Edward's younger brother, George, Duke of Clarence; sent Warwick to France; and, while he was out of the way, made his own peace treaty with the Burgundians. The biggest insult to Warwick came when Edward pulled out at the last minute from his arranged marriage to the French princess.

'For God's sake, why?'

'Because I'm already married …'

This bombshell knocked Warwick for six. To make things even worse, Edward had married a commoner, Elizabeth Woodville. Everyone was flabbergasted and Warwick had been made to look a fool. Nobody could understand why the king had married beneath himself and a conspiracy was cooked up that Elizabeth's mother was a witch who'd used black magic to beguile him. She was put on trial but was acquitted because … well, because she *wasn't* a witch.

It seems that Edward was simply in love with Elizabeth, or at least, sexually infatuated. There's some evidence that Elizabeth only agreed to sleep with him if he married her. But, whatever the case, Elizabeth was formally accepted as queen and Edward embraced something that always made kings unpopular – favouritism. He installed Elizabeth Woodville's large family of unmarried brothers and sisters at court and started giving them land and titles. The Woodvilles, who simply weren't posh enough, became his new inner circle and the old order were losing their status. Warwick, who had so carefully managed everything up to now, found that the young king was no longer toeing the line. When Edward removed Warwick's brother from his post as chancellor, Warwick started to plot against him and covertly switched his support to Edward's brother, the Duke of Clarence, who, soon after, defied King Edward and married Warwick's daughter.

So the war was back on and this time the fighting was between supporters of Edward and supporters of Warwick. Edward's army was defeated at the Battle of Edgecote in Northamptonshire in 1469 and, not long after, he was captured and ended up as a captive in Warwick's castle at Middleham in the Yorkshire Dales. Two of Edward's in-laws from the Woodville family were executed and Warwick and George, the Duke of Clarence, now tried to run the country. But George was useless. He was unreliable, unpopular, none too bright and a drinker. And Warwick himself was becoming increasingly unpopular as well.

The lords, fearing that England might slip back into full-scale war again, forced Warwick to return Edward to power. Warwick continued to plot against Edward but, when he was exposed, fled to France where, amazingly, he started negotiations with his hated enemy, Margaret of Anjou, who was sheltering there at the time, having been on the run since the Battle of Towton.

The pride of Warwick, the self-proclaimed Kingmaker who boasted that he'd single-handedly masterminded the Yorkist strategy, was bruised – and he was consumed by rage against Edward. For her part, Margaret was near destitute but held a trump card: her son, Edward, heir to the throne. Their last chance was to try to reclaim the crown in the name of Henry. To make their deal watertight and ensure

Warwick's place in pole position, he married his daughter, Anne, to Margaret and Henry's son, Edward, Prince of Wales.

Urged on and financed by King Louis, who was revelling in the chaos, Warwick landed an army in England that was joined by nobles discontented with the Yorkist regime. Now, it was Edward's turn to flee – to Flanders, with his little brother, Richard, the Duke of Gloucester.

Warwick was back in charge and he freed King Henry from the Tower of London, putting him back on the throne. If you're finding all this a bit confusing, think about how poor old Henry must have felt. Bewildered from the start, he'd been captured, freed, recaptured, freed, made king, deposed, put back on the throne … After all those years of fighting and bloody battles, everyone had ended up right back where they'd started.

This new state of affairs didn't last long, though. Edward quickly made a pact with Burgundy and landed his own army in England, prompting his slippery brother, the Duke of Clarence, to switch over to his side. The ensuing Battle of Barnet was a miserable affair, fought in heavy fog, with soldiers not knowing who was friend and who was foe. Warwick's army started fighting itself and, in the confusion, the Kingmaker was killed. That's the end of him. He is out of the story. And Edward and the Yorkists are back in power.

Queen Margaret had delayed coming back over to England with her son and landed on the very day that Warwick was killed. She had no choice but to press on, gathering the last vestiges of Lancastrian support. Her army soon met Edward's at Tewkesbury. Her beloved only child, the 17-year-old Prince Edward, was ready to fight in his first battle. This is what Margaret had brought him up for when they'd been exiles in France and the boy thought only of battles and chopping off heads. Now was his chance to fight for his throne … but he was cut down from behind in the rout that followed the collapse of the Lancastrian army.

It was all over. Margaret had lost everything. Her son was dead and soon afterwards her husband – poor, mad King Henry – was killed in the Tower and his corpse brought out to be shown to the people as proof that he was a goner. Many eminent Lancastrians had been slaughtered in the two battles and subsequent executions, and they had no figurehead left. There was nothing left for Margaret except to linger on in France for the next seven years and die in obscurity at the age of 52.

Edward was securely back on the throne and there was to be peace for the next 12 years. As before, he was merciful to his defeated enemies. The only person he came down hard on was his younger brother, George. Edward couldn't forgive the unreliable Duke of Clarence for leading a rebellion against him and, when evidence emerged that he might still have aims on the throne, he was executed in the Tower. The story went around that he was drowned in a butt of Malmsey wine, which may have been a joke about his fondness for the booze. Whatever the truth, execution by drowning wasn't unheard of and George's body was unmarked and still had his head attached to it.

Edward now set up his other brother, Richard of Gloucester, as 'lord of the north' and settled down to finish completing his roster of 10 children with Elizabeth Woodville. Their eldest son, another Edward, was heir to the throne, and his little brother, another sodding Richard, was Duke of York.

As Edward moved into his forties, his lifestyle caught up with him and he began to suffer from numerous illnesses and, in April 1483, his body gave up on him. It may have been pneumonia, or a heart attack, or perhaps apoplexy (which is basically a stroke). Moralists have claimed that Edward was punished for being ruled by his senses – too much eating, too much drinking, too much womanising (much as he loved Elizabeth, he had many mistresses) – but I quite like Edward and don't want to pass judgement on him. He was an able warrior and an able king. If he'd only lived another 20 years, he might have become one of our better-remembered monarchs and we would probably have never had the Tudor dynasty.

Before he died, he decreed that his younger brother, Richard, Duke of Gloucester, should be made protector of the realm until little Prince Edward was old enough to properly take charge. And we'll see in the next chapter just how well that went …

17

Then Who?
Edwards 4–5 (#2)

EDWARD V – 1470–1483
Lived for 12 years. Barely reigned at all (two months).
Died from …?
Remembered for: Being one of the 'Princes in the Tower'.

This is going to be a brief, sorry little chapter, because Edward V had a brief, sorry little life and a brief, sorry little reign. He became king when his father died on 9 April 1483 and ceased to be king 78 days later, on 26 June, when his uncle, Richard, proclaimed himself king. Edward was never seen again.

He may have had a short life, but it ended with an enduring mystery that obsesses people to this day. Most historians are adamant that it's not a mystery at all, that it's all very cut and dried. But nobody can ever say for sure how Edward V died, where he died and when he died because no body was ever found. He and his little brother were the two 'Princes in the Tower' (even though Edward was a king). He might never have had a coronation, but when a monarch dies, their appointed heir automatically succeeds them whether they've been crowned or not.

Prince Edward was born to King Edward IV and his 'commoner' wife, Elizabeth Woodville, when she was taking sanctuary in the Abbot's House at Westminster Abbey while her husband was briefly exiled in Flanders during the complex disruptions of the civil war. Edward was soon to return though and the first 12 years of the boy's life were fairly uneventful. One highlight was when he was knighted and made a member of the Order of the Garter when he was only four years old.

It was customary at the time for sons of noblemen and royalty to be separated from their parents and sent away to be brought up by someone else – a bit like how some people today send their tiny children off to boarding school. I guess the idea is that they'll be toughened up and get a better education if they're not in the bosom of the family, distracted by things like love and affection.

Prince Edward was brought up in the household of an uncle, Anthony Woodville, the 2nd Earl Rivers, at the royal castle of Ludlow in the Welsh Marches. Earl Rivers was one of the members of Elizabeth Woodville's family who'd profited from the titles and favours handed out by King Edward.

A fascinating letter survives in which the king issues a clear set of instructions to Earl Rivers about how the boy should be educated. It gives us a good idea of the typical education of a well-born boy at the time. There's a lot of stuff about 'virtuous learning' and the reading of 'noble stories', there was sport in the afternoons and an order not to expose the boy to anybody in the household who might use 'words of ribaldry', or was a 'swearer, brawler, backbiter, common hazarder, or adulterer …'. This is pretty rich coming from King Edward, who famously had several mistresses on the go at any one time.

Personally, I think the best thing a father can do for a son is give them love, attention, support and security. And if you're a medieval king, all that careful education will be for nothing if you die young and leave your son exposed – which is exactly what happened to poor Prince Edward. He was only 12 when, in April 1483, he heard that his father had died suddenly. Earl Rivers set off to escort the boy safely to London where his mother was waiting for him with his younger brother – Prince Richard, Duke of York.

The king's will named little Edward's uncle, Richard, Duke of Gloucester, as protector of the realm during the boy's minority. At this time, everybody thought that Uncle Dick was a jolly good fellow and a stand-up kind of guy, the perfect person to look after the little boy. Halfway to London, however, Earl Rivers was surprised to be met by Richard at Stony Stratford. The duke wined and dined Rivers and his party, which included another member of Elizabeth's family, but the next day they were all arrested. Richard claimed that the queen's clan were plotting to seize power by force and have him murdered.

When news of these events reached London, the queen once again took sanctuary with her younger children. Richard led little King Edward V into London and put him into the Tower of London *'for his own safekeeping'*,* announcing that he would stay there until his coronation. A date was set for the ceremony, but Richard repeatedly postponed it and even managed (with the help of a pet priest) to persuade Elizabeth Woodville to send his other nephew, Prince Richard, to the Tower, again *'for his own safekeeping'*.

Still, nobody suspected that Uncle Dick might be plotting to take the throne for himself. You could behave as badly as you liked, but it was just not done to depose a rightful monarch – or, worse, have them killed – without a major justification. The coronation never happened, though. Edward and little Richard were moved to inner apartments at the Tower; sightings of them became scarce until, by the end of the summer, they'd disappeared from public view altogether.

A doctor who regularly visited young Edward said that the boy begged for confession every time because he believed that he was facing death. He, at least, realised what was going on, Uncle Richard was, indeed, cooking up a scheme. He got another pet priest to preach a sermon claiming that Edward IV's marriage to Elizabeth Woodville was invalid, thus making their children illegitimate, which meant that Edward and Prince Richard were struck off the royal list and suddenly vulnerable.

Uncle Richard declared himself king in June 1483, not long after which, as I say, the two princes in the Tower were never seen again.†

This all happened so fast, and Richard did it so thoroughly, that people were a bit stunned – 'Wait, what, how did that happen?' King Richard had even mounted a small coup where he rounded up all the surviving supporters of his brother, Edward IV, and either imprisoned or executed them, so that there was no real opposition to his coronation.

---

* The italics here denote heavy sarcasm.

† Soon after Richard's coronation, there was a failed attempt to rescue the princes from the Tower of London and this was what probably led to their deaths. It was too risky to leave them alive.

Richard III has his modern supporters, known as the Ricardians, who are adamant that he was actually a good egg and unfairly besmirched by Tudor propaganda. They always used to claim that he wasn't evil, wasn't in possession of a crook back and didn't really do any of the terrible things attributed to him.* But, quite frankly, looking back at the cold and calculating moves he made, it's very hard not to come to the conclusion that he was the villain of the piece.

But, as I say, nobody will ever know exactly what happened to the two little boys. The most plausible theory is that they were murdered on Richard's orders and their bodies disposed of – probably in the Thames.

Other theories are available.

---

* They had to row back on the 'he wasn't a hunchback' claim when his body was dug up in 2012 and found to have mild scoliosis, as we shall see.

18

DICK THE BAD

RICHARD III – 1452–1485

Richard of Gloucester

Reigned 1483–1485

Lived for 32 years. Ruled for two years.

Died in battle.

Remembered for: murdering the princes in the Tower; having a
crook back; 'A horse a horse, my kingdom for a horse!'

For a man whose reign was so short, King Richard III certainly made
his mark on history. This is partly down to the popularity of the
Shakespeare play, but also because he was the last Plantagenet king
and the last English king to die in battle. His death marked the end of
the Middle Ages and ushered in the Tudors, the Renaissance, the
Reformation, the modern world.

And then there's the small business of the disappearance of his two
young nephews from the Tower of London, and the enduring question
of his guilt – or innocence. The 'Willie, Willie, Harry, Stee' rhyme is
pretty unequivocal in its judgement of him, calling him 'Dick the Bad',
and, for much of history, that's how he's been presented. In the last 100
years, however, there have been moves to reassess him and clear his
name, driven mainly by the Ricardians. It all began with the founding
of The Fellowship of the White Boar in 1924 (the white boar being
Richard's emblem), which changed its name to the more sober-sound-
ing Richard III Society in 1959.

Richard's rehabilitation probably reached its peak in 2012, when a
group of archaeologists from Leicester University, working with the
Richard III Society and amateur historian Philippa Langley, concluded
that Richard III's lost grave was underneath a car park in the middle
of Leicester. They got permission from the council to start digging –

and found the skeleton of a medieval man who'd been hacked to death in battle. DNA proved it was most likely Richard and the discovery caused a sensation. Here was a wronged man, hidden away from the world, buried with the truth. And now he was resurrected!

There's a whiff of north vs south in all this, of a down-to-earth man of the people stitched up by the snobby southern elite. And there's a whiff of the conspiracy theory about it as well. Ricardians tend to believe that they're a put-upon minority who know the REAL TRUTH that's being suppressed by the establishment. The extraordinary thing is that, more than 500 years after Richard was killed at the Battle of Bosworth Field, his reputation is still being fiercely argued about. Indeed, this very paragraph has probably lost me a large number of readers and gained me some angry diatribes on social media.

Let's look at the facts, though. Richard was the 11th of 12 children, another one of those men who never expected to inherit anything and ended up with everything. The Wars of the Roses erupted when he was a child and he was only eight when his father, Richard of York, and older brother, Edmund, were killed at the Battle of Wakefield. The little boy was sent across the Channel to the Low Countries for safety, but when King Henry and the Lancastrians were defeated at the Battle of Towton three months later, Richard returned to London for the coronation of his older brother, Edward, in 1461. Afterwards, although still just a boy, Richard was knighted and made Duke of Gloucester. He then spent some time being looked after and trained as a knight by Warwick the Kingmaker at Middleham Castle in Wensleydale. While Richard was living in Warwick's household, he would have got to know the rest of the Neville family, including Warwick's daughters, Isabel and Anne. It was at this time that Richard developed scoliosis, a curvature of the spine. When his skeleton was discovered under the car park in 2012, the curvature was found to be not very pronounced, but it still blew out of the water the Ricardians' theory that the 'crook back' was a Tudor invention. One of Richard's shoulders might have been a little higher than the other, but this would have been easily hidden under his clothing. He was by no means the caricature, twisted hunchback that he was later personified as, as if a physical abnormality made him an evil person.

When Warwick turned against King Edward IV, Richard stayed loyal to his brother. This was in marked contrast to their other brother, Flaky George, the Duke of Clarence, who sided with Warwick, vainly hoping he might replace Edward as king. To cement this deal, Warwick married his eldest daughter, Isabel, to George. When Edward was temporarily dethroned by Warwick in 1470, he and Richard fled across the Channel to Flanders, which was now controlled by Burgundy. When they returned the next year, Richard was old enough, at 18, to serve as Edward's right-hand man. He proved himself an effective general, winning his spurs and gaining status. By the end of the year, Warwick, King Henry VI and his son, Edward, Prince of Wales, were all dead, the Lancastrians were a spent force and Edward was firmly back on the throne.

Warwick's wealth and estates were up for grabs. Richard was given a number of the Neville estates in the north and also married Warwick's daughter, Anne Neville, the widow of Edward, Prince of Wales. This led to a massive family row involving Flaky George, who'd married Anne's elder sister and had expected to inherit everything. Their dispute was eventually resolved when King Edward had Flaky George killed for his earlier disloyalty. This is one way to deal with the brother you don't get on with.

Edward increasingly gave lands, titles and power to Richard, making him effectively, lord of the north, pretty much splitting the rule of England into two. Richard's job was to unite, strengthen and hold the north against the Scots who would take any opportunity to attack if they felt the king was looking the other way.

Richard was popular in the north. He did much to improve the conditions of the ordinary people by keeping peace and imposing strict law and order. He set up a Court of Requests for men who couldn't afford legal representation. He reformed the bail system to protect the accused from having their property taken from them. He made the buying and selling of land transparent and fair. It was a good training for being a monarch and perhaps, had Richard survived the Battle of Bosworth and reigned for longer, he would have been a just and popular king. Certainly, when he came to the throne after Edward IV's death, he tried to democratise parliament, and make it more accessible to the ordinary people.

Richard had a short but busy reign. He opened up the sale of printed books, which had been greatly restricted. He moved to get English laws and statutes translated from the French. And he wooed the people. But if he'd thought he'd put an end to the wars and could make England safe and secure, he was sorely mistaken.

The threat to Richard's grip on the throne hadn't gone away with the death of the princes. Much as he would have loved to, Richard couldn't imprison or wipe out all of Elizabeth Woodville's clan, nor the Beaufort branch of the royal family. If you remember, the Beauforts were the 'illegitimate' descendants of John of Gaunt, via his third wife, and were staunch supporters of Henry VI and the Lancastrians. In 1483, Henry Stafford, 2nd Duke of Buckingham, launched a challenge to Richard's rule that became known as Buckingham's Rebellion. Stafford's mother was a Beaufort and his wife was a Woodville (Katherine, Queen Elizabeth's sister).

Originally, the rebels claimed that they were trying to put Edward V back on the throne, but when it was clear that he was dead, they switched their allegiance to another contender, Henry Tudor, who had a weak line of royal descent though his mother, Margaret Beaufort (which I'll deal with in the next chapter).

But, when the new Tudor claimant tried to bring an army over to England from France, there were storms on the south coast and, once again, a mighty undertaking was thwarted by bad weather in the Channel. With no proper army to back him up, Buckingham was captured soon afterwards and beheaded. This first rebellion came to nothing.

Richard, needing supporters at court, made the mistake that had derailed many previous monarchs. He got rid of the old guard and surrounded himself with new blood. Satirical pamphlets and mocking ditties started appearing, accusing Richard of favouritism and corruption. Accordingly, support for Henry Tudor grew. Two years after his first thwarted invasion, he tried again, this time with the full backing of the French (any excuse to have a go at the English!).

Henry Tudor landed in southwest Wales and marched eastwards, meeting Richard's army near the town of Market Bosworth in

Leicestershire. Even though Henry's army had been bolstered by Welsh supporters en route, he was still outnumbered by about 15,000 to 5,000. But, as anyone who's ever played Risk will know, it only takes a few bad rolls of the dice for your glorious, unbeatable army to be completely wiped out.

What swung it against Richard was the desertion of two of his chief courtiers, Lord Thomas Stanley and his brother, Sir William Stanley, old hands from Edward's time. They'd fallen out with Richard and had met Henry for secret talks before what became known as the Battle of Bosworth Field. When the fighting started, at first they held back, but, when they saw which way the wind was blowing, they came in on Henry's side.

Richard led his army bravely. Although slight, he was a tough soldier and a good general, riding into battle on his great charger. An hour into the fighting, things were hanging in the balance and Richard tried to end it quickly by leading a cavalry charge into Henry's ranks to try to get at the upstart. Richard cut his way past several famous knights, killed Henry's standard bearer and was within sword's reach of killing Henry when he was surrounded by the deserter, Sir William Stanley, and his men, who hacked him down. Thomas Stanley then reportedly picked up Richard's crown from the battlefield and gave it to Henry Tudor to try on for size.

When Richard's body was dug up in that Leicester car park, they found his skeleton covered in wounds, eight of which were to the skull, including a massive cut that had sliced off the back of his head. So that was the end of Richard. At least he died valiantly in battle, rather than being starved to death in a damp and freezing castle, or having a red-hot poker jammed up his arse.

After the battle, Richard's naked body was tied to the back of a horse and carried into Leicester, where it was displayed in public to prove that he was dead, before being quickly buried in Greyfriars Church with little ceremony. Over the next few hundred years, Greyfriars was redeveloped, before eventually being demolished and built over during the Reformation. Richard's unhallowed grave was lost – until the Leicester University team rediscovered it. For the Ricardians, the rehabilitation of their hero was complete.

It's undoubtedly true that Richard was the victim of Tudor propaganda. To legitimise Henry Tudor's shaky claim to the throne, it was necessary to paint Richard as a villainous usurper. William Shakespeare, writing under Tudor rule, gave us a murderous, scheming, 'crook-backed' monster, who is at the same time one of the most memorable and compelling characters in literature. Richard was no doubt a much nicer man and a better king than the Tudors (and Shakespeare) claimed – but could he not still also be guilty of pragmatically doing away with the princes in the Tower after his coup in order to secure the realm and his place at the centre of it?

We've seen several times how ambitious junior members of the royal family – if they smelled weakness or spotted the chance for personal advancement – didn't hesitate to take a 'rightful' king's throne and justify their actions by claiming it was for the good of the country. Why should Richard have been any different? The Wars of the Roses represented a brutal, ruthless and lethal time for the upper echelons of society.

The facts are pretty cut and dried. Richard imprisoned his nephew, Edward V. He imprisoned or executed key members of Edward's mother's family, the Woodvilles. He did the same to key supporters of Edward IV and declared his brother's marriage to Elizabeth Woodville invalid, thus making Edward V illegitimate. He made himself king and Edward V was never seen again.

In 2015, Richard's remains were reburied, this time with much pomp and ceremony, in Leicester Cathedral. He was at last given a proper tomb and memorial. Which means, that, whatever you think about him, he is now the answer to a very good pub quiz question …

Which English monarch was the last to be buried before Elizabeth II?

19

Harrys Twain (#1)

HENRY VII – 1457–1509
Henry Tudor
Reigned 1485–1509
Lived for 52 years. Ruled for 24 years.
Died from tuberculosis.
Remembered for: defeating Richard III at the Battle of Bosworth
Field; becoming the first Tudor monarch.

The English nobility had realised quite early on that, if they wanted to hang on to their lands, power and wealth from one generation to the next, they needed to keep their estates intact and not divide them up between family members on the death of a patriarch. The English established a system in which eldest sons inherited *everything*, so their power bases and their wealth were passed to the next generation in one lump. Younger sons and brothers might be given smaller estates, or simply had to fend for themselves, but, crucially, the centre held. So, a king hung on to his country and the barons held on to their estates. The Welsh had never adopted this system, which meant that it was almost impossible for one powerful leader to rule the whole country, with the knock-on effect that it was extremely hard for the Welsh to wrest control of the country from their English overlords. By the time of the Wars of the Roses, Wales was a tangled mess of smaller kingdoms ruled by what the English called 'princes'. And it suited the English to keep these Welsh princes at each other's throats by careful use of patronage and support. Divide and rule.

It also meant that the Welsh had been co-opted as vital allies by the two rival factions in the Wars of the Roses. And it was to be the Welsh who decided the final outcome. The bulk of Henry Tudor's army at Bosworth were Welsh and, when the war had started, nobody could have predicted that the crown would eventually end up sitting on the heads of a relatively obscure Welsh family: the Tudors.

So what was the background to this family? Well, that leads me to another problem with Welsh history. Not only did they have a different system of inheritance, they also had a different system of naming, whereby there were no established surnames. Sons would simply be named after their fathers. If (as a non-Welsh-person) you've ever wondered why 'Ap' was part of so many Welsh names at this time, it's because it means 'son of'. So – 'Rhys ap Dafydd', is 'Rhys, son of David', and 'Thomas ap Thomas', is 'Thomas, son of Thomas'. Over time, this system changed and surnames stuck, but it means that it's often hard to trace Welsh ancestry as the names keep changing. The name Tudor (or, more correctly, Tiddwr) started life as a Christian name, leading to an 'ap Tudor' first appearing in Anglesey, before eventually being shortened to 'Tudor' when it started appearing in English records.

Accordingly, not a great deal is known about the early history of the Tudors. Members of the family are first found in England in the retinue of King Richard II, but after Richard was dethroned by Henry IV, they switched their allegiance to the rebel Welsh fighter, Owain ap Gruffydd, now known as Owain Glyndwr (or Owen Glendower in Shakespeare's plays). We've already seen how Glyndwr led an uprising against the English that was defeated by Henry IV. This knocked the Tudors back, but one of them – a guy called Owen Tudor – later turns up as a servant in King Henry V's household.

Because nobody knew how important the Tudor family was going to be, there are hardly any records of the early life of Owen Tudor; most of the fanciful stories that grew up about him – that he fought at Agincourt, that his father was a fugitive murderer, that he was a squire of Henry V – are no doubt apocryphal. There's one extraordinary fact that we know is *absolutely true* about Owen, however. After Henry V died young, his widow, Catherine of Valois, daughter of the mad French king, Charles VI, had an affair with her servant, one Owen Tudor, and then *married* him. Allegedly she'd seen him swimming naked in the local river, had admired his physique, and the rest, as they say, is history. This sort of thing was simply not done by a medieval queen. Owen must have been quite a lad.

Unlike most royal marriages of the time, it was a marriage of love, but that Catherine had stooped to marry the lowly Owen inevitably caused a major scandal. Luckily, he was tough enough to weather the storm and was deaf to the criticism, and they were very happy together. For a while ...

Owen was inevitably drawn into the Wars of the Roses. He'd married into the Lancastrian branch of the royal family and his step-son was King Henry VI, so he knew which side he was going to be fighting on. Sadly, for him, it was the losing side. The handsome serv-ant who'd married a queen was captured by the victorious Yorkist army at the Battle of Mortimer's Cross in 1461 and executed. He was in his sixties, but kept up his macho, devil-may-care image to the end. Just before the Yorkists beheaded him, he said 'the head that shall lie on the stock was wont to lie on Queen Catherine's lap'.

Owen and Catherine had several children, the most important of whom were Edmund and Jasper. Edmund followed in his father's foot-steps and burrowed even deeper into the royal family by marrying the formidable Margaret Beaufort, who was descended from Edward III (see the family tree on page 125).

Edmund died young of bubonic plague (*officially* – he may well have been poisoned) while fighting for King Henry VI in south Wales, but not before fathering a son, Henry. Edmund's brother, Jasper, became a sort of surrogate father figure to the boy, who adored him. Henry was to grow up to become Henry VII and he and Jasper fought alongside each other at the Battle of Bosworth. Amazingly, Jasper made it through the Wars of the Roses unscathed and lived into his mid-sixties.

When Henry was a boy, as a fatherless Lancastrian with royal blood, he was in a dangerous position at such a volatile time. Luckily for him, though, Margaret Beaufort was one tough mother. She was only 12 when she married Edmund, and 13 when she gave birth to Henry – and that was her second marriage! (After Edmund died, she would go on to marry twice more.) Jasper tried to look after the teenage girl and her child, but when Edward of York took the throne in 1461, Jasper fled to France and Margaret and Henry were handed over to the Yorkist Earl of Pembroke, who kept a close watch on them.

For maybe 10 years, Henry was kept under virtual house arrest in Raglan Castle. When all the toing and froing between Edward IV and Warwick the Kingmaker finally ended with Warwick being killed and Edward sitting pretty, Uncle Jasper decided that Henry was in an even more dangerous position. So Henry escaped to Brittany and hid out there for the next 14 years under the protection of the Duke of Brittany. Edward IV tried several times to get assassins into Brittany to bump Henry off, but he survived there until 1483 when circumstances in England improved.

His mother, Margaret, who'd stayed in England, was by now on to her fourth marriage, this time to a staunch Yorkist supporter, Lord Thomas Stanley. Margaret needed Yorkist protection and Stanley profited from a marriage to such a high-born and wealthy woman. King Edward, for his part, wanted to keep this power couple close and needed the Stanley family's support to fight off any challengers to his throne. Margaret worked on Edward and was able to convince him that Henry was no threat and it would be better to have him at court. By 1483, arrangements were being put in place for Henry to return to England, but then the world turned upside down again when Edward IV died at the age of 40.

Enter his brother, Richard of Gloucester, looking shifty (or not, if you're a Ricardian). We know what happens next – Richard launches his coup. Margaret didn't trust Richard and plotted to get rid of him from the start. She'd always fought hard for her son and saw an opportunity to get him to the top of the greasy pole and onto the bloody throne. Remember, she was only 13 years older than Henry, so was more of a big sister to him than a mother and the two formed a very close bond.

Margaret wasn't the only person who didn't like Richard and she was able to start secretly promoting Henry as an alternative to him, even though she was married to the Yorkist, Lord Stanley. The first step was to arrange a good marriage for Henry, who was still over in France at this time, and it was announced that he would marry Edward IV's daughter, Elizabeth of York. This was a clever move on Margaret's part. Elizabeth was sister to the princes in the Tower and the marriage would unite Henry's Lancastrian branch of the family with Edward's

Yorkist branch. Once it became clear that little Edward V was dead, Henry Tudor was one step closer to the throne.

Margaret carried on signing up opponents of Richard to her cause, including the French, the Welsh, Jasper Tudor and King Edward's widow, Elizabeth Woodville. Margaret kept her involvement as quiet as she could and the uprising ended up being fronted by the Duke of Buckingham. As we've seen, the rebellion failed, Henry never made it over from France and Buckingham was executed.*

A couple of years later, however, Henry tried again. This time he landed in south Wales where he was able to recruit a large fighting force with the help of a Welsh defector from Richard's side, Rhys ap Thomas, and marched to England with his uncle Jasper at his side.

Remember how the two powerful Stanley brothers, William and Thomas, swung the Battle of Bosworth Henry's way by switching sides and abandoning King Richard? Well, Thomas Stanley was Margaret Beaufort's new husband, which made him Henry's stepfather. Richard had been worried about the brothers' loyalty and had taken William's son hostage, so it was a gamble for William to desert Richard. If Henry had lost, the two brothers would have been executed, along with William's son. Luckily for them, Henry was victorious. Just as Richard was the last English king to die on the battlefield, Henry was the last English king to win his throne on one. And, thus, the Tudor dynasty was born.

When Henry was crowned king in London, he rewarded his supporters and chose to be lenient towards the Yorkists. A few were executed, while others were imprisoned or fled into sanctuary, but most were keen to make their peace with Henry – at least for the moment. And it suited Henry to make peace with *them*. He had to present himself as the legitimate king, not a violent usurper. And everybody wanted an end to the fighting. The aristocracy had been shattered by the war and there was a danger that the country might descend into total anarchy. Henry needed support from both sides to

---

* If you want to get into the conspiracy theories about the princes in the Tower, Buckingham and Margaret Beaufort are both fingered by many Ricardians as being the real murderers, but this seems very far-fetched.

hold things together and, although he passed laws that made it easy for him to confiscate lands and powers from his lords, he didn't use it. He just left the threat hanging there. He also got many barons to sign bonds over to him and held these substantial sums of money in trust. If they ever turned against him, they'd lose everything. Henry was obsessed with money and finances, and is often accused of being a miserable, grasping miser, but he was a canny man and understood the power that money held.

He was settled enough now to finally go ahead with his marriage to Edward IV's daughter, Elizabeth of York. He had to get a papal dispensation for the union, as they were rather too closely related, both being descendants of John of Gaunt. Their marriage in 1486 was a symbolic union of the Yorkist and Lancastrian branches of the family and Henry invented a new emblem for the monarchy, a combination of the white rose of York and the red rose of Lancaster, that has become an enduring emblem of England. Henry could point to his fancy new Tudor rose and say, 'See, I have every right to rule. I am the party of peace and reconciliation, descended from both the houses of York and Lancaster.' Which was true – if you went all the way back to Edward III.

Henry knew, though, that he'd always have to watch his back and would never be totally secure on the throne. This was a man who, from birth until his death 52 years later, never slept easily. Luckily, he had an excellent spy network and was very well-informed. The first major challenge to his rule came in 1487. One of the reasons Henry had been accepted as king was because so many titled men had been killed in the wars and he was almost the sole surviving member of the royal family. Almost, but not quite …

Edward and Richard's flaky brother, George, Duke of Clarence, had had a son known as Edward, Earl of Warwick (I know, I know, another bloody Edward).* Warwick was only 10 years old when Henry came to the throne but, just to be on the safe side, Henry put him in the Tower of London *'for his own safe keeping'*. People hadn't seen the lad for a while when, in 1487, a 10-year-old boy in Ireland announced that *he* was Edward, Earl of Warwick. The boy, whose real name was

* He was also the grandson of Warwick the Kingmaker, who still cast a potent spell.

Lambert Simnel, was actually just a puppet created by Richard Simmons, a Yorkist priest. Simmons had seen in the boy's features a similarity to Edward IV and had taken him over to Ireland to train him in royal etiquette. When he was ready, Simmons shoved poor Lambert onto the English stage as the Earl of Warwick, with a cooked-up story about how a fellow conspirator, the Earl of Lincoln, had helped him escape from the Tower.

Richard III had been popular in Ireland and the Anglo-Irish lords happily went along with this fake news – any chance to have a go at King Henry. Backed by several thousand Irish troops, Lambert Simnel and his patrons landed in Cumbria. Unfortunately for the hapless Simnel, his claim was ridiculously easy to disprove. Henry simply brought the real Edward of Warwick out of the Tower and put him on display in London. Only a handful of noblemen turned out to support the uprising and, on 16 June 1487 at East Stoke in the east Midlands, Henry's archers launched a withering hail of arrows against the poorly-armed Irish levees. The invading army was destroyed.

Henry showed mercy towards Lambert Simmel, since he was so young and couldn't be blamed for how he'd been used. He pardoned the boy and put him to work, first in the royal kitchens and, later on, as falconer.

There was a very similar rebellion in 1490, when another pretender to the throne, Perkin Warbeck, claimed to be Richard, Duke of York, the younger of the two princes in the Tower. Again, the anti-Tudor movement got behind a rather flimsy, but nevertheless still useful, figurehead. Perkin Warbeck rallied the Irish, some remaining Yorkists and (inevitably) the Scottish king. The so-called 'Auld Alliance' between the Scots and the French meant that the two countries were always trying to make mischief against the English.

In 1496, the Scots king, James IV, crossed the border with Warbeck's troops, but had only got a few miles into England when an English army, led by the historic defenders of the north, the Nevilles, came out to meet them. Warbeck's army broke up and fled, and he went away to plan another attempt. Henry saw this as an opportunity to sort the Scottish out once and for all and began to finance an invasion. But he was having to raise so many taxes that he was becoming very unpopular. In the end, his invasion of Scotland never happened because he had to use the money he'd raised to finance the defence of Cornwall. The locals had risen against him – ironically, because they resented paying all these damned taxes.

Counting on the support of the disgruntled Cornish, Perkin Warbeck landed at Land's End in 1497 and tried again. Ultimately, though, he was no more successful than Simnel. He could never gain *quite enough* support and was eventually captured. When interrogated (and most likely tortured), he admitted to being a Fleming chancer called Pierrechon de Werbecque. His life was spared as he'd confessed to being an imposter, so was no longer a threat. The king made him welcome at his court but, following fresh plots in his name, Henry locked him in the Tower with Edward, Earl of Warwick. And when they tried to escape together, Henry gave in to the inevitable and had them both 'removed from their bodies'.

The king was now able to get back to his favourite pastime: raising taxes. His chief collector of taxes was Archbishop John Morton, who famously had a Catch-22 approach to squeezing money out of the nobility: anyone who spent very little must have hoarded big savings and so could be heavily taxed; anyone who spent lavishly, on the other hand, must have loads of money and so could be heavily taxed. This method was known as Morton's Fork. If you escaped one prong of his metaphorical pitchfork, you'd get skewered by the other.

As I said, Henry was accused of being a greedy, sour-faced miser. He was no hoarder, though. He liked to spend the money he collected. He splashed out the equivalent of £3 million on his own wardrobe in the first two years of his reign, lavished jewels and furs on his wife, and is on record as regularly buying gifts for his children. He kept jesters and minstrels. He had tennis coaches to improve his game so that he would look good when ambassadors visited from overseas. And he didn't only spend his cash on himself. He built or restored several royal palaces, churches and chapels, such as the one at King's College, Cambridge. He strengthened the navy, building new ships and making it a proper fighting force. And a substantial amount of this tax money still made its way into the exchequer. He essentially just wanted peace and economic prosperity, and was largely successful.

Henry made peace with the French and the Scots, and wedded his daughter, Margaret, to King James IV of Scotland, hoping to create 'Perpetual Peace' and break the Auld Alliance. He didn't quite pull that off, but the crowns of England and Scotland were eventually to be united when Margaret's great-grandson, James VI of Scotland, became James I of England.

Henry wasn't finished. Wanting to make an alliance with Spain, the rising superpower in Europe, he married his eldest son, Arthur, to Catherine of Aragon. There was a huge festival to celebrate the wedding with tournaments and pageants, and much celebration. This was the high point of Henry's reign, when both he and the country were at their happiest. After this, things started to go wrong for him and he ended up a broken man.

In 1502, his beloved Arthur died from a respiratory illness known as the sweating sickness, a mysterious, still unidentified disease that did for many people at this time – particularly fit young men.*

Henry was shattered, but he still needed to preserve the Spanish alliance and he persuaded the pope to agree that his second son, Henry, could marry Arthur's widow, Catherine. The following year, King Henry's wife, Queen Elizabeth, gave birth to a little girl who only lived a few days, and Elizabeth herself died soon after. This was another terrible blow to Henry. He'd been deeply in love with Elizabeth and wasn't known for having mistresses and siring illegitimate children all over the place like most kings.

Henry never really recovered from this double shock and, six years later, in 1509, still grieving his wife and son, he died of tuberculosis. He was buried in Westminster Abbey and a bust was commissioned, based on his death mask. There's also an excellent portrait of Henry in the National Portrait Gallery. He looks crafty and inquisitive, and contemporary courtiers described him as being affable, gracious and quick-witted, very much the Renaissance man – which is fitting as his reign introduced Renaissance art and ideas into England. It was a real turning point, the end of the medieval period and the beginning of the modern world.

* Had he lived, he would have been our first official King Arthur.

20

ḤARRYS ṬWAIN (#2)

HENRY VIII – 1491–1547

Reigned 1509–1547
Lived for 55 years. Reigned for 38 years.
Died from pretty much everything.
Remembered for … multiple marriages.

Henry VIII had six wives.

I'm tempted to leave it at that, to tell you the truth. Make this a short chapter and move on. Everyone knows who Henry was and that he married six times, which somehow makes him our best-known king. It seems that if you want to be remembered, you just have to behave like a complete arse. Henry was the typical spoilt brat who inherited everything, couldn't live up to his father's self-made legacy and pissed everything up the wall in an orgy of self-indulgence.

The first thing he did on taking the throne, as a sort of populist move, was to arrest his father's two chief tax collectors and execute them. These were the men who had been behind Henry VII's drive to balance the books and Henry VIII kills them – 'Huzzah, look at me! I'm the man who cut taxes!'. And it's a disaster. For the rest of Henry's reign, he had to borrow money from Italian bankers in the Low Countries to keep afloat; one of the main reasons he turned the country Protestant, closed down all the monasteries and took their wealth was because he needed the money.

The most famous depiction of Henry is the almost photo-realistic painting by Hans Holbein (actually, it's a copy of the lost original). It's an unforgettable image of a monumental figure – legs like tree trunks, standing astride the world – that says, 'This is not a man you want to mess with'. The problem with Henry, though, is that while he wanted to be seen as the big man, the mighty king, strong and implacable –

another Richard the Lionheart, or Edward I, Hammer of the Scots – he never really managed to do anything dramatic on the world stage. He loved the idea of war; he just wasn't particularly good at it. The one successful thing he did on the defence front was build up the navy, which worked out well for England in the long run, so, we'll give him that, but his violence was mainly directed at his own royal court.

But let's start by saying something positive about Henry. When he was younger, he was full of promise. He was an intellectual – well read and curious about the world. He had a great interest in science and scientific instruments, in maps and astronomy. He loved art, theatre, philosophy and architecture. He wrote books, he wrote music. There still exists sheet music written by him and he's a named artist on Spotify, with several tracks to his name (including, erroneously, 'Greensleeves'. Not one of his). His biggest hit was 'Pastime with Good Company', which became a Europe-wide banger and gives you a good idea of the other side of Henry's character – his love of hanging out with his mates, hunting, singing, dancing, having fun.

Part of Henry's problem was that he was more interested in all this stuff than the boring, day-to-day business of running a country. He was hot on big ideas, but he wasn't a details man like his father. His courtiers were always complaining that he didn't read their reports and they had to precis them for him. (Henry VIII has a lot of similarities with Donald Trump. Not just because of his size, his distinctive appearance and his number of wives. In his first term, it was said that Trump used to glance through his paperwork in bed at night while eating cheeseburgers. And I can easily imagine Henry VIII doing that. Well, probably not a hamburger, but you know what I mean. Perhaps some venison, or a swan.)

Like Trump, Henry was a ruthless man, happy to bend the state to his will and rule for his own personal ends. And he was a disruptor, prepared to tear his country apart if it suited his personal needs, to get rid of the old order and throw friends and colleagues under a whole fleet of buses.

As Henry was only second in line to the throne when he was younger – a 'spare' not expected to be king – there wasn't much written about his early life. We know he had a good education and was bright, interested in grammar, poetry, rhetoric and ethics. He spoke French and Latin well, understood Italian and learned some Spanish, but beyond that the details are sketchy.

He only really entered the contemporary accounts at the wedding of his brother, the Golden Boy, Prince Arthur, five years his elder. You can picture the ten-year-old Henry cavorting about at the wedding, getting drunk for the first time and being sick in the bushes. Up to this point, his childhood had been completely overshadowed by his brother, but not long after the wedding, Arthur died of the sweating sickness and their father arranged for the young Henry to marry Arthur's widow, Catherine of Aragon. At first, Henry was too young to marry, and then, when he was 14, he baulked at the idea. He thought the whole thing was dodgy and only finally relented, seven years after the arrangement had first been suggested, when his father died in 1509 and Henry came to the throne as Henry VIII.

The new king could see the wisdom and strategic benefits of marrying a Spanish princess. By this time, the major power blocs in Western Europe were largely consolidated. Eastward imperial expansion was blocked by the burgeoning Ottoman Empire that had burst out of Turkey and now controlled Greece and the Balkans, and was pressing up against Austria. France had sorted out its dynastic disputes and was stable, wealthy and secure. And the rest of Europe was dominated by the Habsburg Empire. For the previous 300 years, the Habsburg family had been taking over central Europe – from Hungary, through Austria to the Netherlands – and they pretty much had the Holy Roman Empire sewn up as well (you can think of it as mainly Germany). The post of emperor was supposed to be an elected one, but a string of Habsburgs had held it for some time. To the south, Italy wasn't a unified country and was made up of many independent city states, including the papal states, who were always at each other's throats. This disunity had allowed France to make major inroads into Italy and take over large parts of the north.

Spain hadn't been a major player on the European scene because for 800 years it had been isolated from the rest of Europe. From the 8th to the 15th century, most of the Iberian Peninsula had been under Muslim rule. Only a thin strip of small countries near the Pyrenees had managed to hold out. The Christian Spanish had gradually fought for their independence, though, and by the 1460s, only Granada in the south remained under Muslim control. In 1469, two powerful Spanish monarchs, Ferdinand of Aragon and Isabella of Castile, married and formed such a strong alliance that they were able to finally drive out the Muslims and become rulers of all Spain.

With no room to manoeuvre in crowded Europe, Spain looked outside the continent for lands to colonise, people to enslave and gold to plunder. In 1492, while broken England was recovering from the Wars of the Roses, Ferdinand and Isabella had financed Columbus's expedition to the New World (although, because he'd got some of his mathematical calculations about the size of the globe wrong, they all thought he was going to Asia) where they started to build an empire and, almost overnight, became the wealthiest country on the block. Ferdinand and Isabella's state income was seven times that of Henry's.

One of Ferdinand and Isabella's daughters, Joanna, married Philip Habsburg, the son of the Holy Roman Emperor, Maximilian, uniting Spain and the Habsburgs of northern Europe. Joanna and Philip's son, Charles, went on to rule as king of Spain, which meant that there were two parts to the mighty Habsburg Empire, a northern one and a southern one – with France sandwiched in between. It increasingly looked like a Europe-wide war was inevitable, with England's old enemies, the French, on one side and the Habsburgs on the other. The pope sided with the Habsburgs while the Italian states kept swapping allegiances.

So, you can see why both Henry VII and Henry VIII thought that an alliance with Spain would be very advantageous and give them an ally against France. This is why Henry VIII eventually married one of Ferdinand and Isabella's other daughters, Catherine of Aragon.

Riven by a 30-year-long civil war that had torn the aristocracy apart, England had been sidelined by the rest of Europe. It was a bit player in the great game. And when fighting broke out in Europe, Henry VIII was keen to make his mark. The real action was in Italy but Henry knew he didn't have much of a chance there. It was too far away and would entail taking an army through France. So, he indulged in the age-old English sport of 'attacking the Frogs'.

Henry received the support of Maximilian, the Holy Roman Emperor and, in 1513, took an army across the Channel where he managed to win a battle – although it was actually more of a skirmish, a cavalry engagement that became known as the Battle of the Spurs.

Henry banged on about the Battle of the Spurs for the rest of his life, boring anyone who would listen, because he didn't really have any other military successes. He and Emperor Maximilian published a joint account of their victory under the catchy title: 'Copia von der erlichen und kostlichen enpfahung ouch früntliche erbietung desz Küngs von Engelland Keyser Maximilian in Bickardy gethon, Unnd von dem angryff und nyderlegung do selbs vor Terbona geschähen. Ouch was un wy vyl volck do gewäsen, erschlagen, und gefangen. Ouch die Belägerung der stat Bornay und ander seltzam geschichten' – which can be roughly translated as 'Max and Harry Twat the French'.

Henry was still the little man in Europe. He had neither the money nor the manpower to properly take on France, whose population was six times that of England. Inevitably, while Henry was dicking about across the Channel, the Scots invaded and it was down to Catherine of Aragon to raise an English army and send it north under the command of the Earl of Surrey. Surrey engaged the Scots at the Battle of Flodden where the Scottish king, James IV, was killed, along with a number of Scottish nobility. So the Scottish threat went away for the time being.

If you remember, Henry VII had married his daughter/Henry VIII's sister, Margaret, to James IV, clearly demonstrating how useless most of these political marriages were as a way of forging alliances and preventing wars. It didn't deter Henry VIII, though, who married another of his sisters, Mary, to the decrepit French king, Louis XII.

Not being interested in the tedious, day-to-day business of running the country, Henry deferred to his chief ministers, making sure he had good, competent men around him. At the start of his reign, Henry's right-hand man was Thomas Wolsey, the lowly son of a butcher who rose to the highest position at court, that of lord chancellor. Henry also made him Archbishop of York, while the pope went one better, making him a cardinal, which put him almost on a par with the king. He was sometimes called (behind his back) Alter Rex – the other king.

Wolsey had significant diplomatic success at the Treaty of London in 1518, when he brought together all of the major European superpowers with the idea of creating universal peace (you won't be surprised to learn that it didn't last). On the back of this, Henry went over to France for a great summit near Calais, a very lavish affair that required so many fancy gold tents that it became known as the Field of the Cloth of Gold. Henry saw this as a total triumph, with himself as a grand international statesman. In the end, though, it all came to nothing.

Meanwhile, the economic situation back home in England continued to deteriorate. In 1517, there were riots against foreigners living and working in London, because, of course, it was all their fault. It's always easiest to blame the immigrants and the affair became known as the Evil Mayday. Henry *did* round up the rioters and execute some of them (Shame! Two-tier justice!), but this was an indication of the discontent that was brewing in the country.

Henry wanted to suck up to the pope and wrote a treatise called *The Defence of the Seven Sacraments*, upholding papal authority and saying that everybody ought to do what the pope tells them. If you look at a British coin (remember them? We used to use them to pay for things), you'll see the words 'FID DEF', or the initials F.D. It stands for 'Fidei Defensor', defender of the faith, a title that can only be bestowed by the pope, and Leo X awarded it to Henry in 1521 for writing such a lovely treatise. It's ironic that Henry VIII, the man who severed England's ties to the papacy, was originally the defender of the Catholic faith.

Henry's marriage to Catherine of Aragon was a long and, until the end, happy one, but there was a problem from the start. A year after she'd married Henry, Catherine miscarried for the first time and, four years after that, in 1514, she miscarried again. She went on to conceive perhaps five times in all, but only two of the pregnancies led to a successful birth. However, Prince Henry died after just a few weeks; only (the future queen) Mary survived to adulthood.

Henry was a man in a hurry. He was all too aware that his father had died when he was only 52, so he perhaps wasn't looking forward to a long and healthy life. He knew he was capable of fathering a son because his mistress, Elizabeth Blount, gave birth to a boy, Henry, in 1519 (Henry FitzRoy was welcomed into the royal court and became the Duke of Richmond and Somerset, but sadly died when he was still a teenager). For now, though, Henry's only legitimate heir was his daughter, Mary, and, unless things changed, England was destined to have a woman on the throne. Catherine of Aragon didn't see this as a problem. She was the daughter of Queen Isabella of Castile, a hugely powerful and influential woman, who jointly reigned with Ferdinand. As far as she was concerned, women could rule just as well as men.

But Henry would settle for nothing less than a boy and started looking at ways to separate from Catherine. There was no such thing as divorce; the only way you could separate was by having your marriage annulled on technical grounds. Henry found a Bible passage that said it was against God to marry your brother's wife and sent Cardinal Wolsey off to see the pope, with the message that Henry didn't believe that his marriage to Catherine was lawful.

But the new pope, Clement VII, dithered and got caught up in complicated European politics, which meant that the permission to annul the marriage kept getting delayed.*

As a cardinal, Wolsey's first loyalty was to the pope and he could do nothing without the holy father's consent and so the first cracks started to appear in his relationship with the king. Henry wasn't deterred, however, and was already looking around for a suitable bride. Another of his mistresses was Mary Boleyn, daughter of a royal courtier, Thomas Boleyn. He'd tired of her, though, and turned his attention to her sister, Anne, a charismatic and self-assured young woman who he became fixated on. But Anne had seen how Henry had treated her sister and refused to go to bed with him unless he married her.

Anne was very interested in the religious reforms that were sweeping through northern Europe. Protestantism taught that people were free to reach God by their own means, the Catholic Church was corrupt and there was no biblical justification for the idea of a pope, or an extensive and wealthy clergy. This wasn't an entirely new idea in

* Clement VII seems to have been quite sympathetic towards Henry. His successor, Paul III, excommunicated him.

England. The Lollards had been preaching against fat-cat priests and wealthy popes since the time of John Wycliffe during the reigns of Edward III and Richard II. Now, though, radicals like Martin Luther had made Protestantism the new cool thing. Freethinkers like Anne Boleyn were fervent that changes needed to be made and she started working on Henry, who saw a way out of his predicament.

Henry had been trying for more than five years to annul his marriage and wed Anne. In 1529, he lost patience with Cardinal Wolsey, stripped him of his titles and had him arrested. This was the first time the king made the mistake of getting rid of a very able statesman. On his way to London for a final showdown with Henry, the broken Wolsey died.

In the end, Henry did something that countless medieval kings would have been envious of: he turned his back on the pope and made himself head of the English church. He no longer had to be told what to do by the pesky bishops and archbishops, which meant he was able to simply annul the marriage himself.

Everything changed for Henry and the country when he embraced both the Reformation and Anne Boleyn. He and Catherine had been (for the most part) happily married for 24 years, and the period of his life that everyone focuses on – his other five wives – took up only the last 10 years of his life.

Henry never really became a Protestant and carried on celebrating the mass until his death. He worried for the rest of his life that he'd committed a terrible sin in rejecting the Catholic faith and was going to go to hell for what he'd done. But worse was to follow.

He'd replaced Wolsey as chancellor with the lawyer and judge, Thomas More, but More was opposed to the Reformation and wouldn't accept Henry as supreme head of the Church of England, nor the annulment of his marriage. Eventually, More was convicted of treason and executed as well. A pattern was emerging. Henry was not a man you wanted to get on the wrong side of.

For some reason, all of the main men in Henry's life were called Thomas; first Wolsey, then More and next Thomas Cromwell, who became Henry's enforcer. Like Wolsey, Cromwell came from a very ordinary background. He'd grown up in Putney, where his father owned a pub. Cromwell had always been an ambitious and clever man and worked his way up to the top by understanding exactly what Henry wanted. He'd been instrumental in getting rid of Catherine and making Anne Boleyn queen and was one of the chief drivers of the Reformation. Henry could worry about his Christian soul all he wanted, but Cromwell was going to Get Protestantism Done. He didn't like the high and mighty. He was an iconoclast, impatient to kick out the old and bring in the new. As a result, he was a hated man.

The Reformation was a massive shock to the English people, whose world was turned upside down. The 'dissolution of the monasteries' is an anodyne term for what was an unimaginably destructive period of English history. Hundreds of monasteries and abbeys were closed down – and in many cases pulled down. Their wealth was appropriated by Henry, who squandered much of it on his useless foreign wars. Furthermore, when all ties with the Catholic Church were cut, money was diverted into Henry's treasury that would normally have been paid to the pope.

The religious houses had been a vital part of English life. Monks and nuns had provided charity, welfare, education, spiritual guidance and healthcare, and made up perhaps 2 per cent of the population. With their institutions closed down, they were turned out to fend for themselves. The desecration was almost inconceivable. We despair when the likes of the Taliban destroy sacred statues and monuments, but it's nothing compared to what Henry did to England. Beautiful buildings were destroyed, stained glass windows smashed, church murals painted over, statues broken up or burned, books destroyed … A whole way of life was torn apart, all so that Henry could get divorced and fill his coffers.

It was also hugely traumatic on an emotional level. England had been Catholic for 1,000 years and now, overnight, people were told that they'd been Getting God Wrong and they were all sinners. Unless they changed the way they worshipped, they would go to hell. People were understandably pissed off. Many couldn't accept Henry and Cromwell's reforms and hated being told that they couldn't worship God the only way they'd ever known. Anne Boleyn argued that money taken from the monasteries should go to the poor. None of it did. The poor got poorer, while the king grew rich on the money he'd stolen.

There were protests and uprisings against Henry, half religious, half economic. One of them, the so-called 'Pilgrimage of Grace', was the largest popular uprising there had ever been in England.

The Duke of Norfolk was despatched with 5,000 men to deal with the situation, but when he arrived in the north of England, he found that his army looked decidedly puny compared to the 50,000 'pilgrims' who'd gathered near Doncaster. He used the time-worn tactic of pretending to negotiate with the rebels and accepting all their demands if they agreed to disband. And then, once they'd all gone home, Henry rounded up the ringleaders and executed them.

He was to execute a huge number of churchmen and Catholic dissenters during his reign. His daughter, Mary, was known as Bloody Mary because when she came to the throne, she tried to reverse the Reformation and started burning Protestants, but she couldn't compete with Henry, who executed more notable Englishmen than any other monarch before or since.

Henry was just as ruthless with his family. Henry passed an Act of Succession in 1534 that declared Princess Mary illegitimate, meaning that any children Anne had would be next in line to the throne. But Anne didn't settle meekly into her role as queen consort. She was headstrong, intelligent, opinionated and forthright. Henry wasn't woke by anybody's standards and began to find Anne's independent manner irritating. She was also pushing him to go further with his reforms, which he might have put up with if she gave him any male heirs. She only produced a girl, though, called Elizabeth.

But, in 1536, Anne was pregnant again and Henry was feeling optimistic as he rode out to give battle in a tournament.* But he was getting too old for this shit. He received a nasty gash in his thigh, was unseated and landed heavily, knocking himself cold. When the news reached Anne, she went into shock and miscarried. Their marriage went steadily downhill after this. Some people have suggested that

---

* Henry enjoyed hunting and jousting, both of which were good training for war, and he left behind some amazing suits of armour that, over the duration of his life, had grown ever larger, until he was so overweight that they had to invent a special mechanical device to hoist him onto his horse.

Henry showed a personality change after his head injury, becoming cold, hard, aggressive and paranoid. His leg wound also debilitated him. By the end of his life, it had become so ulcerated that he couldn't walk unaided.

Whatever the case, Henry was tiring of Anne and already had his eye on one of her ladies-in-waiting, Jane Seymour. Aiming to please his king, Cromwell started plotting to bring down Anne, selling the idea that she was conspiring against Henry and sleeping with all and sundry – including her own brother. In the end, Cromwell was the main driving force behind getting Anne beheaded on 19 May 1536.

Henry announced his engagement to Jane the next day. Their marriage started very successfully. If things had gone differently, we could be talking about the three wives of Henry VIII, not the six, because Jane gave birth to a son, Edward, and Henry was delighted. He'd finally pulled it off. At last, he had a male heir and no doubt there would be many more fine, strapping sons to follow. But you probably know, from the appallingly flippant ditty 'Divorced, Beheaded, Died/ Divorced, Beheaded, Survived' that poor Jane Seymour died. A few days after the birth, she came down with an infection and that was that.

Cromwell pushed for a good political marriage to replace Jane, telling Henry he'd be better off looking overseas for a proper royal wife rather than picking one from among the pretty girls at court whom he just wanted to shag. Cromwell selected Anne of Cleves. Relations between Henry and the Habsburgs had soured and Cleves was part of a Protestant power bloc in western Germany that served as a bulwark against the Holy Roman Empire. Holbein was commissioned to paint a portrait of Anne which was brought over from Cleves for Henry to inspect, and it seems that Holbein's skill at 'photo-realism' had not been called upon. The story goes that when Anne turned up in England to marry Henry, he accused Holbein and Cromwell of a stitch-up. Anne looked nothing like her portrait and she smelled awful. Henry couldn't stand her and she couldn't stand him. It was not a happy marriage but, luckily, Anne managed to get out of it pretty sharpish without coming to any harm. Henry already had the powers in place to be able to annul the marriage himself and Anne was paid off and sent packing six months after their wedding day.

Cromwell had been at the heart of dark skulduggery and plotting at court, and now he was caught in his own net. Henry accused him of steamrolling him into a terrible marriage for his own political ends and saw him as a useful scapegoat for the unpopularity of the Protestant reforms. It suited him to paint Cromwell as the villain who'd pushed it all too far.

So it was Henry's turn to cook up a plot, with the help of the scheming Duke of Norfolk (Thomas Howard, the uncle of both Anne Boleyn and Henry's next wife, Catherine Howard). Cromwell was accused of treason and arrested. Henry used an act of attainder to confiscate all of Cromwell's lands and gave them to his new fiancée. He executed Cromwell on the same day that he married Catherine.

Just as he had regretted falling out with Cardinal Wolsey, Henry soon regretted what he'd done and felt the loss of Cromwell bitterly. His reign never really recovered. He'd relied heavily on the strength, determination and clear thinking of Cromwell, and things went from bad to worse after his death.

Henry still wanted to make a splash internationally. He planned to invade France and, as a warm-up, he attacked the Scots, who were refusing to convert to Protestantism. His army was victorious at the Battle of Solway Moss and it was said that the shock of the defeat killed King James V. Henry now saw an opportunity to unite the English and Scottish thrones by marrying his son, Edward, to James's daughter, Mary (the future Mary, Queen of Scots). The Scots were having none of it, however, and the English spent the next eight years fruitlessly fighting in Scotland to try to force them to change their minds. The war became known as the 'Rough Wooing', which I guess was an attempt at black humour.

Catherine Howard's story is possibly the saddest of those of all Henry's wives. She was a naive teenager who'd grown up in the countryside and had no experience of the royal court and its skulduggery. She'd been sexually assaulted by her music teacher when she was 12 and had been used by men all her life. The man using her now was her uncle, Thomas Howard, Duke of Norfolk. To him, she was a handy pawn and if he could get her promoted to queen, it would also be a huge promotion for his family and himself. Catherine was flattered to be marrying a king – it was like a fairy tale come true! – except, as she was soon to learn, Henry was by now a bloated, bilious, paranoid and vindictive monster. This fairy tale was 'Beauty and the Beast' and Catherine's kiss was never going to change Henry back into the dashing young prince he'd once been.

When Catherine became queen, she had no experience of how to behave at court. She was nowhere near as smart and as switched on as Anne Boleyn and didn't realise just how precarious her position was. She was the queen! She flirted, she enjoyed flattery, she had fun … and, disastrously, she started an affair with a guy called Thomas Culpeper. Eighteen months after becoming queen, poor young Catherine Howard, 19 years old at most, was beheaded.

Henry tried one last time to have another son. This time he married an experienced, sober, older widow, Catherine Parr. It was no use. He died before he could get her pregnant and Parr went on to marry Jane Seymour's brother, Thomas. I'd love to say she lived a long and happy life, laughing about her lucky escape, but unfortunately, she died not long afterwards of puerperal fever following childbirth, as so many women did at the time.

Henry was only 55 when he died, probably of kidney failure. He'd become so obese that his body couldn't cope any longer. He'd been struggling with diabetes and the incurable, ulcerating leg wound he'd received in his jousting accident. What can we say about him? He was a nasty piece of work. He'd wanted to be a Big Man and in a way he succeeded. His waistline at the end was 52 inches.

21
AND NED THE LAD

EDWARD VI – 1537–1553
Edward Tudor/the Boy King
Reigned 1547–1553
Lived for 15 years. Reigned for six years.
Died from some sort of lung disease,
possibly tuberculosis.
Remembered for: dying young.

Everybody thinks of Edward as a pale and sickly, doomed boy king, but, before he came down with a lung infection in his teens, he was a fine strapping young fellow: robust, stubborn and strong-willed, just like his once-athletic and dynamic father. OK, so when he was four, Edward did contract malaria. He survived it, though, and when Henry's personal physician was fussing around him and asked if he felt 'any disposition to vomit', Edward replied, 'Go away, fool'. Which shows that he was quite a self-assured little boy.

Edward was born at Hampton Court Palace, which Cardinal Wolsey had originally built for himself. When Henry turned against Wolsey, he'd 'gifted' his house to him, in a last-ditch attempt to keep the king happy and stay out of the Tower. All in vain. Henry kept the house as his principal palace.

Edward's mother was Jane Seymour, Henry's third wife. The king was so pleased when the boy was born that he showed him off at a window in the palace, very much like modern royals bringing out their newborns onto the balcony at Buckingham Palace. Or Michael Jackson dangling his son out of a hotel window. But Jane fell ill and died, probably from a haemorrhage caused by the placenta remaining in her womb, which the pompous male physicians, having banned midwives from attending Jane, hadn't spotted.

Henry was distraught and became obsessive about his 'most precious' boy's upbringing, insisting on cleanliness, a healthy environment and a proper education. Like his father, Edward was very bright and he was given an extremely rigorous and all-encompassing, humanist education. He learned French, Latin and Greek. He studied the Bible, read the speeches of Cicero and the work of classical historians like Herodotus and Thucydides. He also read Plutarch, Pliny the Younger, Aristotle … He'd basically done a BA Classics degree by the time he was 14.

It wasn't all work for young Ned, though; there was dancing, card games, music and entertainment. No fobbing off the child with an iPad to keep him quiet, Edward had his own group of musicians and a company of players. He was taught the lute, the viol and the virginals (a sort of harpsichord) and sang in a choir.

Edward's childhood notebooks survive and, aside from showing how awful his handwriting was, give us a good idea of what an upperclass education consisted of in Tudor times. He went on to keep a journal throughout his life, which is another useful resource, though sadly it just records facts and figures. We get no sense of Edward as a person or his inner thoughts. At times, it's almost comically mundane and impersonal, with entries almost along the lines of 'They chopped my uncle's head off this morning. Had sausages and eggs for breakfast.'

We've seen how, when Edward was six, Henry tried to get him betrothed to Mary, Queen of Scots, which led to the Rough Wooing. It was a jokey name for one of the most violent campaigns ever unleashed by the English against the Scots, one that would continue almost to the end of Edward's life.

Who knows how much Edward was aware of the shenanigans after his mother died, when Henry married and then quickly divorced Anne of Cleves, but in 1543, when his father married Catherine Parr, his final wife, Edward moved into her household with his half-sisters, Mary and Elizabeth. He seems to have preferred Mary, although this was to change when he was old enough to take charge and push his father's Protestant agenda, as Mary was a devout Catholic from first to last. Edward enjoyed this time of his life. He was well cared for and had, in Catherine, a loving mother figure to look after him. But, four years later, Henry died and Edward, who was only 9, became king of England and head of the church.

On the eve of Edward's coronation there was an endless royal procession through the city, from the Tower of London to Westminster. The part that really stood out for the new king wasn't the cheering crowds, the ranks of marching men in bright uniforms carrying freshly polished halberds, the fanfares and parade of dignitaries. No, it was an Italian acrobat and tightrope walker who did tricks on a rope outside S Paul's, before sliding down onto a huge feather bed. This is understandable; Edward was just a little boy, after all.

The coronation itself was presided over by Thomas Cranmer, the Protestant Archbishop of Canterbury. After hundreds of years of continuity, the wording of those parts of the ceremony that related to the king's religious powers, his relationship with Rome and his relationship with the English clergy were changed. The coronation reinforced the idea that the English monarch was now head of the Church of England, with no higher power above him on earth. There was also quite a lot of anti-papal invective in Cranmer's speech and you could say this was the beginning of the English Protestant war against the head of the Catholic Church, who would become personified as 'the antichrist of Rome, the great whore of Babylon', and, in the process, sanctioned the persecution of Catholics.

There's also mention in the coronation ceremony of the empire of Great Britain, an idea that had arisen in Henry VIII's reign. England was no longer just England; it was part of an empire, which included Wales, Ireland and Scotland. The Tudors were also tentatively starting to look towards North America.

Since Edward was too young to govern by himself, a ruling council was put together, at the core of which were two of his uncles, Jane Seymour's brothers Edward and Thomas. Edward Seymour was given the top post of protector of the realm. Edward was a populist autocrat, not wholly committed to the idea of Protestantism, who liked to think of himself as a great politician. He wasn't. He was a ditherer. His younger brother, Thomas, was something else – a bit of a rogue, a bit of a lad – who was jealous and resentful of his haughty, big brother.

Thomas felt that Edward didn't give him the power, money and status he deserved, and so went behind his back, trying to forge a private and personal bond with the young monarch. He would slip into the king's private apartments at night and pass him secret notes and pocket money so that Edward could tip his musicians and staff. He also stirred the pot by telling the boy that his high-handed brother was making him a beggar.

Edward Seymour grew increasingly pissed off with Thomas and, one night when Thomas was visiting Edward's bedchamber, the king's dog started barking at him. In a panic, Thomas shot it dead, alerting the household. The palace guards arrested Thomas, believing that this was a kidnap attempt. Edward Seymour claimed that this must be a plot, framing it as a treasonous conspiracy, and had his annoying brother beheaded. The Tudors really were a murderous bunch of psychos.

But Edward Seymour wasn't secure in his power. The Rough Wooing had tied up countless troops in Scotland, exhausting both money and patience. With no standing army and no budget for one, taxes were constantly having to be raised. To balance the books, Seymour was also continuing the practice of debasing the English coin that had begun during Henry's reign. This was an early form of quantitative easing. Instead of being solid silver, shillings and sixpences were being made out of base metals thinly coated with silver. It was said that coins were 'blushing with shame', as the copper or brass showed though the silver, and Henry had been nicknamed 'Old Copper Nose' as the silver rubbed off the most prominent parts of the coins.

Seymour's activities weren't helping the English economy and he was now on the verge of bankrupting Edward VI. With discontent fermenting across the land, it was perhaps not the ideal time for Archbishop Cranmer to produce his Book of Common Prayer, the first to be written in English. Nowadays, this is seen as one of the treasures of English literature, but at the time, it was very controversial. Most people hated the very idea of it as they were used to having prayers in Latin and only sermons in English. Nobody likes change. There was also the problem of what today might be called cultural imperialism. The Cornish, for instance, had always felt themselves separate to the rest of England, with their own language and customs. The last thing they wanted was an English-language prayer book imposed on them. They hated being forced to say their prayers in the language of their oppressors, instead of the universal church language of Latin (no matter whether they could understand what they'd been praying for).

In 1549, Devon and Cornwall rose against the king in the so-called 'Prayer Book Rebellion' and the unrest spread all round the country. That year was probably the most dangerous one of Edward's reign. If the whole country rebelled, it would mean the end, particularly as Edward Seymour had all his troops committed to holding Scotland and he'd run out of money.

An uprising in Norfolk was led by a man called Robert Kett, but this rebellion was different to the others. Yes, there was an anti-Protestant angle to it, but the main focus of the rebels' anger was 'enclosures'. Wealthy landlords were constantly expanding their estates, taking over smaller farms, pulling out hedges to make the fields easier to manage and erecting fences. They were also appropriating common land that had been used by villagers to grow crops on and keep animals to feed themselves since before Norman times. Now they were being stopped from using their own land, which was being turned over to lucrative sheep farming. The wool trade was really booming, but the peasants weren't getting any share of it. Robert Kett and his followers had right on their side and (perhaps foolishly) believed that they'd have the support of the establishment, because what the landlords were doing was quite clearly illegal. They knew that honourable men like Edward Seymour would listen to them.

Seymour gave up on Scotland, pulling out his troops and sending enough of them to the West Country to violently put down the Prayer Book Rebellion and execute their leaders. Now he looked east and started negotiating with Kett, making sympathetic noises while he played for time. He agreed that, yes, the enclosures were both awful and unlawful, but once he'd cobbled together an army, he first sent in the Marquess of Northampton, and then, when he failed, a second force under the command of John Dudley, Earl of Warwick. Dudley defeated the rebels in Norfolk and Robert Kett was executed. Dudley became the hero of the day (as far as the powers-that-be were concerned) and Edward Seymour got the blame for everything that had previously gone wrong. He was seen as losing his grip, dithering and negotiating with lefties, so Dudley mounted a coup against him. Seymour panicked, took King Edward hostage and held out in Windsor Castle with him. In the end, though, he had to admit that the game was up. He handed himself over, was tried on trumped-up charges and, guess what, he was eventually executed as well.

You wonder why anybody wanted to get involved in politics at this time. It had been a pattern from the start of Henry VIII's reign that if you made it to the top, you set yourself up for a fall. See Thomas Wolsey, Thomas More, Thomas Cromwell, Thomas Seymour, Edward Seymour …

The new man at the top, John Dudley, was blind to this. His father had been one of the two tax collectors executed by Henry VIII when he came to power, but John still thought, *You know what? I'm going to go into politics. That's the life for me. It'll be a lot of fun. I'll be able to gain fame and influence. What could possibly go wrong?* (I'll give you one guess as to what eventually became of him.)

Dudley took Edward Seymour's place in court as the head of a new radical, reformist faction. One of the reasons that he was able to manoeuvre himself so quickly into a position of authority was that he took King Edward seriously. We've seen before how a lot of boy kings, until they come of age, are at the mercy of their advisers, but Edward was assertive and headstrong from the start. He knew what he wanted: to fulfil his father's legacy and cement both church reform and the reform of the country. If a courtier enabled him to achieve that, then they had a great advantage. Edward wanted things done and Dudley said, 'OK, let's go for it. I won't tell you what to do, kiddo. We'll be a partnership'.

Edward was characteristically tough and decisive in his treatment of his half-sisters. During Henry's reign and on into his son's, the status of Mary and Elizabeth kept chopping and changing. One week they'd be legitimate, firmly in the line of succession, the next they'd be scratched off the list. Now Edward put his foot down. As far he was concerned, neither of them was ever going to rule.

He was growing up to be a forceful king. He would have hastened the acceptance of Protestantism, albeit at the expense of the Catholics, and put an end to all the uncertainty if, at the age of 15, he hadn't caught measles, then smallpox, then a cough. With his immune system weakened, when the cough moved to his lungs, Edward was unable to fight off the infection and it soon became clear that he was dying. He got together with Dudley and they knocked up a document, 'My Devise for The Succession', that set out who was going to rule after Edward. Sure enough, it was neither Mary nor Elizabeth. Edward and Dudley chose Edward's cousin, Lady Jane Grey, a great granddaughter of Henry VII (via his youngest daughter), who just happened to be married to Dudley's son, Guildford.

Whose idea was this? Was Dudley manipulating Edward or was it the king's will? It's difficult to say; there's evidence of some tampering with the document. Perhaps Edward kept changing his mind, or perhaps Dudley kept changing it for him. It certainly wasn't Jane's idea, just as her wedding hadn't been either. Her father, Henry Grey, was a nasty, scheming, violent and very ambitious man who saw in Lord Guildford Dudley a golden opportunity for his family's advancement.*

When she realised that Lady Jane Grey had been chosen to succeed Edward, Princess Mary got out of London as quickly as she could and hurried to Norfolk, where she had large estates and support. This was where Dudley had brutally put down Kett's rebellion, so she was way more popular there than him, especially as she held out the hope of a return to Catholicism, whereas Jane Grey was the poster girl for Protestantism.

Soon afterwards, Edward died coughing up the full spectrum of nasty-coloured gunk from his ulcerated and putrefied lungs. He was

---

* We're so used to people being called by the name of their dukedom or earldom – 'Warwick', 'Norfolk', 'Somerset' – that you might assume 'Guildford' works on the same principle. But, no, Guildford was his actual Christian name. England might have had a King Guildford I. Then what? King Slough? King Croydon?

buried in Westminster Abbey in 1553 with Thomas Cranmer once again presiding. Fittingly, the funeral procession was led by a company of children. There was such political and religious turmoil after Edward's death that his grave remained unmarked for 400 years.

And what of Jane Grey, who he'd appointed as his successor? Well, the 'Willie, Willie' rhyme doesn't include her, except in a jokey addendum at the end: 'Sorry, Lady Jane Grey – you got the chop.' She ended up ruling for nine days before being deposed and beheaded by the woman who became England's first queen, Mary I.

This (partial) family tree might help make sense of it all.

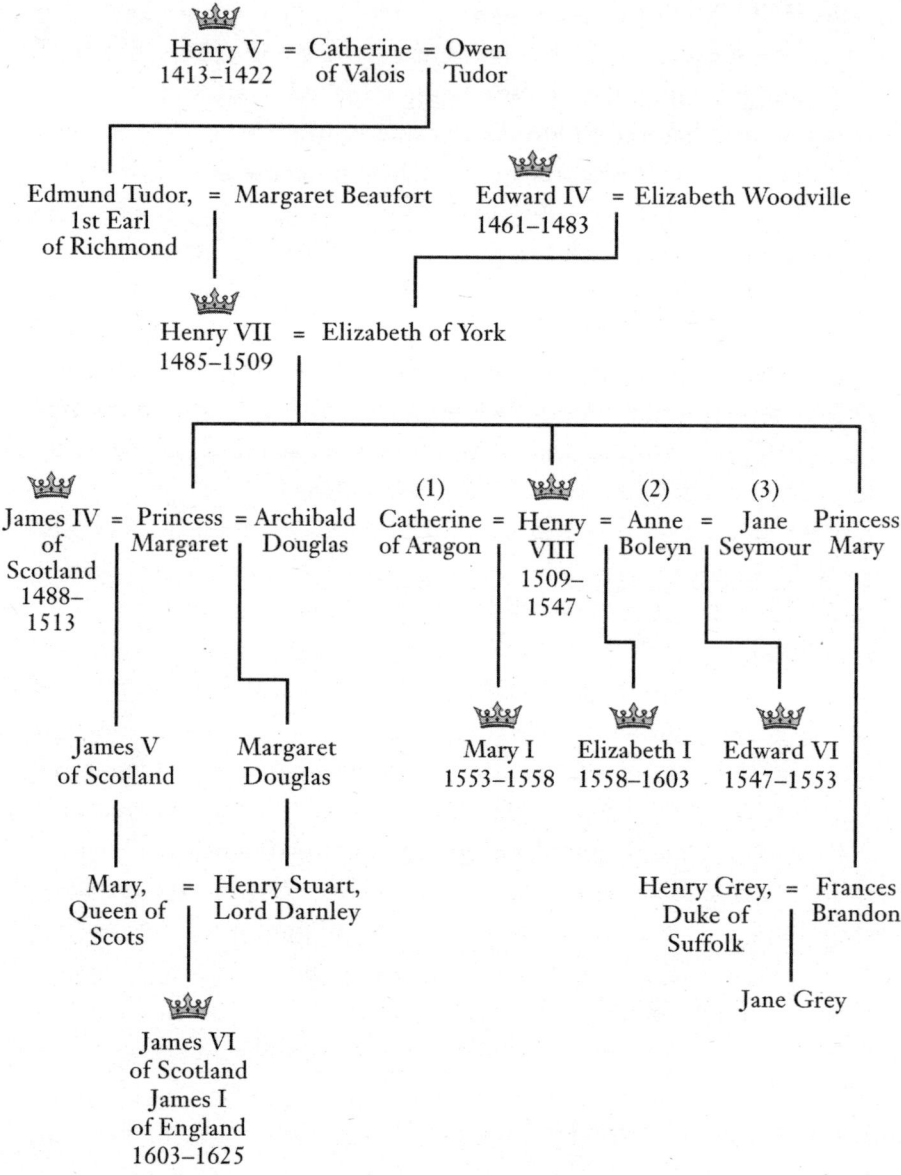

Henry V = Catherine = Owen
1413–1422   of Valois   Tudor

Edmund Tudor, = Margaret Beaufort   Edward IV = Elizabeth Woodville
1st Earl   1461–1483
of Richmond

Henry VII = Elizabeth of York
1485–1509

James IV = Princess = Archibald   (1)   (2)   (3)
of   Margaret   Douglas   Catherine = Henry = Anne = Jane Princess
Scotland   of Aragon   VIII   Boleyn Seymour Mary
1488–   1509–
1513   1547

James V   Margaret   Mary I   Elizabeth I   Edward VI
of Scotland   Douglas   1553–1558   1558–1603   1547–1553

Mary,   = Henry Stuart,   Henry Grey, = Frances
Queen of   Lord Darnley   Duke of   Brandon
Scots   Suffolk

James VI   Jane Grey
of Scotland
James I
of England
1603–1625

22

MARY

MARY I – 1516–1558

Mary Tudor/Bloody Mary

Reigned 1553–1558 (England); 1556–1558 (Spain)

Lived for 42 years. Reigned for five years.

Probably died from cancer.

Remembered for: being bloody and trying to restore Catholicism.

It's 1553. Lady Jane Grey has been declared queen in London, but her champion, John Dudley, Earl of Warwick and Duke of Northumberland, has miscalculated the amount of support she has. Princess Mary is a lot more popular than both Jane and Dudley, and sets off towards London at the head of a small army. The lords in Westminster convince Dudley to try to stop her, but while he's out of London, they stage a coup, declaring their support for Mary. Dudley knows he's had it. There's no point in trying to fight the inevitable. He's arrested and Mary rides triumphantly into London, accompanied by her half-sister Elizabeth and a procession of more than 800 nobles and gentlemen. The commoners are behind Mary as well; their slogan being 'Vox Populae, Vox Dei' ('The Voice of the People is the Voice of God'). This is to be the only popular uprising to succeed in nearly 120 years of Tudor rule. The people are saying, *We are English. We don't like change. We don't want these foreign ways coming over from Germany and the Low Countries. We are Catholics and we want a Catholic queen – a daughter of Henry VIII, Not this imposter, Lady Jane Grey.*

Mary becomes queen and, initially, she tries to be forgiving and lenient. Jane isn't immediately executed, merely kept in custody, like her husband, Guildford Dudley. Mary has no choice, however, but to execute Guildford's father, John Dudley, the mastermind behind the plan to put Jane on the throne and keep Mary off it.

But, within a year, opinion has turned against Mary, mainly because of her plans to marry Philip of Spain (which I'll go into later). A disgruntled Kentish landowner called Thomas Wyatt leads a group of followers up to London, claiming that they want to prevent the marriage, but most historians believe it was an attempt to depose Mary in favour of Elizabeth. Rather unwisely, Lady Jane's father, Henry Grey, Duke of Suffolk, joins the rebellion. But Wyatt is captured and Mary has to accept that she can't risk any of these people staying alive. Wyatt is executed. And now Jane and her husband, Guildford Dudley, both get the chop, as well as Jane's father.

Lady Jane Grey had lasted only nine days as queen and was never properly accepted. She was never crowned, never sat on a throne. She was John Dudley's folly, his big gamble, his big hope for a Protestant succession and to marry the Dudleys into the royal family. And he failed.

Mary realises that she's going to have to change her style and display a ruthless and resolute front, otherwise malcontents will be forever rising against her. From now on, she will rule with an iron hand. There are several portraits of Queen Mary and, in all of them, even those painted when she was young, she stares back at you with a hard, unforgiving gaze, like a Tudor Greta Thunberg. Many courtiers at the time commented on the way she looked at you as if she was trying to stare deep into your soul. As it turns out, Mary was merely short-sighted and could barely see a thing. Her gimlet-eyed frown was the result of her simply trying to work out who you were.

Mary is generally known as 'Bloody Mary' because she put so many Protestants to death. She's partly the victim of Protestant historians writing after her death, though, who painted her in a very bad light because of her religion – and also, it has to be said, because of her sex. It was fine for Henry to slaughter people left, right and centre, but it just wasn't respectable behaviour for a lady. Mary was by no means our bloodiest monarch. She wasn't even the bloodiest Tudor. She just managed to cram quite a lot of killings into a fairly short time. At 37, she was comparatively old by the time she came to the throne and had suffered from ill health all her life. She ended up ruling for only five years but, during that time, she managed to have about 300 religious dissenters burned at the stake, both men and women, which averages out at more than one a week over her reign.

We saw how Edward VI wanted to live up to his father's name and finish the Protestant Reformation that Henry VIII had started. Mary's loyalty was to her mother, the Catholic Catherine of Aragon, who Henry had spurned after 24 years of marriage.

The first few years of Mary's life had been happy enough, while her parents were still married and getting along OK. They were both very proud of Mary, who was the first of their children to survive. She was a lively, bright and precocious child whom Henry was forever showing off to foreign dignitaries. She could dance! She could speak from an early age! She could play the virginals!

As she grew up, Mary learned French, Spanish, Latin and possibly Greek. She studied Scripture and some of the classics, but no medieval romances because, as we know, women can be led astray all too easily. She had her own court at Ludlow Castle and fulfilled the functions of a prince of Wales. She was most use to her father, though, as a pawn in the marriage game. With the help of Cardinal Wolsey, Henry was forever arranging and rearranging betrothals for the child.

When Mary reached puberty, she started getting irregular periods, stomach cramps and long bouts of depression. These health problems were to plague her for the rest of her life. Later physicians put her problems down to the fact that she'd had *some upsets in her life and was a bit down in the dumps*, but Mary had serious underlying issues which eventually killed her. Being taken seriously by male doctors seems to be a perennial problem for women.

Mary's first illness happened around the time that Henry annulled his marriage to her mother, Catherine of Aragon, which made Mary illegitimate, taking her out of the line of succession. But Mary stubbornly refused to acknowledge Anne Boleyn as queen and her half-sister Elizabeth (when she arrived) as a royal princess. Henry was furious, but what he couldn't see was that Mary was very much his own daughter. All three of his children inherited Henry's single-mindedness, implacability and ruthlessness. It was the perfect recipe for family rows and, for three years, Henry refused to talk to Mary (although he still supported her, paying for her clothes and giving her money that she used for gambling at cards, one of her favourite pastimes). When her mother became ill, Mary was refused permission to see her, which meant she wasn't with Catherine when she died. Still Mary wouldn't accept her lot and both her cousin (on her mother's side), the Holy Roman Emperor, Charles V, and Thomas Cromwell tried to get it through to her that, unless she bent to Henry's will, she might well end up following Anne Boleyn to the scaffold.

Unsurprisingly, Mary was never fond of Elizabeth, even after they were *both* declared illegitimate and stripped of any rights of succession. Henry did eventually reinstate Mary as, to be of any use to him in the marriage stakes, she needed to be an actual, legitimate, royal princess. Cromwell first tried to marry Mary into the Cleves family, important German Protestant allies against the might of the Catholic Habsburgs. The marriage never happened and instead it was Henry who married into the family. And we know just how well that went. When Cromwell was arrested soon after the failure of Henry's disastrous marriage to Anne, one of the trumped-up charges against him was that he'd been plotting to marry Mary himself.

Mary had to tread carefully through the rest of Henry's reign, and through that of her half-brother, Edward. She would always be a threat to Edward and a potential figurehead for any Catholic uprisings against his Protestant regime, but when he suddenly died at the age of 15, everything changed again. Now, at 37, Mary became the first queen of England (if you discount Jane Grey, which most people do).

If the people of England who had cheered her to the throne were hoping that Mary would change everything for the better overnight, they were sadly mistaken. Europe was still in the Little Ice Age and Mary's reign was dogged by freezing temperatures, flooding, crop failure and famine. It was a terrible time to be a peasant, but at least the starving, shivering population could go back to their old familiar ways of worshipping God.

Mary was now faced with a big choice. She knew she would have to marry and produce an heir if she wanted her Catholic continuity to last. There were suitable Catholic lords in England she could have gone for, but she rejected them and looked overseas to her mother's homeland for a more high-powered candidate. Prince Philip of Spain was a devout Catholic, the perfect partner to help Mary avenge her mother, launch a counterattack on the Reformation and threaten the growing Ottoman Empire. At least, that's how the short-sighted Mary saw it. She had badly misread the room.

Nothing about Philp was any good. For a start, he was a foreigner, and ten years younger than Mary. He was also a Habsburg, so he suffered from the effects of the famous Habsburg inbreeding. The Habsburgs had a defect that caused family members to have an elongated chin and deformed jaw, making it hard to eat, and even sometimes to talk properly. Philip was also very closely related to Mary, being a grandson of Catherine of Aragon's sister, Joanna, which meant she'd be marrying back into her own mother's family. But that's how the Habsburgs liked it.

For his part, Philip reckoned he'd been gifted an open goal. If he married Mary, he could sideline her and become king of England, making the Habsburg Empire even more enormous. Between the northern and the southern halves, they already controlled Spain, a huge part of central Europe, including Germany, Hungary and Austria, as well as parts of the Low Countries and Italy. Now, they'd control England, too.

Mary had never met Philip, so the Great Renaissance painter, Titian, knocked up a portrait of him and sent it over to England. We have to assume that he tried to show Philip in the best light and perhaps shaved – *just a leedle bit* – off his chin, but it still takes up half the canvas. The half-blind Mary saw nothing wrong with him, however, and went ahead with the union, but not before drawing up a marriage act with Parliament which stipulated that, while Philip was allowed to sign himself king of England on official documents, including acts of Parliament, he wasn't allowed to actually *be* king in any meaningful way.

Furthermore, his title would only last for Mary's lifetime, he couldn't do anything without her agreement and he couldn't appoint any foreigners (particularly Spaniards) to the royal court or any public office in England. It was also made clear that England would *not* automatically support him in any European wars in which he got involved. It did mean, though, that if he and Mary had any children, they'd be heirs to the thrones of both England and Spain. So, it was really only just kicking the can down the road a bit.

The marriage was an incredibly stupid move on Mary's part. It undermined her rule, caused her support base to wobble, her popularity to plummet and led to major long-term problems. It didn't help that she was becoming increasingly hard-line. Her advisers told her not to trust the powerful Protestant bishops and clergymen who'd risen to prominence under Henry and Edward, so she had several of them arrested, including Archbishop Thomas Cranmer, and reversed many of Henry and Edward's reforms in her first parliament. Edward had changed the law to allow priests to marry, for instance, but Mary scrapped the changes and all these poor priests had to break up their marriages or be removed from their positions. Trusting no one, she even put her half-sister, Elizabeth, under house arrest. She also demoted herself from being the head of the church and restored ties with the pope. The one thing she couldn't reverse was giving back the lands from the monasteries and abbeys that Henry had sold off to his cronies to keep them onside. Mary, too, had to keep them sweet; in the end, money trumped doctrine.

Many prominent Protestant lords and clergymen managed to flee abroad, but some stayed, defiantly refusing to renounce their faith, so Mary set fire to them. Burning a heretic at the stake isn't easy. If the fire isn't properly laid, it can take ages to get going. When John Hooper, the Bishop of Gloucester and Worcester, was put on the pyre, for a long while only his legs would burn and he was standing there crying out 'For God's love, good people, let me have more fire'.

The bishops Latimer and Ridley were burnt at the stake together. Ridley had been a very popular Bishop of London who'd helped draft the Book of Common Prayer. He'd preached very well-attended outdoor sermons and given a great deal of money to the poor. As he was set on fire, Bishop Latimer supposedly said to him, 'Be of good comfort, master Ridley and play the man. We shall this day light such a candle by God's grace in England as I trust shall never be put out.' I'm sure that's made up – it's a bit too eloquent and measured for a man on fire. He probably said something more like, 'Ow, shit, that's hot, ow, ow, ow, ow, ow …'

Wealthy families often bribed executioners to tie a bag of gunpowder around the necks of their loved ones, so that when the flames leapt up towards their face, the gunpowder would explode and blow their heads off, ending the ghastly ordeal quickly. But the kindling was too green on Ridley's side and wasn't igniting. The bishop was screaming – 'I cannot burn!' – until a guard pulled away some of the damp upper layer and the flames leapt up and, yes, BOOM.

Archbishop Cranmer witnessed all this and, quite understandably, tried to save his skin. He recanted and said he'd go back to Catholicism. But he was too much of a risk and had been very much Henry and Edward's man, so Mary still sent him to the fire, at which point, Cranmer said, 'Sod the lot of you. I *am* a Protestant' and thrust his 'unworthy' right hand, that had signed false documents, into the flames.

The burning of Cranmer was a turning point. Mary had gone too far. The guy had recanted, FFS. Originally, these public burnings had drawn large crowds to St Bartholomew's Hospital, where many took place. But people were growing sick of it. London was filled with the stench of burning human flesh and the executions were moved behind closed doors.

Meanwhile, Mary was struggling. She didn't see a lot of Philip, who spent most of his time travelling round the Habsburg Empire, but she did get very attached to him, slept with him, fell in love with him (whatever 'in love' means) and, in 1554, stopped menstruating, gained weight, began feeling sick in the mornings … Mary was convinced she was with child. Elizabeth was released from her house arrest and brought to the court to witness the birth and verify that it was all bona fide. Sadly, though, it turned out to be a phantom pregnancy (or signs of Mary's aforementioned health problems) and Mary fell into one of her terrible depressions.

Soon afterwards, Mary's father-in-law, Charles V, abdicated, making Philip the king of Spain and her its queen. Philip thought that, now he was king, he'd better start a war with someone. He picked on France and tried to get the English involved, but Mary's government was against it and sent over only a rather small army. Philip had an initial victory, but the ultimate outcome of this stupid and pointless war was that the French took Calais, that had been in England's hands since Edward III's time and was the last remaining English possession in France. This was a huge blow to Mary's status. The one thing that would have restored her popularity would have been if she produced an heir. Everyone loves a royal baby! And, in 1557, she announced that a child was on the way. This time she really was pregnant.

Only she wasn't. Her stomach had swelled up because she was dying. Weakened by flu, her internal problems got worse and she died in November 1558 in terrible pain. Trying to establish an exact cause of death from this remove is impossible; she may have had ovarian cysts, or possibly cancer of the uterus.

This time, there was no confusion over the succession. Mary didn't try anything clever – Elizabeth would take the throne. Philip immediately proposed to her, but Elizabeth told him to get lost. She was a Protestant and wanted nothing to do with him. All of the fires, all the killing, all the married priests' families torn apart – what a waste. All for nothing. Mary had failed to make England Catholic again. That she had reigned at all, as England's first Queen, was probably her greatest achievement and mustn't be underestimated. She'd shown that a woman could be no worse (and no better) than a man at ruling the nation and had set an important precedent. One that her half-sister Elizabeth was going to have to work very hard to live up to.

23

BESSIE

ELIZABETH I – 1533–1603
Gloriana/the Virgin Queen
Reigned 1558–1603
Lived for 69 years. Ruled for 45 years.
Died from … let's just call it old age.
Remembered for: the Spanish Armada and her 'rallying
the troops' speech at Tilbury.

Elizabeth I's 45-year reign puts her in the Longest-Reigning British Monarchs Top Ten. The period of history named after her, the Elizabethan Age, is seen by many as a golden age, but that depends on who you ask. If you were a nobleman, you could prance about the place in fancy tights, an extravagant doublet, a jaunty hat and shiny silver buckles on your shoes. Maybe you could pop along to the theatre and watch the latest play by Shakespeare or Christopher Marlowe. Or you could have your portrait painted by an expensive foreign artist.

But if you were a peasant, a shepherd, a grunt in the army or navy, a seamstress or a washerwoman, it was a very different story. If you'd asked the average working man or woman at the time what sort of an age they were living through, they'd have said it was a Shit Age. Economic problems and the Little Ice Age hadn't gone away with a change of ruler. Harvests were bad. The plague kept returning. There was high taxation and rampant inflation. Trade with the Low Countries was badly affected by unrest in Europe and real wages were the lowest they'd been for centuries, which led to a rise in crime and begging on the streets, not helped by disgruntled, unpaid soldiers returning from the wars. Elizabeth was famously very slow to pay her troops and had inherited the meanness of her grandfather, Henry VII.

The threat from foreign invasion gave Elizabeth a handy common enemy – in the form of Spain – to blame everything on, but by the end of her life, she'd become a pretty ineffective ruler. Some historians say that the seeds of the civil war that was to tear the country apart 50 years later during the reign of Charles I were sown during Elizabeth's reign.

She was proud to be known as the Virgin Queen, with her zero husbands in marked contrast to her father's six wives, but it meant that Elizabeth would be the last of the relatively short-lived Tudor dynasty.

As we've seen, Henry and his daughters had more in common than their red hair. They were unbending, tough, ruthless and slightly neurotic. Before she came to the throne, Elizabeth had a hard time of it. Regularly declared illegitimate, she had to live with the persistent threat of imprisonment and execution. So many men and women who were close to the throne were wiped out in the Tudor period and the fact that Elizabeth managed to survive the intrigue and come out on top says much about her. Perhaps the very fact that she was accepted as a female monarch was achievement enough.

Elizabeth is one of those instantly recognisable monarchs. She knew the value of a good portrait and tightly controlled her own image. Each painting she commissioned was a piece of propaganda and any that she didn't like, she had destroyed. Her portraits are encrusted with layers of iconography and there's deeper meaning in every detail. What she's wearing, what jewellery is on show, what her rings and brooches signify, what possessions she has around her, what's going on in the background behind her – it all signified something, so it's amazing that anything of her personality shows through. Somehow it does, though. You still get a sense of the real woman underneath, albeit a woman who throughout her life relied on different masks to protect herself, to hide herself and to show the face she wanted to the world.

In some of the paintings, it looks as if she's *literally* wearing a mask. As she got older, she wore heavier and heavier white makeup, almost like a clown's face paint, with bright red lips. She probably started wearing this thick makeup after she contracted smallpox when she was 29, painting her face to hide the scarring. But, later on, she tried to freeze her image at a certain age and become the eternal, perfect, ever-young virgin queen. This 'Mask of Youth' was just one of her many personae.

First, she was Princess Elizabeth. Then, when she was no longer in line to the throne, she was plain Lady Elizabeth. Then she became Queen Elizabeth, Gloriana the Faerie Queen, the Virgin Queen. She was compared to the Virgin Mary and Diana, the chaste huntress from Roman mythology who shot men dead with her arrows. Ultimately, she was Britannia, whose cult she revived, the personification of and protector of Britain, a warrior woman with shield and trident. She was always looking for examples of strong females from myth or history, because she was always having to defend the fact that she was a woman, and people weren't used to having a woman on the throne.

In 1558, the year of Queen Mary's death, John Knox, the leader of the Protestant reform movement in Scotland and founder of the Scottish Presbyterian Church, published a notorious book attacking the idea of women being given power: *The First Blast of the Trumpet Against the Monstruous Regiment of Women*.

Knox was a grim and joyless figure, a bitter, self-important, life-sucking, granite-hard Puritan, usually depicted with a long grey beard and a sour look. Like most male religious extremists who think they're saving the world, he had it in for women and believed their place was to serve and be subordinate to men.

The eye-catching title of his book has endured longer than its now little-read contents, but is usually misunderstood. By 'monstrous', he meant 'unnatural'; by 'regiment', he meant 'regime'. It was specifically an attack on female monarchs, on the unnatural rule of women. It was aimed at both Mary, Queen of Scots and Mary, Queen of England, and as soon as Elizabeth came to the throne, Knox added her to the list. According to the Bible (and John Knox), none of these women should ever have been in power and he was only really spouting the general populist view, which Elizabeth was painfully aware of.

So it suited her to hide behind her masks. The white face paint she used was called Venetian ceruse. It was made from lead and vinegar, and had to be removed with a cleaning solution that included mercury. She also wore thick black kohl around her eyes, which was made of lead and antimony, and her red lipstick contained heavy metals, all of which would have been absorbed through her skin and transferred to her organs. Ironically, in order to disguise the mark of the disease she'd suffered from, she was poisoning herself. Lead and mercury poisoning cause a number of medical conditions, including depression, and Elizabeth certainly suffered from 'bouts of melancholy'. But perhaps it's not surprising she ended up feeling 'melancholy'; she'd led a very stressful life.

When she was only two, her mother was beheaded. Elizabeth would have had very little contact with Anne Boleyn. Children at the time were brought up in other people's households by governesses and tutors. She certainly wouldn't have been suckled by her own mother and, for the rest of her life, never mentioned her in public. No matter what she privately felt about Anne, she had to draw a line under the past.

The young Elizabeth's closest relationships were with her governesses and her ladies-in-waiting. As we've seen, she had no sense of sisterhood with her half-sister and rival, Mary. She was given a good education, particularly in languages, which she seemed to have a knack for, but she wasn't particularly bookish and, despite the fact that her reign saw a flourishing of the arts, particularly literature, she was never actually a great patron. She tolerated playwrights like Shakespeare and Christopher Marlowe, and poets like Sir Philip Sidney, who was also one of her chief courtiers, but didn't necessarily have any great interest in their work, although she did award a pension to the poet Edmund Spenser.

When it comes to religion, Elizabeth was pragmatic, never showing the fanaticism of her Protestant brother, Edward, or her Catholic sister, Mary. She let people get on with things and kept her own worship to herself, allowing England to develop as a Protestant land. That said, however, she did call on God to justify her every act and constantly banged on about how it was God's will that she'd come to the throne and that, as head of the Church of England, she was communicating directly with him.

When her father died in 1547, Elizabeth was only 13 years old and went to live in the household of his widow, Catherine Parr. She was happy there and well looked after, until Catherine remarried to

Thomas Seymour (the more rackety and less reliable of Jane Seymour's brothers). The gossip going round was that before Thomas Seymour married Catherine, he'd proposed to young Elizabeth, who'd turned him down as a bad bet (which he was). He wasn't a great husband to Catherine and was constantly plotting against his older brother, the lord protector, Edward Seymour. He may well have sexually abused the young Elizabeth. There were romps in Elizabeth's bedchamber where Thomas would rush in and start tickling the 14-year-old girl, sometimes joined by his wife. There was one very strange incident when Thomas got Catherine to hold Elizabeth still while he cut her gown into 'a hundred pieces'. He seems to have been a bit of a *Jackass* figure, but it went further than just pranks, and when Catherine caught him embracing the young Elizabeth, she sent the girl away to live in the household of her governess's sister.

A couple of years later, when Elizabeth was 15, things started to unravel at court. Edward Seymour lost patience with Thomas and claimed that he was plotting to put Elizabeth on the throne and then marry her. People close to Elizabeth were implicated in the bogus conspiracy, rounded up and questioned. But Elizabeth held her ground. She was a royal princess and refused to cooperate, maintaining a 'no comment' stance. She survived, but not everybody else was so lucky. Thomas Seymour was executed on the orders of his big brother and, not long after that, Edward Seymour himself was arrested for his disastrous handling of the country in the coup led by John Dudley and executed.

Elizabeth now moved into Somerset Place, a huge residence Edward Seymour had been building on the site of what is now Somerset House. It was a bit of a building site and Elizabeth was never particularly happy there, except that she enjoyed the company of her childhood friend, Robert Dudley, who was looking after the place.

Robert was the son of John Dudley and the brother of Lady Jane Grey's husband, Guildford Dudley. He was tall, handsome, rakish and enjoyed the company of women, and, if there was one candidate for the love of Elizabeth's life, it was him. Later on, both his father and brother were executed by Queen Mary, but that didn't seem to have put Robert off getting intimately involved with the royal family.

As we shall see, Elizabeth toyed with Robert Dudley all through his life, leading him on and then casting him aside. When she was queen, to make him a slightly better marriage prospect, and to keep him sweet, she promoted him to Earl of Leicester (which is why he's usually referred to as 'Leicester'), but he was by no means the only man considered as husband material for her. Ironically, for someone who never married, Elizabeth's name was linked to a bewildering array of men, including ...

1. Philip of Spain (her brother in-law. A total creep)
2. Emmanuel Philibert, Prince of Piedmont and Duke of Savoy (nicknamed 'Iron Head'. Negotiations came to nothing)
3. King Eric of Sweden (not her type; she preferred dark-haired men)
4. Adolph, Duke of Holstein-Gottorp (bit of a long shot)
5. Frederick II of Denmark and Norway (boring)
6. The son of the Habsburg emperor, Ferdinand (you really don't want to marry a Habsburg)
7. Charles, Archduke of Austria (Philip's cousin)
8. Robert Devereux, Earl of Essex (bit of a wide boy)
9. Henry, Duke of Anjou (Hmmmm, he's OK, but French ...)
10. Francis, Duke of Anjou (Henry's brother and another frog, but maybe ...).

This last one was the marriage that came closest to actually happening. Elizabeth seemed to actually like Francis. And *he* liked her, despite the fact that she was about 20 years older than him. They corresponded a lot and he sent her an earring in the shape of a frog.*

But all that is still to come. When Edward VI died in 1553 and Mary came to the throne, it was bad news for Elizabeth. She hastily left London for the royal residence at Ashbridge, accompanied by a retinue of 500 gentlemen. The message to Mary was clear: 'I'm going to get out of your hair, but don't move against me, because I am popular.'

---

* I wasn't being entirely gratuitous when I called him a frog. Elizabeth used to refer to him as her 'little frog'.

But Mary had only been on the throne for a year when the uprising known as Wyatt's Rebellion broke out with the intention of getting rid of Mary and putting Elizabeth on the throne.

There were claims that Elizabeth was complicit in the rebellion and was dealing with the French behind Mary's back, because she knew that she'd never be safe as long as Mary was on the throne. But there was no proof and Elizabeth got away with it once again.

Mary's privy counsellors advised her that Elizabeth was too dangerous to be allowed to live. Mary feared the bad PR however and had Elizabeth arrested and put under house arrest instead. It was while Elizabeth was being kept out of the way in the royal palace in Woodstock near Oxford that Mary made the terrible mistake of marrying Philip of Spain and we've seen how Elizabeth was recalled to the court a year later, because they needed a royal witness to the birth of Mary's first child – but there was no child. One courtier said it was all just a lot of wind, and it certainly left a bad smell in court.

Philip must have been thinking that he'd married a woman 10 years older than him who was never going to give him the child that would secure the Habsburgs' place in the English royal dynasty. He let it be known that if anything should happen to Mary, he'd be there for her little sister and was instrumental in keeping Elizabeth alive and protected. He needed her as a back-up. When Mary died, and Elizabeth rejected his advances, Philip was out of the picture, but he never gave up his ambitions for the English throne.

Elizabeth's coronation – on 15 January 1559, when she was 25 – was an expensive affair. She spent £16,000 of her own money, a huge sum, and she had everything she wanted, except for an Archbishop of Canterbury. Many of the top clergy had died off, or been set on fire by Mary, including our old friend Thomas Cranmer, the former archbishop, so Elizabeth was crowned by the Bishop of Carlisle instead.

She knew that if she wasn't a success, England might well decide never to allow another queen on the throne. The first few years of her reign were pretty shaky, however; when she was staying at Hampton Court in 1562, she contracted smallpox, one of the deadliest diseases of the age. Her ruling council figured she was a goner and started debating which distant member of the Tudor family should succeed her. You'll see from the family tree that Henry VIII's two sisters, Margaret and Mary, had granddaughters. Margaret's granddaughter was Mary, Queen of Scots, while Mary's granddaughter was Katherine Grey, sister of Lady Jane Grey. Both were considered.

Obviously, Elizabeth didn't die from smallpox and when she got up from her sick bed, she was mightily pissed off with her high-handed ministers for jumping the gun and debating the succession without her. Elizabeth eventually learned how to control the condescending big men at court; she flirted, she flattered, she played them off against each other and they learned that she was strong-minded and intelligent. But, to begin with, they would patronise the queen, keeping matters of state from her if they thought the little lady wouldn't understand them, or they weren't suitable for a gentlewoman to discuss.

Her court was a much more settled and safer place than her father's had been, though. She didn't have a habit of executing ministers she fell out with and, once she'd purged her court of Mary's Catholic supporters, she packed it with very able ministers – men like William Cecil and his son Robert, Francis Walsingham (Elizabeth's great spymaster who saved her life on many occasions), Sir Philip Sidney and John Dee, her astrologer, who also worked behind the scenes making sure that Elizabeth was safe. And she also surrounded herself with a lot of powerful, high-ranking women and kept her own female privy chamber. These were women who understood about power and the workings of a royal court and were enormously useful to her throughout her reign.

I don't want to give the impression that it was all sweetness and light under Elizabeth. She was actually 'bloodier' than her sister and killed many Catholic rebels. This was largely down to the fact that, a decade into her reign, the pope excommunicated her and issued the equivalent of a fatwa, encouraging her subjects to rise against her and assassinate her. So the Tower was overflowing with Catholic plotters.

Elizabeth came to the throne unmarried and, in her first Parliament, declared that she would live and die a virgin, wife only to the nation. Nobody believed her, assuming she was just saying it to increase her value on the marriage market. As I say, the closest she came to breaking her vow of celibacy was with Robert Dudley. To begin with, any kind of relationship was impossible, because Dudley was already married, but his wife was diagnosed with breast cancer and then fell down the stairs in suspicious circumstances. Dudley was not accused of her murder, but a lot of people suspected him of giving her a little nudge so that he'd be free to marry Elizabeth.

The queen was serious about not marrying, though. She'd seen what happened if you married the wrong man, as Mary had, and how a man marrying a queen would try to take power and precedence over his wife and make themselves king. So she held off marrying Robert Dudley and, instead, tried to get him hitched to Mary, Queen of Scots, which came to nothing.

Mary, Queen of Scots was to prove Elizabeth right when it came to not trusting a husband. She made two awful marriages. Her third husband, James Hepburn, Earl of Bothwell, even murdered her second and he behaved so badly he pissed off the whole Scottish establishment. Spurred on by the vile John Knox, the Calvinists in Scotland turned against Mary so that, in 1567, she abdicated in favour of her son, James, and fled south of the border, expecting Elizabeth to protect her and help her get her throne back. I would say that Mary threw herself at Elizabeth's feet, but the two of them never actually met. Mary doesn't seem to have been the brightest button in the box. She should have known that Elizabeth had no intention of helping her, since she was the leading Catholic claimant to her own throne. She put Mary in one of her castles and it slowly dawned on the queen of Scots that she was under house arrest and would never make it back to Scotland. Elizabeth didn't want to end up like Mary and so avoided marriage. You could say that Mary followed her heart too much, while Elizabeth followed her head, also possibly too much.

So, she kept Dudley hanging on and, eventually, he got fed up with waiting and remarried to a woman with the splendid name of Lettice Knollys. And Elizabeth, childishly, banished Lettice from court and told Dudley she would never forgive him (she did, eventually, and loved him 'til he died).

The queen had a lot on her plate. England's closest ally and trading partner had always been the Netherlands, a main centre of Protestantism. However, the Habsburg Empire, through marriage and conquest, had spread into the region, much of which was now under their control. Local Protestants were rebelling and while Elizabeth wanted to help, she feared a full-scale war against the Habsburgs, which she didn't have the resources to win. The more bellicose members of her Privy Council, especially Robert Dudley, urged her to intervene, but she could do nothing without European support.

Spain had by now become a much bigger threat to England than France was, because the northern part of the Habsburg Empire, under Emperor Rudolph II, and the southern part, under King Philip of Spain, had France in the jaws of a vice. Elizabeth held talks with her suitor, Francis the Frog, Duke of Anjou, as a potential ally, but mounting a cross-channel invasion while dealing with the worsening economic situation at home was daunting. Elizabeth had serious cash flow problems, while Spain had huge shipments of gold and silver crossing the Atlantic from the Americas.

Queen Mary hadn't wanted to do anything to upset the Spanish and wouldn't allow British ships to attack theirs. Elizabeth had no such qualms. She sent hired pirates, known as 'privateers', to attack the Spanish in South America and steal their loot. The privateers, some of whom were familiar names like Francis Drake and Vice Admiral John Hawkins, the treasurer of the navy, brought home vast amounts of plunder, which Philip of Spain was not at all happy about. Elizabeth also commissioned Drake to circumnavigate the globe and he returned with his ship laden with plunder and spices.

Elizabeth's split of the proceeds was more than her annual crown income. However, it was nowhere near enough to finance an invasion of the Netherlands and, when Elizabeth's potential husband, and ally, Francis the Frog died, there wasn't much chance of anybody in France supporting her. Robert Dudley was nurturing a friendship with Prince William of Orange, the main Protestant ruler in Flanders, but the prince was murdered and, in the ensuing chaos, the Habsburgs made their move. The Duke of Parma, an Italian Habsburg general, took Antwerp.

Elizabeth was now forced to do something and so sent over a small expeditionary force under Dudley. The locals were so pleased to see him they asked him to replace the murdered prince as governor general.

Dudley came back very full of himself, but Elizabeth was furious. The last thing she wanted was for England to be fully responsible for the Netherlands. Plus, Dudley had gone behind her back. She scrubbed Robert Dudley, Earl of Leicester, from her list of potential husbands.

Things quickly went from bad to worse. Philip took over Portugal, creating an even more daunting power block in the Iberian Peninsula, and the Duke of Parma started amassing a huge army in the Netherlands. It was clear that the Habsburgs were preparing to invade England. But, as we've seen, it's difficult getting an army across the Channel, particularly now that the English had built up a very effective navy.

Philip started building a large fleet in Cádiz, with the aim of sailing it up to the Netherlands, picking up the Duke of Parma's forces and crossing to England. Elizabeth acted decisively and delayed Philip's plans for a year by sending Francis Drake down to Cádiz with a small raiding party, where he destroyed much of Philip's armada and burned all the staves that had been amassed to make barrels for carrying fresh water. Drake stopped off to attack other Spanish shipping off the Iberian coast and returned to England with something in the region of £140,000 worth of plunder, the bulk of which he gave to Elizabeth. With classic British 'understatement for humorous effect', the incident became known as 'The Singeing of the King of Spain's Beard'.

In 1587, Elizabeth accepted that she would finally have to do something about Mary, Queen of Scots, who'd been under house arrest for nearly 20 years. There had been serious uprisings in Mary's name, along with assassination plots. Elizabeth's very effective spy network protected her, but it was too much of a risk to keep Mary alive, so she gave in to the inevitable and had her beheaded.

The following year, in July 1588, the Spanish Armada finally set sail with much fanfare, but Philip had foolishly given the command to the Duke of Medina Sidonia, an aristocrat with zero naval experience. It looked like a case of handing the fleet to the poshest man they could find. One hundred and thirty ships, carrying more than 30,000 men, sailed along the north of Spain, up past France and into the Channel, where they started to meet English resistance. The English navy was more up to date than the Spanish and their well-armed ships were much more manoeuvrable than the lumbering Spanish galleons. They were crewed by well-trained, well-seasoned sailors and led by experienced naval commanders who harassed the Spanish all the way along the Channel and sent in fire ships to scatter their fleet. Nothing went the Spanish way; even the winds were against them. They were blown all the way along the Channel and out the other end without even getting close to the Duke of Parma, who was waiting patiently with his troops in the Netherlands, twiddling his thumbs.

Once in the North Sea, the Spanish were battered by terrible storms that pushed them ever northwards up the east coast of England. All they could do now was go up around Scotland and come back down past Ireland, where many vessels were driven onto rocks and wrecked. Out of the original 130 ships, only 70 made it back to Spain and perhaps two-thirds of the men died.

It was a complete disaster. While the English navy played a big part in seeing off the threat, it was the weather that played the biggest part. Nonetheless, Elizabeth made the most of it. She had a shiny, silver breastplate made and, with a silver truncheon at her side, rode a white horse (at least, it was white in the paintings) to where her troops were waiting at Tilbury for the invasion that never came. It was an effective bit of showmanship. Elizabeth told them that, with the full support of God, they would save England together. She went on to praise her subjects, the great men and women of England who had fought off this threat – 'Never before in the field of human conflict has so much been owed to so few ...' type of stuff. And she added that, 'I know I have the body but of a weak and feeble woman. But I have the heart and stomach of a king. And of a king of England, too, and take foul scorn that Parma, or any other prince of Europe should dare to invade the borders of my realm.'

Many British female politicians have tried to make similar speeches and emulate Elizabeth I at Tory party conferences over the years, from Margaret Thatcher to Liz Truss. None of them have come close.

Robert Dudley was in charge of the army and had stage-managed the whole affair, but he died soon after, quite suddenly, at the age of 56, possibly of malaria or stomach cancer. Elizabeth took to her rooms for several days until one of her ministers had to break down the doors. She kept Dudley's last letter to her in a casket by her bed until she died.

Elizabeth's speech at Tilbury was probably her finest moment. She went into a decline after this. Dudley was gone, as was Sidney and, over the next couple of years, she would lose other valuable and important men, such as Walsingham. The war with Spain rumbled on. The Spanish made three more attempts to invade, which all ended just as badly, and the English navy mounted an equally abortive counterattack.

There were further bad harvests and the people were growing ever poorer. And there was also another war to deal with when, in 1593, there was an uprising in Ireland against years of Tudor interference. The English had claimed to rule Ireland since the 12th century, but the Irish never really accepted that. By Elizabeth's time, the area actively controlled by the English was a small patch in the northeast known as The Pale. The Tudors had been trying to expand 'beyond the Pale' and subdue the rest of Ireland. A group of Irish lords fought back fiercely against the English expansionism, with the conflict leading to nine years of bitter warfare, called, imaginatively, the Nine Years' War.

With Dudley, Earl of Leicester gone, the ageing queen transferred her affections to his stepson, Robert Devereux, 2nd Earl of Essex. She promoted him and put him in command of Ireland, a post he was not really qualified for. He was a loose cannon, a wild lad, reckless and vainglorious, the sort of bad boy Elizabeth rather liked. She flirted with him and he flattered the vain old queen, taking her for all he could get. He arrogantly believed he had Elizabeth in his pocket, but he came to grief one morning when he burst into her bedchamber before she was up and dressed.

By now, it was taking Elizabeth's ladies two hours every morning to get her looking as she wanted, with the wigs and the white makeup and all the artifice. What Essex saw was a little old lady in the bed, and for a moment didn't recognise her.*

He did a double take at this hairless, toothless old crone, this 'crooked carcass' as he described her, laughed and got out of there quick. But Elizabeth had seen his look of horror and never forgave him.

---

* She was actually only in her late sixties.

Essex had many enemies at court, jealous of his favour with the queen, and, when he messed things up in Ireland, he launched an all-or-nothing rebellion of his own, hoping that Elizabeth was too old and feeble to hold on to power. This was the most doomed and hopeless of all the rebellions against her. Charging towards London, the rebels stopped for lunch at a pub, got pissed and the next thing they knew, they were surrounded. Essex ended up in the Tower and lost his head not long afterwards.

Essex's rebellion was the last excitement for Elizabeth and, at her final parliament in 1601 she gave another famous speech, summing up her reign: 'Though you may have had, and may have, many mightier and wiser princes sitting in this seat, yet you never had, nor shall have any that will love you better …'

Margaret Thatcher echoed this in her speech when she was kicked out of power. 'We're leaving Downing Street for the last time after 11½ wonderful years, and we're very happy that we leave the United Kingdom in a very, very much better state than when we came here 11½ years ago.'

Elizabeth was slowly beaten down by illness, hot flushes, the black dog of depression and the stress of the succession problem. She had a slow end and died in 1603 from perhaps bronchitis, perhaps pneumonia, perhaps even cancer. We'll never know, because she wouldn't allow any physicians to examine her, nor carry out a post-mortem.*

When she died, there were several people with a claim to the crown. Nearly all of them were women, but predictably a man was chosen – *phew*, huge relief, we've got a bloke back on the throne! This bloke was King James VI of Scotland – son of Mary, Queen of Scots – who became James I of England.

When he took the throne, a joke quickly started doing the rounds – '*Rex fuit Elizabeth, nunc est regina Jacobus*'. Elizabeth was a king, now James is a queen.

---

* This was one of the things that led to the ugly rumours that she was really a man.

24

JAMES THE VAIN

JAMES VI OF SCOTLAND/JAMES I
OF ENGLAND – 1566–1625
Reigned 1567–1625: as king of Scotland
1603–1625: as king of England and Ireland
Lived for 58 years. Ruled England for 22 years.
Died from a bit of everything.
Remembered for: being the first Scottish king of England,
establishing the Stuart dynasty south of the border and surviving
the Gunpowder Plot.

'James the Vain' is what he's called in the rhyme. Was he a vain man? Certainly, he was a proud man who firmly promoted the idea of the Divine Right of Kings that would lead to problems down the line for the Stuart dynasty – and he did have a very high opinion of himself. But was he physically vain? Well, the Stuarts do come across as a bunch of dandies who liked to dress up in the latest, most expensive and extravagant styles, but is there something coded in there as well? 'Vain' implies a certain female quality; real men aren't supposed to care about how they look and what they wear. What I'm trying to say is that James has been characterised as gay – or, at least, bisexual. OK, so he did father seven children with his wife, Anne, and he genuinely seemed to have had a deep affection for her, at least to start with, but obviously that's no proof of a man's sexuality either way. And there's always the danger of seeing the past through the lens of contemporary attitudes.

People today seem more obsessed about James's sexuality than his contemporaries were. It's undeniable that James was emotionally and sexually involved with both men and women in his life (as well as his wife, he kept a mistress, Anne Murray, for instance). And he had a number of 'favourites' whom he confessed to being 'in love' with, most famously/notoriously 'the handsomest-bodied man in all England', George Villiers, Duke of Buckingham.*

Perhaps influenced by the 'Willie Willie' mnemonic, I'd always dismissed James as a 'vain', prissy and dilettantish figure, but he was actually a pretty tough guy who became captain of both the Scottish and the English ships of state under very difficult circumstances, while also managing to navigate very stormy political waters very well. Putting a Scottish king on the English throne was a massive gamble for all involved, a bold experiment that could so easily have gone terribly wrong. That it didn't says a lot about James.

When James took the English throne, the Scots must have been overjoyed. This would be great for Scotland, having one of their own ruling the hated English, but it would end with Scotland being consumed by England, just as the Welsh Tudors coming to the throne had led to the complete subjugation of Wales under Henry VIII.

James pushed for the full unification of England and Scotland under one parliament and wanted to call himself king of Great Britain. But both the Scots and the English resisted, fearing a loss of power for their respective countries. It would be 100 years before England and Scotland were officially united, in the Acts of Union passed during the reign of the last Stuart monarch, Queen Anne.

James also tried to pursue his imperialistic aims in Ireland. The Nine Years' War ended pretty much at the same time as he became king. A scorched-earth policy on the English side had forced the Irish to surrender and James tried to press home his advantage by shipping English people out to colonise more of the country. This 'plantation' process failed, however, when not enough English settlers responded to the call.

Like almost every British ruler, James had problems with the economy and his own personal finances. He had a large household and four countries to run, and was constantly fighting parliament over money. He was determined, at least, to avoid getting involved in any costly

---

* I say his contemporaries weren't too bothered about what James got up to, but there was an obscene ditty – one which made play of a certain rhyme with 'Buckingham' – written about what he and James might have got up to together.

HENRY I: Who knows what Henry I actually looked like. The first English monarch to be painted from life was Richard II, 300 years later. Henry was a fearsome man, laid low by the loss of his son when the <u>White Ship</u> sank.

HENRY V: When I was a boy, Henry V's ludicrous haircut was much mocked; these days footballers seem to have made it fashionable. They'll be playing in George I-style wigs next.

HENRY VIII:
By law, all
books on British
history must
include a picture
of Henry VIII.

ELIZABETH I: *Elizabeth carefully controlled her image and cultivated the 'mask of youth', but can we still see the person behind the mask?*

JAMES I and VI: James I/VI is looking decidedly vain here. Was he gay? Was he bi? He was certainly a bi-monarch, being king of both England and Scotland.

ANNE: Queen Anne has every right to look miserable. She had 17 pregnancies but none of her children reached adulthood. As with so many of these monarchs, you wonder what it was all for.

GEORGE I: *In their own different ways, every Hanoverian monarch was a figure of fun. It would be much simpler if they hadn't all called themselves George (apart from William, who – ironically – is the one that nobody remembers). Even after writing this book I still struggle to remember which George did what. All I can say with any certainty is that George I was the first of the four Georges.*

VICTORIA: Jim has chosen to depict Queen Victoria Mark 2 – the grieving widow, worn down by multiple pregnancies and the loss of her husband. But she eventually reinvented herself as the grandmother of the nation and the grandmother of Europe, as so many monarchs were descended from her.

EDWARD VII and **EDWARD VIII**: A brace of Edwards, both stylish men about town who influenced gentlemen's fashion and tailoring (although Edward VIII's plus-four look is decidedly Bertie Wooster). Edward VII was something of a lounge lizard lothario, but he did seem to have Britain's best interests at heart. The Duke of Windsor, on the other hand, represented the worst side of the British aristocracy.

and wasteful wars in mainland Europe. He ended the war with Spain by signing the Treaty of London in 1604, but other conflicts in Europe hadn't gone away. It was during James's rule that the cataclysmic Thirty Years' War erupted, equivalent in terms of death and destruction to the First World War. Keeping up with these endless European wars is hard work: the Thirty Years' War, the Eighty Years' War, the Nine Years' War (in fact, there were two of these), the Thirteen Years' War, the Anglo-Spanish War, the Austrian-Hungarian War, the War of the Sicilian Vespers, the War of the Spanish Succession, the War of the Austrian Succession … In some ways, they were all just phases of the same war, a never-ending imperial competition over who controlled what in Europe. And it hasn't ended. At the time of writing this, Putin is still fighting a Russian imperialist war in Ukraine.

The spark of the Thirty Years' War (1618–1648) was religion. The Protestant parts of the Habsburg Empire started fighting the Catholic parts, with the Protestants ultimately coming off worst. But, as is often the case, the aims of the war changed as it went on and it escalated into a free-for-all. More than eight million people were killed, mainly in Germany and the German principalities. Most of these casualties were civilians, some of whom were caught up in the fighting, but many more were killed by famine and disease. By the end, Germany had torn itself apart and France had the space to flourish again. Its new boy ruler, Louis XIV, would grow up to restore the supremacy of France and hammer down the Habsburgs as the mighty Sun King.

As I say, James had no desire to get caught up in the war, but as the king of a shakily Protestant nation, many of whose subjects still secretly supported Catholicism, he knew that he'd have to handle matters at home very delicately if he wanted to avoid dissent. Protestants feared, and Catholics hoped, that he would be sympathetic to Catholicism and allow free worship. Luckily, he'd spent a lot of time negotiating these sorts of difficulties and had learned the arts of pragmatism and diplomacy. He'd had a very tough life, after all.

'So, tell me about your mother, James. Do you think your problems all started with her?'

We've looked at how James's claim to the English throne was through his mother, Mary, Queen of Scots. And we've seen how Henry

VIII tried to unite England and Scotland by marrying his son, Edward, to her. The Scots had had to make a treaty with their Auld Allies the French, promising Mary in marriage to the dauphin in return for military aid to help them stand up to the long and bloody Rough Wooing that had been started by Henry.

Mary, who was only five at the time, was sent to Paris and spent the next 13 years at the French court with the dauphin, Francis. When the French king died in 1559, the teenage couple took the throne and Mary became queen of France. It wasn't to last, though. The following year, 16-year-old Francis got an ear infection that spread to his brain, causing an abscess that killed him and Mary was sent packing. She returned to Scotland to find it had gone heavily Calvinist in her absence. Her fancy French manners and Catholicism were not welcome. She even changed the spelling of her family name from Stewart to the French version, Stuart.

Mary made things worse for herself by foolishly marrying a close relative. Henry Stuart (Lord Darnley) was a young aristo, best described as a witless drunkard. In short order, Darnley got Mary pregnant, murdered her Italian secretary David Rizzio out of jealousy, went on the run, came back and was blown up and strangled by a rival, James Hepburn, Earl of Bothwell. Bothwell was another feckless chancer on the make and everybody was aghast when Mary married him. The Scottish people turned against her and forced an abdication in favour of her newborn son, James. After a half-hearted attempt to rally support, Mary fled to England, never to return.

James was only thirteen months old when he was crowned king of Scotland in 1567 and the sermon at the ceremony was preached by our old friend, jolly John Knox. The boy had a harsh and loveless upbring-ing. He was regularly beaten by his sadistic, god-fearing tutor, George Buchanan, who wasn't going to treat James softly just because he was the king. Quite the opposite. James's education was thorough, but he was also encouraged to do sports. He was given a bow and arrows, hunting gloves and a set of golf clubs. It's incongruous to think of Stuart kings playing golf, but it was a very popular sport in Scotland.

As he grew up, James showed himself to be tough and tenacious. Influential lords were forever trying to manipulate him, but he learned to deal with them. It was the same story down in England, where both his mother Mary and Queen Elizabeth also tried to control him from afar, but he politely turned down their offers of help and carried on doing things his own way. Elizabeth grew increasingly furious with him, calling him 'that false Scottish urchin'.

As always happened when a child was on the throne, powerful men started competing with each other for influence and it led to civil war in Scotland. A string of regents came and went: James's first 'protector', James Stewart, Earl of Moray, was assassinated; his successor, James's grandfather, the Earl of Lennox, was killed in the war. Next, John Erskine, Earl of Mar, died of a sudden illness after a meal (he could well have been poisoned – or it might have just been Scottish cooking). James Douglas, 4th Earl of Morton, took over in 1572 and lasted six years before he was ousted in a coup led by Colin Campbell, 6th Earl of Argyll, and John Stewart, 4th Earl of Athol ... Around his 13th birthday, James said, *Enough! Guys, don't worry about it, I'll run things from now on*, and he had a spectacular entry into Edinburgh in 1579 to take control.

It was around this time that the first of the 'significant' men entered James's life, a Scottish/French relative, Esme Stewart.* (Esme also signed some of his documents, 'Amy'.†)

Esme was 20 years older than the 13-year-old James, but they formed a strong male friendship. James had grown up as quite a lonely figure, without any parents and isolated at court, and now here was this friendly, charismatic older man offering companionship. James made him the Earl of Lennox and gave him a central position at court. But, as we know, established courtiers don't like new favourites coming in, so Esme was not made welcome, particularly as he was a pro-French ex-Catholic.

In 1582, a group of hard-line Presbyterian nobles under William Ruthven decided to take matters into their own hands and kidnapped the young king in an attempt to force him to get rid of Esme. It half worked. Esme went back to France and Ruthven held James for more

---

* Don't snigger. At the time, Esme was a male name and meant 'esteemed'.
† Oh, do grow up. Amy was also a male name.

than a year, trying to control him. The king, however, managed to escape and then arrested Ruthven and executed him. This decisive action was typical of James. Whenever there were uprisings against him, he dealt with them swiftly and efficiently, getting rid of the ring-leaders and hanging on to his throne.

Whatever his sexual inclinations, James knew he had to get married. The Scandinavian countries were becoming more important in Europe. Indeed, one of the reasons for the escalation and prolonged bloodiness of the Thirty Years' War was the intervention of Sweden and Denmark on the Protestant side. James saw Denmark as a useful Protestant ally and, as he was always short of money, he thought a nice chunky dowry would come in very handy, too.

His offer of marriage to Anne, daughter of the Danish king, Frederick II, was accepted and, cheekily, he asked for a dowry of ONE MILLION SCOTTISH POUNDS. He was never going to get this, and the Danish bartered him down to £150,000, which was still a hefty wedge (although James managed to spend £100,000 of it on his wedding. Some say he was a miserable skinflint, but he did like to party).

Anne tried to join James in Scotland, but her small fleet was driven back to Norway by storms and James did the only gallant thing he ever did in his life: he set off to pick up his 14-year-old fiancée himself. He married Anne in Oslo and stayed in Scandinavia for some time, having a bit of a holiday. He enjoyed meeting the various intellectuals, scientists, artists and writers who hung out at the royal courts in Oslo and Copenhagen.

The couple eventually sailed to Scotland, where Anne was crowned, and they proceeded to have several children. So James managed to do what Elizabeth had failed to do: he produced heirs and secured his succession. As was usual among the British royals, the children were taken away and fostered almost as soon as they were born. Anne was appalled at this barbaric British custom and argued with the unyielding James.

One of the things that James had discussed at the Danish court was witchcraft. Witch fever was sweeping through Europe, fuelled by the arguments about religion that had led to the rise of Protestantism, with everyone accusing everyone else of being heretics and worshipping God in the wrong way. There was a growing obsession that wicked men and women were inverting Catholic rituals, worshipping Satan and kissing his hairy, demon arse. James got caught up in the witch hunt fever, particularly when stories started circulating that witches had caused the storm that had driven Anne back to Denmark.

There were trials and executions in Scotland, and many confessions of arse-kissing were extracted under pretty nasty torture. James went so far as to write a book called *Daemonologie* in 1597. This was a fairly serious work about witchcraft and the inversion of the sacrament, and James has gone down in history as the scourge of witches, responsible for the deaths of countless innocent men and women. But, within a couple of years, he came to his senses and said, *You know what? In hindsight, this is a load of old bollocks*. He was smart enough to see that people were using the idea of witchcraft for their own ends and exaggerating the threat (OK – he still did believe in witchcraft a *little* bit).

Shakespeare famously picked up on the Jacobean* obsession with witches and put a coven into *Macbeth*, cementing the idea that witches can predict the future and manipulate events. Textbook conspiracy theory material.

Unfortunately for James, Anne, who'd been brought up as a strict Lutheran (which was the whole point of the marriage), decided to convert to Catholicism. Rather than having a huge row with her, James simply asked her not to make a big deal of it. As long as it didn't become an embarrassment for him, he wasn't going to interfere.

James now felt that Scotland needed a major PR campaign to present a better image of the country to the world and he started to big up Scottish arts, traditions, history and, most of all, poetry. He tried very hard to sell the idea that he was the Great King of a Great Country – Scotland the Brave, Scotland the Magnificent. This was something of an exaggeration. Scotland may have been full of fine people, but at the time, it was an impoverished, dilapidated and dour place with virtually no major towns or cities.

---

* Jacobean from 'Jacobus', the Latin version of James. This is also the derivation of the word 'Jacobite', used to describe supporters of King James I's grandson, James II.

At the same time, James was keeping a close eye on what was happening down in England. Elizabeth was on the way out and, like an anxious householder worried about who might move in next door, James was nervous about who his new neighbour might be. What if England chose someone who didn't have Scotland's best interests at heart? From around 1601, he began having secret talks with Elizabeth's right-hand man, Sir Robert Cecil, about the idea that James himself might be the best replacement for the ailing queen.

It paid off. In 1603, when Elizabeth died, the English government offered James the crown. There were some worries that the people wouldn't accept a Scottish king, but there was also a feeling that anything was better than having another woman on the throne. People just wanted things to be settled so they could get on with their lives. They didn't want another civil war with the lords all killing each other. The merchants wanted to carry on with trading and the farmers wanted to carry on working in the fields without armies trampling their crops.

And James did bring stability, even though his arrival in England coincided with a fresh outbreak of the plague, which killed about a quarter of the population of London. Not a very auspicious start. The plague eventually burned itself out, though, and once things were up and running again, the English lords could get back to bickering. Their main concern was that James would stuff the English court with Scottish lords. Inevitably, James had brought some of his Scottish lairds with him, but he tried to maintain a balance to keep both the Scots and English nobility happy. He'd learned diplomacy at home and had the force of personality to hold things together.

Before he left Edinburgh, he'd assured the locals that Scotland would always be the most important thing to him: *I've just got to go and sort out this little thing down in England – I'll be back.* But he never returned. He went native because, as soon as he got to London and saw what it was really like, he thought, *Oh my God, England is like a soft feather bed compared to the hard stone bench that is Scotland.*

James had written a book called *Basilikon Doron* which set out his rather old-school thoughts on monarchy. As far as he was concerned, a monarch had ultimate authority and things would run a lot smoother and more efficiently if everyone just did what their king told them. He had the experience, decisiveness and skills to command respect and just about got away with a haughty, autocratic approach. He still fought with parliament, though, and, at one point, even dissolved it and tried to rule without it. But it didn't go well and, when his finances worsened, he changed his mind.

James saw himself as a great patron of the arts, much more so than Queen Elizabeth, and needs to be given more credit for the so-called 'golden age of Elizabethan literature', which was just as much a Jacobean thing. Men like Shakespeare, Francis Bacon, John Donne and Ben Jonson flourished during James's reign. And the king liked to think of himself as one of them. As well as *Daemonologie* and *Basilikon Doron*, he published many other books and sponsored a group of scholars and translators to write a new translation of the Bible which ended up being named after him – *The Authorised King James Version* – and is one of the great works of English literature.

James's biggest problem was conspirators who wanted to go back to the old ways and put a good Catholic on the throne. The best-known and most serious conspiracy, the Gunpowder Plot, happened early in his reign, in 1605, when the Catholic gentleman, Robert Catesby, tried to blow up the king and the Houses of Parliament. To carry out their scheme, the conspirators hired a Catholic ex-soldier, Guy Fawkes (who was from up north, where everybody hates Londoners). The grand old northern families, like the Percys, were mostly Catholic and felt disenfranchised since power had become centralised in London.

Guy Fawkes stashed 36 barrels of gunpowder in a cellar underneath Parliament. If he'd managed to detonate them, the explosion would have completely destroyed the Palace of Westminster, killing not just James and his wife and children, who were due to be there for the opening of parliament, but the whole of parliament and everyone in it, as well as most of Whitehall and Westminster Abbey, causing a massive loss of life and property, and changing London for ever.

Fawkes has been personified, particularly recently, as a revolution-ary figure: anti-government, anti-establishment, a freedom fighter. On the back of the film based on Alan Moore's *V for Vendetta* comic, the

Fawkes mask has been worn on marches by anarchists, libertarians, anti-capitalists and anti-government protesters. But the real Guy Fawkes was a reactionary, not a forward-looking revolutionary. He didn't like the new way of doing things. He didn't like this new, namby-pamby, Scottish, bloody government.

The plot was foiled when William Parker, the 4th Baron Monteagle, a Catholic lord and the brother-in-law of one of the plotters, received an anonymous letter warning him that he might not want to be at the state opening of parliament. Had one of the plotters got cold feet? Or were they just trying to save someone they thought would be a useful sympathiser after the apocalypse? Whatever the case, men were sent down to search the cellars where they came across Guy Fawkes, who had hidden the barrels behind a stack of wood. He bluffed his way out of it, saying he was just looking after the wood pile, and they went away – 'Sorry to bother you, sir.' But they were persuaded to return and this time they looked behind the stack of wood, where they found Fawkes with a fuse and matches and a shitload of gunpowder. So, the king and parliament and Westminster Abbey were saved. Catesby was killed in a shoot-out soon after and the surviving eight conspirators, including Fawkes, were tried and sentenced to be hanged, drawn and quartered. The worst possible punishment.

It's interesting that we remember this event with Bonfire Night, where effigies of Fawkes – Guys – are burned.* Really, we should be having Hanging, Drawing and Quartering Night. We celebrate *what might have happened*, with fire and fireworks on November 5th. It's a night of chaos and high spirits, with sparks rising into the dark and the air filled with smoke, a night to be devilish and give in to our destructive fantasies.

So James survived the plot and lived another 20 years. His main 'enemy' was obviously the Catholic Church, particularly the radical Jesuits, but he had a growing problem with Protestants as well. Protestantism had been breaking up into sects, and the most radical of them, the joyless Puritans, felt that James wasn't going far enough in pushing the cause. Dissenters were beginning to leave Europe and

* Do people still burn Guys?

set up religious colonies in America. This was the time of the Pilgrim Fathers, disillusioned Puritans who set off in the *Mayflower* convinced that they were never going to see the kind of fully reformed church they'd hoped for in Europe.

It was during the latter part of James's reign that he started his love affair with George Villiers. The Duke of Buckingham became his new favourite, much to the consternation of his court, and he had to defend himself. 'You may be sure that I love the earl of Buckingham more than anyone else,' he said. 'I wish … not to have it thought to be a defect, for Jesus Christ did the same, and therefore I cannot be blamed. Christ had his John, and I have my George.'

Villiers started to manipulate the ageing king, making it clear that if anyone wanted to get to James, they would have to go through him. He also controlled the flow of information that reached the king, who didn't seem to mind. In 1623, he wrote to Buckingham, 'God bless you, my sweet child and wife, and grant that ye may ever be a comfort to your dear dad and husband'. George replied, 'I naturally so love your person, and adore all your other parts, which are more than ever one man had … I desire only to live in the world for your sake and I will live and die a lover of you.'

James seemed happy, but he'd been plagued by illness all his life – arthritis, kidney stones, skin complaints, breathing problems, piles … He was a sickly specimen and, in the end, it was possibly pneumonia that did for him in 1625 – although inevitably there were soon conspiracy theories flying around that the unpopular Duke of Buckingham somehow had a hand in his death.

James was haughty and high-handed, but he was smart and preserved the stability of England, taking the first steps towards what would become the United Kingdom. Yes, he spent a lot of money and raised a lot of taxes, but it's impossible to run a country without a tax system. Yes, he believed in the divine right of kings and relished being head of the church, but he avoided religious persecution (unless you count witchcraft). Yes, he dissolved parliament, but he knew how to play the dangerous game of politics, and he survived.

Unlike his son, Charles.

25

CHARLIE (#1)

CHARLES I – 1600–1649
Reigned 1625–1649
Lived for 48 years. Reigned for 24 years.
Died from parting company with his head.
Remembered for: losing the crown – with his head still attached.

The central fact of Charles I's life was … his death. He is the only monarch in this story who was officially executed. Kings had been killed in battle, murdered, deposed, locked up out of sight and starved to death, but none of them had ever been put on trial and beheaded in full view of their people. Henry VIII had set the boulder rolling down the hill by doing the unthinkable and beheading two of his queens, and the execution of Charles I couldn't have happened if Henry hadn't broken the taboo of formal regicide. If you can execute a queen, you can execute a king.

So what exactly did Charles do to get himself into this position, kneeling with his head on a block on a specially erected platform outside the Banqueting House on Whitehall?* In the end, it wasn't just one thing. His walk to the block took small steps, and nobody really believed it would end the way it did, least of all him, until the axe came down, because this was such a bold line to cross.

I've seen similar scenes in my lifetime with fallen dictators like Ceaușescu and Saddam Hussein ranting in court, *You can't try me! You have no right!! I am your supreme ruler!!!* Like them, Charles I railed against his accusers and only stopped arguing when they separated

---

* Charles was a major patron and connoisseur of the arts. It's largely down to him that the Royal Collection is the largest private art collection in the world. It was Charles who hired Reubens to paint the beautiful ceiling of the Banqueting House.

him into two parts (although they did stitch his head back on when they buried him).

By this time, England had a system of government we'd recognise today, with the House of Lords and a House of Commons with elected members (although there was by no means universal suffrage just yet). Charles, like his father, was also king of Scotland and therefore had to contend with Scottish parliament as well. He spent a large part of his reign arguing with both parliaments and, in many ways, paid the price for the mistakes of every monarch who'd come before him, of every king who'd pissed off the powerful families, the ruling elite, their privy councils, their parliaments, their people, from King John to Henry III, to Edward II, to Richard II, to Henry VI. This was going to happen sooner or later. Charles's father, James I,* had been a very astute politician, a pragmatist, who'd known when to push hard and when to pull back. He'd understood how to keep parliament on side with a combination of carrot and stick. Charles was no James. He came to the throne with a naive overconfidence in his position. He thought that he was king and everyone should do as he said, and got furious when he was denied what he wanted.

To be fair to Charles, he did come to the throne at a very bad time. James might have been good at compromise and working with tricky ministers, but he'd never had a very firm hand on the economy and, like most monarchs who live for a long time, by the end he was feeble and weakened. Just as today, when a government inherits a rotten economy, they're usually blamed for their predecessors' mistakes, so it was with Charles.

He tried to bolster the royal finances when he came to the throne by raising taxes. Parliament inevitably didn't like this, so he tried to rule without their consent, but this only made him more unpopular. He was seen as a tyrannical, absolute monarch, even though England was the least taxed country in Europe, with no system of regular direct taxation in place. We all want a good health service, a good transport system, good schools, law and order, but we want someone else to pay for it.

---

* And James VI of Scotland as we're obliged to call him.

Charles's only method of dealing with his parliament was to dissolve it, believing he could rule without them. He was also never clear about where he stood on religion and was viewed suspiciously by the new hard-line Protestant orthodoxy. Whenever a radically different system of religion or politics comes in, the new men (and it's always men) are the most fanatical, wanting to push things further and further. And, with Protestants under attack through Europe, many doubled down and embraced Puritanism. The very word is uncompromising – this is the *pure* way of doing things, the only way, there's no middle ground – which was where Charles tried to stand. He could never please anyone. He was too Scottish for the English and too English for the Scottish, particularly the Covenanters, the extremist Protestant clique who'd taken over north of the border.

It didn't help that Charles tried to force the Scottish Church to adopt Anglican religious practices and the new Book of Common Prayer, which was seen as Sassenach propaganda and cultural imperialism. The Scots wanted to go fully Presbyterian, which would have meant doing away with bishops, and Charles wouldn't allow that. So they went to war over it. The so-called Bishops' War was essentially between the Scottish king, Charles, and the Scottish Parliament, the Covenanters.

Charles was also having to look towards Europe, which was descending into the extraordinarily destructive Thirty Years' War. Even if he had wanted to get involved, he could never raise the money, which he needed for his various domestic wars. As well as the Bishops' War in Scotland, there was fresh fighting in Ireland and, ultimately, a full-scale civil war in England between the Royalists and the Parliamentarians. These wars have become lumped together under the title of the English Civil War, although historians refer to them officially as the Wars of the Three Kingdoms.

But let's go back and start at the beginning.

Charles was born in Scotland in 1600 and came to the throne when he was 24. He was such a weak and sickly infant that when his father, James, and the rest of his family left for England in 1603, he was considered too fragile to go with them. Cut to a training montage – little Charles toughening up – and the next year he proved he was strong enough to travel by walking from one end of the great hall at Dunfermline Palace to the other all by himself.

When he got to England, the woman assigned to look after him, Lady Elizabeth Carey, made him wear big leather boots, reinforced with brass, to strengthen his weak ankles – and, by all accounts, he grew up to be tough as old boots. Historians have speculated that he possibly had rickets; a diet of deep-fried Mars bars and Irn-Bru can do that. I jest, but people didn't know that much about nutrition back then and there probably weren't a lot of fresh fruit and vegetables knocking around during the Scottish winters. Charles didn't just suffer from physical weakness in his legs, however; his speech development was slow and he had a stammer for the rest of his life.

He was a sporty young man, a good horseman and a fencer, but was no match for Golden Boy, his big brother and heir to the throne, Henry Frederick, Prince of Wales, who Charles very much looked up to. This was the boy Charles wanted to be, and he sort of got his wish when Henry Frederick died of typhoid at the age of 18 and Charles took his place as heir.

Charles and his sister, Elizabeth, comforted each other when Henry died and became very close. In 1613, Elizabeth married Frederick, Elector Palatine, ruler of one of the small states within the Holy Roman Empire, in the Rhineland. There are two things worth noting about Elizabeth.

1. When the English were looking for a Protestant candidate for the throne after the death of the childless queen Anne a century later, they picked Elizabeth's grandson, George, despite the fact that he was about 60th in line to the throne. And German.
2. Although he sounds like an evil *Star Wars* villain, Elizabeth's husband, Frederick, Elector Palatine was a bit hapless. His misadventures sparked the devastating Thirty Years' War and his Protestant palatinate was invaded by the Catholic Habsburgs from the Spanish Netherlands.

Once Charles moved down to England, he barely went back to Scotland and actually spent more time in Spain. He was there for seven or eight months in 1623, trying to get the Spanish court to accept his marriage proposal to Maria Anna, daughter of King Philip III. King James was hoping to get back on good terms with the Spanish, but the marriage never happened. The Spanish looked down on Charles and felt that he was an uncivilised Protestant heretic from a useless backwater.

Charles had gone to Spain with his father's favourite, George Villiers, Duke of Buckingham and, isolated in the snooty Spanish court, the two became firm friends. (After King James's death, when Charles came to the throne, he kept Buckingham on as his right-hand man.) Their trip was a washout, but when they limped back to England, they were greeted by jubilant, cheering, anti-Spanish crowds – so at least it boosted Charles's popularity.

Two years later, shortly before his coronation, Charles married Henrietta Maria of France, sister of King Louis XIII. Henrietta Maria had her head screwed on, unlike Charles, and did much to bolster his reign when things got bad. Their marriage, however, was one of the roots of Charles's problems. First of all, in a secret marriage treaty with his brother-in-law, Charles lent King Louis seven warships to defend France against the Habsburg threat. And then, when Charles was crowned at Westminster Abbey in 1626, the Catholic Henrietta Maria was absent. She refused to participate in a Protestant religious cere-mony, which wasn't a good look. And then King Louis used his seven new warships to attack the Protestant Huguenot community in La Rochelle,* which put Charles in a very awkward position. He'd prom-ised to protect the Huguenots, but needed to keep on good terms with Louis.

Buckingham stepped up and dashed over the Channel with a war party to help the Huguenots. The raid was a dismal failure, the Huguenots were defeated and Buckingham was humiliated. This

---

* Protestants in France were far less successful than in England and the Low Countries. The Huguenots, as they became known, suffered such violent persecu-tion that most of them fled the country, many ending up in England.

wasn't his first unsuccessful and vainglorious European expedition, so parliament, whose members had never liked him, ordered Charles to impeach him – ostensibly for abusing his power and damaging British interests, but mainly because he was a royal favourite. The king refused to do what he was told, tried to save his friend and shut down parliament. Charles figured he could rule quite happily as long as he avoided spending too much money, because only parliament could raise taxes. So he came to terms with France and Spain, and for the next 11 years, England was at peace. Which was no bad thing.

The Stuart family called this long period of rule without a parliament the Personal Rule; the Parliamentarians (and pretty much everyone else) called it the Eleven Years' Tyranny. Charles did still need *some* money, so he started looking at unconventional ways to raise funds, methods that had fallen out of use over the years. He found a few loopholes and old acts that he resurrected in order to squeeze money out of people without needing parliament. He was just about scraping by when the war in Scotland kicked off. Without a standing army, Charles had to recall parliament, hoping they'd be so grateful they'd give him whatever he asked for. Thinking this was all a ruse by Charles to create an army he could use against them, parliament refused. So Charles shut them down again; this brief session became known as the Short Parliament.

Charles's problems around Buckingham were solved when the duke was shot dead by a disgruntled veteran of one of his ill-fated campaigns. So that was the end of the divisive (but gorgeous) man whom King James had called his 'sweet child and wife'. Charles replaced him as his right-hand man with Thomas Wentworth, 1st Earl of Strafford, a tough soldier and a very capable, if ruthless, politician. The king sent him to sort things out in Ireland where Strafford established a strong authoritarian administration. As far as the new English colonists were concerned, Strafford was very successful and he started generating a large income for the king there. As far as the local Irish were concerned, though, he was a tyrant.

Back in England, the lords grew suspicious of Strafford, fearing that he was getting too powerful and wealthy, and was creating a private army in Ireland for Charles. Believing that Strafford was the best man for the job, the king sent him to Scotland to sort out the war there, but it went very badly. The Scots had learned their lessons from all their battles with the English and managed to not only send Strafford's troops packing, but went on to invade England and capture Newcastle.

Charles had to call another parliament, which became the Long Parliament. He brought Strafford to London as an ally, but parliament announced that they were going to impeach him for his high and mighty behaviour in Ireland and for raising an army to attack them. Charles swore to Strafford that he wouldn't let anything happen to him but, in the end, and to keep parliament on side, he broke his word. 'Put not your trust in princes,' Strafford said shortly before he was executed, and Charles never forgave himself for not standing up for him. At his own end, on the scaffold, Charles would wonder if God was punishing him for deserting his friend.

Things were falling apart. The country was rudderless and unruly gangs of anti-Royalist apprentices with shaved heads were marauding around the lawless streets of London.* Charles was seeing plots against him and his family on all sides (perhaps justifiably) and made the ultimate mistake of taking soldiers into the House of Commons to arrest the five men he saw as the chief conspirators. But they'd been tipped off and had done a runner. Members of parliament are as touchy and entitled as monarchs, so Charles's intrusion into their space was just not the done thing. The affronted speaker of the house refused to cooperate with him and he was left spitting with impotent rage.†

Charles, realising he'd overstepped the mark and only made things worse, fled London and headed north, while parliament started raising an army. Charles had support in the Midlands, Wales, the West Country and northern England, while parliament controlled London, the southeast and East Anglia.

The first battle of the English Civil War was at Edgehill in Warwickshire in October 1642, where Charles's nephew (by his sister,

---

* This was the origin of the term 'roundhead'.
† Many of the bewildering traditions surrounding the state opening of parliament (such as the doors being slammed in Black Rod's face and the monarch initially being barred entry) stem from this incident.

Elizabeth) – the dashing but reckless Prince Rupert of the Rhine – led the cavalry. He argued with Charles's generals and was forever chasing after people in battle and not coming back. At Edgehill, he managed to plunder the parliamentary baggage train. It wasn't enough to give Charles a victory, though.

The English Civil War is often portrayed as being fought by long-haired, foppish aristocrats (the Cavaliers) on the king's side, and tough, shaven-headed, ordinary working-class men of the people (the Roundheads) on the Parliamentarian side. But this isn't really accurate. The Parliamentarians were from the nobility just as much as the Royalists. Many them were the equivalent of tweedy country gentlemen.

The war followed the same course as every previous English Civil War: each side took it in turns to win and lose, a lot of men were killed, families were torn apart, property was destroyed and crops ruined … What tipped the balance in favour of the Parliamentarians was that they found a good general, Oliver Cromwell, who was instrumental in making their army better organised, better equipped and more professional.*

After the collapse of the king's army at the Battle of Naseby in 1645, Cromwell decisively held the upper hand. The following year, Charles found himself under siege in Oxford and narrowly escaped, dressed as a servant. In an act of desperation, he gave himself over to the Scots, hoping that the Covenanters might form an alliance with him and bring a fresh army south to take on the Parliamentarians. But it didn't go the way he hoped and the Scots ransomed him to Cromwell for £100,000. Charles still refused to compromise, hoping to exploit disunity on the opposing side, with parliament and the army falling out with each other and Scotland threatening them from the north. Charles briefly managed to escape before being recaptured, but it was enough encouragement for his supporters to reignite the war, with the help of the Scots, with whom Charles had cut a deal. The almost

---

* As we'll see in the next chapter, Cromwell was another country squire type, forever railing against 'the elite' (that he was part of). A kind of Nigel Farage on horseback.

invincible New Model Army knocked out all-comers, though, and Charles was forced back to the negotiating table. By now, parliament had been taken over by hardliners and negotiations gradually turned into a trial, leading to Charles being charged with treason. He put up a clever and spirited defence, although the central core of his argument was that they had no right to try him, which was never going to fly.

Charles went bravely to his execution. He insisted on wearing two shirts so that he wouldn't shiver from the cold and have people think he was shaking with fear. His was a dignified end that left the country without a monarch for the first (and last) time since the days of Alfred the Great. After the execution, there was a sense of shock: What have we just done? What happens next?

Charles had left behind several children, including his sons, Charles and James, and his daughter, Mary, but they were barred from the throne. So eventually parliament decided to give Oliver Cromwell the job of lord protector, which led to a lot of fun and games. Well, no fun and no games, actually.

26
THE INTERREGNUM

OLIVER CROMWELL – 1599–1658
Ruled as Lord Protector: 1653–1658
Lived for 57 years. Ruled for five years.
Remembered for: executing King Charles I.

RICHARD CROMWELL – 1626–1712
Ruled as Lord Protector: 1658–1659
Lived for 86 years. Ruled for one year.
Not really remembered at all.

Oliver Cromwell doesn't make it into the Willie Willie rhyme, because he wasn't a monarch. His title was 'Lord Protector' – king in all but name. He interrupted our pageant of monarchs in spectacular fashion and you can't tell this story without looking at the part he played in it, so I hope you'll indulge me if I deviate from the mnemonic.

Cromwell's reputation has fluctuated wildly over the centuries. Many think he was a hero of the people who got rid of a corrupt and irrelevant monarchy; others will tell you that he was a military dictator who ushered in a period of unpopular Puritanism and wrecked much of British culture and society, destroying a huge amount of beautiful art and architecture in the process.

The Irish, in particular, are unequivocal in their judgement of Cromwell. To them, he was a bloody monster who represents everything that was nasty, unjust and brutal about English colonial rule in Ireland.

Whatever your view, Cromwell was at the heart of a revolution that had to happen. It was a necessary reset, a useful pause to consider what the monarchy is for and how it should function. It also showed what the alternative might look like, without a monarch as head of state. In the end, there was a typically mild British conclusion – OK, we've had our little revolution and cleared the air. Can we get back to normal now?

There are only three statues directly outside the Houses of Parliament. One is of the suffragette Emmeline Pankhurst, one is of a monarch, Richard the Lionheart, and the other is the 'great hero of parliament', Oliver Cromwell. (Here comes the 'but'.) But Cromwell was by no means an all-purpose man of the people and champion of democracy. For a start, he didn't want everyone to have the vote. He was very much on the side of the landed gentry and fell out with his more radical supporters who wanted equality for all. He tried to rule through the democratic process as it stood and didn't want to extend the vote to include all and sundry – not even the loyal soldiers who'd fought for him. He ended up behaving in a very similar fashion to Charles I: when parliament didn't give him what he wanted, he kicked half of them out and instated military rule.

Cromwell was 54 when he became Lord Protector and held the post for only five years before he died, so he'd lived most of his life before he took control. He grew up in East Anglia, mostly in Cambridgeshire, and is often thought of as coming from a lowly back-ground. He hadn't. He was a stout gentleman farmer. His great-great-grandfather, Morgan ap William, had married Thomas Cromwell's sister, Catherine, and their sons had taken her family name. Cromwell's grandfather had been a wealthy landowner, but, by Oliver's time, the family had come down in the world. Oliver had started studying at Cambridge University when his father died in 1617 and he had to leave to take charge of the family holdings.

He married a woman called Elizabeth Bourchier and they had nine children together. In 1628, he went into politics and became the member of parliament for Huntingdon, sponsored by the wealthy Montagu family, who expected him to look after their interests.*

It was a terrible time for Cromwell to get into politics, however, as it coincided with King Charles dissolving parliament. Cromwell was

---

* At this time, you had to prove a certain level of wealth before you were allowed to become an MP, which was an unpaid job.

in the House of Commons for only about a year – not enough time to make his mark. The parliamentary records have him down as only making one (poorly received) speech. Charles went on to rule the country by himself for the next 11 years.

Up to this point, Cromwell hadn't shown any strong religious beliefs, but soon after becoming an MP, he was being treated for 'melancholy'. He was to suffer heavily from depression throughout his life and it seems that he turned to God to get him through his first bout. Afterwards, he thanked the Lord for his recovery and was to become increasingly religious over the years, believing that he was God's chosen man and that everything that went well in his life was thanks to Him.

One of the factors that exacerbated his condition and led to a mental breakdown was stress caused by a local land dispute in Huntingdon that he got embroiled in. Cromwell came off worst and had to sell his property and move out of the area into a smaller house, where he eked out a living selling eggs and wool, and started writing letters to his family full of biblical imagery, eventually describing himself as having been the chief of sinners who had turned his life around.

As a born-again Christian, he got caught up in the religious fervour that was gripping the nation, with hard-line Protestants disappointed that the Reformation hadn't gone far enough and insisting that all Catholic beliefs and practices should be purged from the church. In 1634, Cromwell tried to emigrate to one of the new Puritan colonies in New England, but, as a member of parliament, he was barred from leaving the country. Things improved when he inherited some property from an uncle that came with the job of tithe collector for Ely Cathedral.*

When King Charles hastily reconvened parliament in 1640 to try to raise taxes to fight the Scots, Cromwell was in with a second chance and re-entered parliament as the member for the borough of Cambridge. Alas, this was to be the Short Parliament, which only

---

* A tithe being a religious tax that churchgoers (basically everyone in the community) paid to the church. So he became a tax collector and a landlord with a fairly respectable income.

lasted three weeks, so it looked like Cromwell was destined never to be a sitting MP. Luckily, Charles realised he couldn't keep shutting down parliament. His attempts to raise money by unorthodox means, such as the 'Ship Tax', were largely unsuccessful and were only making him more unpopular, so he convened what became the Long Parliament. It soon became clear, however, that religious and political extremists, which included Cromwell, were never going to agree with anything that Charles wanted and the king looked for a more extreme solution to his problems.

If you ask people 'Who started the English Civil War?', most would probably say that parliament declared war on King Charles. But it was actually the other way round. Charles raised an army in Oxford and sent it to attack his own government.

Cromwell's military experience only began when the war started. He saw his first action in 1642 when he led his local county militia to Cambridge to prevent the Royalists from getting their hands on a store of arms and a load of silver that had been collected from the colleges to fund their forces. On the back of this, Cromwell then set up his own cavalry regiment and was involved in various military actions in East Anglia, most notably at the Battle of Gainsborough in 1643. By the time of the Battle of Marston Moor the following year, he'd proven himself to be a very able soldier and had risen to be a senior commander of the Parliamentarian army.

He'd finally discovered, at this late point in his life, what he was good at. He was an excellent military commander who instilled great loyalty in his men. Royalist troops tended to be undisciplined, with hot-headed commanders, like Prince Rupert of the Rhine, charging about trying to gain personal glory for themselves, but Cromwell was organised and level-headed, and began forging a more modern, disciplined army. He wasn't yet the overall commander of the Parliamentarian forces, however; the two chief men in charge were Thomas Fairfax, Lord of Cameron, and Edward Montagu, Earl of Manchester. Cromwell was fast rising to challenge these established members of the nobility, though. At the Battle of Marston Moor in 1644, his cavalry played a decisive role in defeating the Royalists when they got round behind their infantry and attacked them from the rear, causing the king's army to collapse. This victory secured the north for the Parliamentarians, but wasn't quite decisive enough to completely crush Royalist resistance and, at the Second Battle of Newbury, Manchester cocked up, letting the king and his defeated army slip away.

Cromwell had a massive row with Montagu, accusing him of not being fully committed to the war – and, possibly, Manchester *wasn't*. This was the worst kind of conflict: families against families, brothers against brothers. It was hard for people to say definitively that they were *completely* against the king and wanted nothing more than to grind him into the dirt. Cromwell was different. He was fired up with reformist, Puritan zeal and, as far as he was concerned, Manchester was a useless toff. In return, Manchester accused Cromwell of recruiting men of low birth as officers into the army, to which Cromwell replied: 'If you choose godly, honest men to be captains of horse, honest men will follow them. I would rather have a plain russet coated captain that knows what he fights for and loves what he knows, than that which you call a gentleman and is nothing else.'

Cromwell had that familiar, man-of-the-people, middle-England distrust of the fancy 'elite', who always betrayed them. Impatient, he pushed through a new law called the 'Self Denying Ordinance' of 1645, which forced members of parliament to choose between either staying in government or serving in the army. Parliamentarians could no longer do both and had to make their choice. Cromwell was hoping to flush out untrustworthy aristocrats from his army and ensure it was led by men who genuinely wanted the defeat of the king. All the lords chose to give up their positions in the army. One man didn't have to choose, however: Oliver Cromwell. He was allowed to stay in both parliament and the army because the 'Roundheads' had realised that he was the man who was going to win the war for them and hold parliament together.

He set about remodelling the army. Up to this point, it been made up of militias, who were only expected to fight in their local area, which made it very hard to move large armies around the country. Cromwell changed all that and built a national army, properly trained, uniformed (in red, as it was the cheapest dye), sheltered, fed and expected to go and fight wherever they were needed. This was the

New Modelled Army (it was a while before it became known as the New Model Army).

This professional, well-run fighting force made a huge difference at the Battle of Naseby in 1645, when The New Modelled Army smashed the Royalists in what proved to be the last major battle of the First English Civil War. The Royalists lost their artillery, their equipment, their stores, all of Charles's personal baggage, and his private papers. Among his documents were letters that revealed he was planning to hire foreign mercenaries and build an alliance with Irish Catholics and bring them into the war on his side. Parliament seized on this and published a pamphlet, 'The King's Cabinet Opened', which exposed Charles's secret plans and massively undermined his cause.*

After Naseby, the Royalists were pretty much beaten. While mopping up the dregs, Cromwell laid siege to a Catholic fortress known as Basing House where he was accused of killing a quarter of the 400 men who surrendered to him – which didn't endear him to his enemies. When the Scots entered the war on Cromwell's side, Charles knew it was all over and surrendered to them, vainly hoping he might persuade them to switch allegiances. As we've seen, they sold him to Cromwell instead.

Charles tried to negotiate with parliament, but Cromwell fell into one of his depressions and was out of action for a month. When he returned, he found parliament in disarray. Many different factions were vying for control of the country and the military. One of the knock-on effects of creating a national standing army was that it had become a powerful force in its own right (which was exactly why England had resisted having one before) and the generals were ominously influential in parliament.

Revolutionary England had very similar problems to Galilee in *Monty Python's Life of Brian* with its bewildering number of variants of the Judean People's Front.† You had the Presbyterians, the

---

* Before now, it would have been difficult for ordinary people to know what was going on in a war being fought all around the country. But this was the first 'media war', in which newspapers were widely available and people were literate enough to read them, so information was getting out there.

† Including the Popular Front of Judea, which only had one member.

Episcopalians, the Quakers, the Baptists, the Anabaptists, the separatist Brownists (most of the Puritans on the *Mayflower* were followers of Robert Brown, aka 'Brownists'), rivals to the Brownists called the Barrowists (followers of Henry Barrow) ... Quite a lot of these Puritan sects, like the Fifth Monarchists, were Millennialists, waiting for the rapture, which they believed was imminent. The conditions for the second coming of Christ appeared to be just as they were prophesised in the Book of Daniel, including Cromwell's victory.

Cromwell himself got caught up in this millennialist fervour and, when he allowed the Jews back into England later on, in 1656, it was partly because he'd observed how useful they'd been to the booming Dutch economy, but also to try to fulfil the part of the prophecies that said the Jews needed to be converted to Christianity.

Alongside the religious extremists, there were new radical political factions, the most famous being the Levellers who'd begun life as a protest group opposing enclosures and had gone around tearing down (levelling) the fences and hedges that landowners were putting up. And there was an even more radical faction called the Diggers, who thought the Levellers weren't going far enough (the Diggers had got their name by farming on common land). The more radical elements were pushing for the complete deposition of Charles and giving the vote to ordinary men and ... I was about to say 'women' but, of course, it was just men.

To complicate things further, there was still a significant pro-Royalist faction. And all of these groups were fighting each other, so nobody could agree on what to do with the king. Most members of parliament wanted to disband the New Model Army and pay off the Scots to get them out of northern England. But the army had become radicalised by Puritan and egalitarian elements and wanted recognition for the part it had played in deposing the monarch. The soldiers were also owed backpay and, as Cromwell was as slow to pay as past monarchs, they were loath to disband as it would reduce their bargaining power.

Now it was Cromwell's turn to be stuck in the middle of warring factions and, in the midst of all the bickering, King Charles managed to escape. He was quickly recaptured, but this was enough encouragement for the Royalists, supported by the Scots – who were furious with the way that their king was being treated by Cromwell and had made a deal with Charles to establish Presbyterianism in England – to rise up again. So a Second Civil War kicked off in 1648.

The New Model Army went in hard. The Scots were decisively defeated at the Battle of Preston where Cromwell was the supreme commander of the army for the first time. After the battle, he started firing off heavily religious letters full of Bible quotes and claims that he was doing God's work. He seems to have become more driven by faith than by political ideals. He demanded that Puritan military commanders, known as Grandees, were given more power. Parliament, fearing a military takeover, demurred; their fears came true when Cromwell sent Colonel Thomas Pride into the Palace of Westminster to forcibly remove anybody in the government who didn't support the Grandees.

This military coup left only a tiny number of members sitting, who became known as the Rump Parliament. Cromwell forced them to agree that Charles should be tried for treason and the king was executed on 30 January 1649, at which point a republic was declared and the Commonwealth of England was created.

Cromwell couldn't rest, though. First, he put down two Leveller mutinies within the English army, executed the leaders and then set sail for Ireland where Royalist supporters were trying to recruit the locals. *Cromwell's killed the king. They'll come for you next. They're rabid Puritans. They hate Catholics. They hate the Irish.*

The Royalists were correct. Cromwell had never forgiven the Irish for massacres they'd committed when they rose against the English in an uprising of 1641 and, filled with protestant zeal, his campaign was brutal and ruthless. When he captured Drogheda after a bitter siege in 1649, his troops killed more than 3,000 people. Many of them were Royalist soldiers and many of them were townsmen carrying arms, but civilians were massacred as well.

Cromwell was undaunted. He had God on his side after all: 'I am persuaded that this is a righteous judgement of God upon these barbarous wretches.' A similar thing happened when Cromwell's soldiers sacked Wexford. Perhaps 1,500 civilians were killed and much of the town was burned to the ground. Cromwell has never been forgiven for his actions in Ireland. He'd behaved pretty ruthlessly in England, and in Scotland too, but, fired by his religious certainties, he went much further in Ireland. He also stepped up the process of colonisation, confiscating land and giving it to Protestant settlers. There were mass evictions and killings, with more than 50,000 men, women and children deported to the West Indies as indentured servants, one step away from being slaves.

Cromwell left Ireland in 1650 because Charles I's son had tipped up in Scotland where he'd been declared King Charles II by the Scottish parliament. Cromwell smashed a Scottish army at the Battle of Dunbar, and grandiloquently gave thanks to God, but when he tried to pursue the war in Scotland, he got bogged down and Charles II took a small force south into England. Cromwell came rampaging down after him and destroyed his army at the Battle of Worcester, after which Charles only just escaped back to the continent where he stayed for the next nine years.

When Cromwell returned to London, he found that the Rump Parliament was still sitting, on its rump, doing bugger all. He tolerated them for another 18 months before he lost it and stormed into parliament with 40 musketeers (just as Charles I had done 10 years earlier), commanded the speaker to leave the chair and accused members of parliament of being prostitutes with no more religion than his horse, and who had sat too long without doing any good. 'Depart, I say, and let us have done with you. In the name of God, go!'

He then grabbed the ceremonial mace – 'that shining bauble there' – the symbol of parliament's power and threw it to the floor, demanding that it be taken away before clearing the chamber, locking the doors and storming off to brood in Whitehall. Unlike Charles I, Cromwell got away with abusing parliament and cobbled together a new parliament who gratefully made him Lord Protector for life. The powers that be, even though they'd got rid of the monarchy, still liked the idea of having a strong man in charge.

Cromwell turned down offers to become king, although he very much ruled in the style of a monarch, and Puritans all around the country raised a glass and toasted 'His Highness'. 'No, no!' I hear you cry. 'The Puritans banned drinking.' Actually, even though they banned

CROMWELL HURLS HIS MACE TO THE FLOOR

almost everything else that was fun – singing, dancing, sport, maypoles, parties, feast days, Christmas, adultery (now punishable by death) – they didn't ban drinking. The Puritan ethos is that if it's not in the Bible, it's not Christian. So, no pope in the Bible, no transubstantiation, no Catholic rituals, but there *is* booze. Christ turned water into wine, after all. (Best to avoid public drunkenness, though; the Puritans came down heavily on that.)

Cromwell attempted various types of government to keep all the factions happy. He tried instituting a parliament of religious leaders (the Parliament of Saints), but they voted to dissolve themselves in case they got too tyrannical. He tried putting the army in charge, but that lasted less than two years. Despite all of this disruption, England was doing well enough economically for parliament to declare war on both England's traditional allies, the Dutch and the Spanish. The first Anglo–Dutch War and the Anglo–Spanish War were essentially fought over commerce and trade, and spread all round the world, reaching as far as the Persian Gulf and the Americas, where the English seized Jamaica from the Spanish. Apart from a few land grabs, though, the wars would eventually come to nothing for the British.

Cromwell was still trying to figure out how to make this new system work when he suddenly became quite ill in 1658. It was probably a combination of malaria and some kind of kidney disease, and it was soon obvious that he was on the way out. Despite the fact that he wasn't a king and had got rid of dynastic rule, he decided that his son Richard should take over as Lord Protector on his death.

Richard Cromwell fell out with everybody and didn't last very long in the job he'd never asked for. Parliament didn't like him, the nobility didn't like him, the army didn't like him, the people didn't like him … But I quite like 'Tumbledown Dick'. This book is a bloody parade of ambitious and ruthless people fighting, killing, betraying, marrying, usurping and generally doing anything they could to get on the throne. Richard is just about the only man who didn't want it. He stepped away from it and escaped the infighting, the back biting and the intrigue, going off to live a very simple life, first in France and then in Hertfordshire until he was almost 90. When visitors came to his house, he'd show them souvenirs and tell them how he used to be Lord

Protector – and how he was better off out of it. Until Queen Elizabeth II, he was our longest-lived head of state.

So what happened after Richard stepped down? Who was now in charge? There was never any suggestion that the country could simply be ruled by parliament, perhaps because none of the members of parliament could ever agree on anything. In the end, George Monck, commander of the Scottish army, marched on London, restored parliament and forced everyone to agree at gunpoint to restore the monarchy, telling them that the only way to avoid another civil war and stop the country falling back into chaos was to invite Charles II back to England.

So England's brief flirtation with rebellion and the abolition of the monarchy was over. And everyone decided the best thing to do was to forget it ever happened and carry on as normal. It had been useful to let off steam and, if the Interregnum hadn't happened, England might have exploded much more violently later on down the line and had a full-fat French-style revolution.

Cromwell had been buried in Westminster Abbey in 1658, but when Charles II took the throne, he had his body dug up and hung in irons before being taken down, beheaded and reburied under Tyburn gallows.* His head was stuck on a pike and displayed outside Westminster for about 25 years until the pike broke and the thing fell down. A guard on duty stuffed the head up his coat and took it home.

It passed through several hands over the years. At one point, three brothers displayed it as a sort of Madame Tussaud's exhibit (except this was the *actual* head, not a waxwork). They went bust and apparently died under mysterious circumstances, leading to a myth that the head was cursed. Eventually, it ended up back at his old college in Cambridge, where it was finally laid to rest and buried in a secret location.

And so we move on from the dour Oliver Cromwell, dressed in black, warts and all, to Charles II with his frippery, foppery, finery and fornication, his elaborate wigs, his pencil moustache and his 14 mistresses.

---

* There's a macabre symmetry in this. Charles's head was stitched back on after his execution; Cromwell's was cut off after his death.

27

CHARLIE (#2)

CHARLES II – 1630–1685

The Merry Monarch
Reigned 1660–1685
Lived for 54 years. Reigned for 25 years.
Died from kidney failure.
Remembered for: hiding in a tree, the Restoration
and Nell Gwyn.

The rhyme could so easily have stopped at the first Charlie and, by now, our monarchs would probably have all been long forgotten as some weird anomaly of The Olden Days, like scrofula, Blemmyes, cod pieces and burning witches. But Oliver Cromwell never worked out a viable alternative, so, when General George Monck, the military governor of Scotland, marched down to London and said it was time to restore the monarchy, nobody argued with him.

When Charles II came to the throne, he was smart enough to know he couldn't act in the same high-handed way as his father and antagonise parliament. He accepted checks and restrictions on his powers and wanted an easy time. He's often accused of being lazy and careless, more interested in his women than in governing. It used to appall his counsellors that he would cancel meetings for an afternoon enjoying himself with one of his mistresses.

When he came to the throne, he lifted the Puritan military boot off the country's neck and it sprang back into life. There was a flowering of science, art, music, theatre and literature. England became an all–singing, all-dancing, all-fornicating society. This can perhaps best be exemplified by the new style of 'restoration comedy'. The theatres had been closed for 18 years under the Puritans and there was a hunger for entertainment. People wanted to laugh at authority. Writers like

William Wycherley, John Dryden, John Vanbrugh, and England's first female playwright, Aphra Behn, fed the public's appetite for scurrilous, bawdy, satirical plays that poked fun at the high and mighty. Charles also wanted to be entertained. He loved the theatre and allowed female actors on stage for the first time. In fact, he insisted on it. The theatre was a good place to ogle young women and, in the king's case, have sex with them after the show.

One of the stock characters of restoration comedy was the rake, a free-and-easy, witty, drunken, womanising gentleman. There was a 'Merry Gang' of rakes at court that included Charles himself, along with John Wilmot, George Villiers (son of the other George Villiers) and Charles Sackville. I suppose they were a bit like the infamous Bullingdon Club. They liked to drink, gamble, act inappropriately, make lewd jokes, drop their trousers, damage property, roar and fight. There was a famous incident when Sackville and another rake, Charles Sedley, preached a sermon to a crowd of onlookers from the balcony of a boozer in Covent Garden (the appropriately named Cock Tavern), stark naked and pretending to roger each other.

Charles's reign, however, wasn't all fun and games. He had to deal with an economic depression, the Great Plague, the Great Fire of London, war with the Dutch and the expansion of the British Empire fuelled by the burgeoning slave trade. And it all ended with another succession crisis. The final years of his life were also tarnished by disputes with his government – and he did exactly what his father, and Oliver Cromwell, had done before him: he shut parliament down.

Charles was tall for the time, a little more than six foot, and was considered to be rather handsome, in a dark-complexioned, Mediterranean way, with the pencil moustache of a comic-book gangster. Popular and affable, he tried not to impose rules on how people behaved and worshipped. He was probably more Catholic than Protestant in his own beliefs, but he very wisely kept it to himself.

One of his childhood tutors was William Harvey, the physician and scientist best known for describing the circulation of blood. Science was blossoming and new discoveries were being made every day about how we work and how the universe we live in works. Charles was fascinated by science and scientific equipment. He stuffed his bedroom full of clocks and was one of the founders of the Royal Society. He also loved telescopes and had his own one made. It was some 35 foot long and Charles liked nothing better than getting his posh mates round and showing them astronomical wonders like the rings of Saturn. He commissioned the building of the Greenwich Observatory on a site chosen by Christopher Wren, who was just one of the many clever people Charles encouraged in this post-Catholic time of intellectual exploration. Others included the chemist Robert Boyle, who studied the nature of air, and the biologist Robert Hooke, who built his own microscope and discovered microorganisms.

There's not a lot to say about Charles's childhood, except that it was inevitably dominated by his father's relationship with parliament and the civil war that started while he was still a boy. His father was a family man who loved his wife and children, and he tried to keep Charles and his younger brother James alongside him when war broke out. When Prince Charles was old enough, he was nominally given charge of the Royalist army in the west. When the war became deadly serious, however, the king urged his son to get to safety in France. The 16-year-old prince refused. He wanted to stay and fight, but his army was steadily driven westwards, right down into Cornwall, at which point he thought *Sod this for a game of soldiers* and hopped in a boat. He eventually ended up in Paris with his mother and James. They were all still out of the country when the king was beheaded three years later, sending shock waves through Europe, not least in Scotland.

The radical Presbyterian Kirk Party was now in control of Scotland. The Scots had never been able to make their minds up about whether to support the Royalists or the Parliamentarians. The Kirk, however, didn't think that Cromwell was doing Protestantism properly and feared his army would become too powerful, so now they fixed on the exiled Prince Charles. He was essentially Scottish, and if they could get him to support their religious and political agenda, they would all be winners. So they brought him over from the continent. At first, Charles rejected the Kirk's extremist demands, but in the end realised that, if this was his only hope of getting onto the throne, he would have to at least pretend to accept their demands. So it was that, on New Year's Day 1651, Charles was crowned at Scone in Scotland and became, at least as far as the Scots were concerned, King Charles II. Cromwell had other ideas, taking a break from committing atrocities in Ireland to rush over to attack the Scots. 'King Charles II' saw an opening and took a separate Royalist Scottish army down into England. He got as far as Worcester virtually unopposed, hoping to gain popular support and spark an uprising. But the English didn't like the Scots and didn't really know Charles, who they suspected of being a Frenchified Catholic. Cromwell followed Charles down from Scotland and the Battle of Worcester in 1651 was the last major conflict of the English Civil Wars.

Charles's subsequent escape from England has become part of colourful, schoolboy history. At least it was when 'Colourful Schoolboy History' was still taught. It was the most exciting part of Charles's whole life. In later years, he would bore people to tears telling them about his exploits when he was on the run. Helped by secret supporters, who disguised him as a peasant and taught him how to act like one, the somewhat conspicuous six-foot-tall royal prince zigzagged his way down through England, evading Cromwell's troops. At one point, he famously hid in an oak tree, which became dubbed the Royal Oak (this is why we have so many pubs called that today). He was on the run for six weeks, at last crossing to Normandy from Shoreham in Sussex, and it looked like that was it, the end of the royal cause.

Charles, who was now in his twenties, did what most modern young men do: he moved in with his mother, who was living in the Louvre, which at the time was still a royal palace. The family weren't exactly living the high life, though, as they were completely broke and reliant on the charity of the French king and occasional small donations from supporters in England.

Charles amused himself by having affairs with as many women as he could from the community of English aristocratic expats in Europe, who, like him, weren't welcome in England. He'd fathered his first child in Rotterdam, a son called James, in 1649, before his ill-fated attempt to retake the throne, and didn't stop there. He had at least three children in exile, all with different women. A charming rogue or a serial, womanising abuser? Take your pick. He did at least support his illegitimate children, ennobling some of them, and was never ashamed of them.

CHARLES II   HIDING IN THE OAK TREE

His lack of money was a big problem, though, and he tried everything to raise funds and gather support for his cause. European monarchs were appalled by what had happened in England and feared that it would set a precedent, but the age-old rivalries between them made it difficult for Charles to pick a reliable patron without antagonising all the others. As well as the French, he sought help from the Germans, the Spanish and the pope, before finally trying the Dutch, who'd been at war with Cromwell.

And then Cromwell snuffed it and, when his son Richard became Lord Protector, everything changed. The unstable coalition in England between the army, the moderate Protestants and the hard-line Puritans that had been held together by the force of Cromwell's will began to crumble and, in the end, George Knox brought the republican experiment to an end.

The great Samuel Pepys, who kept an extraordinary record of life at court and at home in Restoration England, began writing his diary in January 1660.* On 23 May, he recounts how King Charles, set sail from Holland with a small flotilla and regaled everyone on board with stories of his great escape. Charles had many supporters with him on his flagship, the newly rechristened *Royal Charles*, including his brother, James.

Once he was crowned, at an extremely opulent, expensive and wine-fuelled ceremony, Charles tried to draw a line under the political upheavals that had gripped the country. He announced that he had no plans to arrest any of the people who'd been in charge during the Interregnum and even invited many of them back into government. He was, however, determined to punish all of the men who had ordered his father's beheading and relentlessly tracked them down.

Charles had spent nine years in exile, much of it in Paris, and he'd been very impressed by the court of the awesome Sun King, Louis XIV, who ruled as an absolute monarch. Charles had fallen in love with everything French: the style, the manners, the art, the scientific

---

* Pepys was a politician who became the chief secretary to the Admiralty. He had a large group of influential friends, regularly visited the theatre and had a very active sex life – with his wife and various mistresses – so his diaries have something for everyone.

advances … it was all so *civilised*. He started to style his own court in similar fashion, which caused suspicion. Was Charles too Francophile? Might he be a secret Catholic? Dealing with all this would preoccupy his reign, but he just about got away with it.

One of the first big decisions he had to make was which European princess to marry. He chose Catherine of Braganza, daughter of the Portuguese king, John IV. After 60 years of rule by the Spanish, Portugal had recently regained its independence and was becoming an important world player through its empire-building in the Americas and the Far East. The Portuguese would be a good counter to the Spanish, and Catherine came with a substantial dowry that included Tangier in north Africa, trading privileges in Brazil and the East Indies, and Bombay (now Mumbai) in India. It turned out to be very expensive to administer all these places, however, so Charles sold the islands of Bombay to a trading corporation, the East India Company.

The Company, which was run from a small office in London, had been founded in 1600 with the aim of exploiting the wealth and vast natural resources of the Indian subcontinent. As it grew richer and more powerful, it started to take control of India and became the largest corporation in the world, with one of the most extensive armies in the world, numbering more than a quarter of a million soldiers, twice the size of the British Army. It's extraordinary to think that, by selling these insignificant islands to the Company, Charles accelerated a process that would lead to the eventual founding of the British Raj, the most significant part of the British Empire.

Charles sold off pretty much all of the overseas territories he'd got from Catherine of Braganza's dowry. Tangier was abandoned and a large area in North America was handed to a similar corporation to the East India Company, the Hudson's Bay Company.

Inevitably, British imperial interests rubbed up against those of the Dutch, not only in Europe but also in the Americas. This made things tricky for Charles because his sister, Mary, had married the latest prince of Orange, William. Soon the two countries were at war again. It started well for the English. Charles's brother, James, was in charge of the navy and had a spectacular victory at the Battle of Lowestoft in the North Sea, but the Dutch retaliated by sailing up the Thames

Estuary and into the River Medway where the British fleet was anchored at Chatham and Gillingham. The incident became known as 'The Raid on the Medway', perhaps in an effort to underplay what happened. 'Oh, don't worry about it. It was just a little raid. It wasn't *that* important.' In fact, this was one of the worst naval defeats the British have ever suffered. The whole fleet was sunk, apart from the flagship, the *Royal Charles*, which the Dutch captured and symbolically sailed back to the Netherlands as a prize.

This was a massive loss to Charles and he was left with no option but to sue for peace and bring the costly war to an end. Not before triggering a serious economic depression, however, which wasn't helped by an outbreak of the plague in London in 1665. Many of the wealthiest Londoners were able to escape the city, including Charles, and the plague ran its course within a year, but thousands died and, to compound the king's woes, the following year a fire started in a bakery in Pudding Lane that burned down most of the City of London, and about a third of the city as a whole.

The city had been packed with decrepit, timber-framed buildings, many dating back to the Middle Ages, so a catastrophic fire was going to happen sooner or later. It was useful to clear it all out and make space for a new London. The original St Paul's Cathedral was one of the iconic buildings that went up in flames, but Christopher Wren's classical replacement is one of the wonders of British architecture.

The fire was also an opportunity for Charles and James to play the hero as they conspicuously led the firefighting effort. Soon afterwards, a conspiracy theory emerged that the fire had been started by the Catholics. Like all conspiracy theories, it wasn't true and played on the belief that everything that happens must be caused by some malevolent human agency. That the theory took hold is an indicator of the uneasy, distrustful atmosphere in the country. The situation wasn't helped by an odious charlatan called Titus Oates, a conman who weaseled and lied his way into a position of huge influence by pretending to be far better qualified than he was. He claimed to have uncovered a popish plot to assassinate the king and he named names. There was a wave of arrests and many innocent men and women were executed on zero evidence. Oates was a populist disrupter, good at whipping up the ordinary people of England into a fury and getting them on his side by blowing the rusty old dog whistle. *It's all the fault of nasty outsiders who are trying to undermine the good, stout, Anglican folk of England.*

Charles considered it all as poppycock, but in the 1660s parliament forced through a series of measures known as the Clarendon Code that clamped down on nonconformists and any 'extremist' religious group (i.e. non-Anglican) and prescribed what they were and weren't allowed to do, and what their priests and preachers were and weren't allowed to say. (The later Test Act of 1773 was to focus more on Catholics and excluded them from holding many important posts.)

By 1673 Charles had been married to Catherine of Braganza for 11 years, and while he'd been having children left right and centre with his mistresses, his wife was yet to deliver an heir to the throne. His most famous mistress was Nell Gwyn, who'd started out as an orange seller before becoming an actress, then a royal mistress and all-round celebrity. She was tough and witty, a very funny actress, and became the embodiment of restoration society. She also had two sons by the king, proving yet again that it wasn't Charles who was infertile. He didn't do a Henry VIII, however, and stuck with Catherine, accepting that the crown would pass to his brother, James.

Unfortunately, though, James came out as a Catholic. An 'Exclusion Bill' was proposed in 1679 to keep him off the throne, which enraged Charles, split the government down the middle and led to years of argument. The unforeseen consequence of this was the birth of a two-party system in the English parliament.

The two factions were loosely based along Civil War allegiances. The 'Cavalier' faction was made up of wealthy, traditionalist, high-church Anglicans, with a slight Catholic bent. Opposing them was the more liberal, forward-looking Protestant faction, who didn't want any return to the old ways and supported a constitutional, rather than an absolute, monarch. They derisively nicknamed the conservatives 'Tories' from an Irish word, *toraí*, a generic term for an Irish brigand or an outlaw that had been used to smear anti-Parliamentarian Catholic and Royalist guerrillas in Ireland. Titus Oates had introduced the word to England when he used it to describe the plotters against the king. The 'Tories' retaliated by coining a similar insult for their liberal opponents, calling them Whigs. Whig derives from the word *Whiggamore*, a derisive term for Scottish horse thieves that was applied to the radical Presbyterian hard-liners who opposed the king. Over the years, both the Tories and the Whigs owned their insulting nicknames and kept them when the two factions solidified into actual political parties – the Conservatives and the Liberals.

The succession crisis inevitably led to trouble. In 1683, a group of extremist Whigs plotted to assassinate Charles and James on their way back from Newmarket races. The brothers were due to pass Rye House, where the conspirators planned to lay in wait for them. But a fire broke out in Newmarket, so Charles and James went home a day early and completely missed their appointment with death.

This sort of thing might have gone on for years, but in 1685, Charles fell ill. Instantly there were rumours that he'd been poisoned – 'Oh, it's the Catholics again … Or perhaps James wants to get onto the throne more swiftly …'. The root of Charles's illness was some kind of kidney problem, caused by his unhealthy lifestyle and overindulgence of the booze. There were many scientific advances during his reign, but the practice of medicine was still pretty medieval. Physicians spouted mumbo jumbo and superstition, and, for the most part, didn't have a clue what they were doing. The cures that Charles's doctors used on him included bloodletting and deliberate blistering of the skin – evidence that the illness and 'bad humours' were being drawn out. These deluded physicians might do very well in today's 'wellness' culture – obsessed as it is with purging 'toxins' from the body – but the sad fact is that they basically tortured the king to death and he had an utterly miserable end, wasting away in great pain. Towards the end, he got a Catholic priest to secretly take his confession and called his brother to his bedside and famously said to him, 'Let not poor Nelly starve …'

Charles was, in many ways, a decent fellow – unless you were married to him. His wife probably thought he was a bit of a tosser. He didn't really do a great deal during his reign, except hold things together and bring back a sense of fun, a joy in life, believing that we're not put on this earth to suffer, so let's try and enjoy it while we're here.

And, for me, that's achievement enough.

28

James Again

JAMES II (AND VII) – 1633–1701
James the Shite
Reigned 1685–1688
Lived for 68 years. Reigned for three years.
Died from syphilis (possibly).
Remembered for: being forced to abdicate for being too Catholic.

'New York, New York/So good they named it twice', according to the song, but the man whom the city was named after, King James II – who was Duke of York from birth – was so terrible, they named him simply James the Shite, and he lasted only three years on the throne. He did live on after he was deposed, however, dying when he was 68, making him one of our longer-lived monarchs.

As a prince who was never expected to take the throne, James's early life isn't as well recorded as big brother Charles's. He was a classic duke of York, the second son, the 'spare' who cocks everything up. He didn't have a particularly rigorous education, but at the age of three, he was appointed lord high admiral, an honorary position at first, but, after the Restoration, he did properly take charge of the navy.

James was with his father and brother at the Battle of Edgehill when he was only 11 years old. He and Charles came close to being captured by the Parliamentarian forces and the incident was portrayed in romantic accounts of the war as two brave young princes hiding out on the battlefield, trying not to be captured by Cromwell's rough, tough soldiers.

While Prince Charles was commanding the army in the west, James stayed with his father in Oxford, where he attended the university (while still rather young). In 1646, Oxford surrendered to the Parliamentarians and James was captured. He was taken to London where his servants were dismissed. As one commentator put it, everyone had to go, 'not so much as excepting a dwarf whom his Royal Highness was desirous to have retain'd with him'.

He was placed in the guardianship of the Earl of Northumberland at St James's Palace. As the king was still on the loose in the north, and Prince Charles had fled to France, parliament thought about making the 15-year-old James a puppet king. Fearing the worst, Charles I got word to the boy via a friend, Colonel Joseph Banfield, that he should escape. So, one day, while James was pretending to play hide and seek in the palace gardens with his younger brother and sister, he slipped out of the grounds into St James's Park, where Colonel Banfield was waiting for him. Banfield smuggled him away, disguised as a girl, down the Thames to the docks at Tilbury from where a waiting boat took the prince to Holland.

James was to spend a third of his life in exile – first as a young man during the Civil War, and later after he was deposed. In Holland, he met up with his big sister, Mary, who'd married Prince William of Orange, ruler of the Dutch Republic. James stayed with them for a while and got very excited when some ships in the Parliamentarian navy went over to the Royalist side and sailed for Holland. He was still head of the Admiralty and was looking forward to taking command, but his brother Charles put their dashing cousin, Prince Rupert of the Rhine, in charge. This was a sensible move: James was still only 15 and had no naval experience. As it turned out, the fleet was too small to have any impact anyway.

In 1649, James spent a month at a Benedictine monastery in France where he became drawn to the religious life. He then met up with his mother and elder brother, Charles, in Paris, where he learned that his father had been beheaded.

What happened next was a sort of royal soap opera, or perhaps sitcom, as James, Charles and their mother, Henrietta Maria, were holed up together in Paris, almost destitute and at each other's throats, arguing about what to do with their lives. To keep himself occupied, James first joined the French army, and then the Spanish army (when Charles got fed up with Louis XIV for not supporting the family and switched his allegiance to the king of Spain). James enjoyed his time as an officer, proving himself to be a pretty good soldier, and was about to accept the post of high admiral of the Spanish navy when Oliver Cromwell died – which meant he could finally become lord high admiral of the English navy, when his brother, Charles, took the throne two years later.

James wasn't expecting to become king, so figured he could behave however he liked. It turns out he was an even worse serial shagger than his brother. Pepys described him as 'the most unguarded ogler of his time' – although this does seem to have been his only vice. He was a regular racegoer but didn't gamble. Neither did he drink very much, and, as he got older, he became more and more ascetic, particularly after he embraced Catholicism. He even took to wearing a hair shirt and a spiked necklace to do penance for his sins.

Charles's chief minister was a man called Edward Hyde, whose daughter Anne was a famous beauty. She and James had an affair, and when she became pregnant, he agreed to marry her. The public was appalled, not that he'd got her pregnant, but that he'd married a commoner. People wanted a nice, posh Disney wedding with a foreign princess. Even Anne's father tried to stop the marriage.

But James went ahead with the wedding and his first child, Charles, was born less than two months later. The baby sadly died in infancy, as did another five children. Only two daughters survived – Mary and Anne – both of whom would go on to become queens of England.

Samuel Pepys wrote that James was very fond of his children (not a given in royal households) and lived like an ordinary family man. Dammit, he even showed affection to his wife in public, which was just not done. However, being in love with Anne didn't stop him sleeping around. When he wasn't chasing women, James was chasing foxes two or three times a week and had extensive buildings to house his horses and hounds.

He may have become almost a hermit in his later life, turning his back on the pleasures of the world, but he and Anne enjoyed a recklessly lavish lifestyle. She'd been in exile in France at the same time as James, and they'd both experienced what it was like trying to get by without any money. They now seemed hell-bent on spending as much as they could. And James enjoyed the status, prestige and perks that came with being both lord high admiral of the navy and the Duke of York.

In 1664, in a bloodless raid, a British fleet captured the Dutch settlement of New Amsterdam on Manhattan Island in the Hudson River. They renamed the town New York in honour of James and he became the first ruler of the colony. He was also granted colonial rights on the northeast American mainland, which was renamed New England.

Provocations like this were one of the factors that led to the Second Anglo–Dutch War; another major factor was a struggle for control over the lucrative slave trade. The Dutch had built fortified ports in west Africa, where they'd established martial law to control the trade, and the British were trying to muscle in on it. They established the Royal African Company who joined with the navy to attack the Dutch outposts and take them over. The Royal African Company shipped more African men, women and children to the Americas than any other single institution during the entire period of the transatlantic slave trade. And many of these slaves were branded with the letters 'DY' for Duke of York, as James had been made the proud governor of the Company.

James was riding high and his naval reputation went up a few more notches when he commanded the British fleet that defeated the Dutch at the Battle of Lowestoft, but Charles removed James from active service in the navy on safety grounds, so he wasn't involved in the debacle of the Dutch raid on the Medway soon after. He managed to lay the blame at the feet of Edward Hyde, who was now lord chancellor, which suited James, who was not on good terms with his father-in-law.

Nobody's quite sure exactly when James converted to Catholicism because he kept it secret for a long while. He survived a severe illness in 1670, which is often a trigger for people to convert. He was also disgusted by the divisions among Protestants and the explosion of different sects: Presbyterians, Baptists, Anabaptists, Anglicans, Puritans, Levellers, Diggers, Millenarians ... It looked to him that people couldn't decide on the right way to be a Protestant. At least there was only one way to be a Catholic. James was quite a dull man, and was perhaps a little dull-witted as well. He didn't like complexity.

He liked things to be straightforward. His memoirs consisted of tedious lists and facts; nothing personal comes through.

By the mid-1670s, James was fully out as a Catholic and rather reluctantly allowed King Charles to arrange for his daughter, Mary, to marry the Protestant prince, William III of Orange – not to be confused with his *sister* Mary, who had married the previous William of Orange.

The family tree overleaf might help.

This was one of those incestuous royal marriages. As you can see, William III, Duke of Orange, was simultaneously James's nephew and his son-in-law, making William and Mary first cousins. It was a terrible time for James to announce that he was a Catholic. Charles II had to dissolve parliament three times in an effort to stop it bringing in anti-Catholic laws and this was exacerbated by the fact that even though Charles had enough illegitimate children to start his own football team, he hadn't managed to produce any legitimate ones. So James was heir to the throne and, if he had a son, he would be the next heir.

James was becoming ever more unloved by the public, but after he narrowly avoided assassination in the Rye House Plot, his popularity soared (which always happens after failed assassinations attempts). It swiftly plummeted again and, when Charles died young in 1685, James found himself on the throne. Coronations are another good way of improving the royal family's ratings. There was cheering in the streets on the big day, but it was thought to be a bad omen when the crown slipped as it was being lowered onto James's head.

Soon after the coronation, there were two dangerous rebellions – one in Scotland, led by anti-Catholics, which was quickly put down, and another in the West Country, led by James Scott, Duke of Monmouth. Monmouth was the eldest son of Charles II, the illegitimate one who'd been born in Paris. He was a popular figure, just not quite as popular as he thought. Lacking the support he'd anticipated, his small army was defeated at the Battle of Sedgemoor and he was taken to London. Despite begging for mercy, poor, illegitimate James was beheaded on Tower Hill by the notoriously ham-fisted executioner, Jack Ketch, who tried eight times to chop his head off and had to finish it by sawing though the last part with a knife.

STUART MONARCHS

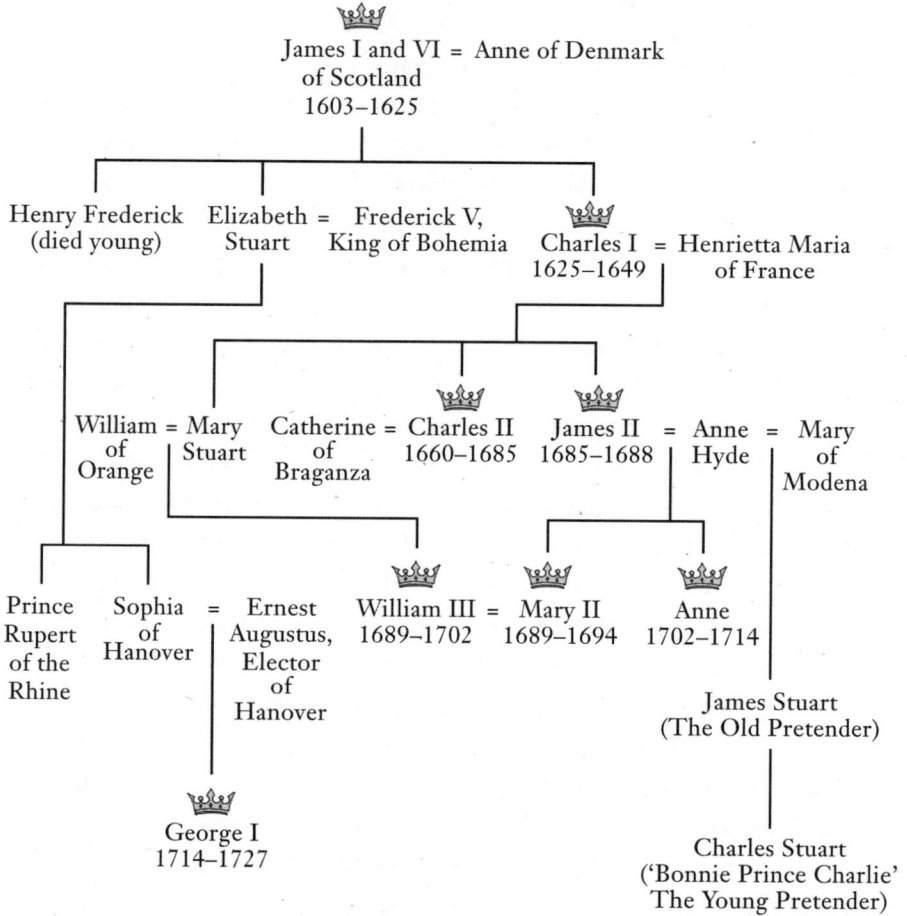

James I and VI = Anne of Denmark
of Scotland
1603–1625

Henry Frederick   Elizabeth = Frederick V,   Charles I = Henrietta Maria
(died young)   Stuart   King of Bohemia   1625–1649   of France

William = Mary   Catherine = Charles II   James II = Anne = Mary
of   Stuart   of   1660–1685   1685–1688 Hyde   of
Orange   Braganza   Modena

Prince   Sophia = Ernest   William III = Mary II   Anne
Rupert   of   Augustus,   1689–1702   1689–1694   1702–1714
of the   Hanover Elector
Rhine   of
                   Hanover   James Stuart
                                                        (The Old Pretender)

George I
1714–1727   Charles Stuart
                                                        ('Bonnie Prince Charlie'
                                                        The Young Pretender)

In response to the Monmouth Rebellion, James sent the infamous Judge George Jeffries to the West Country to preside over a series of trials that became known as the Bloody Assizes. Jeffries, nicknamed the 'Hanging Judge', was ruthless and unforgiving, and the Bloody Assizes didn't go down well with the general public, particularly as people had liked the Duke of Monmouth, just not enough to join his cause in any great numbers.

So, despite having quashed these rebellions, James was not sitting comfortably on the throne. Trying to enlarge the army and make it a permanent standing force didn't help endear him to the nobility either and there were riots in Scotland where the locals thought he was trying to turn them all Catholic. James was actually quite liberal in his views and tried to promote freedom of worship for everyone – including Catholics. He might have had his way and held on to power if he hadn't had a son. His first wife, Anne Hyde, had died and he'd married an Italian noblewoman, Mary of Modena, who was seen as a Catholic interloper. And when they had a boy, James (if only these monarchs wouldn't keep giving their children the same bloody name as themselves), everybody feared this was the birth of a Catholic dynasty.

A conspiracy theory even started doing the rounds that Mary of Modena hadn't been pregnant and the child was some commoner's baby, smuggled into the royal bedchamber in a bed-warming pan.

A group of lords got together and started figuring out if there was a viable alternative to keeping James as king. As I said, he had two daughters, Mary and Anne. Mary didn't have as strong a claim as James's newborn son, James, but because there were laws in place banning Catholics from taking the throne, there were ways round this. People were still averse to the idea of having a queen again, but Mary was married to the Protestant Prince William. What if they ruled jointly?

And so, in 1688, William and Mary were invited to come over to England and take the throne. James was seeing his support fall away and now his own daughter had turned against him. He wanted to resist the invasion, and this could have been the start of another bloody civil war, but when one of his chief generals, John Churchill, turned against

JAMES II FLEES IN A BOAT

him and took a substantial part of his army over to William's side, the king knew the game was up.

James was swiftly deposed without a fight and William and Mary took the throne. This narrowly avoided war became known as the Glorious Revolution, and people have argued about it ever since. Was it glorious? Was it a revolution?

King William didn't want to risk another controversial royal execution, particularly as James had done nothing wrong, apart from being a Catholic, so he allowed James to escape. Stopping only to chuck his royal seal in the Thames in a petty fit of pique, James made his way to France where he regrouped. He decided that his best chance of winning his throne back was to rally support in Catholic Ireland where there was no love for the heavily Protestant monarchy in London and where the people still considered James their king. So James sailed to Ireland and raised an army, but William of Orange wasted no time in leading Anglo–Dutch troops over there himself and comprehensively defeated James at the Battle of the Boyne.*

Instead of staying to fight on, James abandoned his Irish supporters and fled the country, earning him the Gaelic nickname 'Seamus an Chaca' – James the Shite. Back in France, he gave up and lived out his days quietly. Nobody was going to support him again. In 1701, he died of a brain haemorrhage – possibly caused by syphilis. He was still a hero to the Catholics, almost a martyr, so his body was cut into pieces and gifted to different religious institutions. His brain was buried in the Scots College in Paris, his heart in a nunnery at Chaillot, his body in the English Benedictine church in Paris, and the final bit of him was cut off and sent to some Augustinian nuns, who must have been over-joyed when the postman knocked.

'Oh, look, sister Mary. A package has arrived in the post.'

'What is it?'

'Well, it looks like … It looks like the flesh from King James's right arm.'

'Oh, that's nice.'

During the French Revolution, James's tomb in Faubourg was broken up and his body was displayed for a few months as a tourist attraction before being destroyed. But his heart, his entrails, hair cuttings, some linen dipped in his blood and the flesh from his right arm were taken to England as holy relics.

---

* If you don't know your Irish history and have ever wondered what on earth was going on with the marches, and the Orangemen, and the murals of King Billy, it all goes back to this short war. This was the crushing of the Catholics and the return of the heavy boot of English Protestantism, stamping down on the Irish once again.

29
WILLIAM & MARY

WILLIAM III – 1650–1702
William of Orange
Reigned 1689–1702
Lived for 51 years. Reigned for 13 years.
Died from pneumonia.
Remembered for: the Battle of the Boyne and being killed
by the 'little gentleman in the velvet waistcoat'.

MARY II – 1662–1694
Reigned: 1689–1694
Lived for 32 years. Reigned for five years.
Died of smallpox.
Remembered for: the Glorious Revolution and
joint rule with her husband.

So, we've come to our first, and only, joint rulers, William and Mary, who are always presented as a pair rather than as two individual people. As grandchildren of Charles I, they both had a claim to the throne, though their marriage was pretty incestuous. To complicate matters further, they were also the second generation of William and Marys to run the Republic of Holland.

Let's start with Mary. She had a standard, upper-class female education for the time, not heavily intellectual, but with a lot of singing and dancing and playing of the harpsichord, and dominated by some heavy religious indoctrination. A string of Anglican bishops instructed her in the principles of the Church of England and she grew up to have a strong Protestant faith and a dislike of her father's Catholic leanings.

Mary was only 8 when her mother, Anne Hyde, died of breast cancer and she was sent to Richmond to be brought up by a governess,

Lady Frances Villiers. Lady Frances treated Mary as one of her own children and the little girl made good friends with her daughters, particularly Elizabeth. It was while Mary was in Richmond that she became obsessed with an older girl, Frances Apsley, and started sending her floods of (very badly spelled) romantic letters, expressing her love and devotion. This is an extract from a letter she wrote when she was 14:

> *I love you with more zeal then any lover can, I love you with a love that ner was known by man, I have for you excese of friandship more of love than any woman can for woman and more love then ever the constanest love had for his Mrs, you are loved more then can be exprest by your ever obedient wife vere afectionate friand humbel sarvant to kis the ground where one you go to be your dog in a string, your fish in a net your bird in a cage, your humbel trout.* *

Mary's younger sister, the future Queen Anne, joined in this curious romance, writing letters of her own. Anne has been brought to wider attention by the Oscar-winning film *The Favourite*, in which she's unequivocally presented as a lesbian, and there's much discussion about whether Mary also had lesbian tendencies. Or was this just a confused adolescent crush for an older girl? A sort of play acting? Mary didn't know any boys, so perhaps she projected her romantic fantasies onto Frances. At first, Frances went along with the 'game' and wrote back, but she got fed up with the younger girl and, after a while, basically said, 'Mary, I think you need to stop sending me these letters'.

As Mary grew up, she became fond of dancing and even performed in a ballet at court, *Callisto*, or *The Chaste Nymph*. She also enjoyed the typical pursuits of a lady of leisure: she liked to play cards, she liked to do needlework (embroidering all the curtains in the royal bedchambers, for instance) and was very interested in gardening. This wasn't pruning the roses; it was gardening on a grand scale, organising the layout of the grounds at royal palaces. For instance, she worked with

---

* 'Your humble trout' – I must remember that as a term of endearment. 'I am your humble trout, madam.'

Sir Christopher Wren planning the gardens at Hampton Court and Kensington Palace.

Mary was next in line to the throne after her father, so was very valuable to her uncle, King Charles II, as a diplomatic tool. She couldn't be married to members of either the French or the Spanish royal families as they were Catholic.*

The Dutch had historically been Britain's closest allies and most important trading partners, and were, crucially, Protestant, and now, despite having been at war with them (or perhaps to patch up their differences), King Charles announced that his 15-year-old niece was going to marry the 26-year-old William, Prince of Orange. Mary's father, James, hated the idea, but Charles bullied him into accepting the deal.

Mary had met William of Orange before and hadn't taken to him. He was a cold fish. According to her chaplain's diary, when she heard the news that she was betrothed to him, 'she wept all that afternoon and the following night'. In fact, she probably wept for weeks. A girl of her romantic nature would have loved to marry a strapping, golden-haired Prince Charming, but William was not a prepossessing figure. She was tall, at five foot eleven; at only five foot six, he was shorter than her by several inches. He had blackened teeth, a hooked nose, curvature of the spine and terrible asthma that gave him a hunched stance. He was also prone to coughing fits and nose bleeds. Mary's sister Anne called him Caliban (after the monster in Shakespeare's *The Tempest*) and 'that Dutch abortion'. I think you can tell she didn't like him.† He came across as a horrible, rude, little man who made no bones about the fact that the marriage was purely for political ends. The French king, Louis XIV, was a permanent threat to the Dutch republic and William needed British support.

So, who exactly was William? And why was he called Prince of Orange?

---

* There weren't any Spanish princes, anyway. The king of Spain, another Charles II, was ailing and childless, having been done in by the notorious Habsburg inbreeding. The rest of Europe was gearing up for a war over his succession.
† In fact, nobody seems to have liked him much.

It's all a result of one of those peculiar quirks of history. Orange was originally an independent principality based around the city of Orange in Provence, southern France, but, through a complicated (and, I have to admit, quite bewildering) series of wars, marriages and shifting inheritances, the ruling princes of Orange ended up in Holland, running the Dutch Republic. Orange remained an isolated Dutch satellite state until it was annexed by Louis XIV in 1713. To this day, the Dutch royal family is the House of Orange-Nassau.

The ruler of Holland was officially the stadtholder, an elected position, but the title had been passed down by members of William's family for generations. It was the Orange family who had clawed back control of Holland from the Spanish after they'd taken over much of the Netherlands and absorbed it into the Habsburg Empire.

So that was the world William had been born into. His father, the previous William, Prince of Orange, died of smallpox eight days before the boy was born. He didn't have a very happy childhood; his mother, Mary, the eldest daughter of King Charles I, was cold and distant, which is possibly an explanation for William's own chilly demeanour.

Holland was staunchly Protestant and increasingly republican, with many people wanting to get rid of the title of prince of Orange and the influence of the family. The leader of this republican movement was Johan de Witt, who controlled the Dutch parliament and spent the first 22 years of William's life trying to make sure he never took power. He may have succeeded if Louis XIV hadn't invaded the Netherlands in 1672, which became known as the *Rampjaar* – the Disaster Year.

De Witt was a firm believer in appeasement and tried to negotiate with Louis, who ignored him and pushed on with his blitzkrieg. William put himself forward as the man who could save Holland; after all, his family had freed the republic from the Spanish. He took control of the army and quickly became a very popular figure. His early battles didn't go too well, but he managed to get the blame shifted onto the prevaricating de Witt and then decided to flood the dykes. Huge parts of Holland had been reclaimed from the sea by draining water and building great ditches, dykes and dams. By simply opening a few gates, you could flood a huge area and essentially create a vast moat around the centre of Holland. Louis XIV's advance literally got bogged down and ground to a halt. The French started talking about peace and William coined a phrase when he proclaimed that he'd defend his country 'to the last ditch'.

William turned the Dutch against de Witt and, when Orangist supporters attacked him in The Hague, the civic militia shot him and his brother and left their bodies to the mob, who stripped them, mutilated them and strung them up on a public gallows. There were reports that they even cut out their livers, roasted them and ate them.

William claimed he'd had nothing to do with the riot. He might not have given the order, but his bloody fingerprints were all over those mutilated corpses (there are echoes of the storming of the Capitol in Washington in 2021 – although that was without the cannibalism). So now, with William firmly in control, he and King Charles II arranged the marriage to Princess Mary in 1677.

The actual wedding took place at nine in the evening in Mary's bedchamber at St James's Palace in London. Significantly, it wasn't her father, James, who gave her away. It was her uncle, King Charles II. At this time, the royals had what was known as a 'bedding ceremony' as a way of making sure that the wedding was consummated. There were still parts of Europe where the close family and village elders would stand around the bed and watch, but the ceremony by this point in England, and certainly at the royal court, had become a ritual formality. Now it was enough to discreetly draw curtains around the bed and wait for the witnesses to depart. I'm not sure the couple were even expected to start banging the headboard, yelping and moaning.

It was Charles who drew the curtains round Mary and William's bed. It seems he was very nice about the whole thing, and very jolly, but he was making no bones that this was a good political alliance for the family and they'd better start producing heirs. Mary's teenage romantic illusions had been scraped away.

William didn't completely treat his 15-year-old wife with cold indifference. He gave her jewels and an allowance, even if he didn't give her his heart. After the wedding, they planned to move to the Netherlands, but their departure was delayed when Mary's sister,

Anne, came down with smallpox. Neither commoner nor royal was immune; both of William's parents had been killed by the deadly virus. Luckily, Anne survived though and the newly married couple belatedly arrived in Holland to a magnificent reception. Mary didn't get off to a great start, however. Holland was a republic, not a monarchy (although the ruling princes were kings in all but name) and the Dutch court was more modern and informal than the English one. At first, Mary was seen as being stiff, snooty and standoffish. She later admitted that she really hadn't known what she was doing. The poor girl was only 15 and knew nothing of court protocol in Holland. But she was a fast learner, soon getting to know the ropes and becoming very popular in Holland, perhaps because she was such a better specimen than her wretched husband.

Even at a young age Mary had seen enough of the world to know what men were like. In one of her teenage letters, she wrote to Frances Apsley that 'in two or three years, men are always wary of their wives and look for mistresses as soon as they can get them'. And after the wedding, William did nothing to disabuse her of this opinion. To rub salt into the wound, he took as his mistress Mary's childhood friend, Frances Villiers's daughter Elizabeth.

There's a story that, early on in their marriage, Mary was tipped off about William and waited to catch him coming out of Elizabeth's room in the middle of the night. When she confronted him, he gaslighted her, saying he'd simply had some late-night household business to discuss with Elizabeth and walked away. And Mary, as people often do in these relationships, found it easier and less distressing to believe the lie than accept the truth.

When she'd first arrived in Holland, Mary had been homesick and confused by Dutch customs, but she gradually grew to appreciate life in the republic, where she was able to live quietly and do all the things she enjoyed – playing cards, needlework, gardening. And she slowly grew more affectionate towards William until she was able to convince herself, and many others, that she was truly, madly, deeply in love with him. Perhaps it was easier for her to write letters to friends about how devoted she was to him than to admit that, actually, he made her miserable.

She imported a string of Anglican priests from England and it's through their journals and letters that we get a glimpse of Mary's life in Holland. One of them wrote that 'the Princess's heart is like to break, and yet she … everyday counterfeits the greatest joy. The Prince hath infallibly made her his absolute slave.'

Mary and William *did* have a physical relationship, and Mary *did* get pregnant, but she unfortunately miscarried twice in 1678. The same thing happened a year later and, after the second miscarriage, she never conceived again. There's inevitably a lot of speculation about this. Perhaps James II had syphilis and passed it on to his daughters? Perhaps Mary had suffered complications from her second miscarriage? Maybe she decided she couldn't cope with another pregnancy? Or maybe she stopped sleeping with William? We'll never know.

Mary's faith led to her falling out with her increasingly Catholic father, James, who barely visited her after she left England and they became estranged. When James married Mary of Modena and they had a son – who technically replaced Mary as legitimate heir to the throne – it was the last straw for Mary, and for the English establishment. James and his Catholic heir had to go.

Anne tried to get Mary to buy into the conspiracy theory that the child wasn't James's and had been smuggled into the bedchamber in a warming pan, and in public, at least, she had to get behind her Protestant husband against her father. James – and the Catholics – never forgave her for the way she deserted him and supported William. And Mary herself struggled with the betrayal.

A group of six English noblemen and one bishop, known as the Immortal Seven – a kind of Protestant superhero team – officially invited William to bring an army over to England in 1688 and 'rescue the nation and the religion'. William readily accepted the offer, because it meant that he'd get what he'd always wanted: full English support and resources for his wars against Louis XIV.

Mary went down to wave William and his fleet off from the naval port of Hellevoetsluis and she made a big show of doing the whole 'Oh my goodness, I can't bear for my darling William to leave. I'm going to watch him to the far horizon until he has disappeared' routine, behaving like the heroine of a romantic novel. Unfortunately, a storm forced the fleet back home and they had to go through it all over again a few days later.

William's fleet was enormous, at least twice the size of the Spanish Armada, and was packed with Dutch soldiers and foreign mercenaries. There was no doubt that this was a serious invasion force, prepared for war. Sailing westwards, when they got to the narrowest point of the English Channel, the 20 miles between Dover and Calais, it was said that the sailors in the ships on the northern flank of the fleet could salute Dover, while the sailors on the southern side could salute Calais.

William landed at Brixham in the West Country and marched towards London. King James, realising he didn't have enough support to fight William, wisely surrendered and was allowed to flee to France. And thus the bloodless Glorious Revolution brought about regime change.

Once England was secure, Mary followed her husband over the North Sea and they were jointly crowned at Westminster Abbey in April 1689. They'd already agreed to a pre-nup 'Declaration of Rights', which stated that William and Mary would rule together with equal status as king and queen, and that if Mary died before him, William would still be king. This gave him considerably more rights and powers than King Philip of Spain had been allowed when he'd married Mary I. Mary II seemed happy to go along with this. 'My opinion', she wrote in her memoirs, 'has ever been that women should not meddle in government.' Although, as we'll see, she did end up getting very involved with parliament.

Not long after the coronation William signed the Bill of Rights, a declaration that Parliament takes precedent over the monarchy. This was another document in the tradition of Magna Carta and perhaps the closest thing that the UK has to a constitution. It set in stone the institution of a constitutional monarchy, officially declaring that the monarch can't rule without the consent of the people/parliament. It also states various universal legal rights, and guarantees frequent parliaments and free elections.

William wasn't too bothered about losing some of his rights as a monarch. He was sort of going, 'Yeah, yeah, yeah, whatever. Can we just sign this piece of paper and move on?' He was Dutch, after all, and didn't give a shiny shite about the finer points of the English constitution. He was quite happy to rule by government rather than royal decree, because all he wanted was what England could give him: soldiers to go off and fight Louis XIV.

William was not exactly welcomed to England with open arms and he didn't try to make friends. Very soon, supporters of the ousted James II put around the rumour that, on top of being a bloody foreigner, he was a sodomite to boot. William knew he'd have to suppress any Jacobite dissent. We've seen how he went over to Ireland, where he defeated James and his Irish Catholic supporters at the Battle of the Boyne, but before that he had to deal with some business in Scotland, where there was a Jacobite uprising led by one Viscount Dundee. Dundee had raised troops mainly in the Highlands, with the aim of getting James back onto the throne. The Jacobites won a victory at the Battle of Killiecrankie, but Dundee was killed and a Scottish Presbyterian army fought back, putting an end to the uprising at the Battle of Dunkeld.

William ruthlessly exploited divisions within Scotland and successfully used a policy of divide and rule. The highland clans all seemed to hate each other, but not as much as they hated the lowlanders, while the Protestants mutually hated the Catholics.*

William offered to pardon any Scottish clans that had taken part in the uprising, as long as they agreed to accept his rule with Mary, but the MacDonalds of Glencoe weren't able to declare their oath before the deadline ran out, which was used as an excuse by rival clans to hit back at them (with the support of William's army). The MacDonalds were bottled up in the Glencoe Valley and thirty-eight of them were slaughtered on 13 February 1692 in an incident that became known as the Massacre of Glencoe. This made William very unpopular north of the border, even though, as with the murder of Johan de Witt, he claimed not to have been directly responsible.

---

* This sectarianism still persists in the rivalry between the two big Glasgow football clubs, aka the 'Old Firm' – Rangers (Protestant) and Celtic (Catholic).

Having sorted out his problems at home, William left Mary in charge and returned to Holland which, since 1688, had been involved in a new war with France. It was down to Mary to woo the nation and make this unconventional new regime acceptable. At first, she really didn't know what to do. She was unused to English court life and wasn't up to speed on all the latest laws and rules. But she was smart and quickly became popular. William had put in place a ruling council roughly divided between Tories and Whigs to run things for her, but they struggled to agree on anything, and Mary described them variously as – weak, obstinate, lazy, mad and 'of a temper I can never like'.

Mary learned how to manipulate these men, privately working with the different factions and flattering them so she could get them to do what she wanted. One courtier described her as 'another Queen Elizabeth' – and maybe she would have gone on to be just that, one of our most revered queens, if, in the run up to Christmas 1694, she hadn't come down with a fever and a rash. She hoped that it might be the lesser scourge of measles, but by Christmas it was clear that she had smallpox and the Archbishop of Canterbury visited her. Mary had a terrible end; smallpox is as horrific as the plague. The Jacobites were crowing – *See how this evil woman has been punished for the way she treated her father. This is the judgement of God upon her!* The Archbishop of Canterbury said, *No, no, don't be silly. It was the sin of the nation which caused it – the immorality and licentiousness at the court of Charles II. She is paying for her family's sins, not her own.*

It was all a load of old bollocks. Smallpox is not a religious or a moral judgement. It's an extremely nasty disease. It's amazing how, even today, illnesses are still seen in many quarters as some kind of judgement. William did show affection towards Mary before she died. He set up a bed in her room so he could be near her. Having already survived smallpox himself, he assumed he couldn't catch it again. Afterwards, he kept a lock of her hair on his person at all times … Or, so his PR machine claimed. Were the stories of his devotion put about to make the English look more kindly on him? He certainly made a public display of being heartbroken and, while Mary had asked that her funeral wouldn't be too expensive and should be kept simple, William insisted on dropping £50,000 on the lavish affair and had a funeral anthem specially written by the court composer, Henry Purcell.

The Jacobites dismissed Mary as 'too bad a daughter and too good a wife', but she did much to stop the country descending into chaos after her father was kicked off the throne, as well as helping to mitigate the damage caused by William's abrasive personality. After her death, he went on to rule for the next decade, most of which involved fighting the French. He was a better soldier than he was a ruler and politician, but he still lost more battles than he won and the war with France turned into a nine-year-long slugfest (imaginatively called the Nine Years' War). To aid his war effort, William helped put together the Grand Alliance, a union between England, Holland and the Habsburg Empire, with the aim of halting Louis XIV's expansion.

William had initially supported the Tories in government, but when they proved reluctant to support the war, he switched his allegiance to the Whigs. To finance the whole undertaking, William established the Bank of England in 1694. This was a major step in the City of London becoming the pre-eminent financial, banking and trading centre in Europe, and towards Great Britain becoming an economic superpower.

The other function of the Bank of England was to service the new-fangled idea of the national debt. Now the government and the royal family could simply borrow money from the bank whenever they needed it. Easy.

William had a number of young male friends at court, who he liked to give promotions to, in particular a pair of good-looking young Dutch noblemen, who sound like an old-school music-hall act: Bentinck and Keppel. Keppel started out as a lowly pageboy and ended up as an earl without ever actually doing anything other than being a *young friend* of William. This is such a familiar pattern with monarchs and was inevitably resented by rivals at court who felt these positions should have gone to them. Bentinck and Keppel became the greatest rivals of all, though, accusing each other of being rather too close to the king. Bentinck wrote to William in 1697 that 'the kindness which Your Majesty shows for a young man and the manner in which you seem to authorise his liberties and impertinences, make the world say things I am ashamed to hear'.

William had never been a healthy man and he grew progressively shrunken and stooped as he got older and battled various diseases. And then he was out riding one day when his horse stumbled on a molehill and fell, throwing William to the ground and breaking his collarbone. The break never set and, as the king was lying in bed, infection set in, moving to his lungs and causing his death from pneumonia. Ever since then, the Jacobites (and, indeed, many ordinary Scotsmen who simply don't like the English) have raised a glass to the 'little gentleman in the velvet waistcoat' (i.e. the mole).

William died without a male heir, so the first Anglo–Dutch dynasty died with him. Needless to say, there was the usual horse-trading towards the end of his life over who would succeed him, and the job of monarch went to his sister-in-law, Anne, the oldest of King James's surviving children from his first – Protestant – marriage.

30

ANNA GLORIA

QUEEN ANNE – 1665–1714
Reigned 1702–1714
Lived for 49 years. Ruled for 12 years.
Died of disputed causes, probably lupus.
Remembered for: being the last Stuart monarch,
the Act of Union and the Battle of Blenheim.

There was only ever one Queen Anne, so she has no regnal number, and it has to be said that, despite being a one-off, Anne isn't one of our better-known monarchs. If you mention her name, people are probably more likely to think of architecture and furniture than the woman herself. She did get a little more recognition when Olivia Colman won an Oscar for portraying her in *The Favourite*, but the film only gave us a tiny glimpse into Anne's life and the history of the time, and was perhaps rather flippant about her personal tragedies.

This was a woman whose mother died when she was six, who lost six siblings at an early age, who was troubled by illness all her life, who got pregnant 17 times in 17 years but didn't see a single child survive to adulthood, and who died before she was 50. Despite all that, she steered the country through some extremely important events, including a major international war and full union with Scotland, and was by no means the weak, ineffectual ruler that she's often characterised as.

Anne was interested in art and science. She knighted Isaac Newton, whose contribution to mathematics, physics and astronomy is mind-blowing. She was a patron of theatre, poetry and music (George Frideric Handel composed music for her).

Perhaps if she'd been a bit wilder and more disruptive, she might have made a deeper impression, but, like the style of architecture that bears her name, Anne liked things neat, orderly and balanced. Under her rule, the country grew ever more prosperous and developed into a major player on the world stage. Her crowning glory came in 1707 when her parliament passed the Act of Union, officially uniting Scotland and England into a single entity under one monarch and one parliament – Great Britain.*

The Stuarts were essentially a Scottish family and Anne had always been passionate about making the two countries one. She wasn't alone; there were many in both England and Scotland who'd been pressing for a full union, particularly since Scotland had bankrupted itself trying to found a big colony in Panama under the so-called Darien Scheme. Full union would mean that wealth, power and influence would be shared between the two nations and there would be an end to the debilitating wars that had blighted the north for hundreds of years. At least, that was the hope.

The traditional picture of Anne comes from the memoirs of her childhood friend, Sarah Jennings, who grew up to become Duchess of Marlborough. The two of them were extremely close for many years and Sarah became Anne's favourite at court before they fell out, leading to bitterness on both sides. Sarah wrote her memoir after the split and it was very unfair to Anne, negatively colouring our view of the queen. Sarah was trying to settle old scores. More recently, Anne has been re-evaluated by historians who have painted her in a more favourable light, as I will try to do here.

Anne was plagued as a child by excessive watering of the eyes, and she had terrible eyesight all her life. When she and Sarah were girls, they had a furious argument about whether a distant object was a man or a tree and, even when Sarah dragged her over to show her it was a man, Anne stubbornly still claimed it was a tree. She was a royal princess, after all, and if she said it was a tree, then it was a tree.

After her mother died, Anne was brought up in Richmond with her sister, Mary, in the household of Lady Frances Villiers, and we've seen

---

* I really wish they hadn't called it that, because it's led to so much bullshit over the years – 'We're Great Britain. We're really great. They wouldn't have called us great if we weren't great. And we need to be Great again!'. It's simply a geographical term that refers to size rather than status – the land mass of England, Scotland, Ireland and Wales.

how the two girls became obsessed with an older girl, Frances Apsley. It was while Anne was in Richmond that she first met Sarah, and she formed a similarly intense attachment to her new friend. In 1673, her 39-year-old father, James, married the 15-year-old Mary of Modena, who was only six years older than Anne and four years older than her big sister, Mary. When James introduced the three girls to each other, he said, 'I have brought you a new playfellow', which all seems rather dodgy. Anne got on quite well with her new stepmother, however, and James was a loving father despite everything.

Over the next 10 years, Mary of Modena had 10 pregnancies, but suffered several miscarriages and only one of her children lived beyond infancy (Isabel, who died aged four). This left Mary and Anne second and third in line of succession after their father.

In 1677, when her sister Mary married William of Orange, Anne missed the wedding because she was quarantined in her room with smallpox. She recovered, unlike her guardian, Lady Frances Villiers, who died of the virus. Soon afterwards, Charles II moved James to Scotland to keep him and his dangerous Catholic leanings out of the way. Anne visited him in Edinburgh in 1681–82, when she was 16. This was to be the last time she ever left England, mainly because she was plagued all her life with serious health problems.

Historians have tried to diagnose what Anne's main problem was. For a long while, it was assumed to be gout, but many now think she may have also suffered from the autoimmune disease lupus, where the body attacks itself. She developed a nasty leg ulcer in later life too; her health got so poor she couldn't walk and had to be carried around in a sedan chair. She also had a little one-horse cart, which she drove madly around her palace grounds. The lack of mobility led to her becoming obese and she turned to what we would now call 'comfort eating'. The upshot was that foreign travel was off the bucket list.

Charles II inevitably wanted to marry his niece off to a potential ally. He'd already married Mary to William of Orange and was now thinking that he needed to counterbalance Dutch dominance and so looked to Scandinavia. Protestant Denmark was becoming a wealthy and ambitious nation, and Anne was married off to the confirmed

Lutheran, George, Prince of Denmark, younger brother of the Danish king, Christian V.

George was 12 years older than Anne and had trained as a soldier. He wasn't exactly *Love Island* material, but was more warm-hearted and better-looking than the cold and hunched William of Orange (almost everybody in Europe was better-looking than William). George was dismissed as a bit of a nonentity. Charles II famously said of him, 'I have tried him drunk, and I have tried him sober, and there is nothing in him.' Like William of Orange, George suffered from asthmatic wheezing and a certain Lord Musgrave said that 'he was forced to breathe hard in case people took him for dead and buried him'.

This was all mainly just bitchiness among the tight-knit, snooty aristocrats at the English court. It seems to me that old George was just a nice, decent bloke who didn't want to overshadow his wife. A bit of a Denis Thatcher figure. He stuck by Anne and supported her in parliament, even when, privately, he disagreed with her. And, crucially, he showed no signs of wanting to be regarded as king. He was always only ever Prince George.

After their wedding, Anne and George were given a royal residence, a set of buildings in the Palace of Whitehall known as the Cockpit, so called because it had been, well, a cockpit – where people went to watch chickens fighting each other to the death. But the couple were comfortable there and Anne appointed her childhood friend, Sarah, as one of her ladies of the bedchamber, her inner circle. Sarah had herself married the soldier John Churchill, and was now Sarah Churchill.

Anne quickly became pregnant after the marriage, but sadly the baby was the first of many to be stillborn. Over the next two years, however, she gave birth to two healthy daughters, Mary and Anne Sophia. So these were happy times for her.

In 1685, Charles II died and James took the throne. Anne had been brought up as an Anglican and was very disappointed when her father started giving important positions in the military and the government to Catholics, which went against the Test Acts that Charles's government had passed. It wasn't that James was trying to promote Catholicism, though; he simply supported religious tolerance and wondered whether it really mattered what type of Christian you identified as.

The year 1687 was a terrible one for Anne. She miscarried again, George caught smallpox, and their two young daughters died of the disease. This must have been absolutely devastating for Anne. Luckily, George survived, but this established a pattern of disappointment and heartbreak that would run through her life. To make matters worse, Mary of Modena gave birth for the first time since James II had come to the throne.

The royal princesses exchanged letters, discussing whether the whole thing had been faked, and they turned against their father, largely because of their Protestantism, but no doubt also because the king's new son, Bedpan James Junior, had knocked both sisters down the line of succession. They didn't have to worry about it for long, though, because parliament stepped in, ousted both Jameses, father and son, and invited William of Orange to invade.

We saw in the chapter on James II that the crucial event that stopped him from engaging William in battle was his general, John Churchill, switching sides. Churchill's wife, Sarah, was influential in this decision and had plotted in advance with Anne and her husband to support William. This was a major gamble and, in the fevered atmosphere at court, nobody was safe. As it was, Anne and Sarah had to do a moonlight flit from London to avoid getting caught up in the fallout if it all went wrong.

James was heartbroken when he found out about Anne's desertion and cried out, 'God help me. Even my children have forsaken me.'

For the rest of her life, Mary felt horribly guilty about betraying her father, but Anne displayed no great concern for him. On the evening when James threw in his hand, she carried on having her usual card game with her ladies. The following summer, she successfully gave birth to a son, Prince William, who became the Duke of Gloucester. He was a sickly child, but managed to survive infancy and, because William and Mary had no children, it looked as though Anne's son would eventually inherit the crown.

William and Mary were very suspicious of this rival power base at court. They'd never shown any respect for Prince George and refused to give him a senior position. Sarah Churchill, however, was a very different proposition. She was an astute and able young woman, better versed in court intrigue than Anne. She helped her childhood friend navigate these choppy waters and became her right-hand woman. So that they could have a relationship on an equal footing and not be queen and subject, they started calling each other Mrs Morley and Mrs Freeman. Just two ordinary women.

William and Mary initially rewarded John Churchill for his support and made him Earl of Marlborough, but then they became suspicious of him as well. They feared he might become too powerful and even suspected him of plotting with the Jacobites against them. He'd done the dirty on one king; what would stop him doing it to another? So, three years after making him an earl, they kicked him out of some of his offices and banished him from court (he remained an earl, however). At the same time, Mary banished Sarah, declaring her *persona non grata*. Anne was furious and blamed William, who she hated, writing to Sarah: 'Suppose I did submit, how would that Dutch abortive laugh at me and please himself with having got the better…? No, my dear Mrs Freeman, never believe your faithful Mrs Morley will ever submit.'

She refused to dismiss Sarah from her household and openly took her along as her plus one to a big do at the palace, as a result of which she was punished by her sister, who stripped away many of Anne's privileges and staff. Perhaps it was the stress of all this that led Anne to give birth prematurely to another son, who almost immediately died.

Mary came to visit her but, instead of offering sisterly comfort and support, she laid into her for her friendship with Sarah Churchill and the two sisters never saw each other again.

Tragically, for Anne, things never improved on the childbearing front. In January of 1700, she gave birth to another son but the doctors told her it had been dead inside her for a month. That was her final pregnancy and, sadly, in that same year, her only surviving child, William, Duke of Gloucester, died. One moment he was happily celebrating his 11th birthday with his family and, six days later, he was dead. It was possibly smallpox, but he'd also had a weird, liquid-filled lump on the back of his head. It's possible his doctors had tried to interfere with it and caused an infection. Whatever the cause, William died and Anne never recovered.

In 1701, Parliament passed the Act of Settlement, an attempt to clarify how the line of succession worked. It boiled down to ... NO CATHOLICS. Family trees were consulted, lists were drawn up and it was concluded that if Anne didn't produce any heirs, the crown would go to the Protestant Sophia, Electress of Hanover, who, even though she was a descendant of James I (& VI), was something like 60th in line to the throne behind loads of Catholics.

It was a pretty desperate measure. Sophia was from an insignificant little offshoot of the family who ruled a tiny patch of land in Germany called Hanover. She excitedly started to make arrangements to visit England, the country she may rule one day, but was kept away. Once again, nobody wanted a member of a rival royal family at court.

A year after the Act of Settlement was passed, in 1702, King William died. He was not greatly mourned, but Anne was a very popular choice for queen and she made a big point in her first speech to parliament of saying that she was very much an *English* queen – not Dutch in any way (or Italian, like Mary of Modena). 'I know my own heart to be entirely English.'

Like Elizabeth I (another childless queen), Anne genuinely believed that she was the mother of the country and that everyone loved her. She put her husband, Danish George, in charge of the navy and John Churchill in charge of the army. Sarah Churchill was given a promotion and new titles. She became groom of the stool, mistress of the robes and keeper of the privy purse – the three highest positions in the royal household.

Anne's health certainly wasn't getting any better and she had to be carried to her coronation in 1702 in a sedan chair, and, before she was even sitting comfortably on the throne, she had to contend with a major European war.

The feeble-minded, blank-firing Charles II of Spain had died childless in 1700 and there were two contenders for his throne, neither of them Spanish. Each had their supporters. Jaffa Charlie had nominated a Frenchman, Philip of Anjou, his great-nephew and grandson of Louis XIV. This was not a popular choice with the other European rulers as it would unite France and Spain into one massive power bloc. So, they'd formed their own power bloc, the Grand Alliance, to get behind the rival contender, Archduke Charles of Austria, from the Austrian branch of the Habsburg Empire.

The resulting War of the Spanish Succession ended up dragging on for 13 years (from 1701 to 1714), spilling over into the Americas where most of the countries involved had colonies. The end result was more than a million deaths and a rebalancing of power in Europe. The British ended up with Gibraltar and trade concessions in the Americas that broke the Spanish monopoly on the slave trade. This would be a major step towards Britain becoming the largest slave-trading nation in Europe.

The Englishman who came out of the war best was John Churchill, who proved himself to be a brilliant and audacious general. His greatest success came in 1704, at the Battle of Blenheim, where his Anglo–Dutch army surprised a French force that been threatening Vienna and totally overwhelmed them. Churchill had brought his troops 350 miles down from Holland in secret, largely marching at night. The French were knocked sideways by their defeat and Churchill's victory turned public opinion around and kept England in the war (for better or worse).

During the war, Churchill was promoted from earl of Marlborough to duke of Marlborough and a 'grateful nation' gave him a gift of a large estate in Woodstock, near Oxford, and the money to build a house. 'House' is perhaps not the best word to describe the humongous pile he built: Blenheim Palace.*

The war ran throughout Anne's reign while, on the home front, she had to deal with the day-to-day grind of running a country. When she'd come to the throne, her ministers were rubbing their hands thinking, 'Great, we've got a weak and unwell woman on the throne. She'll basically do whatever we tell her.' But it wasn't to be. Anne was as able a politician as her sister, Mary, and, like her, after a shaky start, got the hang of playing the Whigs and the Tories off against each other.

---

* In 1874, it became the birthplace of Winston Churchill, a descendant of the first Duke of Marlborough. If certain family members had fallen off the perch, he could have inherited the title and estates, and may never have gone into politics.

Anne tried to keep the status quo and not come down fully on one side, although she inevitably leaned towards the traditionalist, pro-monarchy Tories. Her friend and favourite, Sarah Churchill was more radical and kept trying to pull her towards the Whigs, who were greater supporters of her husband and the war. Under John and Sarah's influence, Queen Anne removed many high Tories from office in 1704 when they refused to back the war, but Mrs Morley was beginning to feel that Mrs Freeman was pushing her around and trying to take control. As the war dragged on, Anne gradually lost heart in it and, as the Duke of Marlborough's triumphal gleam began to wear off, Anne distanced herself from Sarah.

Sarah said their falling-out was simply because she was the only person who dared to tell Anne the truth. In the end, though, it was Anne, not Sarah, who was queen, and if she said that a man was a tree, then a man was a tree. Finally, Sarah's own cousin, Abigail Hill, replaced her in Anne's affections. Abigail was as ambitious as Sarah, but was better at sucking up to the queen. She became more influential and worked her way ever closer to the heart of Anne's court. Gossip started doing the rounds that her relationship with Anne was sexual; it seems that Sarah Churchill was one of the main instigators of these scandalous rumours. She somewhat hypocritically accused the queen of having a lesbian affair and warned her that if she didn't get rid of Abigail, it would destroy her reputation, which didn't endear her to Anne.

By 1707, a series of setbacks in Scotland had brought the country round to the idea of accepting full union with England. First, the ill-fated Darien Scheme had ruined many leading Scottish families. Then, when the English parliament passed the Act of Settlement, the Scots were furious about the idea of being ruled by a German without any consultation and ignored it, passing a rival Act of their own. The English parliament hit back with the Alien Act, the equivalent of Trump's tariffs. If Scotland wanted to behave like a separate country, then they'd be treated like one. Free trade between the two countries was stopped and all Scottish imports blocked. Scottish landowners were also threatened with having all their lands and property in England confiscated. The Scots quickly realised they couldn't survive without England's support and caved in. The English parliament pushed its advantage and, on the back of a campaign of bribery, economic blackmail, flattery and coercion, got the Acts of Union passed. Many Scottish noblemen now became part of the English establishment and the English parliament, and found themselves at the heart of the newly blossoming British Empire, able to share in its wealth and influence.

The Union Jack – a combination of the crosses of England and Scotland, that had been used by the monarchy since the crowns had been joined during James I's reign, now became the official national flag of Great Britain (the red Irish saltire was added in 1801). There were, of course, still many Scots who hated the idea of a union and felt that Scotland had been betrayed and diminished. Many English people also felt the same sense of betrayal. They hated that England wouldn't be a sole sovereign nation any more and would have to share everything with the Scots.

Anne was jubilant, but, in 1706, her husband, the ever-supportive Prince George, started coughing up blood. By 1708, he was too ill to attend a thanksgiving service at St Paul's to celebrate Churchill's latest victory. Anne, who was fraught and exhausted from caring for George, refused the heavy clothes and jewellery that Sarah insisted she wore and, after a long coach ride, the two of them had a blazing row outside the cathedral doors, in full view of everyone. Finally, Sarah snapped 'Be quiet!' and immediately regretted it.

You do not speak to a queen like that in front of her subjects.

George died soon after, from a combination of asthma and oedema, and Anne was broken. Sarah didn't help. She turned up at the royal apartments and removed a portrait of George from the Queen's bedchamber, saying Anne needed to get over it, pull herself together and not be reminded of her late husband. Anne felt differently. She'd had enough of being told what to do and it was Sarah who was removed from her life.

Anne was also fed up with the war. She was sick of the bloodshed, the expense and the fact that there didn't seem to be any way of ending it decisively. And, as she saw it, if the newly-powerful Austrian contender, Archduke Charles, did take the Spanish throne, then Britain would simply end up having to go to war with him. In 1709, the allied army lost around 20,000 men at the Battle of Malplaquet, although it was considered another victory for the Duke of Marlborough, albeit a dangerously narrow one, and morale hit rock-bottom. The Grand Alliance was breaking up, thinking the war wasn't worth carrying on with, particularly as the French army was getting stronger. Everyone sat down to negotiate a peace treaty, a process that dragged on until 1714. But then, at last, it was all over. Britain was at peace, and business and trade (particularly the ghastly slave trade) could flourish again.

Anne was becoming increasingly unwell and had such a horror of death that she couldn't bring herself to sign her will. On top of all her other health problems, she suffered a series of strokes in 1714 and her poor, beleaguered body gave up. She was only 49 and died intestate and childless, so her estate was absorbed by the crown. At least it had been agreed long ago who was going to succeed her.

Sophia, Electress of Hanover, had waited all her life for this moment and was ready for her close-up, but – wouldn't you know it – she dropped dead just before Anne. And so it was that her son, the unprepossessing George, came to the throne as Britain's first German monarch. It was the end of the Stuarts and the beginning of the Hanoverians.

31

4 GEORGES (#1)

GEORGE I – 1660–1727

George Louis (Georg Ludwig)
Reigned 1714–1727
Lived for 67 years. Ruled for 13 years.
Died from an exploding brain.
Remembered for: being the first Hanoverian King, struggling to
speak English, and having two mistresses – one fat, one thin.

It's apt that the Georges are all dumped together in the rhyme as '4 Georges', because they're all quite similar and I have to confess that I struggle to remember which of them did what. We've come to the time in this story when parliament had become much more important in the day-to-day running of the country than the monarch, and it was during George I's reign that Britain got its first prime minister, Robert Walpole, who arguably had a lot more influence on British history than the king.

So, George I was born Georg Ludwig in Hanover, but when he took the English throne, he was urged to anglicise his name to George Louis (Ludwig being the German form of the name Louis).*

George has a reputation for not speaking English, being a bit dull (bordering on the stupid), having very little interest in Britain, spending half his reign back home in Hanover and being quite happy to leave the day-to-day business of running the country to his government so that he could sit and play cards with his mistresses – the fat one and the thin one. As we shall see, though, most of this is not exactly true.

---

* It's interesting that Hanoverian names – George, Louis, Sophie – are very popular now with the British royal family.

George should never really have come to the throne in the first place. Many in Britain believed that the son that James II had with Mary of Modena should have been the one wearing the crown. This was James Stuart, the bedpan baby, the great white hope of the Jacobite movement, who I'll refer to as 'James the Old Pretender', to avoid confusion with King James. As a Catholic, he was barred from the throne by the Act of Settlement of 1701, which set in stone that no future monarch could be a Catholic – a law that remains in force to this day.

When George was invited over from Hanover, James the Old Pretender was living in exile in France where he'd been kept by the 75-year-old Sun King, Louis XIV, as a useful idiot. If Louis wanted to make a deal with the British, he'd offer to get rid of Pretender James, and, if he wanted to go the other way and rattle the British cage, he'd claim to be supporting him as the legitimate king of England. So the Pretender was a constant threat to George.

At 54, George was the oldest monarch to have ever come to the throne, but he'd have been delayed even longer if his mother, Sophia, Electress of Hanover, who was busily picking out what to wear for her coronation, hadn't been caught in a sudden downpour while taking a walk, got chilled to the bone and died. She'd been lobbying for the crown half her life and missed wearing it by a few weeks. Sophia was a clever and ambitious woman who'd brought George up to think of himself as the little prince in waiting. George's father, Ernest Augustus, had been a bully who'd made the boy's life miserable and suffered from classic Competitive Dad Syndrome.

George had a fairly conventional upbringing. He had some interest in science, but his main passion was for all things military. He loved organising and reorganising the army, like a boy playing with toy soldiers. When he was quite young, his father wanted to show him what a real war looked like and took him off to fight in the Franco-Dutch War, and, later on, the Great Turkish War.

The Ottoman Empire had been expanding and pushing up into Europe since the 15th century and large parts of the continent were much more preoccupied with what was happening in the east than they were with Little Britain, off to the west. The Turks had overrun north Africa, the Crimea, Greece and the Balkans, getting as far as Austria. George was present when the Turks were defeated at the Battle of Vienna in 1683, which marked the point at which the war turned against the Ottoman Empire and its westward expansion was halted.

Ernest Augustus had been keen for George to learn about military matters so that he would be able to look after Hanover, which was considered by the English establishment to be a pretentious and unimportant little German principality, but to George was home and had to be defended.

The Greater Hanoverian state (properly known as the Duchy of Brunswick-Lüneberg*) was made up of smaller districts ruled by George's uncles. Ernest Augustus wanted to unite the whole of the state under his son, so he arranged for him to marry his first cousin, Sophia Dorothea of Celle (a part of Greater Hanover ruled by George's uncle George†).

Nobody, least of all the 22-year-old George, was pretending that his semi-incestuous marriage was any kind of love match. George and Sophia didn't like each other very much and were very different. George was short, stout and – even in his most flattering portraits, tricked out in fancy togs and elaborate wigs – was not a pretty sight. He was a grumpy, retiring homebody who liked to spend his evenings playing cards. Sophia was a great beauty and a party animal, full of life and laughter. But the couple did knuckle down and manage to produce two children, a daughter and a son.

George is often accused of being dull and unimaginative, so you can imagine how the conversation went with Sophia.

'Oh, George. What are we going to call our daughter?'

'I have the perfect name for her – Sophia Dorothea.'

'So … The same as me …?'

'Ja, and let's call our son, George. That's a good name. I like the name George.'

---

* As if you cared.

† You're going to have to get used to everybody being called George in the next few chapters.

Having produced a healthy male heir, George and Sophia's marriage dragged on for a few years before they went their separate ways. He took a mistress and she took a lover, a handsome Swedish count called Philip Christoph von Königsmarck, a colonel in the Hanoverian army.

Men at the time were expected to take mistresses; nobody batted an eyelid. It was very different for women, however. Perhaps, had Sophia been discreet, she might have got away with it, but she made no secret of her relationship with Königsmarck and George and his father were having none of that.

The affair between Sophia and Königsmarck became one of those great romantic royal love stories and was the model for several novels and films. It was a classically doomed romance, though. One day, Königsmarck disappeared, in the South American sense. One story went around that he'd been cut up and hidden under the floorboards of a castle. Another more plausible story was that he'd been murdered, his body weighted with stones and chucked in the local river.

George officially separated from Sophia and locked her up in Ahlden Castle, a stately home surrounded by water, where she remained for the next 33 years until her death in 1726. Her children, who were eleven and seven, were taken away from her and she never saw them again.

George also never saw her again.

This was the sordid past that George drew a veil over and left behind when he travelled to England for his coronation in 1714. He and his entourage arrived in London in 260 horse-drawn carriages that took three hours to pass by. He brought his Hanoverian guards, his German courtiers (including his turbaned Turkish servants, Mehemet and Mustapha, whom he'd picked up on his campaigns) and those two mistresses – the Elephant and the Maypole. At least that's the joke that went around. One of them was indeed his mistress, the 'maypole' Melusine von der Schulenburg. She and George lived as husband and wife and had three children together. The other woman, Sophia Charlotte von Kielmannsegg, was actually the daughter of one of George's *father's* mistresses, making her George's half-sister. George had taken her under his wing and she'd become part of his inner circle.

She was a clever and ambitious woman, described by one courtier as like a spider at the heart of the great web.

OK, so George may have been a bit of a shit, but he was the victim of British xenophobic propaganda all his life. At the end of the 1600s, in a fit of liberalism Parliament had allowed the Licensing Act to lapse. This meant that many restrictions on newspapers, pamphlets, prints and posters were lifted, and people could publish whatever they wanted, as long as it wasn't openly treasonous. Suddenly, you were allowed to poke fun at the monarchy and, during the Hanoverian period, there was a great flourishing of political cartoons, plays and satirical prints that reached its height towards the end of the 18th century with satirists like James Gillray, Thomas Rowlandson and Isaac Cruikshank coming to prominence.

So, poor old George was the victim of the equivalent of the tabloid press of his day and had to suffer the jokes and the gossip in silence (although, when provoked, he had a filthy temper). The mocking began on day one, at the coronation itself. The Great British Public were bewildered and put out. Why was this German turnip being crowned as their king in Westminster Abbey? A spectator was arrested for actually waving a turnip on a stick at the coronation procession.

It got worse than a turnip on a stick, however. There were more than 20 riots around England, stoked by the Jacobites. George was equally unpopular at court. He was a private man who came across as awkward, cold and standoffish (as a shy man, I can recognise another shy man. Shyness is often misunderstood as rudeness. So, I'll let him off). It didn't help that he spoke no English. He tried to learn, but learning a new language in your fifties is no easy task. It must have been like one of those awful stress dreams for George: you inexplicably find yourself on the throne, you've got to rule a country, but you can't speak the language …

The Tories particularly didn't like George. As traditionalists, they believed deep down that there should be a Stuart on the throne, although they couldn't openly come out as Jacobites. The Whigs were rubbing their hands with delight. Here was this clueless German, with little interest in Britain or its governance, and they'd be running the country, not him. But George wasn't as much of a pushover as they'd hoped and they resorted to devious methods to undermine him, such as anonymously writing scurrilous political pamphlets and feeding information to the 'tabloids'.

Another problem for George was that he was still elector in Hanover and had to keep an eye on what was going on back home. He couldn't just let the old place go. The oft-told tale is that George spent most of his reign in Hanover and was never in England. Actually, he only spent about a quarter of his time in Hanover (whereas William of Orange had spent more than half of his reign on the mainland fighting for Holland).

The year after George's coronation, James Stuart, the Old Pretender, made the second of three ill-fated attempts to rally Jacobite support and overthrow the king (having not even managed to get off his ship back in 1708). He tipped up in Scotland in 1715 to rally his troops, but he'd spent so much of his life in France that he'd taken on the ways of the French court and came across as another bloody foreigner, like George. And, worse than being German, he was basically *French*. The Old Pretender was an uninspiring fop with no stomach for war who could never get enough men onside. At his third attempt, he had to resort to hiring Spanish mercenaries. That final rebellion was put down at the Battle of Glenshiel in 1719, after which the cause was taken up by his son, the Young Pretender, Bonnie Prince Charlie.

Talking of fathers and sons, the Hanoverian kings had an odd trait: every single one of them hated their eldest son, and vice versa. George I had had an uneasy relationship with his overbearing bully of a father, Ernest Augustus, but his relationship with his own son, the future George II, was disastrous. There was a mutual hatred between the two of them from the off.

George I possibly hated George junior because he reminded him of his mother – the unfaithful, incarcerated Sophia Dorothea. And, in return, young George hated his father for the way he'd treated his mother. The boy had been separated from Sophia when he was young and banned from ever seeing her. There's a fanciful story that he once tried to swim across the moat to where she was being held captive, but failed. George junior was 30 when his father was crowned, so already an adult. We've seen so many times down the years how kings distrusted their sons and feared they'd rise up and take their place on the throne prematurely, and King George certainly seemed resentful and suspicious of his son. When he had to go over and deal with matters in Hanover, he refused to appoint the prince as regent. He didn't trust him to rule the country in his absence and preferred to let parliament run things. Their relationship got so bad that King George eventually banished the prince from the royal court, only for him to set up his own court at Leicester House. Prince George's rival court became a focus for anyone who was discontented with the king. Many politicians got in with the prince to further their own careers. After all, he would be king one day.

The man who rose to the top of early Georgian politics was Sir Robert Walpole, a wealthy country squire from Norfolk who cultivated the image of a simple, rough-hewn countryman. He was a master of the Nigel Farage schtick: a member of the establishment pretending to be just an ordinary, pint-swigging bloke. Walpole was landed gentry and knew how to play the political game, eventually becoming the most powerful person in England. Even more powerful than George.

Walpole was such a force that his party, the Whigs, ended up running the country for nearly 50 years. From 1714 to 1760, a period known as the Whig Supremacy, Britain was effectively a single-party state. In 1721, Walpole became first lord of the Treasury, the most senior position in government and a post he held for 20 years. This was more than a little controversial and the scandal sheets took the piss out of him, saying he saw himself as the 'prime' minister. And, just like how the mocking insults 'Whig' and 'Tory' had been adopted by the two parties, the slur of 'prime minister' eventually stuck. (The post is still not actually an official position. Technically, the leader of the UK government is the first lord of the Treasury, but we just call them prime minister). And Walpole set the template for later PMs. He'd been offered 10 Downing Street by George, for instance, but only agreed to live there if it became the official residence of future PMs.

George was lucky enough to come to the throne at a time when there was a clever politician at the heart of government. He'd have been sunk without Walpole, who was a big figure in every sense of the word, weighing in at 20 stone. People tend to enjoy strong governance and where George wasn't providing it, Walpole stepped up to the wicket. It was Walpole who steered the country through the enormous crisis that almost brought down the government, the monarchy and the entire financial system – the 18th-century equivalent of the Wall Street Crash, the Dotcom Bubble of the 1990s, the 2008 collapse of the subprime mortgage market and the subsequent recession. It was the granddaddy of all bubbles: the South Sea Bubble.

Now, I'm no expert on finance, banking, stocks and shares, hedge funds, etc. I'm as bewildered as the next man by the massive complexity of global finance. But at the heart of many financial crashes are two simple ideas that even I can get my head around: you can only get rich on someone else's money, and the value of things is whatever people are prepared to pay for them.

All those crashes of the modern world have resulted from wild speculation leading to overinflation of worth caused by people not really understanding the product but being convinced that they've found the secret of free money.

The South Sea Bubble was in many ways a classic pyramid scheme. We've looked at how the Bank of England was set up to manage government debt. The model was simple: people who put money into the bank got a reasonable return on their investment. The bank then lent to the government at a higher rate of interest, which meant the bank made money and was able to carry on lending and borrowing. The Bank of England was independent of the government and the monarchy, and became hugely successful. Anyone who invested in it early on made a good profit.

Inevitably, a group of envious and corrupt city men decided to set up a rival. So it was, that in 1711, three years before George came to the throne, the South Sea Company was launched with the original aim of supplying slaves to South America and 'the South Seas'. This was on the back of the deal Britain made with the Spanish at the end of the War of the Spanish Succession to open up the slave trade in South America. The South Sea Company also grandiloquently announced that it would underwrite and consolidate the national debt. So how did they get these concessions? Mainly through dodgy dealings, brown envelopes and gifts of stock to ministers. Everybody got in on it, including King George's two card-playing companions, Melusine and Sophia Charlotte, who then encouraged George to do the same. The king invested a substantial amount and the grateful South Sea Company made him one of the governors (which was further, excellent PR for them).

This royal seal of approval started a stampede of people eager to drop their own money into the company. The share price rocketed and start-up investors who withdrew their money early got huge returns, which encouraged ever more people to invest. As long as this continued to happen, the South Sea Company appeared to be a runaway success. Nobody seemed bothered that the promised trading concessions never materialised, or that the South Sea Company didn't actually do anything other than collect other people's money and use it to pay out dividends to existing investors.

It also became an umbrella concern for many smaller speculative undertakings, including a company set up to import walnut trees from Virginia, another that aimed to develop the Greenland fisheries, and even a 'Company for carrying on an undertaking of great advantage, but nobody to know what it is'. That sums up the financial world in many ways.

The frenzy to get in on this magic money-making scheme got out of control, with wealthy landowners, small traders and shopkeepers taking out loans and selling their homes to raise cash to invest. The South Sea Company knew this couldn't last and the directors started to sell their own shares when they were at their highest. Inevitably, word got out and there was a classic 'run on the bank' as people clamoured to get their money out before the whole thing collapsed. Most failed.

The bubble burst, revealing that there was nothing inside it except hot air. The South Sea Company didn't own even a single ship. The catastrophe ruined thousands of people from all levels of society, leading to suicides and to the redistribution of wealth in Britain. This could have been the end of the whole modern system of banking, share trading and city finance – and might have led to societal collapse – if the panicked George hadn't handed over control to Walpole, who worked with his government and the Bank of England to stabilise things and reassure the public.*

He took control of the economy, helped many people in difficulties and prevented the City of London from going bankrupt. He was even able to save George and his 'mistresses' from the mob, but the king never again got involved in any financial schemes and left the running of the county to Walpole. George lived quietly for another six years until, on one of his trips back to Hanover in 1727, he suffered a stroke and died. He was buried in Germany and his son, George II, refused to go to his funeral.

---

* Walpole was one of the lucky ones who made a killing early on and managed to save his fortune, with which he built himself a huge country pile in Norfolk.

THE HANOVERIANS

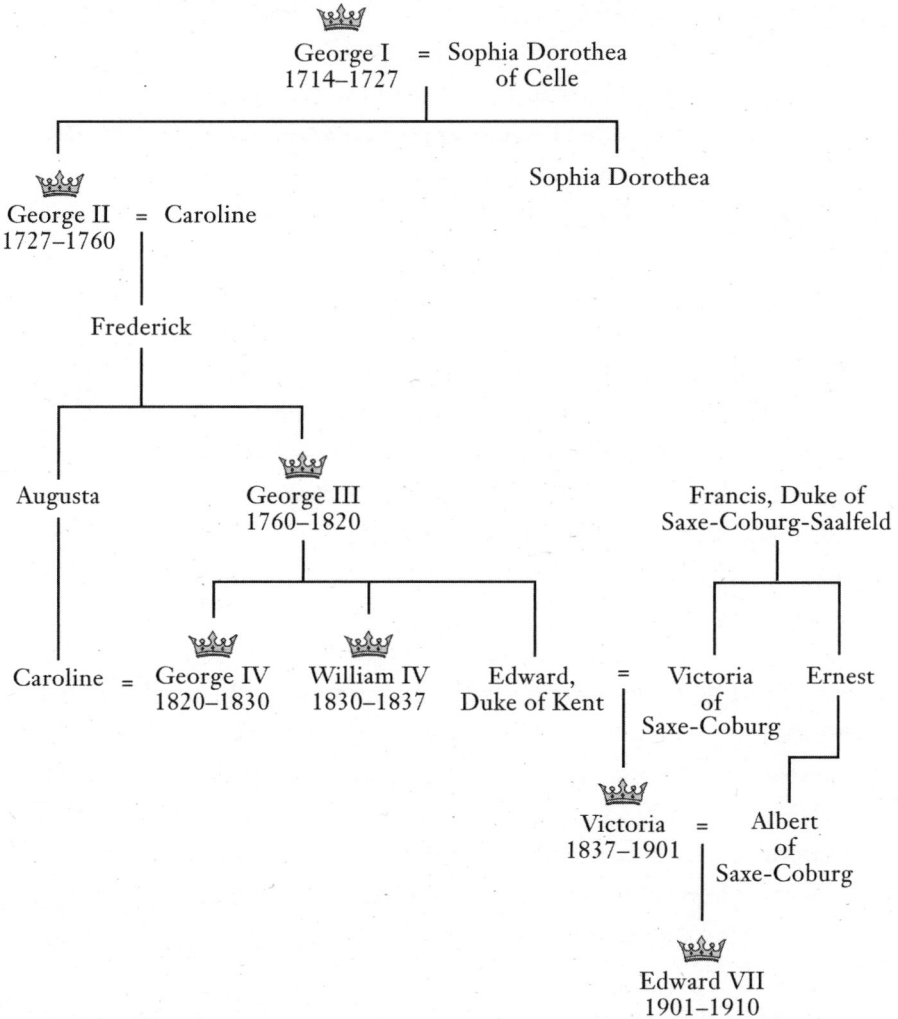

George I = Sophia Dorothea
1714–1727   of Celle

Sophia Dorothea

George II = Caroline
1727–1760

Frederick

Augusta

Caroline = George III
1760–1820

Francis, Duke of
Saxe-Coburg-Saalfeld

Caroline = George IV   William IV   Edward,   =   Victoria   Ernest
1820–1830   1830–1837   Duke of Kent   of
Saxe-Coburg

Victoria = Albert
1837–1901   of
Saxe-Coburg

Edward VII
1901–1910

32

4 GEORGES (#2)

GEORGE II – 1683–1760

Reigned 1727–1760
Lived for 76 years. Ruled for 33 years.
Died from an exploding heart.
Remembered for: snuffing out the Jacobite cause at the Battle of
Culloden and being the last British monarch to lead troops into
battle (though not at Culloden).

When he heard that his father, George I had died, the incoming George II retrieved his mother's forbidden portrait, hung it on the wall and read through her papers, including love letters to her Swedish lover, Königsmarck. He then burned the letters, burned the portrait and never mentioned her again. Make of that what you will. But I suppose if they were filthy letters, well, no son wants to believe their mother ever had a sex life.

We might be tempted to feel sorry for George II because of his unhappy childhood – his mother locked away when he was 11, the boy banned from seeing her – but it has to be said that there was a lot about him that was ridiculous and he grew up to be a hapless figure of fun.

When he was 17, the Act of Settlement in England changed his life dramatically. As an heir to the English throne, it was important for him to marry. A few candidates were considered, one of whom was Caroline, the daughter of Johann Friedrich, the Margrave of Brandenburg-Ansbach.*

George I had had a miserable, loveless, arranged marriage with the doomed Sophia Dorothea of Celle and didn't want that for his son. So,

---

* I'm not even going to begin to try to explain where she fitted in the ludicrously complex world of German principalities.

he did the unthinkable and encouraged the boy to actually *meet* his prospective brides and choose the one he got on with best. It might be assumed from this that George I had a soft spot for his son, after all, but his only concern was to secure the succession. A good marriage would lead to lots of children.

So, the prince secretly visited the court of Caroline's father in Ansbach under the name of Monsieur de Bush. Whether anyone fell for this flimsy subterfuge I don't know, but George Bush hung around long enough to discover that he actually rather liked Caroline and announced that he wouldn't think of marrying anybody else. For once in this story of bad monarchs and bad marriages, we have a pretty good marriage. It has to be said that George didn't remain faithful to her. He thought it was his duty as a king, particularly an English one, to have a mistress, and he kept several over the years, although still remained devoted to Caroline until her early death.

Caroline was eight months older than George. Well-educated, she comes across as the smarter of the two in this relationship. They were married in 1705 and their eldest son, Frederick Louis, was born in January 1707. In all, they had seven surviving children. The Hanoverians were considerably better at producing healthy offspring than the Stuarts, or, indeed, the Tudors. Sadly, though, George grew to hate Frederick in the same way that his father hated him, as we'll see later.

Prince George was keen on warfare and had been itching to fight in the War of the Spanish Succession. His father hadn't allowed him to take part, however, until he'd produced a son and heir. Once Frederick was born, George was ready to fight, but had to delay his departure when Caroline came down with the dreaded smallpox – and he then caught it off her after insisting on staying by her side during her illness. They both recovered, though, and, in 1708, George hurried off to serve under the Duke of Marlborough in the cavalry. He fought well and bravely at the Battle of Oudenarde, where his horse was killed under him, hit by cannon shot, and the officer next to him was also killed, splattering the prince with his blood and gore. As a result, George became something of a hero in both Hanover and England, which his father resented.

When he accompanied his father to England in 1714 for his coronation, he was made Prince of Wales and it seemed that everybody in

England much preferred him to the new king – another reason for his father's resentment. One cause for the mutual antagonism between Prince George and *his* son, Frederick, was that when Prince George came over to England, the king ordered him to leave Frederick behind. He didn't see the boy for 14 years.

Prince George spoke better English than his father, albeit with a thick German accent, and claimed to love England. He was apparently a very good dancer, the John Travolta of the Hanoverian court, who all stood back to admire his slick moves. He also showed a lot of interest in the ladies-in-waiting and promised them a fun and colourful court.

His father, who was not a people person and was terrible at connecting, grew ever more jealous of the sociable Prince of Wales, keeping him at arm's length and not allowing him to get involved in the workings of government. It was made clear that the prince wasn't welcome at court, either, and, even though he'd been further ennobled, he wasn't allowed to take his place in the House of Lords. His titles sound like the sort of cod, made-up English titles you get in American films or comedy sketches. He was the Duke and Marquis of Cambridge, the Earl of Milford Haven, Viscount Northallerton and Baron Tewkesbury.

When George I went over to Hanover, he gave his son only very limited powers to govern while he was gone, and the prince set up camp at Hampton Court from where he did a grand tour of several towns in southern England. He entertained lavishly and even invited people to come and watch him dine (apparently a hot ticket). His star rose even higher when he helped to put out a fire in London in 1716 and then kept a cool head when a man broke into his box at Drury Lane Theatre and tried to kill him. The would-be assassin shot one of the prince's attendants dead before he was overpowered. As we've seen, surviving an assassination attempt is a sure-fire method of gaining instant popularity.

It seems that father and son were in the process of patching things up when, in 1717, Caroline gave birth to a second son, imaginatively christened George. I do wish they wouldn't keep doing this. I've lost count of how many sodding Georges there are in the story now (don't worry, though, the poor baby died three months later, so that's one less). King George appointed the Duke of Newcastle as the little boy's godfather, and it seems the Prince of Wales hated the man. The two of them had a huge row at the christening that ended with the prince shouting at the duke, 'You are a rascal!! But I will find you!!!'

The Duke of Newcastle, who was highly strung and a little deaf, thought that Prince George had said 'I will fight you' and was challenging him to a duel. To prevent it all kicking off, the king forced his son to apologise, which he did grudgingly, and then kicked him out of St James's Palace (the royal residence at the time), where he'd been living. Caroline and the Prince of Wales had to leave their young children behind in the care of the king (their eldest boy, Frederick, was still in Hanover).

George and Caroline set up camp at Leicester House and now everyone – ministers, courtiers and family – had to choose who to show their loyalty to: king or prince. At first, the prince was in a panic, fearing he might be disinherited. Luckily, though, he had a secret weapon – his wife, Caroline. She was very canny and understood politics and the intricacies of court intrigue better than her husband. She cultivated a close relationship with Robert Walpole and they built a firm power base together over the next few years, gathering opponents of the king at Leicester House. And then, in 1727, King George I died unexpectedly, and the prince was crowned George II.*

George I had left extensive instructions about the succession and family inheritances in Britain and Hanover, but the new king wasn't going to be told what to do any more. The first thing he did on becoming king (after burning his mother's letters and portrait) was to get hold of his father's will and hide it. It was never seen again. It didn't really make a lot of difference to the British line of succession because the monarchy didn't actually have any say in that – it was all controlled by parliament – but it might have split the family power in Hanover, where the British government had no control.

George II settled down to a life of dull routine at Saint James's Palace. He had two prime mistresses – Henrietta Howard, Countess

---

* This was the first time that the rousing anthem, *Zadok the Priest*, by court composer Handel, was sung at a coronation. And it's been sung at every coronation since.

of Suffolk, and Mary Scott, the Countess of Deloraine. Just like his father, however, he mainly just wanted partners to play whist with and didn't seem to have hankered after a raunchy sex life. He had a strict calendar and played cards with different women on different nights. The whole thing was like a light-comedy sex farce (Walpole once reported that George's mistress, Lady Deloraine, was in disgrace because she'd pulled the chair from under him just as he was trying to sit down).

George enjoyed music, but had very little interest in art or literature. He was always complaining that Queen Caroline read too many books and insisted on having soirees with intellectuals and men of learning, making her more like a school mistress than a queen.

He was a fastidious, meticulous man, obsessed with order and routine. He ran his domestic life like clockwork and behaved like a bad-tempered child, flying into terrible rages at the slightest provocation, usually over some tiny, pedantic point. Today, he might be diagnosed with OCD and placed somewhere on the autistic spectrum, perhaps with Asperger's. For instance, he had his underwear numbered, according to days of the week, and it had to be laid out in the correct order or he'd throw his wig on the floor and kick it around in frustration. He knew every detail of the palace, where each painting should be hung, where every ornament and vase should be placed. And he had a love of lists, like royal family trees and military regiments, which he delighted in reciting. He could bore for England. And he did.

Even George's sex life ran to a strict schedule. He would visit the apartments of his chief mistress, Henrietta Howard, at exactly seven o'clock every evening, pacing about and checking his watch beforehand to make sure he entered as the clock struck the hour.

Henrietta was one of the longest-serving royal mistresses in history (nearly 20 years) and held the title as an official royal appointment. She received a salary, and a pension when she retired. It was all very ordered and civilised. Henrietta had been married to an abusive husband when she first became George's mistress and it was an escape for her. Queen Caroline liked getting a break from the obsessive George as well. It meant she didn't have to listen to him going through his lists of regiments every night. Henrietta was fine with that. She was deaf.

In 1728, Prince Frederick, aged 21, finally came over to England from Hanover and was soon made Prince of Wales. As I said, George hadn't seen him for 14 years and absence certainly hadn't made the heart grow fonder. They despised each other. Frederick didn't allow his parents to be present at the birth of his first child, Augusta, which led to a major falling out, with the prince being kicked out of St James's, just like his father before him.

In 1736, George went back to Hanover. He wasn't a regular visitor, but it was still a very unpopular move in England. There was a suspicion that the Georges cared more about Hanover than they did about England and that their foreign policy was solely focused on protecting Hanover. Somebody stuck up a satirical poster at the gates of St James's which read: 'Lost or strayed out of this house. A man who has left a wife and six children on the parish.' The truth is, though, that while George had very little actual control over the government in Britain, it was a different story in Hanover, where, as elector he was the effective ruler.

Queen Caroline rode shotgun for him, holding things together in England and keeping relations with parliament sweet. Unfortunately, in 1737, she died after a long illness. The king was at her deathbed, hovering about and telling her how much he loved her, when Caroline told him that he must marry again. George protested that he was a decent man who would honour her memory. He wasn't going to take a wife. 'No! I shall have mistresses.' This was a man with no filter.*

The wars for control of Europe were never ending. Whenever there was any dispute, everyone got together and said, 'I suppose we'd better have a war about this.' There were three wars over succession in Spain, Poland and Austria, the last one set in motion by the War of Jenkins' Ear, which at least had a fun name. It had started in the Americas where the Spanish were aggressively guarding their trade, boarding and searching any suspect English ships. A furious row broke out on one ship and the Spanish cut an ear off the captain, Robert Jenkins. Nothing much more happened at the time but, seven years later, when

---

* Not long after Caroline's death, George imported another mistress from Hanover – Countess Amalie Sophie Marianne von Wallmoden-Gimborn, whom he made countess of Yarmouth and with whom he had an illegitimate child.

bellicose elements of the English government were looking for an excuse to start a trade war against Spain, they dragged Jenkins into the Houses of Parliament and said, 'Look what those dirty foreigners did to this poor man. We must declare war on them.'

George had had a pretty successful military career in his younger days and, in 1743, decided that he was going to go over to Europe for one last hurrah and to remind his people of past glories, even though he was now 59. He led an allied army of British, Hanoverian, Austrian and German troops against the French at the Battle of Dettingen in the War of the Austrian Succession. This was, famously, the last time a British king led an army into battle. The battle was otherwise pretty unmemorable and it was hard to tell who'd actually won (probably George).

The King was told that he mustn't put himself in danger like this again and gave command of the army to his favourite son, Prince William Augustus, Duke of Cumberland. The war didn't go well for the British, however, and Cumberland was badly beaten by the French at Fontenoy.

The Jacobites had been keeping a close eye on developments and thought *OK, England's in a precarious position, let's go for it!* And, in 1745, the Old Pretender's son – Charles Edward Stuart, Bonnie Prince Charlie, the Young Pretender, who'd been trying to drum up backing in France – set sail to Scotland, where the support for his cause was greatest.

Charlie and his Scottish army were initially very successful. They beat the English at the Battle of Prestonpans and marched south, getting as far as Derby, where they stopped. We've seen this happen so many times – a Scottish army raids northern England, gets up the courage to press south, but then wavers. Like many before him, Charlie was dissuaded by his nervous commanders from pressing on into the English heartlands and trying to take London.

Charlie had been in a bubble and believed the yes-men around him. He'd been expecting thousands of secret Jacobites in England, who'd had to remain silent, to rise up and join his army. In the event, one man and his dog turned out. By now, hardly anybody in England wanted the Jacobites back. They didn't want the disruption. Things were calm and orderly under the Hanoverians. So Charlie turned round and went back to Scotland – hotly pursued by the Duke of Cumberland. The English army took the fight across the border and, on 16 April 1746, smashed the Jacobites to pieces at the bloody Battle of Culloden near Inverness, the last pitched battle fought on British soil.

There was no mercy given. Cumberland wanted to put down the Jacobite threat for ever and Charlie's troops were mostly ill-equipped Scottish Highlanders. They were brave, tough men, but they stood no chance. This was the end for the Jacobites, who never again tried to take the throne. The song 'God Save the King' had been written for a play and became so popular after the victory at Culloden that it was adopted as the national anthem.

George relaxed and went back to his mistresses and his card playing and boring people with his recitals of lists. Everything was sorted. The Jacobites were no longer a threat, the War of the Austrian Succession had ended in 1748, parliament was getting on with the business of running the country, and the king had a male heir in the shape of Frederick, Prince of Wales. OK, so the two of them hated each other, but at least the succession was secure … And then, in 1751, Frederick was hit by a cricket ball and died at the age of 44 (that's the fun version – as ever, I have to spoil the party by saying it was possibly just a pulmonary embolism).

King George shed few tears. In fact, he seemed quite happy at the way things had panned out. Frederick had left behind a healthy 12-year-old son, George, and the king could bring up his grandson however he wanted.

It wasn't long, though, before Europe was at war again. The Seven Years' War was a fearsome conflict, perhaps the first *world* war, fought in Europe, the Americas, India and the Far East. It also spread to Africa, where the British took territory from the French and further tightened their grip on the slave trade.

Spain was top dog in South America and the dominant force in the Caribbean. Their allies, the French, controlled large parts of North America, in particular Canada. Britain's main ally was Prussia, which, under the leadership of Frederick the Great, was becoming an extremely dominant force in Europe. And Frederick's main enemy was Austria.

The Seven Years' War was a big step towards Britain ruling a vast, international empire, and many heroes of the British Empire emerged from it – men like General Wolfe, who was instrumental in taking Canada from the French, and 'Clive of India', who was instrumental in taking India from the Indians. These were names that every pupil knew when I was a boy but which have fallen out of fashion as their reputations have tarnished, alongside the reputation of the empire. Wolfe was an insane squirt with a death wish, Clive was a greedy plunderer who cared nothing for the Indian people.

Despite the fact that George was growing blind and deaf, he enjoyed the war and was always encouraging his commanders to go in harder and more ruthlessly. He had Admiral John Byng shot by a firing squad on board the HMS *Monarch* for 'failing to do his utmost' to relieve a British garrison in Minorca. He even had a go at his favourite son – William, Duke of Cumberland, the Butcher of Culloden, not otherwise known as a softie – for being insufficiently aggressive towards the French in Hanover.

On 25 October 1760, the 76-year-old king got up at his regular time, went into his bathroom at his regular time and had his regular dump, but when he didn't emerge at his regular time, his valet became anxious. Then there was a mighty thud and the valet rushed in to find that George had fallen off the toilet and hit his head.

Just to complete his comedy ending, George whispered 'Call Amelia' and his daughter, Amelia, was summoned to his side, only for him to complain, 'Not that one …' He'd meant for them to fetch his mistress, Amalie, Countess of Yarmouth.

George's reputation is full of contradictions. He had mistresses but adored his wife. He was blunt and plain-spoken, which meant he could be offensive, but he was never deceitful. He didn't do much politically, but (albeit rather grudgingly) allowed strong politicians like Robert Walpole and William Pitt the Elder to flourish. He was a figure of fun, but the British were proud of their country's achievements under his rule.

Britain, with its expanding empire and dominance of the slave trade, combined with the rise of industrialisation at home, was becoming a wealthy and prosperous world power. The Hanoverians had been accepted.

33

4 GEORGES (#3)

GEORGE III – 1738–1820
Farmer George
Reigned 1760–1820
Lived for 81 years. Reigned for 59 years.
Died from pneumonia.
Remembered for: going mad and losing America.

George III was on the throne for 59 years and, until Victoria beat his record, he was both the longest-lived and the longest-reigning monarch. He's still the longest reigning *king*, which means a lot of history happened while he was on the throne: the Acts of Union officially unified the British Isles into the United Kingdom of Great Britain and Ireland; the American War of Independence kicked off and led to the founding of the USA; the French Revolution tore Europe apart; Napoleon rose and fell … George just wasn't always aware of what was going on because his life was blighted by spells of madness, which increasingly made him incapable of functioning.

During his longest spell of madness, his son (the future George IV) ruled in his place as Prince Regent from 1811 until the king's death in 1820. When people talk of the 'Regency Era', they're usually referring to the longer period from 1795 to 1837, spanning the latter part of George III's reign and on through his two sons, George IV and William IV. As with all the other Hanoverian kings, George III and IV both hated each other, which made the early regency quite fraught.

George was the first Hanoverian king to be born in Great Britain and the first who spoke English as his primary language. He didn't like travelling and never actually visited Hanover. He also never visited the north of England, Scotland, Wales or Ireland, staying pretty much in the south of England. He took his holidays in the coastal town of

Weymouth in Dorset, which he popularised as one of the first resorts in England and made it fashionable to go to the seaside, which is why you have so many Georgian and Regency buildings in English coastal towns, most famously Brighton.

The satirists of the day nicknamed him Farmer George, portraying him in a silly country hat and smock. They laughed at him as a simpleton who was only interested in mundane things like growing vegetables. George was very modern in a way, though. Because of the war with Europe, he insisted on what we now call food security, saying that farmers should be able to grow enough food to sustain the nation. 'Farmer George' ended up as a term of endearment and he was seen as a simple, decent man of the people.

As I say, George spoke English as his first language and, in his accession speech in 1760, made a point of explaining that he 'was born and educated in this country. I glory in the name of Briton.' He was basically saying, 'I'm even more English than the last George.' He also became caught up with the idea that monarchs should behave in a 'royal' manner. They should be an example to us all, a paragon of virtue and dignity.*

George was very unforgiving of members of his family who didn't live up to his high standards. It has to be said that a lot of his brothers and sisters, and his own children, *did* behave in a rather unreconstructed manner and their personal lives were pretty fruity. George was forever ticking them off and complaining that it was his misfortune to live in particularly wicked times (but, let's face it, since the dawn of mankind, people have thought that).

George was considered not to be a particularly bright child and was accused of laziness and occasional melancholy. He was also sullen and distant, so people didn't warm to him. He blossomed as he grew up, however, and when he was a young man, the Duchess of Northumberland described him as tall, robust, graceful and dignified, with blue eyes, thin, light brown hair, good teeth and 'a noble openness

---

* Queen Victoria also promoted this idea, which persists to this day, particularly in the Tory press, who are always getting hot under the collar about members of the royal family who don't behave 'properly'.

in his countenance, blended with cheerful, good-natured affability' and a ruddy complexion.

The main thing George did take from his schooling was an interest in science, particularly astronomy, and he was involved in setting up the King's Observatory in Richmond, where he was forever dragging people in to look at things like the transit of Venus.

His life took an unexpected turn in 1751 when his father, Frederick, Prince of Wales, died from a lung injury, caused by either being hit by a cricket ball or from a pulmonary embolism. This meant that the 12-year-old George became next in line to the throne and his grand-father, King George II, began to take more of an interest in him (relieved that the despised Frederick was out of the picture). Then, in 1760, George II himself died and George III came to the throne at the age of 22, at which point it was decided that he really ought to get married. To promote his Englishness, George initially said that he would marry an English noblewoman, but he was talked out of it; a political marriage to a foreign princess would be far preferable. Eventually they settled on the 17-year-old Charlotte of Mecklenburg Strelitz, who was considered a safe bet: she was sensible, sweet-natured, compliant, Protestant and had little interest in politics. The only thing she didn't have going for her was 'regular beauty' (although, like George, she was judged to have good teeth). That didn't seem to matter to George – the marriage lasted 57 years and they had 15 children.

George didn't meet Charlotte until the day they married in September 1761. They were introduced to each other at three in the afternoon, were married at nine and then it was off to bed. I'm not sure Charlotte was particularly fond of George at first, but she did grow close to him. He was a much more likable man than the other three Georges. He could be stern, and preferred the more judgemental parts of the Bible, but he was kind to his wife, who lived up to her promise. She was supportive of him, didn't cause any problems and, well, did very little, really.

George had liked one of his otherwise spectacularly dull tutors, John Stuart, 3rd Earl of Bute. In fact, he liked him so much that one of the first things he did on becoming king was help manoeuvre him into becoming prime minister. Bute became the first ever Tory PM after more than 50 years of Whig supremacy, but, inevitably, he was a disaster. Other politicians didn't like the king interfering and Bute was not an able politician. A lot of scurrilous gossip went around that he'd been having an affair with George's widowed mother. He was hanged in effigy and assaulted on the street, so he didn't last long, and George was scalded in his dealings with government. This was his one and only attempt to be a proper, old-fashioned king, a mover and shaker who ruled the country and kept a firm control of parliament. He had to accept that his role was largely ceremonial. He was a constitutional, not an absolute, monarch, and needed to learn how to deal with politicians more diplomatically. Parliament was now more important than the monarchy and prime ministers were the new kings. That being said, people were ambivalent about the power of these new 'prime ministers'.

The autocratic and arrogant William Pitt the Elder had taken over from Robert Walpole during the reign of George II. The public liked Pitt when he helped them to win wars and kept the economy afloat but turned against him in less turbulent times, which would make him throw a fit and resign. Then other, lesser, men would take over and fail, get thrown out and Pitt would be invited back.

The Seven Years' War ended in 1763, three years into George's reign, and left Britain as the dominant European power. The defeat of the French not only gave Britain sole rule of Canada and the eastern parts of North America, but it also became the main European force in India, pretty much by accident. The British army had initially gone to India to fight the French and try to stop them taking over there. Once the French were beaten back, however, it left India open to imperial exploitation by the British, who, within a remarkably short time, were ruling almost the entire subcontinent.

Now that Britain was at peace, trade could open up again and the treasury was under less strain, allowing George to settle down to married life. He bought Buckingham House as a more comfortable London residence for Queen Charlotte than St James's Palace, renaming it the Queen's Residence. (It's not exactly the same building as it was back then; the public-facing frontage, of what is now called Buckingham Palace, is a later extension.) None of the royals have ever liked the place. It's big and cold and uncomfortable, very hard to maintain and not very pretty. Queen Elizabeth II famously lived in a small suite of private rooms that she made as homely as she could and really only used the larger rooms on state and ceremonial occasions.*

When George came to the throne, the Crown Estate, the royal lands, didn't produce enough income, so the monarchy was reliant on taxes. George worked with parliament to rejig this system. He surrendered the revenues from the Crown Estate in return for an official, regular sum given to the royal family to run their household and cover expenses, called the civil list. Despite the new arrangement, during the course of his long reign, George still managed to amass more than £3,000,000 in debt, which was paid off by parliament.

He didn't spend all the money on himself. He helped out the Royal Academy of Arts, he gave a large amount to charity and he was a patron of the sciences. Pretty much every institution with 'Royal' as part of its name was founded by George III. But he's best known as a collector of books. His King's Library was accessible to scholars and more than 65,000 volumes from his collection are now housed at the British Library in London.

France had been economically crippled by the war and then wrung dry by the subsequent Treaty of Paris. In much the same way that Germany struggled after the First World War, leading to societal collapse and the rise of Hitler, France underwent a similar process after the Seven Years' War. The severely damaged economy brought about radicalism, which in turn led to the French Revolution and then the rise of a dictator – Napoleon Bonaparte.

The Seven Years' War also directly led to the American War of Independence and the end of British rule there. The war hadn't only been expensive for the French; the British needed to claw back some cash and started heavily taxing all their colonies. The king's army had fought against the French alongside the British colonists in America.

---

* I've attended a few functions at Buckingham Palace and always leave with the feeling that I really wouldn't want to live there. The state rooms are heavy and soulless and weirdly anonymous, despite displaying some rather fabulous paintings, such as Vermeer's *Lady at the Virginals with a Gentleman* and some fine Canalettos, acquired by George.

One local man who came to prominence in the war was a young officer in the British army called George Washington.

After the French were driven out, their previously held territories were technically up for grabs, but the British government put limits on westward expansion because they'd made treaties with the Native Americans, who'd fought on their side in the war. In a royal proclamation of 1763, the government created what were essentially the first 'Indian reservations'.

The British colonists didn't like this one bit. They figured it was up to them to decide whether or not to take more land from the original inhabitants. They also didn't like paying taxes without having any direct representation in Westminster. Parliament argued that saving the colonies had been a pretty bloody, expensive undertaking, so the least the colonists could do was pay some something towards the cost.

This didn't wash in the colonies and there was talk of separating from Britain. The government didn't take this very seriously at first and further enraged the colonists by imposing stamp duty on all paper documents and custom duties on trade. When relations got even worse, George insisted that parliament removed these duties from everything except tea (to maintain the precedent).

In 1773, a group of colonists dressed as Native Americans boarded tea ships moored in Boston Harbour and threw all the cargo overboard in an incident that became known as the Boston Tea Party. Instead of trying to negotiate with the locals, the British government went in heavily and soon there was fighting between rebel Americans, who saw George III as a tyrant, and loyalists. George sent the navy and an army over from Britain to try to support the loyalists and preserve the colonies. A dispute over taxes, stamp duty and customs tariffs had blown up into a full-scale war. It was only later that concepts like idealism, liberty and patriotism were attached to the conflict (a lot of it retrospectively) to promote the idea that the founding fathers of American independence were fighting all along for high-minded democratic principles.

King George stubbornly refused to give up the fight, even though it was almost impossible to sustain a major war on the other side of the Atlantic. The logistics and the cost were just too hard to support, and it became clear that the rebels were totally committed. People started telling George that he had to let it go. There was unrest on the streets and rioting. In 1776, the Americans declared themselves independent, but George only admitted defeat in 1783, after two of his sons died in infancy and he was at a very low ebb.

William Pitt the Elder had eventually died in 1778. His son, William Pitt the Younger, eventually filled his boots when he was only about 11 years old. Well, not quite that young, he was 24 when he became prime minster in 1783.

The loss of America was humiliating, but it has to be said that there were economic advantages for Britain who no longer had to spend huge amounts of money supporting the colony. The removal of the American problem meant that British politics could settle down without constantly arguing about how to handle the situation, allowing the imperial drive to be directed towards India (as well as Australia and Africa).

The loss of the American colonies, on the back of losing two children, was enormously stressful for George and, in 1788, his mental health suddenly deteriorated. Until quite recently, a diagnosis of porphyria was commonly accepted, a blood disorder with many symptoms, including anxiety, confusion and discoloured urine (George purportedly had purple piss). The more accepted diagnosis is now bipolar disorder, the main symptom of which is cycling between deep, debilitating depression and irrational euphoria.

George was plunged into terrible despair and then lifted to the heights of incredible mania, where he felt he was a godlike figure, filled with incredible energy and insight, spouting flowery language that made little sense to anyone other than him. When in a manic part of his cycle, George would talk for hours on end until he was foaming at the mouth and his voice was hoarse and cracked. He would be consumed by wild flights of fancy and then plummet into anguished despondency: *I'm going mad. What's happened to me? I'm losing everything. This is a disaster …*

His doctors didn't know how to deal with it. They tried putting him in a straitjacket until he calmed down, and they tried putting caustic poultices on him and cupping them 'to draw out the evil from within', which, of course, did nothing beneficial and only exacerbated his unbalanced mental state.

His first bout of mania was not as extreme as the attacks he suffered in later years. He was well enough to leave London and visit Cheltenham Spa for recuperation in the summer of 1788. But his condition worsened and, for the first time, a regency was discussed in parliament, although the competing factions couldn't agree on the terms and George recovered before they came to any decision.

People were happy to have their king back and talking sense, and he became even more popular when a fellow madman shot at him at Drury Lane Theatre, in an extraordinary repeat of what had happened to his grandfather. The would-be assassin, James Hadfield, was an officer who had received severe head injuries at the Battle of Tourcoing in 1794. He'd then got heavily into deluded conspiracy theories and joined a millennialist cult, becoming convinced that if he was killed by the English government, it would lead to the second coming of Jesus Christ. But his suicide mission went wrong. He failed to kill the king and he failed to get himself killed. Realising that the man was obviously insane, George treated him humanely.*

The year before Hadfield's failed assassination, in 1789, the French decided to have a revolution. At first, many in Europe, including the Whigs, cheered on the revolutionaries. This was progress towards true Parliamentarian rule and many in Britain asked why it had taken the French so long. The British had had their revolution 150 years earlier under Cromwell; although the monarchy had eventually been welcomed back, it was with severe restrictions.

Unlike the British, the French had had an absolute monarchy and when their kings were strong and victorious, like the awesome Louis XIV, nobody much complained. But since the Sun King's death in 1715, the French had been saddled with a couple of duds – Louis XV and Louis XVI. No longer the dominant force in Europe, when France lost the Seven Years' War and many of its overseas possessions, the writing was on the wall. The country was in economic tatters, people

---

* He also didn't seem to have been that traumatised by the incident. He fell asleep during the interval.

were hungry, the social order was breaking down and the blame was pinned on the monarchy. A group of radical politicians, journalists and free-thinkers harnessed the public mood and, in 1789, the whole thing exploded. Three years later, the monarchy had been abolished and Louis XVI was locked up. When a Prussian army bolstered by French loyalists threatened Paris, the revolutionaries panicked. Fearing that the old regime would get back into power, as they had done in England, they started massacring aristocrats and anyone they caught on the streets who they thought might be counter-revolutionaries, or just didn't like the look of.

There was no going back from this. The king's execution the following year, in 1793, was followed by the Reign of Terror when the guillotines worked flat out.

Across the Channel in London, even the Whigs who'd originally supported the revolution were thinking that it had gone too far and worried that anarchy and violence might spread to Britain. It was almost a relief when the French revolutionaries declared all-out war on all non-revolutionary countries – including Britain.

A 28-year-old Corsican called Napoleon Bonaparte, who had shown a great flair for warfare as an artillery officer and had quickly risen to prominence in the revolutionary army, was sent off to Egypt with orders to cut a way through the Ottoman Empire to India and take on the British there. However, he'd been followed by a British fleet under Rear Admiral Horatio Nelson. Nelson was an unconventional naval commander whose very successful but rather unsubtle tactic was to split his fleet into two, go in hard against enemy ships from both sides and Attack! Attack! Attack! He smashed the French fleet to pieces and they never really recovered for the duration of what became the Napoleonic Wars.

Understandably, the British people were none too happy when the prime minister, William Pitt the Younger, increased taxes and raised armies. Consequently, crowds demanding an end to the war and lower bread prices attacked King George's carriage in 1795 on his way to opening Parliament. George and his government hastily passed the 'Treason and Seditious Meetings Act' that banned large gatherings.

GEORGE III
IN HIS
STRAIGHT JACKET

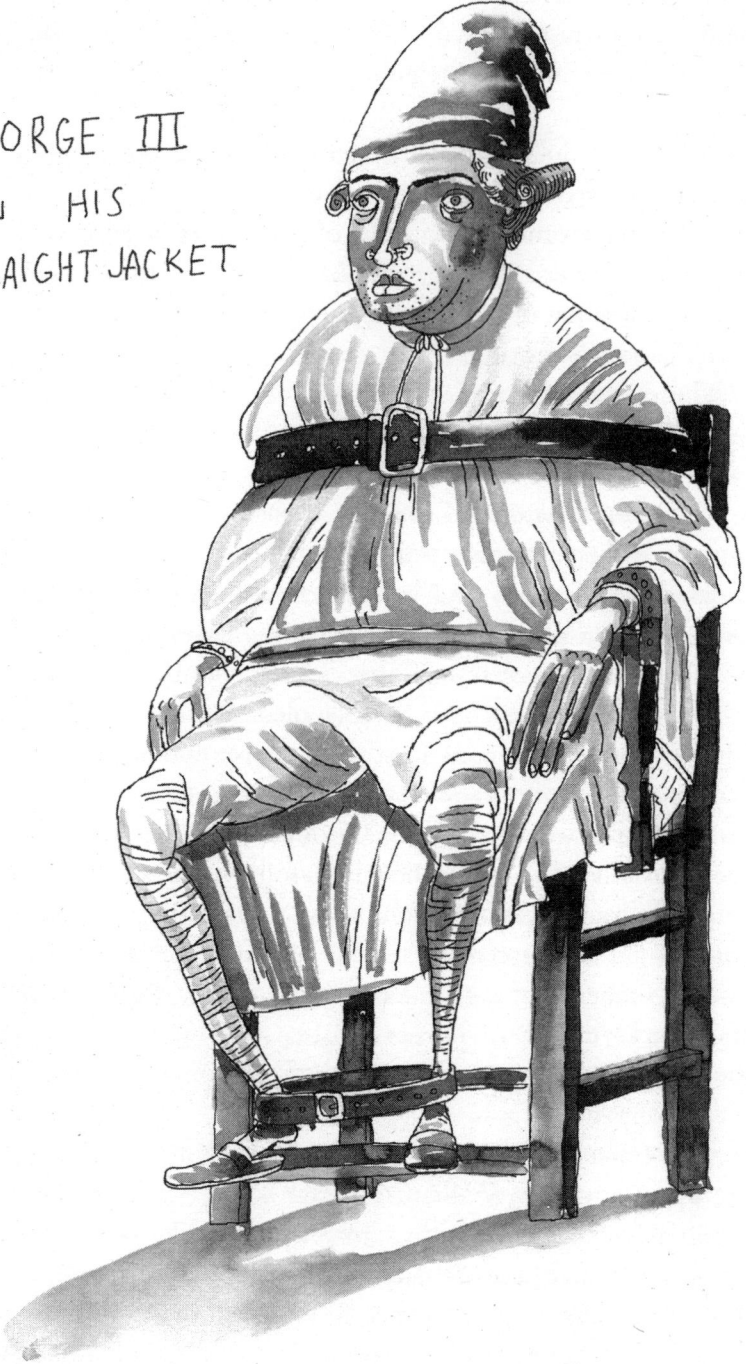

The French Revolution descended into mindless self-destructive violence. Nearly all of the original leaders ended up dead, which allowed Napoleon to seize power in a military coup in 1799. The French may have got rid of a king, but they'd ended up with an emperor. And Napoleon wasn't content with just taking back control of France; he wanted to rule the world.

To counter the threat, Britain made a series of coalitions with different foreign powers. There were seven in all and the first five didn't work. In 1800, the second coalition was defeated and Britain was left to fight alone for a while. That same year, the British and Irish parliaments passed the Act of Union, binding Great Britain and Ireland into a single entity with no separate parliaments. Great Britain officially became the United Kingdom of Great Britain and Ireland. William Pitt the Younger wanted to give more freedom to the Catholics, arguing that the restrictions on them were outdated and unjust. George fiercely resisted, saying that he'd made a coronation oath to uphold Protestantism and couldn't allow the emancipation of Catholics, causing Pitt to threaten to resign. The stress of all this, on top of a major war, tipped George into another period of madness.

There was by now a serious threat of an invasion by Napoleon. Coastal defences were improved, with forts, known as Martello towers, being built everywhere. But the navy was Britain's greatest defence. It was the best equipped and best trained in Europe, commanded by skilled, experienced and ambitious officers eager to prove their worth.

In 1805, Napoleon made his move and launched a combined Spanish–French fleet to take control of the English Channel in preparation for an invasion. His nemesis was once again the brilliant and ruthless admiral, Horatio Nelson, who used similar tactics to those that had served him so well at the Battle of the Nile, seven years earlier. Near the Cape of Trafalgar off the coast of southern Spain, he split his fleet into two and went in hard, breaking up the line of enemy ships and sinking 20 of them. Nelson didn't lose a single ship but was killed in the battle, which went down as one of Britain's greatest naval triumphs.

George recovered enough to return to public life, but he was by now 66 and in ill health, and attended parliament supported by walking sticks and wrapped in blankets. The victories against Napoleon had made him popular again. Of course, his popularity varied depending on who you asked. A Georgian-era popular drama like *Bridgerton* will show you the nice frocks and the lovely houses, but there was a huge mismatch between the layers of society.

The upper classes, the landowners and the slave traders were doing very well, thank you very much – as were middle-class traders, merchants, bankers and the money men in the city. The lower levels of society weren't exactly profiting from any of this, though. So many of them had lost access to common land during the enclosures that they weren't able to feed themselves. The big shots who'd taken the land for themselves, however, were beginning to exploit what was *underneath* it. Mineral rights in the rest of Europe mostly belonged to the state, even on private property. Rights in Britain belonged to the landowners and many of them were sitting on coal, which was firing a newly industrialised nation. People were leaving the countryside and moving into the towns to work in the steam-driven factories. And, in turn, due to the 'triangular trade', there were cheap goods coming in from the Americas to fuel these workers, chiefly sugar, tobacco and coffee.

The triangular trade was a useful euphemism for the slave trade, which must have seemed almost miraculous to people in England. Ships would set off from English ports like Bristol and Liverpool laden with cheap goods – cloth, knives, guns, beads, cooking pots, beer, cider etc. – and would return months later weighed down with cotton, gold and, yes, sugar, tobacco and coffee.

But there was a third leg of this journey that the British people saw nothing of. When the ships left England, they sailed to West Africa and exchanged their cargo for slaves who were transported across the Atlantic to the Caribbean to be sold. Finally, the human cargo was replaced by local goods.

In the 1790s, almost 400,000 Africans – men women and children – were shipped to the Americas in the most appalling conditions. One in eight of them died on the way. And this awful business did very well for Britain.

George himself never owned any slaves but, like most well-off people in Britain, he massively benefited from the trade. When he was young, he wrote that slavery was a ridiculous, terrible idea and shouldn't be allowed, yet, ironically, as king he resisted efforts to end it.

There had been a growing anti-slavery movement in Britain since the middle of the 18th century, largely driven by religious groups like the Quakers and the Methodists. William Wilberforce is credited with being the driving force behind the abolition of slavery, but he didn't act alone, and many Africans, such as Olaudah Equiano, were vocal and influential in the ongoing debate.

In 1807, King George finally gave in to pressure and signed the Slave Trade Act. What's interesting is that the act didn't ban slavery – which had not been allowed on British soil since William the Conqueror's time – only the transatlantic trade. British overseas land-owners were barred from acquiring any new slaves but were allowed to keep those they already owned. It was to be another 35 years before slavery itself was abolished in the Slavery Abolition Act of 1833, although, even then, there were certain places within the British Empire that you were allowed to keep slaves, such as the territories governed by the East India Company.

Indeed, slavery still existed in parts of the British Empire into the 1930s.

Passing the Slave Trade Act was the last significant undertaking George III managed. By 1810, he was nearly blind from cataracts, in terrible pain from rheumatism and showing signs of dementia. It was then that he suffered his worst descent into madness. This was the start of the official Regency period that lasted until the king's death in 1820.

Lost in a world of his own, George knew nothing of the ultimate defeat of Napoleon, or that he was declared king of Hanover when it was made a monarchy in 1814, or that his beloved wife Charlotte died in 1818. At Christmas 1819, he apparently spoke nonsense for 58 hours non-stop, not dissimilar to what a Russell Brand podcast feels like.

For the last few weeks of his life, he couldn't walk, he was totally blind, manic and demented. He eventually died of pneumonia at Windsor Castle at the beginning of 1820.

The British liked Farmer George. He would happily chat to his subjects about the market price of their cattle, or their favourite apple pudding recipes, and he gained a reputation for being normal and approachable (when he wasn't locked away out of sight in a strait jacket). This contributed greatly to the stability of the institution of the monarchy. The British also loved George because he stayed married to one woman, didn't have any mistresses and was very pious. It seems that the standards for why you would love a monarch were quite low at the time.

His son, George IV, was a very different kettle of rotting fish.

34

4 GEORGES (#4)

GEORGE IV – 1762–1830

Prince Regent/Prinny/the First Gentleman of Europe
Reigned 1811–20 (as prince regent); 1820–30 (as king)
Lived for 67 years. Ruled for 19 years
(including his time as regent).
Died of just about everything.
Best remembered for: being an odious, obese dandy and
commissioning Brighton Pavilion.

And so we come to the notorious George IV, a king whose reign was soiled by scandal and extravagance. He was the sort of lazy, dissolute, frivolous, noisy, selfish, self-centred, self-indulgent, gluttonous, unreliable, irresponsible, out-of-touch, wealthy toff that gives the upper classes a bad name. Many started saying that Britain should go down the French route, have another revolution and get rid of the royal family altogether.

George ruled as regent for the last ten years of his father's life, impatient to take the throne, and then, when he eventually did become king, he moaned about it, saying it was too much work. He just wanted to eat and drink and spend vast amounts of money. He struggled financially all his life, spending too much on horses, on women, on various buildings, on the art he filled them with, on clothing and on banquets. At one feast, with a gold and silver theme, he had a huge table specially made with a canal down the middle filled with live fish.

George just couldn't stop racking up the debts, hitting a staggering £630,000 (about £65 million today) before he'd even become regent, and parliament had to keep on bailing him out with a series of grants.

His full name was George Augustus Frederick, but he was called many things in his lifetime. He started out as the Prince of Wales, then became Prince Regent, which many people shortened to Prinny. His preferred epithet was 'the First Gentleman of Europe', but the writer, Charles Lamb, wrote a lampoon about him in which he dubbed him the 'Prince of Whales' – which is how most people saw him.

On the plus side, George was an unlikely fashion icon and trend-setter, and he could be very entertaining. He was constantly telling funny anecdotes and impersonating people, trying to make everyone laugh. It was said that he was witty, not only when he was drunk but also while he was sober, which is a hard act to pull off.

The Duke of Wellington, who was prime minister for a couple of years during George's reign (after he'd become a national hero for defeating Napoleon), called him 'the worst man I ever fell in with my whole life, the most selfish, the most false, the most ill-natured. The most entirely without one redeeming quality'.

Wellington was a very serious and self-important man and, while he admired George's wit, he had less time for his buffoonish side. George loved to wind him up by pretending that he'd fought at Waterloo disguised as a German general, so perhaps we can't rely on the duke for an unbiased view of him.

Wellington's opinion, though, was shared by pretty much everyone, sharpened by the fact that George was the complete opposite of his father, George III, who'd been a decent, God-fearing, well-behaved sort of chap. It has to be said, though, that George IV was a lot more fun than his father who was, let's face it, just a little bit dull (when he wasn't raving and foaming at the mouth in one of his periods of insanity).

Prinny's upbringing was fairly brutal. As is often the way with the upper classes, his parents insisted that his tutors didn't go soft on him or pamper him in any way: any signs of laziness or being untruthful, and they should severely beat the boy. One of George's sisters recalled seeing George and his brother, Frederick, held by their tutors like dogs and flogged with a long whip.

He was a bright but lazy boy and didn't apply himself to his studies (surprisingly, the floggings didn't work), but still somehow managed to learn three languages. When he came of age at 21 in 1783, he was given his own court at Carlton House, where he threw himself into

GEORGE IV AT HIS LEISURE

the debauched lifestyle of a wealthy young rake, which revolved around drinking, overeating and fornicating (once again, I'm amazed that regularly thrashing him as a boy hadn't forged him into a healthy, well-adjusted young man). Parliament also gave him a grant of £60,000 (the equivalent of about eight million quid today) and he was given an annual income of £50,000 (you do the maths), but it was still nowhere near enough for George. His stables alone swallowed up a huge chunk of his income – more than £30,000. And this led to a big falling-out with his frugal, lentil soup-eating father and disapproving mother.

Prinny managed to up the game for Hanoverian monarchs by having a terrible relationship with *both* his parents. Their constant criticism of his extravagant and wanton lifestyle inevitably had the opposite effect to what they were hoping. Like all good teenagers, George embraced the politics that his dad most disapproved of. The king was an out-and-out Tory, but Prinny was a supporter of the radical Whig politician, Charles James Fox. The wily Fox was the perfect ally for the prince and they set themselves up in opposition to the king's court.

Fox had a parliamentary career that spanned nearly 40 years from the late 18th into the early 19th century, with most of his time spent in opposition. He was the sort of self-promoting politician who wasn't too bothered about being in power as long as he had a lot of attention and influence. He'd been the arch-rival of William Pitt the Younger, and regarded George III as a tyrant. He was a fan of the French Revolution and an opponent of the slave trade and, well, anything really that the Tories, or King George III, supported. He pushed for religious tolerance and individual liberty. Puh. Talk about being infected by the woke mind-virus. What a libtard snowflake.

Through his life, Prinny had a string of affairs with aristocrats, actresses and servants. In his early twenties, he fell for a woman called Maria Fitzherbert, and proposed to her. Maria was a twice-widowed Catholic who was six years older than him, and not quite at the top of the social ladder. Knowing that his stuffy parents would be horrified, George kept the relationship secret from them. The Act of Settlement, however, barred any monarch from marrying a Catholic, while the later Royal Marriages Act of 1772 prohibited any royal heir from marrying without the ruling monarch's consent, which put Prince George in a tricky position. His solution was to say 'Sod the lot of you' and marry her anyway, privately, at her house in Mayfair in 1785, even writing out the marriage certificate himself. Legally, the marriage was void and the prince had to keep it secret. Inevitably, though, the story got out and it became a field day for the satirists.

George was getting further and further into debt and, this time, Daddy, incensed by his son's stupid marriage, refused to bail him out, which led to a quite extraordinary state of affairs. The Prince of Wales quit his royal residence at Carlton House, which he'd been doing up on a massive scale, and moved in with Maria, who had to help support him. George hoped that his political chums would come to his aid, because it would suit the Whigs, the party in opposition, to have the heir to the throne in their debt. But the Whigs could only push through a government grant and send some cash his way if George's illegal marriage was never exposed. Fox made a grand speech in parliament, effectively saying 'This is fake news. George never married anyone. What are you talking about?'. This placated parliament but pissed off Maria, who protested to George that she *was* his wife and couldn't he show her some respect.

To keep her quiet, the playwright and Whig politician, Richard Brinsley Sheridan, put the squeeze on parliament and got them to cough up £161,000 (equivalent to about £22 million today) for living expenses and an extra £60,000 for improvements to Carlton House.*

The money that George spent on Carlton House was extraordinary, buying up property on either side and knocking it all into one, like some 18th-century rock star (although he stopped short of digging out the basement to put in a swimming pool and cinema). It was a colossal waste of money, particularly considering it was demolished only a few years later.

In 1788, George III had the first of his breakdowns and wasn't able to open parliament. It was clear that somebody needed to rule in his place, but without the king's stamp of approval, this couldn't happen.

---

* This feels a lot like Boris Johnson putting up expensive new wallpaper and curtains at 10 Downing Street when he was prime minister.

Fox said that the Prince of Wales was automatically in charge if his father was incapable (it would have suited him very well to have his pocket prince as regent). The Tories naturally opposed this but had to concede that establishing a regency was the only solution. In the end, as we heard already, they argued about the Regency Bill for so long that, by the time they passed it, the king had recovered, so the whole thing had been a big waste of time.

Prinny had been hoping that, as regent, he could sort his debts out and so now had to go back to daddy with his begging bowl. The king and parliament would only release more funds if the prince separated from Maria Fitzherbert and married properly. In 1795, Prinny caved in, saying, *All right, I'll marry some bloody princess if it makes you happy. I'll have that one, there.*

Nobody has ever been able to work out exactly why, of all the eligible princesses in Europe, George chose his cousin, Princess Caroline of Brunswick, who was a gauche, hearty, unsophisticated German fräulein with a big laugh and poor standards of hygiene. When they first met and embraced, Caroline was appalled at how fat George was, and George was appalled at how ugly and unwashed she was, causing him to blanche, retreat to the corner of the room and ask his friend, Lord Malmesbury, for a large glass of brandy.

To be fair, neither of them would have made it as a catwalk model. Even in contemporary paintings and prints (which must have been intended to be flattering), Caroline looks like a demented fishwife who's let herself go, while George looks like an overstuffed sausage. The marriage was, predictably, a disaster. George was pissed at the ceremony and had to be supported by pals. On the wedding night, he got so drunk that he fell into the fireplace and slept there until the morning when he recovered sufficiently to climb into bed with his wife. It seems to have been the first and last time they had sex, and, exactly nine months later, she gave birth to their daughter, Charlotte.

To make matters worse, George became convinced that his new bride wasn't as inexperienced in bed as she ought to be. As soon as their daughter, Charlotte, was born, George separated from Caroline and went back to his unofficial wife, Maria Fitzherbert. His other lovers included Mary Robinson, an actress who he paid to leave the stage, and then paid to bugger off when he got tired of her, destroying her career. Another was Grace Elliott, the divorced wife of a physician. Then there were a few aristocrats, such as Frances Villiers, Countess of Jersey, Isabella Ingram-Seymour-Conway, Marchioness of Hertford, and Elizabeth, Marchioness Conyngham. Between them, George was rumoured to have fathered several illegitimate children.*

In 1810, the king tipped over into his final and most severe bout of mental illness and, luckily this time, Parliament already had the blueprint for a Regency Bill ready to go from before, allowing Prinny to smoothly upgrade from Prince of Wales to Prince Regent in 1811, a role he filled until he became king 10 years later.

I mentioned before that George was a trendsetter. His influence on fashion came about largely because of decisions he made that had little to do with aesthetics. He desperately wanted to be a stylish man about town, but was cursed with being overweight. Traditional Georgian clothing – tailored shirts and coats, tight knee britches and stockings – left nowhere to hide. George did away with britches and replaced them with loose pantaloons to hide his thick legs and, once the king was wearing pantaloons, everyone followed suit. He also started wearing high collars and a cloth, wrapped around his neck, to hide his surfeit of chins. The other change he made that made him look so radically different to his Hanoverian predecessors was to dispense with the ubiquitous white powdered wigs that had been so recognisably a part of Georgian men's fashion.

This was something of a political move. Governments are always looking at innovative ways to tax people – and people are always looking at innovative ways to avoid paying tax. William III, for instance, had introduced the very unpopular window tax as a way of targeting the wealthy. The more windows you had, the higher tax you paid, which is why you see so many bricked-up windows in grand old houses. In 1795, during the reign of George III, the government passed the Duty on Hair Powder Act, which brought in a tax on the powder used to keep wigs white, so it became a lot more expensive to

---

* The apparent similarities between him and Boris Johnson keep on coming. They even look quite similar; cartoonists enjoyed depicting George with dishevelled hair.

wear them. George hated all this and basically just stopped wearing wigs, which led to all the upper classes abandoning them.* George started to wear his hair brushed forward in a distinctive manner, which is pretty much the hairstyle sported by posh, English public-school boys today.

George loved to dress up in mad, colourful and very theatrical outfits. He loved uniforms and designed many of his own. He once bought 83 pairs of boots and 74 pairs of gloves on a single shopping trip and arrived for his first appearance in the House of Lords wearing black velvet with pink high heels. When he visited Scotland in 1822, he sported an elaborate and rather Disney-fied tartan outfit, it led to a tartan craze in Scotland (where tartan had been banned for nearly 40 years after the Battle of Culloden and had fallen out of favour).

So people copied George, but he was nowhere near as influential as his friend, George 'Beau' Brummel. Brummel was the epitome of the dandy: unconventional, witty, waspish and dressed to kill. He completely changed men's fashion and his name is still used today as a mark of style and elegance.

Sadly, when George came to power with the arrival of the Regency, he went down the age-old route of abandoning teenage radicalism for middle-aged conservatism. Beau Brummel and most of George's friends were Whigs and George gradually cut them out of his life as he became increasingly more right-leaning. Things came to a head in 1813 at a fashionable masked ball where the 'Dandy Club', as Beau Brummel's inner circle were known, were gathered. Brummel was hanging with the most fashionable people in London: Lord Alvanley, Henry Mildmay and Henry Pierrepont. George came over to the group, who, like him, were all wearing masks. He greeted Alvanley and Pierrepont, but cut Brummel dead, saying nothing to him, prompting Brummel to remark to Alvanley, 'Who's your fat friend?'

After that, Brummel was shunned by royal society. He fell deep into gambling debt and eventually fled from his debtors to France, where

---

* Wearing wigs was an innovation that had been brought in by Charles II. The only place it didn't die out was in the law courts.

he died in a lunatic asylum in Caen – shabby, forgotten, penniless and driven crazy by syphilis.

The other man who defined Regency style was the architect, John Nash. When we talk of Regency buildings, we think of Nash, who designed Regent Street and the terraces around Regent's Park, as well as the Orientalist fantasy of the Brighton Pavilion that he built for George.

It was during George's time as regent that the Napoleonic wars came to an end. On 18 June 1815, near a Belgian village called Waterloo, Napoleon fought his final battle against an allied army of British troops under Wellington and Prussian troops under Prince Blucher. Wellington and Blucher's army held out against the French onslaught and eventually broke them. The game was up for Napoleon who was exiled to Saint Helena, in the middle of the Atlantic, never to return.

Once again, Britain was emerging from a long and costly war and there was economic and political disruption to deal with on the home front. George, who normally left parliament to get on with running the country so that he could devote more time to carnal pursuits, had to get involved. He was no doubt extremely drunk, however, and cracked open a fortifying bottle of brandy to help him deal with the problem of Catholic emancipation. There were unjust and out-of-date laws still in place barring Catholics from holding any influential positions, such as politicians, lawyers or judges. People were calling for change but, inevitably, the backward-looking Tories, under their new prime minister Spencer Perceval, were opposed to any loosening of the laws.

Perceval was assassinated in 1812, however – the only British PM to have suffered this fate. It was feared that this might be the start of a revolution, but his assassin, John Bellingham, was a classic 'lone nutter', an unhinged merchant with a grudge against the government.

He wasn't the only one. The issue of parliamentary representation was a hot topic. George worked his way through a crate of nice Riesling and a few bottles of gin while the arguments raged. Landowners and factory owners were growing increasingly wealthy and the men and women (and even children) who were deserting the countryside to work in the factories and mills had no parliamentary representation.

The problem was that you would have a newly populous city like Manchester with no members of parliament at all, whereas many tiny medieval villages, whose populations had migrated to the cities, could have two members of parliament representing them. These villages were known as 'rotten boroughs' and in the smallest of them, the 'pocket boroughs', wealthy landowners would bribe the seven or eight voters in town to vote for them. So, it was a pretty messed-up situation.

Growing grassroots movements were demanding better representation and a fairer system. In 1819, 60,000 people gathered in St Peter's Field Manchester to vent their frustration and listen to speeches. Of course, this was seen as a great threat by the powers that be who sent in the militia (mainly mounted cavalrymen) who indiscriminately attacked the crowd, injuring and killing many people. This wasn't long after Waterloo and the militia's actions led to the incident becoming known as the Peterloo Massacre.

At the same time, landowners were putting pressure on parliament to bring in protectionist tariffs on corn imports. Before Britain started importing sweetcorn from the Americas, 'corn' simply meant cereals – wheat, oats and barley – which in the 19th century were the staple diet of most ordinary people, alongside potatoes. But the men who owned the land on which the grain was grown had for a while been moaning about cheap foreign imports, saying they were undercutting their profits. Parliament bowed to the lobbying and introduced laws that heavily taxed and restricted the import of corn. The Corn Laws were designed to keep prices high and favour domestic producers, which meant that the landowners' profits went up massively. The system was completely inflexible, so even when domestic food supplies were low, and therefore already hugely expensive, the tariffs stayed at the same rate, which led to periods of starvation.

Big profits for the few gave them increased political power, but food prices shot up and the cost of living rose, with a knock-on effect in other sectors, such as manufacturing, as it reduced people's disposable income. Obviously, this was all very unpopular, particularly in the urban areas, where nobody was profiting from homegrown corn. George had a good stiff drink and wolfed down a tray of pastries to get over it.

He was human, though, and was genuinely devastated when his only legitimate child, Princess Charlotte, died soon after giving birth to a stillborn baby in 1817 at the age of 21. He was too upset to attend her funeral. He was considerably less upset when his father, George III, died in 1820. The regent was, by then, already 57 years old and nothing really changed when he came to the throne as he'd pretty much been acting as king for the last 10 years.

He was now hugely overweight, with a 50-inch waist, and addicted to laudanum (essentially liquid opium). He was taking ever larger doses to help him deal with severe bladder pains, leaving him in a drugged and mentally confused state for days on end.

His relationship with his wife, Caroline, was a total mess. They'd been living apart for 25 years and had both been having affairs. George instigated a divorce trial, but abandoned it when he realised how unpopular it was making him. As this was all going on, Napoleon died on St Helena in May 1821. When George was told 'Sir, your bitterest enemy is dead', he replied, 'Is she, by God!'.

Caroline had moved back home to Germany, but when she found out that George was finally going to take the throne, she hopped on a ship and hurried to make sure she was crowned queen alongside him. George was furious and banned her from attending the ceremony. She still tried to get in, though, hammering pitifully on the doors of Westminster Abbey screaming, 'I am the queen! Let me in!' The crowds were split between those who were cheering her on – 'Go on, Caroline. Get in there! He's a fat wanker' – and others who were enjoying the spectacle. 'What's the silly cow doing now?'

George was inside, decked out in a special coronation outfit of his own design, consisting of layers of heavy embroidered cloth, a fur-lined robe and several gangsta-style gold chains, topped off by a fancy new crown studded with more than 12,000 diamonds. He was so hot and sweaty, and his girdle was so tight, that he almost passed out. The coronation cost £250,000, which adjusted to today's money is about £24 million (in contrast, George III's coronation had only cost about £10,000, a fraction of what his son spent).

Despite the enormous cost, it was a very popular event. The fact of the matter is, The Great British Public *like* pomp and ceremony, they like spectacle, they like glitter and crowns, they like a gaudy coronation and they like a good royal wedding. So, George got away with it. That night, Caroline fell ill, and, convinced 'til the end that she'd been poisoned, died three weeks later.

The coronation was probably the high point of George's reign. His health went into steady decline and he spent most of the rest of his life secluded at Windsor Castle. When Wellington pushed through the Catholic Relief Act in 1829, George was too unwell to resist. He'd become a target of ridicule. The satirists portrayed him as a gross, self-indulgent monster and, if he went out in public, people would jeer at him.

He had just about everything wrong with him that he could have: gout, arteriosclerosis, peripheral oedema (which back then was known as dropsy), porphyria, stomach pains and cataracts. He spent days in bed and took to bleeding himself. Bloodletting had been the most common medical practice performed by doctors since antiquity and was based on the spurious idea that disease was the result of an excess of blood. In George's case, it led to awful breathlessness, and his fingertips would go black as oxygen wasn't getting into his bloodstream. By 1828, he had such bad gout in his arm that he couldn't even sign documents. At his worst, he was taking more than 100 drops of laudanum for public appearances and had to sleep upright in a chair. His doctors frequently stuck a tap into his abdomen to drain off the excess fluid.

He was very much like Mr Creosote in *Monty Python's The Meaning of Life*, though, and just couldn't stop stuffing himself. In 1830, the Duke of Wellington wrote in his diary that he'd been to see the king, who had eaten for breakfast a pigeon and beef steak pie, three parts of a bottle of Moselle, a glass of dry champagne, two glasses of port and a glass of brandy (all no doubt washed down with a large glass of laudanum). And he died not long after from eating a wafer-thin mint.

Well, that's almost what happened. A blood vessel in his stomach ruptured and he died of intestinal bleeding. When surgeons carried out an autopsy on him, they found a large tumour the size of an orange attached to his bladder, which explained his stomach pains. His heart was also surrounded by a thick layer of fat and had calcified valves.

So that was the glorious and romantic end of the charming monarch, King George IV, the First Gentleman of Europe. What should George's epitaph be? One of his aides, Charles Greville, the clerk to the privy council, wrote in his diary: 'A more contemptible, cowardly, selfish, unfeeling dog does not exist ... There have been good and wise kings, but not many of them ... And this I believe to be one of the worst.'

35

WILLIAM

WILLIAM IV – 1765–1837

Sailor Bill/the Sailor King/Silly Billy/the Pineapple
Reigned 1830–1837
Lived for 71 years. Reigned for seven years.
Died from pneumonia.
Remembered for: not much really.

Since George IV's only legitimate child, Charlotte, had died in 1817, his brother, William, the Duke of Clarence, became king. William is one of those obscure monarchs who most people don't know much about. He didn't really make any mark on history. He sat on the throne for seven years, trying (and mostly succeeding) to avoid controversy and was a bit of a palate-cleanser between the unsavoury reign of the monstrous George IV and the great, heavy feast that is Queen Victoria.

His only real claim to fame is that, at 64, he was the oldest person to come to the throne, a record eventually broken by Charles III. Poor old William – when most people are thinking about retirement, he had to suddenly rule the country. Unlike his self-important older brother, he hated all the fuss and ceremony and theatricality of being king. He'd been in the navy, hence his nickname, Sailor Bill, and he had that sort of bluff, no-nonsense, Navy Man character. *Oh, I don't need all this frippery and finery. I'll just wear my tatty old jumper.*

When he realised that he was going to be king, he questioned whether he even needed a coronation. Wouldn't it all be too much bother? In the end, he was persuaded that he really should be officially crowned. His coronation, however, cost a fraction of George's. In fact, there was a law that stipulated the *least* amount you could spend on a coronation (£30,000, which he slightly exceeded). And, apparently, he

chuckled and arsed about all through his coronation, embarrassed by
the absurdity of it all and determined not to take it seriously.

As well as Sailor Bill, or the Sailor King, a lot of people called him
'The Pineapple' because of the odd shape of his head (which was very
similar to that of Grampa Simpson). By the time he came to the throne,
he had a shock of white hair sprouting out of the top to complete the
pineapple effect.

William was not an intellectual giant and, unlike his brother,
George, had no interest in arts and culture. He rarely picked up a book
and was one of those 'I speak my mind, take me as I am' types. He
didn't always think about what he was going to say and would blurt
things out, unafraid of making a fool of himself.

He was considered quite eccentric. He was fond of strolling about
town and meeting his public. And whenever he stayed at his brother's
amazing folly, the Royal Pavilion in Brighton, he'd get an aide to visit
all the local hotels to see who was staying there. If there were any old
chums, or anyone William fancied meeting, he'd invite them over to
dinner with a note saying not to bother about clothes.

He wasn't a totally cuddly simpleton, however. He had an insane
temper, particularly when he was a boy. He was quick to anger and was
always getting into fights. He mainly tried to steer a middle path,
though, and keep things simple. There was a revolutionary spirit
rampaging through Europe and all the monarchies were looking
precarious, so it was wise for William to keep his head down and try
to avoid controversy. He did manage to prevent Britain from descending into the chaos and widespread violence of revolution. The only
time he almost lost his grip was during arguments over political
representation in the early 1830s which led to rioting. William
appeared to be against change and had to curtail his public perambu-
lations for a while to avoid people jeering and throwing things at him.

Because he was a spare, who'd never expected to be monarch,
William had been able to experience life outside the royal bubble. As
a boy, he was sent off to join the navy, which gave him a greater understanding of the lives of others. George III had that stuffy, old-fart
attitude: young people should be forced to join the army, bring back
National Service, very character building, toughen them up, what.

OK, so maybe they'll get shot and killed, but they'll go to their graves with nice short haircuts and a respect for discipline. His father explicitly told the officers in the navy not to go soft on young William and make a man of him.

So, when he was 13, William joined the Royal Navy as a midshipman, the entry level for officers. It seems extraordinary that 13-year-olds could be naval officers; conditions on a navy ship at the time were pretty brutal.

He was fairly rapidly promoted during his 11 years at sea and mostly served in the West Atlantic, from the Caribbean up into Nova Scotia, with a two-year stint in Europe in the middle. He threw himself into this life and gained combat experience at a couple of naval engagements. It seems he was as happy fighting foreigners as he was his fellow crew members. Once, like a bunch of Bullingdon toffs, he and some other junior officers drunkenly smashed up a brothel in Barbados, leaving Daddy to pay the bill. On another occasion, after a drunken brawl in Gibraltar, he was thrown into prison and had to pull the classic 'Do you know who I am?' line before being swiftly released.

He served in New York during the American War of Independence, and, while he was there, George Washington put together a plan to kidnap him. Luckily for William, the details were leaked and the heist never happened. Not long after that, he was moved back to the West Indies where, in 1785, he was made a lieutenant and later a captain, and, for a while, served under Horatio Nelson. Nelson wrote that William was superior to two-thirds of his fellow officers. They dined together almost every night and, when Nelson got married, William insisted on giving the bride away.

Their friendship waxed and waned over the years, but William was always proud to have been close to the admiral. Later on, as an ageing ex-naval man, he would bore his guests at dinner parties about the good old days with Horatio.

In 1790, still in his mid-twenties, he was made a rear admiral. Despite what Nelson had said about him, he wasn't the greatest officer in the world though and, behind his back, he was known as Silly Billy. There were also concerns about his safety. He may have been a spare, but it was increasingly looking like he might be needed if his older

WILLIAM IV AND HIS ICECREAM HAIRDO

brother didn't knock out some heirs. So, he was brought back to England and, although his father and parliament kept promising that he might one day go back to sea, it never happened.

William longed for a meaning to his life, though, and wanted to engage in some kind of useful political activity; he also needed money. He pestered his father to make him a duke, which would not only give him status but also guarantee him a decent income, but George refused. He was fed up with his sons spending stupid amounts of money and wanted to keep them under control.

In retaliation, William declared that as he couldn't get into the House of Lords without a title, he would simply stand as an ordinary member of parliament and get himself elected to the House of Commons. Appalled, King George quickly made him the Duke of Clarence, and supposedly complained 'I well know it is another vote added to the opposition' since his sons were all rebelling against their Tory father and supporting the Whigs. Later in life, William vacillated between the two parties and no one was ever quite sure what his politics were – if, indeed, he had any.

When Britain declared war on France in 1793, he was desperate to be given a command of some sort and serve his country. It didn't happen, partly because he broke his arm falling downstairs while drunk, but mainly because he foolishly (he was prone to foolishness) made a speech in the House of Lords opposing the war, which is not a good look for an admiral.

William never saw active service again and, in 1811, was given another meaningless, honorary position, admiral of the fleet, where he basically commanded his desk. He did get close to the action, however, while visiting British troops fighting in the Low Countries in 1813. He was watching the bombardment of Antwerp from a church steeple when he came under fire and a bullet went right through his coat. Again, another fruity anecdote for the dinner table.

In 1799 William had spoken in the House of Lords *against* the abolition of slavery – ironically, on humanitarian grounds. He'd seen the living standards among dirt-poor free men in places like the Scottish Highlands and believed that their conditions were worse than among the slaves in the West Indies. And, actually, when the slaves *were* freed in the Caribbean, many of them *did* end up in indentured labour, which is almost as bad as slavery.*

Yes, indentured workers were technically free, but they were treated very badly, paid very badly and were often neither fed, sheltered nor clothed, but that sort of misses the point about the injustice of slavery. When William had been in the West Indies, he'd got to know local plantation owners who'd obviously nobbled him. In the end, he just didn't want the established way of doing things to be upset. He didn't want trouble. He even insulted William Wilberforce in the House of Lords, saying, 'the proponents of the abolition are either fanatics or hypocrites, and in one of those classes I rank Mr Wilberforce'.

William's private life was quite curious. In 1790, he fell in love with an Irish actress called Dorothea Bland, who was better known by her stage name of Mrs Jordan. Dora was older than William and already had a few children, he moved her into Clarence Lodge nonetheless. At the beginning, she was partially supporting him as he wasn't getting enough money from his father or from parliament, whereas she had an income as an actress. Later on she was granted an annual stipend of £1200.

They lived together for 20 years and had ten children. Everyone knew about this state of affairs and the satirists went to town on it, particularly as his older brother, George, had an almost identical relationship with Maria Fitzherbert.

For the time being, the relationship was tolerated in royal circles. In 1797, King George even gave William the keys to Bushy House to accommodate his steadily growing family. His illegitimate children were all given the surname FitzClarence and William had a very contented domestic life until 1811 when he told Mrs Jordan that he was leaving her. He explained that it was looking highly likely that he was going to end up ruling the country and needed to reorganise his life. His biggest problem was that he wasn't getting enough to

---

* The services of an indentured worker are basically bought in advance by an employer. They must then work for a number of years to pay off the debt. Sometimes the wages wouldn't be paid until the end of the period of service – and employers often reneged on the deal.

live on, and needed an official royal wedding to bring in some dosh. So, Mrs Jordan was paid off with a settlement of £4,400 a year (about £300,000 in today's money) and custody of her daughters (as long as she never went back on the stage). She liked William and understood why he did what he did. In fact, she felt rather sorry for him, giving up so much. Sadly, her life afterwards was pretty miserable and she died penniless in France five years later, having been fleeced by one of her daughters and her husband.

William, meanwhile, tried to get married to a string of wealthy heiresses, young women with money rather than titles, but his family kept blocking him, saying he had to marry a proper royal. Until it looked like he might one day become king, however, proper royals had little interest in him. Eventually, in 1818, he settled on Adelaide of Saxe-Meiningen. It was a happy marriage that lasted nearly 20 years until William's death. Adelaide took him in hand, sorted out his finances, organised his life and filled in the gaps in his personality. You can tell how popular she was as a queen by how many pubs are named after her (as well as the city of Adelaide in Australia and several other places around the Commonwealth). For their first year together, William and Adelaide lived in Germany, enjoying a fairly frugal lifestyle, which pleased George III. Adelaide gave birth to two daughters early on, but sadly they were short-lived and she went on to have two stillbirths. Once again, William was following in his brother's footsteps: producing countless illegitimate children but no official heirs.

George III died in 1820, George IV died in 1830 and William came to the throne aged 64, declaring: 'Who's a Silly Billy now?' He was keen to give the public a different kind of king to his brother, wanting to do the right thing and quickly established himself as a conscientious plodder who at least tried to make things run smoothly.

Wellington, his first prime minister, said that he'd done more business with King William in 10 minutes than he had with George IV in as many days and that 'everything he has done has been benevolent'. William oversaw plenty of social advances. The Poor Law was updated and slavery was eventually abolished (mostly …). The child labour laws were also updated. Kids still went to work, but conditions for them improved.

One of the first things William did was make the royal court more traditionally British. He got rid of George's French chefs and his German band and replaced them with British ones. The public approved. He was the sort of simple man who enjoyed marching bands, but couldn't sit through a classical concert. He gave much of George's art collection to the nation, cut back on the Royal Stud and completed the renovation of Buckingham Palace. He hated the place so much he tried to give it to parliament after the original medieval Houses of Parliament burned down in 1834.*

The only real crisis of William's reign was over the hot potato of political representation. As we've seen, constituencies hadn't been updated since they were established in the Middle Ages and members of parliament were very unevenly and unfairly distributed. Rotten boroughs had undue influence (the most famous of them, Old Sarum, in Salisbury, had just seven voters), so it was very easy to manipulate the vote, particularly as vast numbers of working men in the big towns and cities often had no representation at all. And even where they had representation, not everyone was allowed to vote. Unless you had substantial property, you were barred.

There was a growing Whig movement in parliament to redistribute seats, remove restrictions and consider universal suffrage (for men, that is; it would be a while before women got a look in). And, of course, there was massive pushback from the wealthy landowners who didn't want to lose their corrupt authority.

A first Reform Bill got bogged down in a divided house in 1831, but a hastily called general election later in the year gave the Whigs a landslide victory and enough of a majority to pass a second bill – only for the House of Lords to block it. This led to rioting and fresh fears of revolution. William was caught up in all this and, as he wouldn't pick a side, the public turned against him. The Whigs had a quiet word with William and told him that if he wanted to hold onto his crown he'd have to stuff the Lords with a load of newly

---

* The current Houses of Parliament are a Victorian creation. Charles Barry, a keen Gothic revivalist, was the architect chosen for the rebuild, with a lot of help from Augustus Pugin.

ennobled Whigs to ensure that the bill would get through at the third attempt.

The king reluctantly did what he was told and the bill finally passed. It wasn't perfect. A lot of working-class men still had no representation. Indeed, even by the time the suffragettes were fighting for women's electoral rights in the 20th century, not all men had the vote.

Once William had navigated these choppy waters, the rest of his time at the helm of the ship of state was plain sailing (do you see what I did there?). But he still didn't have an heir, so it looked like his niece, Victoria, daughter of his deceased younger brother, Edward, Duke of Kent, was going to succeed him. Unfortunately, William had fallen out with Victoria's widowed mother (his sister-in-law, the Duchess of Kent, also annoyingly called Victoria). William thought she had ideas above her station and was acting like a Queen mother before he was even cold in his grave. Young Victoria liked her uncle William, even if he was a bit odd and eccentric and occasionally quite angry, but she was rarely allowed to see him. The Duchess of Kent kept the girl very close.

William, who had suffered from asthma all his life, was unwell and knew that if he died before Victoria came of age at 18, her mother would rule as regent. He did manage to cling on until a month after his niece's 18th birthday, which gave him some satisfaction. Victoria wrote in her diary: 'Poor old man. I feel sorry for him. He was always personally kind to me.'

William died, aged 71, of pneumonia on top of heart and liver problems. He had avoided a French-style revolution and instead helped a different kind of revolution to roar on: an industrial one. The United Kingdom was rapidly changing and many new men were growing wealthy.

There are no direct descendants of either George IV or William IV in the royal line, although, a recent prime minister is descended from Lady Elizabeth FitzClarence, one of William's illegitimate daughters.

A certain David Cameron.

36

AND VICTORIA

QUEEN VICTORIA – 1819–1901
Mrs Brown/Eliza/The Widow of Windsor/
Grandmother of Europe
Reigned 1837–1901
Lived for 81 years. Reigned for 63 years.
Died of old age.
Remembered for: being Queen Victoria.

Queen Victoria sits there, like an unmovable lump of granite, through much of the 19th century and into the first year of the 20th. There's no getting around her.

She represents the traditional idea of Great Britain, of empire, of monarchy, but it's interesting that, when she was young, the name 'Victoria' was considered a weird foreign German import that sounded ugly and a little bit showy off to British ears. Calling yourself 'The Victorious One' is rather blowing one's own trumpet, don't you think? Tut-tut. The name proved to be prophetic, however. There was a massive expansion of the British Empire during Victoria's reign and, in 1876, the prime minister, Benjamin Disraeli, pushed the Royal Titles Act through parliament and Victoria was crowned Empress of India.

She was the first of our first monarchs to be photographed and the first to be filmed; there is blurry footage of her diamond jubilee in 1897. She may only be a black blob sitting in an open carriage under a big white parasol, but there she is, preserved for ever, as a ghost made of light. She was nearly 80 when the film was shot, and she'd been on the throne for 60 years, so there's a lot to fit into this chapter.

Victoria's was a reign of two halves. She came to the throne aged 18, young, vivacious, a feminising influence on the royal court. She woke the palace up and brought in life and youth and colour. And then she fell in love with Prince Albert, with whom she had a very happy marriage and nine children. Victoria and Albert presented the image of being a traditional British family. All was sunny and bright, but then Albert died young at 42 and everything changed. Dark clouds descended as Victoria became engulfed by mourning. On went the black widow's weeds and, for the second half of her reign, she was a very different woman. Traditionally, the latter image of Victoria – dumpy, grim-faced, swathed in black – is the one that people had fixed in their minds. She even had her own catchphrase: 'We are not amused.' Over recent years, however, several films and TV series about her early reign have redressed the balance and shown viewers that Victoria wasn't always a sour-looking old widow with a little white bonnet.

She never actually said 'We are not amused'. In her younger days, she was very amused, indeed. She was described as laughing a lot – although one of her older and more stuffy male courtiers complained that she showed her teeth and gums too much when she did.

Perhaps recent dramas have swung too far the other way and have made Victoria out to be more glamourous than she actually was. And taller. I think the four foot eleven queen would have been very flattered by the portrayal of her in *Young Victoria* by five foot seven Emily Blunt. As Victoria got older, her distinctive Hanoverian features began to get more pronounced – the little bulging eyes and the prominent nose in the egg-like face. In the earliest known photograph of her, taken in 1845 with her eldest daughter Princess Victoria (who was always called Vicky), Victoria looks about 40, but was only 25.

We talk of the 'Victorian era' as if it were just one thing. But the country changed just as much over the 60 years of Victoria's reign as the queen herself did. It was a period of industrial, scientific, military and political development, fuelled by the Industrial Revolution and the expansion of the British Empire. As fast as things were moving forwards, though, there was a compulsion to look backwards. A craze for historical fiction gripped the nation, and there was a new interest in British history. The love of classical architecture that had flourished during the Georgian period fell away and in came neo-Gothic architecture that harked back to the Middle Ages. A lot of weird, faux-medieval flummery (that had started with George IV) took over royal events and coronations.

The Victorians told British history as a colourful pageant, a sanitised, romantic fantasy of brave, tartan-clad Scottish warriors and chivalrous knights wooing their fair ladies, where every great man from the past (women didn't get much of a look-in) was a perfect hero. There was a revival of interest in the likes of King Alfred and the legendary King Arthur. The Victorians remoulded the past to fit an image of the British as benevolent empire-builders, the bringers of civilisation, the justified rulers of the world. It's an image that we're only really now trying to pick apart and properly reassess.

Victoria prudently tried not to get too involved with politics. She knew that, to keep her throne when so many others in Europe were being lost, she needed to not look like a meddling monarch. She learned the gentle art of having a quiet word, which Queen Elizabeth II used to such good effect. Rule by nudge rather than by decree.

Like Elizabeth II, Victoria saw several prime ministers come and go: Lord Melbourne and Lord Palmerston; Robert Peel, who created the first professional police force (known colloquially as Peelers); William Gladstone (after whom the Gladstone bag was named); and Benjamin 'Dizzy' Disraeli (after whom the board game 'Dizzy, Dizzy Dinosaurs' was named*).

Victoria, of course, had countless things named after her: cities, states, waterfalls, lakes, plums, a moth and the pub in *EastEnders*. Her actual first name was Alexandrina, but she never liked Alexandrina and insisted on being called Queen Victoria.

Her father, Edward, Duke of Kent, the fourth son of George III, died in 1820 when Victoria was less than a year old, so she never knew him. A week later, her grandfather, the king, died as well. Her mother, the widowed Duchess of Kent, gave the little girl a miserable childhood. Helped by her close friend Sir John Conroy (who was rumoured to be the duchess's lover), she put together a very strict regime, called the Kensington System. The duchess hardly let Victoria out of her

---

* Actually, I don't think anything was named after Disraeli, but he *was* nicknamed Dizzy.

sight, concerned that she might come to harm or be corrupted in some way. The young princess was accompanied all the time. She slept in her mother's bedroom and wasn't even allowed to go down the stairs by herself without holding an adult's hand.

Victoria hated Conroy and grew to hate her mother, who prevented her from seeing anybody she didn't think suitable, trying to keep her weak and dependent. Her only real childhood friends were her governess, Louise Lehzen, her older half-sister, Feodore, her dolls and her King Charles Spaniel, Dash.

As Victoria grew up, the duchess and John Conroy made plans for her marriage. They consulted the duchess's brother, King Leopold I of Belgium, who suggested she should marry his nephew, Prince Albert of Saxe-Coburg and Gotha (another one of those confusing little German dukedoms), despite the fact that Albert was Victoria's first cousin.

Albert met Victoria in Kensington in 1836 and, luckily, they hit it off straight away. She wrote extensive journals and letters that are a great insight into her life. (Unfortunately, after she died, her daughter Beatrice dutifully went through them and expurgated them, removing all the most interesting stuff.) According to Victoria's 1836 diary, she really liked Albert and considered him to be 'extremely handsome … his eyes are large & blue & he has a beautiful nose & a very sweet mouth with fine teeth'.

Not long afterwards, on 20 June 1837, Victoria wrote her best-known diary entry. 'I was awoke at 6 o'clock by Mamma, who told me the Archbishop of Canterbury and Lord Conyngham were here and wished to see me. I got out of bed and went into my sitting room (only in my dressing gown), and alone, and saw them. Lord Conyngham then acquainted me that my poor uncle, the king, was no more, and had expired at 12 minutes p.2 this morning. And consequently that I am queen.'

The first thing she did on becoming queen was ask for a blessed hour alone and then she got rid of the hated Conroy, saying he was to stay out of her presence. Victoria was the first monarch to actually live in Buckingham Palace, but she exiled her mother to apartments in Belgrave Square (they were later reconciled and grew much closer when Victoria had her first child).

Coming to the throne at 18 after a childhood wrapped in cotton wool, Victoria knew nothing about dealing with parliament or running a royal household, so she worked very closely with the Whig prime minister, William Lamb, aka Lord Melbourne. The two of them got on very well and became close. Melbourne patiently taught her all he could – advising her, updating her on the news and the business of parliament – and Victoria grew to rely on him. She had no father and Melbourne had no daughters, and a familial relationship developed between them. In soft-focus versions of her story, there are hints of this being something more than just a father-and-daughter relationship, but that seems far-fetched. In romantic historical fiction, everybody in the past was shagging everybody else.

Victoria's coronation took place in 1838 at Westminster Abbey and more than 400,000 visitors came to London for the celebrations. This was the biggest crowd that the city had ever seen, brought into town by the railways, a fairly recent innovation that allowed people to travel much more freely, faster and more inexpensively than they'd ever done before. The railway was just one of the aspects of industrialisation that was completely changing the country.

The streets were heaving and Westminster Abbey was packed to the rafters – literally: stadium-style seating had been installed to accommodate all the royals, toffs and foreign dignitaries. After a series of botched coronations, efforts had been made to ensure that Victoria's went off smoothly (although they didn't bother with a rehearsal) but the whole affair became a torturous 5-hour ordeal. The Archbishop of Canterbury never seemed to quite know what was supposed to happen next and Victoria struggled to keep up. The ring had been made for the wrong finger and was too small, but the archbishop persevered and jammed it onto her ring finger anyway.* An elderly peer, aptly called Lord Rolle, fell down the steps to Victoria's podium that he'd climbed to kiss the ill-fitting ring. When he tried again, Victoria hurried down to meet him to save him the effort, which everybody thought was a charming and gracious gesture.

---

* Some accounts say that the ring was fine but the Archbishop forced it onto the wrong finger. Whatever the case, Victoria had to soak her hand in iced water to get it off.

The music didn't get a five-star review, either. The general opinion was that it was ramshackle and out of tune. At one point, the archbishop declared that the whole thing was over and Victoria went into a side chapel to recover, only to be hastily dragged back – several pages of the script had been accidentally skipped. When it was finally over, the treasurer of the household, the Earl of Surrey, tossed some silver coronation medals into the crowd, which caused a small riot as people fought each other to get their hands on one.

Once Victoria was queen, she kept a lively court, with many balls, dinners and parties. She was having the time of her life. She was a teenager. She was popular. She was seen as a burst of spring sunshine. But, barely two years after she'd come to the throne, there was a major scandal at court that became known as the Hastings Affair. One of her mother's cronies, a young lady called Flora Hastings, who'd been involved in the cruel and rigid Kensington System that had made young Victoria so miserable, appeared to have got herself pregnant. Victoria had never liked Flora and encouraged the rumours that Sir John Conroy was the culprit. It was disgraceful that an unmarried woman should be pregnant and visibly swelling, but Flora insisted that she wasn't carrying a child and only consented to be medically examined when Victoria forced her. It turned out she wasn't pregnant, she was a virgin, and she was dying of cancer. The post-mortem discovered a large tumour on her liver that had caused her abdomen to swell. Victoria didn't come out of this looking very good at all.

Flora's family and Conroy openly accused Victoria of making false accusations and hounding the poor girl to her death. When the Queen went out in public, people jeered at her, hissed and called her Mrs Melbourne. Not long afterwards, following a series of defeats in Parliament, Melbourne resigned as prime minister and was replaced by the Tory Robert Peel. The first thing that Peel did was try to purge any Whig supporters from Victoria's household in what became known as the Bedchamber Crisis. Victoria stood her ground, refusing to change anything and told Peel that he could run the country, but she was going to run her own household. Peel was backed into a corner and he resigned, allowing Melbourne back into 10 Downing Street.

In 1839, Prince Albert visited Victoria, who, realising that she liked him even more, promptly proposed to him. They were married the next year and Victoria wrote in gushing, teenage style that she 'never, never spent such an evening. My, dearest, dearest, dear Albert, his excessive love and affection gave me feelings of heavenly love and happiness I never could have hoped to have felt before he clasped me in his arms and we kissed each other again and again. His beauty, his sweetness and gentleness … Oh, this was the happiest day of my life.'

It also turned out to be one of her happiest nights. She had a very healthy sex life and really enjoyed being in bed with Albert. Unfortunately for her, she immediately became pregnant and her marriage with Albert was to be a succession of pregnancies and births, which she hated. She detested being pregnant. She didn't really like babies. She was disgusted by the idea of breastfeeding. She suffered from post-natal depression. She hated the demands that her children put on her and that she couldn't enjoy herself with Albert as she used to. But she did her duty. Over the following 17 years, she and Albert had a further eight children.

Of course, getting pregnant and churning out royal babies made her very popular with the sentimental British public, who love nothing more than a royal wedding, followed by a royal birth. The other thing that made her popular was being shot at during her first pregnancy, in 1840, while she was riding in her carriage through London. It was to be the first of eight attacks on her. None of them seem to have been political (apart from when a young Irishman had a go) and her assailants were either disaffected young men with mental health problems or were trying to get deported to Australia (if you couldn't afford the travel costs, you could simply fire a blank at the queen and you'd be on your way Down Under for a new life free of charge). Victoria later said that it was worth being shot at 'to see how much one is loved'.

In 1853, when Victoria gave birth to her eighth child, Leopold, her doctors gave her an experimental new form of anaesthetic: chloroform. She loved it so much that she started to promote it and used it again for the birth of her ninth, and last, child, Beatrice. The church opposed it, saying that women were born to suffer the pain and danger of childbirth as their punishment from God for original sin. It also has to be said that many doctors were against it because it was actually pretty dangerous. But Victoria was desperate. Her post-natal depression became worse with every birth and she became increasingly short-tempered and petulant. She would fly into rages with Albert, claiming from the start that she didn't want a large family and 'could not be more unhappy'.

Her relationship with Albert is often portrayed as a great romance, but, like all marriages, it was more complicated than that. Albert (like Prince Philip during Queen Elizabeth II's reign) felt a bit like a spare prick at a wedding. He didn't have an official function and wasn't allowed to be called king. So he took on the role of Victoria's private secretary and started to deal with her royal paperwork: *Oh, Victoria, you're pregnant again. You can't cope with all this. You need to look after the children. Let me get on with running things.* He became quite controlling and saw it as a way of coping with Victoria's emotional outbursts. She, at least on the surface, acquiesced: *Oh, I'm so lucky to have Albert to do all this for me.* She put on the facade that he was perfect in every way, and she was just this silly little woman, but if there was ever a disagreement over something, she'd have a quiet word. *You must remember, Albert. I'm the queen.*

So, what was going on on the political stage while Victoria was drowning in babies? The argument about the Corn Laws was still raging because grain prices were still being kept artificially high, and then, in 1845, there was a potato blight in Ireland. The Irish couldn't get hold of cheap grain to replace the diseased potatoes so there was a massive famine. More than a million Irish died and another million emigrated, largely to the US. The Irish started to call Victoria 'the Famine Queen', even though she did try to help by personally donating £2,000 (about £200,000 today). These events inevitably put pressure on parliament to repeal the Corn Laws. The Tories were, of course, largely opposed to reform because many of them were major landowners who benefitted hugely from the current system, but Robert Peel, with Victoria's support, eventually managed to get the laws scrapped.

In 1848, republican revolutions ripped through Europe. There were popular uprisings against monarchies in Italy, France, Germany, Denmark, Hungary, Sweden, Switzerland, Belgium, Spain and Ireland.

One country that didn't have a revolution was Britain. As I say, there was one in Ireland, which was part of the United Kingdom, but Britain as a whole – because it was stable, because people liked Victoria, because she handled things with a light touch, because the government repealed the Corn Laws, because the bourgeoisie already had a great deal of power, because they'd experimented with (and rejected) republicanism under Cromwell – avoided serious revolt. They didn't want revolution, but British people *were* calling for change, particularly the Chartists, so called because they had a charter of six aims.

1. All males over 21 to have the vote.
2. Secret ballots.
3. Annual elections.
4. No property ownership qualifications for becoming an MP.
5. Payment for MPs.
6. Constituencies of equal size.

This sounds like a perfectly reasonable template for democracy, but the Chartists were seen as dangerous revolutionaries. The oldest surviving photograph of a protest in British history is a picture that was taken when the Chartists organised a mass meeting on Kennington Common in south London, with the aim of marching to the Houses of Parliament to deliver their petition. The size of the crowds panicked the establishment and Victoria and Albert were sent for their safety to the Isle of Wight, where Albert had built a property called Osborne House. The government used all their powers to prevent the crowd getting anywhere near parliament. They declared the procession illegal and many public buildings were boarded up, their custodians armed with muskets and swords. In the end, the leader of the Chartists, Feargus O'Connor, folded under pressure, left his followers kettled in Kennington in heavy rain, and delivered his damp petition by cab. It was inevitably rejected and the Chartist movement collapsed. After her slightly bathetic escape to the twee Isle of Wight, the queen was able to safely return to London.

Having weathered the political squalls at home, Victoria was faced with a fresh outbreak of imperial warfare. The Ottoman Empire, which had been such a dominant force in eastern Europe, was starting to collapse, leaving a power vacuum. Russia (this might sound familiar) pushed down through what is now Ukraine into the Crimea, trying to take over Ottoman territories. Victoria, who had already been suspicious of Russia, believed that they were planning to expand into the Middle East and might even threaten India. The British allied with the Ottoman Turks and the French to try to hold Russia back.

I don't have the space to go into the subsequent Crimean War in any detail. The most famous engagements were the Battle of Balaklava,* the Battle of Alma (after which many pubs are named), the Battle of Inkerman and the Siege of Sebastopol. It was not a glorious war for anybody involved, but it did halt Russia's imperialist expansion.

The next major conflict was in India, where the East India Company had been running things and keeping control with its gigantic private army, largely made up of local Indian soldiers known as sepoys. In 1857, the sepoys rose against their overlords. The British called it the Indian Mutiny, while the Indians called it the Indian Rebellion (it's now known as the First War of Independence). Parliament, with the blessing of the queen, decided that the only thing to do was remove the East India Company from power and take over. A large British Army deployment was sent to India, the locals were defeated and India formally became part of the British Empire. Victoria hated the violence on both sides and wrote of her feelings of horror and regret at what she called 'this bloody civil war.' But she had the notion that once the good old British Empire was running things, everyone would be much happier. We could make it all nice and British, there wouldn't be any more of these damned civil wars and India would benefit from our civilising influence and thank us. In the end, Britain ruled India for a little less than 90 years.

There were other colonial wars – in Afghanistan, Egypt, China, even New Zealand. And in South Africa there was the Anglo–Zulu War and two Boer wars (which I'll deal with in the next chapter).

---

* The British typically managed to create a heroic myth out of a pitiful disaster when the Light Brigade embarked on a doomed charge against Russian artillery during the Battle of Balaklava.

Known as the Opium Wars, the two wars with China were particularly interesting and shine a light on the devious workings of empire. Basically, China had a lot of goods that the British wanted – spices, silk, tea, porcelain, whatever – but Britain didn't have anything much that China wanted. The Chinese preferred to have nothing to do with the West and had no interest in free trade. It was economically unsound to send empty ships to China that came back stuffed with Chinese goods, so the British decided to force them to buy opium, produced in India. British gunboats easily beat the inferior local navy and the Chinese had no choice but to sign very unfavourable trading treaties. The end result was that the British ended up with Hong Kong and a roaring trade, while the Chinese ended up addicted to opium.

On the domestic front, Prince Albert, who was very aware of the anti-monarchical feelings raging in Europe, had the idea of trying to make the royal family appear ordinary. He felt they should engage with the public and appear to be like them. Building Osborne House on the Isle of Wight had been part of this process – *Look! We live in a house just like you. Not a castle or a palace.* (Although, it has to be said, it's pretty bloody massive.) To the same end, he built another house in Scotland, the more modest Balmoral, which became Queen Victoria's favourite place to be (as it was Queen Elizabeth's).

Victoria had become subservient to Albert, even slightly infantilised, and the royal household made up a nickname for her: 'Eliza' (similar to how Elizabeth II was nicknamed Brenda in parts of the UK press). Albert was extremely bright and Victoria would claim that she was stupid and knew nothing – *He's the brainy one.* At the same time, she demanded his undivided attention. There's a suspicion that he was keeping her pregnant because as long as she was carrying a child, he could sideline her. She'd have to go into confinement around a birth for many weeks and, once she was nursing and suffering from her depression, she was rendered powerless, leaving him to fill the gap. But after the birth of Princess Beatrice in 1874, her doctor advised her that she shouldn't get pregnant again, to which she responded with a line that gives us an insight into her sex life: 'Oh, Sir James. Can I have no more fun in bed?'

In fact, fun was running out. Albert developed a stomach complaint, exacerbated, as Victoria saw it, by stress that was brought on by problems with their eldest son, Edward. The Prince of Wales was generally known as Bertie and was a bit of a throwback to George IV. He had large appetites and an eye for the ladies. He'd been having a very open student affair with an Irish actress, Nellie Clifden, and Albert had waded in to try to sort out the mess. The two of them had a man-to-man in the rain and Albert died soon after, in December 1861.

The royal doctor, William Jenner, noted the cause of death as typhoid fever (Victoria forbade them from carrying out an autopsy). There's speculation that what actually killed Albert was more likely Crohn's disease (or possibly kidney failure, or even some form of abdominal cancer … why are the royal family always so secretive about their health problems?).

The queen was overwhelmed by terrible grief. Officially, women were expected to go into mourning for a while, but Victoria was in mourning for the next 40 years. She completely withdrew from public affairs, dressed herself in black and didn't connect with her people or her parliament. She became known as the Widow of Windsor, staying secluded there (or at Balmoral, or the Isle of Wight), and only very rarely visiting Buckingham Palace. Prince Albert's room at Windsor Castle, the Blue Room, was kept exactly as it was the day he died. Servants would put out clean clothing, fresh flowers and hot water for him to wash and shave every morning, while also making sure his pen was filled and ready on his blotting paper. This continued until Victoria died.

The queen had always had a tendency towards comfort eating and her weight increased, which made her even less keen to appear in public. In 1864, a wag stuck a notice to the railings of Buckingham Palace saying: 'These commanding premises to be let or sold in consequence of the late occupants' declining business.'

Victoria was accused of being too emotional, of wallowing in her grief in an un-British manner and losing touch with her people.*

---

* When Princess Diana died in 1997, Queen Elizabeth II was accused of being *not emotional enough*. How times had changed.

The only person who seemed to have any positive influence on the queen was her manservant in Scotland, John Brown. It's a big thing these days to connect with nature, to go on long walks and enjoy the natural world as a way of dealing with mental health problems, and that's just what John Brown did with Victoria, helping her to get over her crippling depression. The two of them were painted together by Sir Edwin Landseer and it was seen as not the done thing for the queen to be getting so pally with an ordinary working-class man.

They grew so close that people began to gossip that they were having an affair. Satirists started referring to her as Mrs Brown and there were ridiculous rumours that she'd secretly married – and had had a child with him. Victoria outlived John Brown and, after his death, she started to write a biography of him. But she was dissuaded by her private secretary, Sir Henry Ponsonby, and the manuscript was destroyed. Which is a shame.

Even though Victoria had withdrawn from public life, the business of running the country went on. In 1867, a second Reform Act was passed, which almost doubled the electorate, giving many more urban working men the vote.

The prime minister that Victoria got on best with after Melbourne was Benjamin Disraeli. He was Jewish and hadn't come from the aristocracy, but he worked out how to charm Victoria. He was good at flirting with her, letting her think she was getting her way when he was calling all the shots. He called her his 'faery' and knew that the best way of managing the spoilt child was by humouring her. 'Everyone likes flattery,' he said. 'And when you come to royalty, you should lay it on with a trowel.'

Disraeli's greatest rival was Gladstone, who served as PM a record four times and each time he came back more obstinate, more tyrannical, 'older and madder', as Victoria saw it. She hated dealing with him because he talked to her not as a woman, but as if she were a public meeting, forever speechifying and mansplaining to her.

Disraeli and Gladstone were constantly fighting for pole position, and they both urged Victoria to reengage with her public. Partly to flatter her, Disraeli pushed through the Royal Titles Act in 1876, making her Empress of India to much celebration. The British (mostly) loved the idea of the empire, of Britannia ruling the waves, of Great Britain being the most powerful and glorious nation on God's Earth.

Ten years later, in 1887, the whole of the empire celebrated Victoria's golden jubilee. She had a huge banquet to which 50 kings and princes were invited and went on a very popular procession across London. The public started loving her again and Victoria had become 'the grandmother of the people'.

Ten years after her golden jubilee, she had her diamond jubilee in 1897. And, not long after, in 1901, at the age of 81, she died of 'old age'. You can find memorials to her almost everywhere you look and, of course, Albert was immortalised as well. Victoria commissioned the bizarre and rather gaudy Albert Memorial that sits opposite the Royal Albert Hall, the huge concert venue beside Hyde Park in London. And they are remembered together in the name of the world's largest museum of decorative arts and design: the Victoria and Albert in South Kensington, which opened in 1852. And let's not forget there's also a piece of intimate, gentleman's jewellery named after him – the Prince Albert cock ring (although the idea that he wore one to keep his parts in place during official functions is sadly an urban myth).

Between them, her children gave Victoria 42 grandchildren, and she had 87 great-grandchildren. So many members of her family ended up on European thrones that she became known as 'the Grandmother of Europe'. By the turn of the 20th century, she had grandchildren on the thrones of Germany, Russia, Denmark, Greece, Norway, Romania, and Spain. The three main leaders during the First World War – Tsar Nicholas, Kaiser Wilhelm and George V – were all grandsons of Victoria, not only making them first cousins but making the war the biggest family feud ever.

37

ℰDWARD ...

EDWARD VII – 1841–1910

Bertie/Edward the Caresser
Reigned 1901–1910
Lived for 68 years. Ruled for nine years.
Died from smoking too much (heart attack).
Remembered for: being a 'ladies' man', having a sex chair and
establishing the Entente Cordiale with the French.

Edward died just short of his 69th birthday, a relatively ripe old age for a monarch, but because his mother lived for so long, he'd barely sat down on the throne before he keeled over from a heart attack, brought on by a lifetime of smoking and overeating.

Queen Victoria always thought that her oldest son was a bit thick and would make a terrible king. Edward actually turned out to be one of our more benign monarchs who presided over something of a golden age. The Edwardian era is seen as a brief period of innocence and gaiety, when men picnicked in punts wearing stripy blazers, white flannels and straw boaters, while women in wide hats rode bicycles. It was a bright, fresh and fun time after the heavy, gloomy, Gothic-revival Victorian era that had been weighed down by crusty medievalism. Edward's reign heralded a new dawn of motor cars and aeroplanes, of the birth of the suffragette movement and of early moves towards creating a more caring, welfare state.

You can't help but wonder what would have happened if war hadn't broken out soon after Edward died. The catastrophic descent into violence, death and destruction that was the First World War snuffed out that golden dawn and a generation of young men were lost.

Edward VII was actually christened Albert, after his father, Queen Victoria's beloved Prince Albert, but he said in public that he could never live up to his father's name – there could only ever be one Albert! I'm not sure he liked his father that much, however, and hated living in his 'perfect' shadow, so perhaps there was more to his not wanting to be the first King Albert, as his mother had always hoped.

Edward's family and friends called him Bertie, but he was also known by various nicknames. He famously enjoyed the company of women and had a string of mistresses, so he was dubbed Edward the Caresser and even Dirty Bertie. He was also called Tum Tum (although not to his face). Edward always had big appetites – for food, for sex, for cigars – but, unlike the similarly greedy George IV, he didn't actually drink that much. He enjoyed the occasional glass of champagne but wasn't known for getting drunk. He did like his grub, though. He ate a full breakfast, then lunch, tea, dinner (usually 12 courses) and, finally, supper, a snack before bedtime, just in case. He stuck to this regime all his life and also got through 12 huge cigars and 20 cigarettes a day. Eventually, all of this killed him, but he did enjoy himself along the way.

Just like George IV (again), Edward was famous for his interest in male fashion and uniforms, and was a stickler for the correct way of dressing. He established many of the 'rules' for menswear that still hold today. Because of his 48-inch waist, for instance, he had to leave the bottom button of his waistcoats undone, which became the 'correct' style. Inspired by his family trips to Balmoral, he made tweed fashionable (his favourite pattern became known as the Prince of Wales check) and it remains the material of choice for upper-class country clothing. He also popularised the Norfolk jacket, the Homburg hat and black bow ties with dinner jackets, rather than white tie and tails.

He had a miserable childhood. Victoria never really liked him. I mean, she never liked having children in the first place. They made her sick and depressed and stopped her from enjoying herself with her husband. So, perhaps she resented Bertie for coming between her and Albert?

Victoria had had a miserably strict upbringing herself, under the Kensington System, and she and Albert were determined to give Bertie more of the same. Inevitably, their attempts to make their son toe the line had the opposite effect. Victoria became appalled by her son's appetites and sexual escapades, while Albert thought him depraved.

The boy did very poorly in his lessons, developed a nervous stammer and was prone to sudden rages like his mother, who quickly wrote him off as a lazy half-wit – and ugly to boot. Victoria said of him: 'Handsome I cannot think him, with that painfully small and narrow head, those immense features and total want of chin.' (She could talk.)

Bertie was brought up to speak English, German and French. He enjoyed German the most and spoke it so much as a child that he ended up with a slight German accent. He was more like his mother than his father. Neither was an intellectual and Victoria dismissed herself as stupid. Perhaps this was another reason why she disliked the boy. She saw too much of herself in him, and not enough of Albert.

But, despite Victoria and Albert's terrible parenting, Bertie turned out to be a genial fellow who made an effort to be pleasant with everyone and was splendid company. He would happily chat to politicians, writers, scientists, musicians and ordinary people. He enjoyed the simple pleasures. He liked to play cards, particularly a new game that was becoming a craze called bridge. He liked to travel and he enjoyed the theatre and sports, particularly blood sports, but also yachting and golf. He was apparently a very good goalie in ice hockey – probably because he was so huge that nobody could get a puck past him.

He was fond of horse racing and loved attending meetings. For the Great British public, this humanised him. There was much rejoicing when, in 1900, his horses won the Grand National, the 2000 Guineas, the Newmarket Stakes, the Eclipse Stakes, the Derby and the St Leger, making the prince the top owner that year with nearly £30,000 in winnings and bets.

He was a much more relaxed and pleasure-loving monarch than his complicated mother, and his personable nature put him in good stead when he became a sort of roving ambassador for the royal family. He was related to most of the crowned heads in Europe and was forever visiting them, helping them out and maintaining relations, while his mother retreated from the world. Victoria, for her part, wanted to keep him away from the everyday running of parliament and royal business, so worked hard to keep him busy overseas.

This diplomatic role gave Bertie's existence some meaning and purpose, and allowed him to see the world. He travelled to the US, Canada, Russia, France and Germany, and particularly loved Biarritz, where he went every year to enjoy the climate, the sailing and the socialising.

His urge to do something useful made him want to join the army, hoping to train like any other young officer at Sandhurst. But the royal court demurred. *Oh, no, no, Bertie, you don't need to do that. You're the prince of Wales. We'll simply have you made a lieutenant colonel.* So he ended up with a meaningless position and his boot camp ambitions were thwarted.

Despite his lack of intellectual prowess, he did manage to go to university. In fact, he went to three: Edinburgh, Oxford and Cambridge. After a summer at Edinburgh he started at Oxford, where he was very disappointed that his father wouldn't let him live in a college like any other student but insisted he stay in a house in town with a minder, Colonel Robert Bruce, who strictly controlled his social life. So, once again, his chance of mucking in and being like everyone else was thwarted.

After some time at Oxford, he moved on to Cambridge. Despite attending three universities, he didn't come out any brighter than he'd gone in, and his time at university is remembered more for his sexual antics than his studying.

While he was at Cambridge, his pals arranged for him to lose his virginity and sneaked the actress, Nellie Clifden, into his rooms. Soon afterwards, Edward had a brief shot at being an ordinary soldier. In the summer of 1861, he went to an army camp at Carragh near Dublin. He loved the uniforms and the parades and the ceremonial side of things, but his commander-in-chief said he would never make a useful officer. While he was at the camp, his fellow soldiers smuggled Nellie into his tent several times, with inevitable consequences. Word got out and it blew up into a royal scandal. We saw in the previous chapter how, when Bertie returned to Cambridge, Prince Albert went huffing and puffing up there to have a stern, fatherly talk with him and Edward must have said the right things because Albert came back saying, *I think he's going to be alright. I think I've straightened him out ...* And then he went and died.

For the rest of her life, Victoria blamed Edward for Albert's death. She never let Albert go and didn't let anyone speak of him as if he was dead, so Edward was never able to replace him in his mother's heart or step out from under his shadow.

Before Albert's death, it had been agreed that Edward would marry Princess Alexandra of Denmark in the hope it would curb his philandering. An alliance with a Scandinavian country was always useful as a counterbalance to the dominance of France and Germany. Luckily, Edward and Alexandra both liked each other. She was a notable beauty with a charming, warm and fun-loving personality. She liked dancing, ice skating and horse riding, despite suffering from regular attacks of rheumatic fever which caused her to limp.

The couple were married at St George's Chapel in Windsor in 1863 and went on to have a happy marriage, despite the fact that Edward was a terrible womaniser who was pretty open about his sex life. (Edward was notorious for spending time in the brothels of Paris, where prostitution was legal. One lavish bordello, Le Chabanais, even built him a love chair that supported his great weight and allowed him to have sex with two women at once without crushing them to death.) Alexandra chose to turn a blind eye to his infidelities and threw herself into bringing up their children, which, unlike Victoria, she very much enjoyed.

Although Alexandra enjoyed Edward's company, she didn't like her mother-in-law. On paper, all of her children were born prematurely and it's been suggested that Alexandra and Edward lied about the due dates to make sure that Victoria was never around for any of the births.

When Victoria went into seclusion after Albert's death, Edward and Alexandra became the public face of the royal family, which they both enjoyed. They lived at Marlborough House in Pall Mall and Victoria also bought a house for them in Norfolk – Sandringham – where there was very good shooting. For the rest of his life, Edward would spend a great deal of his leisure time at Sandringham, killing things. He even brought in a system known as Sandringham Time, where all the clocks in Sandringham were set to a different time to the rest of the country to allow more hours of daylight so he could see what he was shooting at.

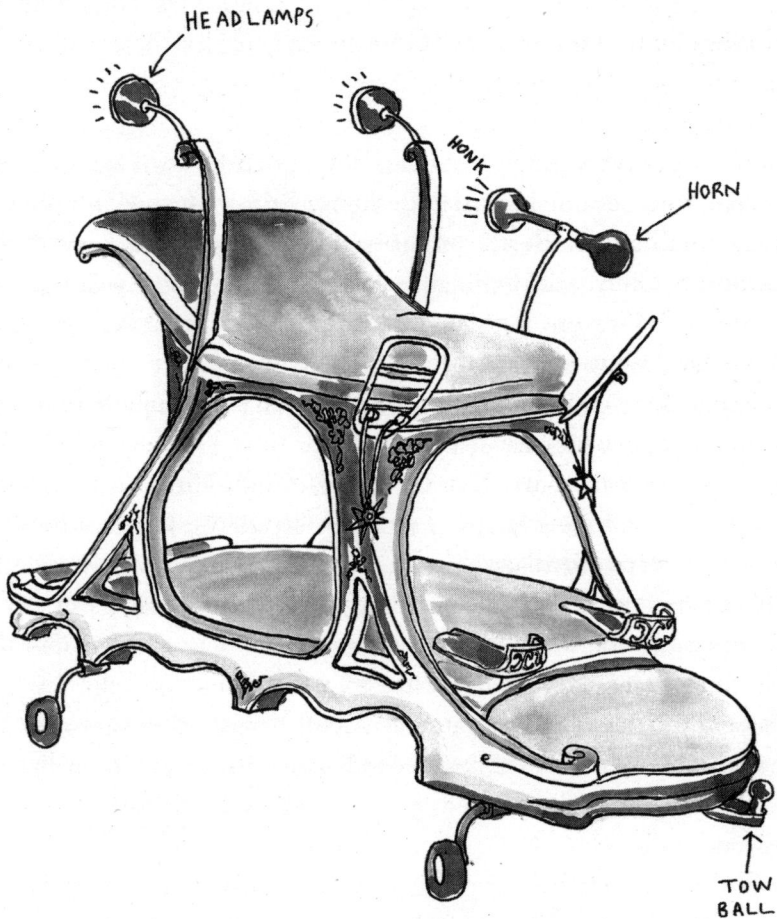

HEADLAMPS

HONK

HORN

TOW BALL

EDWARD'S LOVE CHAIR

Edward also loved schmoozing people and throwing parties at both Marlborough House and Sandringham, which became *the* places to be. While Edward was partying, Queen Victoria sat and brooded, jealously guarding her own power and keeping him at arm's length from parliament. But the prince befriended the foreign secretary, Lord Rosebery, who began secretly passing him documents and information. It didn't help Edward's relationship with his mother that he sided with the liberal Gladstone, who she hated, over the conservative Disraeli. Another classic case of a child choosing the opposite politics to their parents.

As I say, Prince Edward had many mistresses, including the actresses Lillie Langtry, Sarah Bernhardt and 'La Belle Otero', but his preference was for other men's wives, perhaps because there was less chance of them getting too attached to him. Among his aristocratic lovers were Alice Keppel, Patsy Cornwallis-West and Lady Brooke, who became known as Babbling Brook for spilling the beans on her dalliances. Bertie possibly even had an affair with Lord Randolph Churchill's wife, the American heiress Jennie Jerome, mother of Winston. The two of them certainly had a very 'close friendship'. Edward's tactic of sleeping with other men's wives blew up in his face a couple of times. He was even sensationally called as a witness in a divorce case in 1870, the first time a prince of Wales had given evidence in court since Prince Hal in the 15th century. People booed Edward in public and there was a real fear that Edward might bring down the monarchy.*

But when, in 1871, Edward caught typhoid fever and nearly died, everyone loved him again. This was the same disease that his father was thought to have died from, and suddenly a reverent hush fell across the land: was Bertie going to pull through? The poet, Alfred Austin, who went on to become the poet laureate, wrote some immortal lines about this incident.

Flashed from his bed, the electric tidings came. He is not better. He is much the same.†

Even though the queen was told to prepare herself for the worst, Edward miraculously pulled through and there was cheering in the streets. The threat of republicanism went away. (Bertie's flagging popularity was to be given a similar boost during a later rocky patch in 1900 when he was shot at in Belgium.)

On his travels as a royal envoy, he toured the Middle East in the early 1860s, and a decade later, when he was 34, he visited the Indian

* This is a sentiment that still rears its head in some quarters of the British press when one of the royals (usually Harry) is thought to have stepped out of line.
† That first line refers to the new invention of the electric telegraph.

subcontinent, where he had a splendid time hunting, although the others in his party found it hard to keep up with him. On his very first day, he shot six tigers. He enjoyed India but was disgusted by some of the racist attitudes he came across among British administrators. He wrote that 'because a man has a black face and a different religion from our own, there is no reason why he should be treated as a brute'. When he returned to England, he got at least one of these colonial nobs removed from their posts.

Edward seemed to have been free of any prejudices. It's telling that in a country where one of his ancestors had thrown out the Jews, Edward was happy to count several among his friends. They were part of the group of important and interesting men that Bertie gathered around himself and who became known as the Marlborough House Set.

He was also something of a reformer and, for a royal, quite progressive. He got involved in a royal commission on housing that was concerned with improving the terrible living conditions for the poor and secretly visited the East End slums in disguise to see the situation for himself without the 'fresh paint' effect (it was joked that Queen Elizabeth thought everywhere smelled of paint because whenever she made a royal visit, the local dignitaries would redecorate before her arrival). So he was genuinely trying to do good alongside sleeping with other men's wives.

Alexandra and Bertie were very worried about their eldest son, Prince Eddy, the Duke of Clarence. He was a bit of an untrustworthy cad who behaved even more scandalously than his dad and was suspected of sleeping with both men and women. Nevertheless, Bertie was still absolutely heartbroken when Eddy died of pneumonia brought on by a bout of flu a week after his 28th birthday in 1892. Bertie was a very warm father figure and had a very good relationship with all his children. He loved them and they loved him in return. But there was relief in the royal court that Edward's second son was now in line to the throne. Prince George was considered a much safer bet as monarch, being a serious, studious and reliably dull boy.

Queen Victoria eventually died in January 1901, having just scraped into the 20th century. When Edward came to the throne, he was almost 60 and overweight, but still filled with energy. He was raring to go and needed to be active; he got bored very quickly otherwise. He entertained or dined out almost every evening and set about remodelling, rebuilding and updating the royal palaces, helped by the fact that he was the highest-paid British monarch ever.

He was older than most of the other European monarchs and had an avuncular relationship with them, tending his flock and helping them weather the revolutionary storms. He liked all of the monarchs, except his nephew, Kaiser Wilhelm of Germany, whom he thought was stuck-up and pompous. He complained that the kaiser genuinely thought of himself as a mighty emperor ruling by God's will, saying that he 'needs to learn that he is living at the end of the 19th century and not in the Middle Ages'.

Probably Edward's greatest diplomatic achievement was the establishment of a better relationship with England's old enemy, France. He was a driving force behind the Entente Cordiale, a friendly, and lasting, alliance between the two countries. The talks had stalled, so Bertie went on a goodwill trip to Paris, shaking hands, slapping backs and being generally chummy. Initially, the French were resistant to this bluff, tweedy English monarch and didn't think too kindly of a royal coming over and trying to butter up the post-revolutionary French republic. What swung things in Edward's favour was a visit to the theatre. During the interval, the king was socialising in the foyer when he spotted a French actress he'd once had an affair with – Jeanne Granier. He approached her and said in fluent French, 'Mademoiselle. I remember applauding you in London where you represented all the grace and spirit of France.'

Even though this was almost inevitably a set-up, the king's gesture and his words about France went round Paris and the visit became a triumph. Finally, the deal was signed and, after nearly a thousand years of mutual aggression, France and Britain were officially best mates. Not that it really made that much difference in the long run. The deal couldn't halt the inexorable slide towards the First World War.

Edward always feared Germany's imperialist intentions. And when his nephew Kaiser Wilhelm built several steam-driven ironclad battleships, the British government responded by building their first dreadnought. Several steps up from the wooden-hulled ironclads, dreadnoughts were made entirely of iron. Wilhelm answered back by building some dreadnoughts of his own, and a deadly arms race was on.

The Conservatives in the British parliament argued for more dreadnoughts, while the Liberals wanted to reduce the military budget and increase social spending. They proposed an early version of a welfare state to support the poor. Under Herbert Asquith, the Liberals gained control of the House of Commons, something of a high point for the party who would never hold power like this again.

The Conservatives cared little for the working classes and wanted more battleships, even coming up with what they thought was a catchy slogan: 'We want eight and we won't wait!' A war cry, it has to be said, that was taken up by jingoistic and bellicose citizens from all levels of society. The Liberals bargained with the Tories, pulled back on some of their demands and agreed to commission some more dreadnoughts in return for the establishment of an old-age pension, the whole package to be funded by a big hike in taxation for the super-rich.

The House of Lords, which was weighted towards the Conservatives, repeatedly refused to pass any of Asquith's bills. The Duke of Beaufort even threatened to set his dogs on the chancellor, David Lloyd George, and his radical colleague, Winston Churchill, who was at the time a Liberal politician (he had a tendency to swap sides to make sure he was always on the winning team). This led to a constitutional crisis and Asquith and Lloyd George urged Edward to create more liberal peers to overwhelm the Conservatives in the Lords. Edward baulked at the idea, arguing that it wouldn't look good, and instead told the Liberals to call a general election and see who the people supported.

Unfortunately, the election was inconclusive and, in the end, the Liberals had to form a coalition with both the Irish Nationalists, who were pushing for Home Rule, and the nascent Labour Party, under Keir Hardie, a Scottish coal miner (whose father was a ... well, we don't know – he was illegitimate). Edward's main concern was to avoid war. Britain had just come through the Second Boer War, where a bunch of Dutch farmers had been able to hold their own against the

British Army.* The British had only narrowly won and annexed the Boer-occupied lands into the empire. They'd had to resort to using some pretty brutal tactics to beat the Boers, though. They'd taken the fight to their families, implementing a scorched-earth policy and building concentration camps. The war had exposed a harsh and pathetic reality. Despite posters showing proud, strapping young soldiers, the British Army was useless. British working men were undernourished, diseased and (there's no polite way of saying it) *shrivelled*, growing smaller with each generation. One of the reasons Edward supported the Liberals' social reforms was to make sure the army had healthier soldiers. Something needed to be done to give workers better living conditions, better health and better nutrition.

Unfortunately, Edward's relationship with his nephew, Kaiser Wilhelm, never improved. The mutual antagonism between England and Germany grew worse and the constitutional crisis was still rolling on when Edward's lifestyle caught up with him. In 1910, he suffered a series of heart attacks and died. His last words were about a horse of his that had done well at Kempton Park races – 'I am very glad'.

---

* Both Boer wars had been fought over the same things – land, power and mineral rights – between British and Dutch (Boer) settlers. Of course, the rights of the native Africans weren't considered, especially since they'd been beaten down in the Anglo–Zulu War of 1879.

38

GEORGE ...

GEORGE V – 1865–1936
George Frederick Ernest Albert/Grandpa England
Reigned 1910–1936
Lived for 70 years. Reigned for 25 years.
Died from a massive speedball overdose.
Remembered for: the First World War and
collecting stamps.

George V was the first of the Windsor monarchs (although, technically, he was still a Saxe-Coburg and Gotha). He was advised to change the family name during the First World War, when there was such an outpouring of anti-German sentiment that it was deemed prudent to go with something more English-sounding. It wasn't the only aristocratic German name to be changed; others included the Battenbergs who became the Mountbattens.*

George V has a reputation for being the most boring man in England whose only interests were stamp collecting and shooting things. People would break a leg or feign a bout of typhoid fever to avoid sitting next to him at dinner. This stems partly from the extremely dull journals he wrote. He's been reassessed recently (hasn't everyone?) and presented in a more sympathetic light. It seems he wasn't necessarily boring; he was just a very guarded and private man. He didn't feel it was his place to put anything emotional or personal in his journals, so for the most part we get no glimpses of the man that wrote them. This means you get entries along the lines of 'Two eggs for breakfast. Stuck some stamps from Mauritius into my album. The

---

* George's cousin, Kaiser Wilhelm, thought this was hilarious and said he looked forward to seeing a production of *The Merry Wives of Saxe-Coburg and Gotha*.

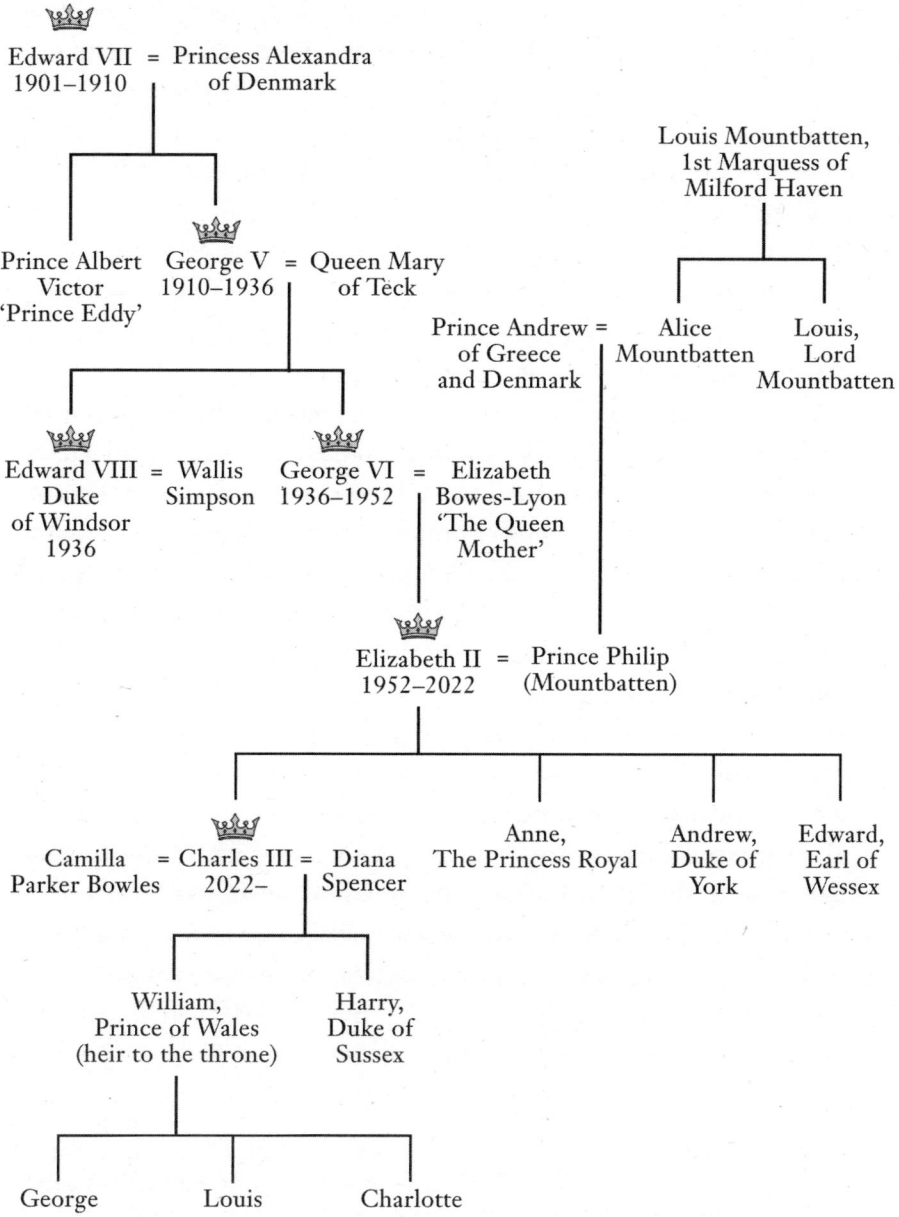

THE WINDSORS

Edward VII = Princess Alexandra
1901–1910   of Denmark

Louis Mountbatten,
1st Marquess of
Milford Haven

Prince Albert   George V = Queen Mary
Victor   1910–1936   of Teck
'Prince Eddy'

Prince Andrew =   Alice   Louis,
of Greece   Mountbatten   Lord
and Denmark   Mountbatten

Edward VIII = Wallis   George VI =   Elizabeth
Duke   Simpson   1936–1952   Bowes-Lyon
of Windsor   'The Queen
1936   Mother'

Elizabeth II =   Prince Philip
1952–2022   (Mountbatten)

Camilla   = Charles III = Diana   Anne,   Andrew,   Edward,
Parker Bowles   2022–   Spencer   The Princess Royal   Duke of   Earl of
                                                        York   Wessex

William,   Harry,
Prince of Wales   Duke of
(heir to the throne)   Sussex

George   Louis   Charlotte

12-cent green with a nice picture of me on them. Pheasant for lunch. Informed that we are at war with Germany.'

So what sort of a man *was* he? He seems to have been quite a down-to-earth, unshowy bloke who wanted to live an ordinary, upper-middle-class life. He was honest, dutiful, placid, and – oh God, I'm sorry – HE WAS DULL. Just the man that Britain needed on the throne during a time of great upheaval: a steady, stable, reliable, calming (and dull) presence.

At his silver jubilee in 1935, he was so moved by the cheering crowds that he remarked, 'I cannot understand it. After all, I'm only a very ordinary sort of fellow.' On the whole, the British tend to like their monarchs as long as they don't do anything more than stand around looking stately at official functions. George V was very fond of his eldest granddaughter, Princess Elizabeth, the future Queen Elizabeth II. He nicknamed her Lilibet and she called him Grandpa England, which was how many of the British thought of him.

If the First World War wasn't enough, George's reign also saw the Parliament Act of 1911 (which established the supremacy of the House of Commons over the unelected House of Lords), the Russian Revolution, the rise of both communism and fascism throughout Europe, votes for women, the first Labour government in 1924, the general strike in 1926 and the Great Depression of the early 1930s.

The British Empire also reached its height during George's reign. By 1922, it was the largest empire the world had ever seen, covering around a quarter of Earth's landmass and ruling almost a quarter of its population, some 458 million people. Of course, if 1922 was its peak, that meant that the empire started to decline during George's reign. He witnessed the growth of both the Indian and Irish independence movements, the latter of which encompassed a civil war.

So perhaps it helped to have a conservative, unflustered, stolid (and dull) ruler like George to stop the country sliding into extremism. He was the embodiment of KEEP CALM AND CARRY ON.* You still wouldn't want to be stuck next to him at dinner, though.

---

* This was never actually used as a campaign in the Second World War. Posters were printed but never issued. The slogan first saw the light of day when an old poster was found in a Northumberland bookshop in 2000.

As a boy, George didn't expect to become king. He and his older brother – the heir, Prince Eddy – had a fairly normal upbringing until 1877, when his father sent the siblings off to join the navy, believing this was the very best possible training for life they could have. George was only 11. He stayed in the navy for some time, visiting various British colonies around the empire. When he was 16, he and Eddy got tattoos on a visit to Japan. This was de rigeur for navy men and, of course, the Pacific is just the place for getting inked up. When I first read about this, I assumed George probably had a little anchor or maybe 'I love Gran' and a picture of Queen Victoria. But no. He had a dragon all the way down one arm and a tiger down the other. This led to a craze for tattoos in upper-class society.

When George and Eddy returned to Britain from one voyage in 1882, Queen Victoria was so appalled her grandsons couldn't speak French or German that she sent them away for six months of language lessons in Lausanne, where they both completely failed to learn anything. Prince Eddy, as next in line to the throne after his father, was then removed from the navy, just in case, and enrolled at Trinity College, Cambridge, where he also failed to learn anything. But George, as the spare, returned to sea. He went on to command a few vessels, including a torpedo boat, and his last active service was in command of HMS *Melampus* between 1891 and 1892. After that, he kept his naval rank, but it was largely honorary. In most photographs of George, he's wearing some kind of military uniform, particularly during the First World War when, a little like President Zelensky of Ukraine, he insisted on wearing a uniform in public until the war was over.

George was dogged by health problems throughout his life. Like his father, Edward VII, he was a heavy smoker and suffered regular bouts of bronchitis, chest problems and heart problems. In 1891 he was struck down by a bad bout of typhoid fever and only just survived. As we've seen, his elder brother, Prince Eddy, wasn't so lucky. George had barely recovered from his illness when Eddy got engaged to his second cousin once removed (whatever that means) Princess Victoria Mary of Teck (yet another one of those annoying little German principalities). But, six weeks later, Eddy came down with flu and died, leaving George as heir to the throne.

GEORGE V DISPLAYS HIS TATS

Just like Henry VIII, another monarch who'd never expected to take the throne, George ended up marrying the woman who'd been lined up for his older brother, Princess Victoria. He didn't want his wife to be called Queen Victoria, so she became Queen Mary. George, in his undemonstrative way, loved Mary. He had no mistresses, there were no scandals (apart from one time where there was a false accusation of bigamy from a republican journalist that was easily disproved) and they went on to have five sons and a daughter. That's how a marriage should be, but I'm nodding off just writing it down.

Some of his children did say that George was cold and strict, particularly his eldest son, who went on to become (briefly) Edward VIII, but we need to treat the flaky Edward as an unreliable narrator. However, as George apparently once remarked to a friend: 'My father was frightened of his mother. I was frightened of my father, and am damned well going to see it that my children are frightened of me.'

The family mainly lived in Sandringham in Norfolk, where there was a smaller house in the grounds of the estate called York Cottage, which Edward had given George as a wedding present. George loved his cosy life at York Cottage, which he said was 'like three Merrie England pubs joined together'. And they lived there like a well-to-do, ordinary middle-class family rather than royalty. It wasn't all bucolic bliss, though. We saw how Victoria hadn't allowed Prince Edward to get involved in politics and the business of being a monarch. Edward VII did the opposite with George, making sure he learned what his job would entail.

In the early 1900s, George and Mary toured the British Empire, doing their bit for the monarchy. In 1905, they visited India, where, like his father, George was appalled at the racial discrimination he observed there. And, again, just like his father, he supported Indians in their efforts to be given a greater say in the governance of their own country.

In 1906, the royal couple attended the wedding of King Alfonso XIII of Spain in Madrid and were nearly killed when an anarchist, Mateu Morral, threw a bomb at the procession as it left the church. Twenty-four people were killed, but none of the royals were among the dead.

Four years later, in 1910, Edward VII died and George wrote in his diary, 'I have lost my best friend and the best of fathers.' If he'd felt he had a strict upbringing or resented being sent away to join the navy at 11, he didn't mention it. He was now king and, at his coronation, he refused to say some lines that he considered offensively anti-Catholic. They were officially removed by the Accession Declaration Act. Although George was very much a conservative, he was no stuffy tyrant and conceded that changes would have to be made for the good of all.

He did, though, inherit a massive political snarl-up from his father. The Liberal prime minister Asquith was still trying to push through his parliamentary reforms to increase income tax and death duties, but the House of Lords were still busy blocking everything. George was advised, like his father, to create more liberal peers and overwhelm the conservatives in the lords, and Asquith was rounding up anyone he could to maintain his majority in the Commons. To get Irish politicians onside, he had to promise that he would seriously consider home rule for Ireland, which opened up a whole new can of worms. These problems were still being batted backwards and forwards when, in 1914, war broke out, putting everything on hold for the next four years.

As I've said before, in some ways you can view all of the wars in Europe since 1066 as being individual conflicts within a wider, never-ending war: a battle between the major countries for dominance, land, influence and wealth; a battle for empire. There have always been specific reasons why each individual war has started but, really, countries have always been on the lookout for an excuse to have another go and grab whatever they can get their hands on.

The First World War is too big and too well-known a subject to properly deal with here, but I will try to explain how it started. In 1914, there was a complex web of edgy alliances in Europe. Edward VII had been the driving force behind the Entente Cordiale with France, and Britain also had an alliance with Belgium. Russia was allied with France, as well as Serbia, while Germany had an alliance with what remained of the old Austro–Hungarian Empire. When the Ottoman Empire had lost the last of its European territories, Austria–Hungary had taken over part of the Balkans, including Bosnia Herzegovina. Serbia had been independent since 1878 and factions were pushing for a wider Serbian state/empire. It was a tense time. The anarchist bomb attack in Spain was by no means an isolated incident and it wasn't a great idea for Archduke Franz Ferdinand, heir to the Austro–Hungarian throne, to visit his troops in Sarajevo, the capital of Bosnia Herzegovina. A young Serbian nationalist, Gavrilo Princip, who felt that Serbia should be in control of Bosnia, assassinated the archduke and his wife. Austria–Hungary declared war on Serbia and the Russians declared war on Austria–Hungary. In no time at all, a chain reaction dragged allies in on all sides and the conflict spread to Africa, China and Japan; the last major power to get sucked in was the US. By the time the smoke cleared, up to 22 million people were dead, almost a million of which were British and Empire troops.

I think everyone knows about the trench warfare across the traditional battlegrounds of northern France and Belgium, and how the invention of tanks broke the deadlock there.* It was the involvement of the US, in 1917, that brought the war to an end, though. Americans had originally been strongly against joining the war in Europe, which they felt was nothing to do with them, but U-boat attacks on American shipping, along with a propaganda push from King George and the British government, eventually persuaded President Woodrow Wilson to change his mind. It was also a chance for the US to show what it was capable of. Lloyd George, the British prime minster at the time, pointed out that by joining the war, the US had 'at one bound become a world power'.

More than 100,000 American soldiers were killed in the war and by the outbreak of flu in 1918, but perhaps the greatest US contribution was financial. As we've been reminded recently, war is INCREDIBLY EXPENSIVE. There had been a big effort in Britain to raise money through taxes and war bonds (a system of essentially borrowing from the British public and institutions), but it wasn't enough. We still needed a massive loan of $4 billion from the US in order to get through it. It was much trumpeted that Britain only finished paying off this war loan in 2015, with a final payment for the outstanding amount of £1.9 billion, but the awkward secret is that this didn't

---

* A lot of innovative new ways to kill people were perfected during the war: aeroplanes, gas, submarines, machine guns ...

include repayment to the USA. Britain stopped paying the US First World War debt during the Depression. The US Treasury is keeping a tab, though – we currently owe them $16,669,221,062 (which helps explain why British PMs have to keep kissing US presidents' arses).

The war deeply affected King George. He spent a lot of time in Europe inspecting troops and raising morale but had a nasty accident when he fell from his horse, badly fracturing his pelvis, a wound from which he never fully recovered. He was visibly aged by the end of the war (heavy smoking didn't help) and his health was poor. His doctors tried many remedies over the years and in 1928 they sent him away to the seaside resort of Bognor in Sussex, down on the English Channel, for a period of recuperation, after which the town changed its name to Bognor Regis. There's a wonderful story that his last words were 'Bugger Bognor', but unfortunately there seems to be no evidence that he actually said it. Shame.

The fallout from the First World War was huge. In 1916, the Irish rebelled against British rule, but the Easter rising in Dublin ultimately failed. The revolution in Russia in 1917 was significantly more success-ful. George's cousin, Tsar Nicholas, was overthrown and, soon after, he and all his family were executed. The old regimes were toppling across Europe, with the thrones of Austria, Germany, Greece, Russia and Spain all lost. George V was almost the only royal to hold on to his crown. As a constitutional monarch, he wasn't seen by the British people as being personally responsible for the war, plus it helped that he was on the winning side. His other cousin, Kaiser Wilhelm, was forced to abdicate, bringing an end to the Second Reich in Germany.

There were changes on the home front in Britain, too. Women, who had played such an important role in keeping the country and its industry running during the war, were finally given the vote in 1918.* It was only for women over the age of 30 with a certain income, though; equal suffrage would have to wait another 10 years.

---

* It had been a year before the war, on 4 June 1913, when the suffragette Emily Davison stepped out in front of King George's horse at the Epsom Derby. She'd probably only meant to stop the race and publicise her cause, but was trampled to death. Tragic for her, but votes for women became the big talking point in the country.

In 1921, the question of Irish home rule was (partially) settled by the Anglo–Irish Treaty. The largely Protestant population of Ulster, in the north, chose to remain part of the United Kingdom. Northern Ireland became a loyalist stronghold, governed from Belfast. The rest of Ireland (the Irish Free State) became an independent country, ruled from Dublin. This compromise led to a lengthy period of civil war in Ireland between moderates who saw this as a first step towards full independence and radical elements who thought it was a sell-out and hadn't gone far enough.

There had been a large miners' strike before the war and George and his conservative advisers were frightened of socialism and the growing labour movement, mistakenly thinking it was also a republican movement. He made an effort to get out and to meet the ordinary working people, which went down very well. The king had something of a common touch – he liked to chat with farmers and country folk about horses and pigs, and became very involved in sport. He was the first monarch to present the FA Cup, for instance. And, as it turned out, most of the working classes quite liked having a king. In 1924, the UK got its first Labour prime minister, Ramsay MacDonald, and, you know what, the country didn't fall apart. George's fears had been groundless.

He remained popular right through to 1936 when his recurring lung problems worsened. It was clear that he was in great pain and on the way out. His doctor, Lord Dawson of Penn, wrote in his diary that the last thing the king said was 'God damn you ...' to his nurse who was coming at him with a big syringe. He was right to fear the needle. It came out in 1986, when Dawson's private diary was made public, that at 11pm on the night of 20 January, the doctor injected the king with a fatal dose of morphine and cocaine into his jugular vein. An hour later, George was dead (no doubt with a big smile on his face).

His death had been 'brought forward' not only to relieve his suffering, but also so that it could be announced in the morning edition of *The Times*, rather than in the evening. The morning papers were much more reputable than the evening ones, which were more like today's tabloids – sensationalist and gossipy. The family wanted it to be announced at just the right time so that civilised people could read about it at breakfast.

39

Then Ned the 8th Quickly Goes and Abdicat'th

EDWARD VIII – 1894–1972

Duke of Windsor/David

Reigned January–December 1936

Lived for 77 years. Reigned for 325 days.

Died from cancer of the throat.

Remembered for: abdicating. And hanging out with Hitler.

Edward VIII is the only king whose biography is summed up in the Willie, Willie, Harry, Stee rhyme.

Perhaps it was all foretold?

At King George V's funeral, as his body was being taken to lie in state in Westminster Hall, the cross fell off the Imperial State Crown (which had been placed on the coffin) and rolled into the gutter. The young man who'd become king the moment George died, Edward VIII, witnessed the incident and wondered whether it was a bad omen for his own reign. It was. Edward, although briefly king, never got to wear the crown. There were only two other monarchs who were never crowned: Edward V, one of the princes in the tower, and Lady Jane Grey, whose head was cut off before the crown could be fixed to it.

Edward's 325-day reign was the shortest since Jane's, and he was the first monarch to give up the throne since James II, almost 250 years previously.

George V had always had a poor relationship with Edward. The two of them didn't see eye to eye on anything, and it got worse as George got older and Edward failed to knuckle down and prepare himself for his future role as monarch. He was a throwback to his grandfather and namesake, Edward VII, who lived the life of an international playboy and had a series of affairs with married women as the Prince of Wales. In a letter to the prime minister, Stanley Baldwin, King George wrote that 'after I am dead, the boy will ruin himself within 12 months'.

And he was right.

George had always preferred his second son, Albert (Bertie) ... Actually, I'd better stop here and sort out these names. Edward VIII was christened Edward Albert Christian George Andrew Patrick David: Edward being the most popular name for a British king (and a nod to his uncle, Prince Eddy); Albert, after his great-grandfather Prince Albert; Christian to cover the Scandinavian side of his family; and then George, Andrew, Patrick and David, the patron saints of the four countries that made up the United Kingdom. For some reason, out of all those names, the family chose to call him David. So, technically, before he came to the throne, I should refer to him as David. I'll call him Edward, though, for clarity. His younger brother, who would go on to reign as George VI, was christened Albert Frederick Arthur George. And, as I say, the family called him Bertie. I'm going to stick with that for now so as not to confuse him with George V.

We've seen how George V was very fond of Bertie's daughter, Elizabeth, who he nicknamed Lilibet, and apparently told a courtier: 'I pray to God that my eldest son will never marry and have children, and that nothing will come between Bertie and Lilibet and the throne.'

Edward/David might not have been popular with his father, but the public loved him. He was everything a dashing young prince ought to be. The feeling wasn't mutual. Edward wrote to his sister-in-law, Alice, in 1925 that he was heartily sick of being cheered and yelled and shrieked at by the general public. When he became king, it was far worse than he'd ever imagined. He looks bored to tears in many photographs and admitted something that no monarch ever should, that it was 'one of the most confining, the most frustrating and, over the duller stretches, the least stimulating jobs open to an educated, independent minded person'.

A constitutional monarch has to deal with an enormous amount of paperwork and bureaucracy, and perform endless tedious rituals and public duties, while totally lacking any kind of real power or the ability to influence any meaningful matters of state. What Edward discovered after his abdication, though, was that he missed the status, respect and glamour that being the top royal had bestowed on him. His consolation title of Duke of Windsor meant very little and, for the rest of his life, he was a bitter and resentful outsider. The 'Firm', as some have called the royal court, is very unforgiving. Once you're out, you're out, as Prince Harry is no doubt discovering.

Edward/David was born in 1894, while his great-grandmother, Queen Victoria, was still on the throne, but he comes across as our first 'modern' monarch, particularly in the way he dressed and styled his hair. Like nearly all monarchs, he influenced fashion and became a style icon not just in Britain but also in the US, where he was a frequent visitor. In the 1920s, he was the equivalent of a Hollywood star and you can imagine many of his outfits being worn by male models in the pages of *Vogue* magazine, lounging around in the Riviera. (Perhaps the only look that dates him was his fondness for Bertie Wooster-ish plus fours.)

Edward was bullied by his nanny and claimed to have had a miserable childhood, full of hardship. He later suggested that this was why he didn't want children of his own (his childlessness was one of the reasons he was deemed unsuitable to be king). He claimed that his father had been cold, distant and given to violent bouts of anger. It's hard to know how much of his feelings stemmed from his later resentment of the royal family in general. Certainly, George V and Queen Mary were emotionally undemonstrative. Edward liked to blame all of the problems in his life on a harsh father and an unloving mother, to whom he wrote some fairly nasty letters in later life.

He was educated at home alongside his little brother, Bertie, in York Cottage at Sandringham. Their tutor, Henry Hansell, doesn't seem to have pushed the boys very hard and was more interested in trying to teach them sport. They did OK with modern languages, but grew up with zero grasp of mathematics and even struggled to write their own names. Edward never had any serious interest in arts and culture. He did learn to play the bagpipes, though, and his party trick was to jump up and play a tune after one of his dinner parties. What does it say about a man that he has no interest in intellectual pursuits, in theatre, literature and science but really enjoys the bagpipes?

In 1907, at the age of 12, he was sent away to naval college, where he gained the nickname Sardine. I have no idea why. Even as a boy, Edward was good-looking and charismatic. He was slim and frail, with a dreamy look about him, and was able to charm both sexes, but he was also very sensitive and was inevitably picked on and bullied in the navy.

When his grandfather, Edward VII, died in 1910, 15-year-old Edward became heir to the throne. He was made Prince of Wales on his 16th birthday and had his investiture the following year in a bizarre, cod-medieval ceremony at Caernarfon Castle in north Wales. The ceremony was put together by the Welsh politician David Lloyd George and had elements of olde worlde cosplay, pantomime, Welsh pageant and Ruritanian royal fantasy.

Despite being bullied, Edward had been hoping to stay in the navy, but his father sent him to Oxford University instead, where he doesn't seem to have learned anything. It was just a rubber-stamping process. When war broke out in 1914, he joined the army and served in Europe, mostly behind the lines, doing royal things like inspecting the troops. He was mainly there to boost morale and show that they were all in this together.

The main reason that Edward was kept away from the front was not that he might be killed (although that was obviously a consideration) but that he might be captured. He would have been a very useful and valuable hostage. He preferred to get around by bicycle, but sometimes travelled in the Royal Daimler, in which he did finally manage to visit some frontline troops. Unfortunately, however, his driver was hit by shrapnel and killed.

Later in the war, Edward was sent on various diplomatic missions to the Middle East and spent a lot of time in Paris, drinking and dancing to jazz bands in the nightclubs and visiting high-class brothels. This was more like it. But when the war ended, the process of finding him a suitable bride swung into action. He wasn't particularly interested in any of the various princesses who were presented to him, however. Public tastes were changing, as was protocol. Edward felt that these arranged, political marriages were all a bit medieval and that marrying for love might be a better bet. By this time, he'd already started to have affairs with other men's wives and had also had a fling with a French courtesan, who he'd met in Paris in 1917, called Marguerite Alibert. He became absolutely infatuated with Marguerite and wrote her a series of rather explicit letters which she astutely kept hold of.*

The chief among Edward's mistresses was Freda Dudley Ward, the socialite wife of a Liberal MP. His relationship with her lasted until 1934 when he dropped her for Wallis Simpson. The king and queen, who had a very upstanding, stuffy, dull lifestyle, were appalled by Edward's womanising and sent him away to act as a royal ambassador to keep him out of the public eye. Edward was the first monarch to do a royal walkabout, mingling with commoners at events, shaking hands and engaging them in small talk. He was a big hit everywhere he went – the US, Canada, Australia, New Zealand, India …

Edward might have given off an aura of being a suave, stylish, modern, bright young thing, but he had some extremely retrograde views and was less troubled by imperialist racism than his father and grandfather. Believing that whites were innately superior to other races, he made some horrendous comments. For instance, in 1920, during his visit to Australia, he wrote that the indigenous people 'are the most revolting form of living creatures I have ever seen. They are the lowest known form of human beings and are the nearest thing to monkeys'.

He started out with a youthful, modern outlook and promoted the idea that royalty should be relaxed and populist, but he moved further and further to the right as he got older and ended up as a snobbish, out-of-touch, fully signed-up member of the establishment. In the 1920s, though, he was still very much the louche party boy and, as his father's health began to decline in the 1930s, people started asking whether he was going to turn his back on his wastrel playboy ways to settle down and do his duty when he became king.

---

* In 1923, while they were staying at the Savoy, Marguerite shot her husband several times from behind, resulting in a sensational murder trial at the Old Bailey. There's much speculation that Marguerite blackmailed the establishment, threatening to drag Edward into the trial and publicise his letters if they didn't pull some strings. She was acquitted.

As it turned out, the answer was no. On 10 January 1931, at a party hosted by one of his mistresses, Lady Thelma Furness, he was introduced to Wallis Simpson. Even though she was with her second husband, Ernest Simpson, an American businessman, Edward decided that this was the woman he was going to marry. He felt she was the perfect partner for him: bright and witty, a great conversationalist and an excellent hostess who was very good at gathering the right people around her.

Wallis had spent some time in China and there were a lot of scurrilous rumours going round that she'd been very promiscuous out there and had learned secret oriental sex techniques. How else to explain her hold on Edward? She was certainly no more beautiful than his previous lovers. There's zero evidence that Wallis misbehaved in China, however. In the end, perhaps, as an American, she had fewer of the repressed hang-ups of English women. Or perhaps Edward was simply in love with her.

Whatever the case, Wallis set about divorcing her husband so that she could marry Edward, but he must have known that this would be problematic. The Church of England didn't allow divorcees to marry in church while a former spouse was still living and Wallis would have two of them. Edward was also the future head of the Church of England and sworn to uphold its values. The Archbishop of Canterbury, Cosmo Gordon Lang, told Edward that he couldn't marry a divorcee. Edward could be either king or Wallis's husband. He couldn't be both.

It was tacitly understood that even though the press knew all about what was going on, they wouldn't break the omerta. This meant that the British public were kept in the dark and had no idea that Edward was blithely strolling into a full-on constitutional crisis when George V died in 1936 and he became king.

Edward had grown up watching his father at his desk, opening the red boxes filled with paperwork from the government and diligently reading it. From the off, the now King Edward VIII skim-read official documents or ignored them or pushed them to one side. The government started sending him less and less paperwork, but it was clear that he was never going to engage. Perhaps they preferred him not to?

Edward had sympathetic views of Nazi Germany and didn't think too deeply about what Hitler represented. He was pro-appeasement. He thought that another war would be a terrible thing – and he was right, *nobody* wanted another war. Beyond that, though, Edward was fairly naive about politics. Later on, he wrote (actually, it was ghost-written) a fanciful and self-aggrandising memoir called *A King's Story*, in which he said the best advice he had from a courtier was 'never miss an opportunity to relieve yourself, never miss a chance to sit down and rest your feet'. So that was his takeaway from being king at one of the most volatile moments in British history.

Wallis Simpson hadn't gone away. Fed up with the goldfish bowl of Buckingham Palace, Edward set up his own separate court at a folly in the grounds of Windsor Castle called Fort Belvedere, where he could carry on partying and spending time alone with Wallis away from the prying eyes of royal courtiers. He tried to bargain with Stanley Baldwin, suggesting a morganatic marriage in which Mrs Simpson would be married to him but wouldn't actually be queen. Even though this idea was supported by Edward's friend, Winston Churchill, it came to nothing. Stanley Baldwin pointed out that Edward would have to convince not just him but the whole government, the British people, the British establishment, the rest of the Commonwealth and, indeed, the whole empire. All these parties would have a say in the proceedings because he was their king. Rather flippantly, Edward said that there weren't that many people in Australia, so their opinion didn't much matter, which wasn't very helpful.

In the early thirties, Edward had campaigned for the less well off in society, making several rousing speeches and radio broadcasts, and had seemed to be genuinely concerned for the lot of the working man. In November 1936, he visited the shuttered Dowlais Iron and Steel Works in south Wales, an area devastated by the depression. He engaged with the mostly unemployed locals, noting that 'these works brought all these people here. Something should be done to get them at work again'. Baldwin saw this as an attack on his government and an attempt to intervene politically and he became even less keen to accommodate the king's wishes. So, how genuine was Edward's concern for the workers in his kingdom? Well, not long after his visit, he abdicated and ended up doing nothing for them. In the end, he cared more about himself and Wallis Simpson.

We may never know the full truth of why Edward went through with his abdication. Was he calling Baldwin's bluff? Was he hoping the PM would beg him to stay and work out a compromise? Or did Wallis Simpson call Edward's bluff? Did she want to end the relationship and gave Edward an ultimatum – 'Marry me, or I'm off' – hoping he'd choose monarchy over marriage? Did the government think that Edward was making idle threats and it would all blow over? Or were they thinking that this would be a good way to get rid of a potentially harmful monarch who was going to be nothing but trouble?

To make matters worse, the newspapers were wobbling. They couldn't risk looking foolish if the news got out before they broke it, and on 3 December they reneged on their vow of silence and began reporting on the affair. Eventually, on 11 December (the same date on which James II had given up the throne in 1688), Edward threw in the towel. His reign had lasted only 325 days. He broadcast to the nation saying, 'You must believe me when I tell you that I have found it impossible to carry the heavy burden of responsibility and to discharge my duties as king, as I would wish to do, without the help and support of the woman I love.'

Most of the public thought the speech very romantic and touching, like something out of a Mills & Boon novel.

So, Edward's younger brother, Bertie, was thrust, blinking and stammering into the spotlight and Edward was demoted to Duke of Windsor. Wallis Simpson became a duchess but was never allowed to be addressed as Her Royal Highness, which rankled Edward 'til his dying day, believing this to be a terrible slight.

After abdicating, he moved to France and married Wallis. Not a single member of his family showed up. When you're out, you're out, Buster. Edward moaned that he wasn't given enough money to live on and was always sending begging letters to Bertie, who took pity on him and sent him large amounts of cash. It came out later that Edward had lied about his wealth and had actually amassed a substantial fortune while he was Prince of Wales and during the short time that

EDWARD AND MRS SIMPSON AND HERR HITLER

he was king. He and Wallis lived a very comfortable life as moneyed expats.

One of the first things the happy couple did was visit Nazi Germany in 1937, where they toured factories and were introduced to high-ranking Nazis. They also met Hitler and Edward gave a slightly fey Nazi salute. He and Wallis enjoyed being treated like royalty, they liked the flattery and attention, while Hitler and the Nazis felt that their visit was a PR coup and gave them the stamp of approval.

When France fell to the Germans, Edward and Wallis fled first to Madrid and then to Portugal, which was neutral at the time but was maggoty with spies, counter-spies, Nazis and Germans of all stripes. Joachim von Ribbentrop, the German minister of foreign affairs, put together a plot to kidnap the duke, called Operation Willi. The Nazis' idea was to set him up as a sort of alternative English king, just as they'd done when they'd installed Marshal Pétain as their puppet ruler of France.

The plot was never put into action, but Edward was very vulnerable in Portugal and so the British government appointed him governor of the Bahamas, which he hated. He felt he'd been sent to a third-rate British colony in the middle of nowhere. Despite seeing the local black population as inferior, he did try to do something for them. He looked into the problems of poverty, civil unrest and low wages, which he blamed on mischief makers, communists and Jews. He also took on a black Bahamian, Sydney Johnson, who later became his valet.

Edward remained ostracised from The Firm and resigned his governorship as soon as the war ended to go back and live in Paris. He hardly ever saw his family again. In 1952, he was allowed to attend the funeral of his brother, George VI, but he wasn't invited to Queen Elizabeth's coronation the following year.

Edward aged rather quickly. He'd always been a drinker and a heavy smoker, and, in 1972, he died from throat cancer. His body was brought back to England with a certain degree of royal ceremony and lay in state in St George's Chapel in Windsor, where it was visited by a huge procession of the public.

Wallis Simpson lived on longer as something of a recluse, occasionally giving interviews as this strange royal curiosity. Eventually, after a long period of dementia, she died in 1986 at the age of 89.

40

L̲E̲AVING G̲EORGE 6

GEORGE VI – 1895–1952

Bertie

Reigned 1936–1952

Lived for 56 years. Reigned for 15 years.

Died from lung cancer.

Remembered for: the Second World War.

George VI only reigned for 15 years and, for six of those, Britain was at war. The Second World War was the central and defining event of his reign. But what sort of a man was he? Well, he modelled himself on his father, the dull but dutiful George V, rather than his glamorous but deeply flawed and self-centred older brother, David, who had little sense of duty and would have been a terrible wartime king. Bertie wanted to come across as an ordinary family man, who, like his subjects, was just trying to get his wife and children safely through a terrible war – *We're all in this together*. In public, he came across as plain and straightforward; behind the scenes, though, he had a violent temper (so many similarities with his father). He was shy, self-conscious and enjoyed all the same things as his daughter Elizabeth – horses and dogs and everyday country pursuits. He was by no means an intellectual, but then the British have always been suspicious of intellectuals.

George had been christened 'Albert' to keep Queen Victoria happy and soon became known as Bertie. There still seemed to be an aversion among the royals, however, to having a King Albert. So he was crowned George VI, although his family carried on calling him Bertie. As he wasn't expected to become king, he led a fairly simple life before his brother abdicated in 1936. Bertie was a few days shy of 41 when it happened, and, because of his awkwardness and self-consciousness, he hated the prospect of being king. He told his mother, Queen Mary, that when he heard that Edward was going to abdicate, he burst into tears. When he came to the throne, however, he tried hard to be diligent and to dutifully carry out his royal tasks to the best of his abilities. The part he dreaded most was having to deliver speeches in front of thousands of people, particularly as he had a bad stammer and a difficulty pronouncing his Rs.

Bertie was sent away to naval college while still a boy. He was not academically minded and only just scraped through his entrance exam. At the end of his training period, he managed to come 67th out of 68 – and, even then, some strings had been pulled to make sure that he *did* actually graduate as a junior officer.

He enjoyed life in the navy and got on with his fellow officers, even though he suffered badly from seasickness and developed a mysterious stomach complaint. He'd never been very robust. He'd been so knock-kneed as a child he'd been made to wear splints. And now, despite having his appendix removed, his stomach problems didn't go away. He stayed in the navy, though, and when the First World War broke out, he served as a turret officer on HMS *Collingwood* during the Battle of Jutland in 1916 – a key naval battle of the war, from which the German navy struggled to recover. His brother, David (Edward), who never saw active service, was eternally jealous of him.

In 1917, Bertie joined the Royal Naval Air Service (which eventually became the Royal Air Force) and although he liked flying no more than being at sea, he qualified as a pilot and, two years later, became a squadron leader. After the war, he was sent to Trinity College, Cambridge, where he enjoyed the freedom more than the studying. Even at Cambridge, Bertie had staff around him, including an equerry called Louis Greig, who'd previously been one of his tutors. The two of them started playing tennis together and turned out to be pretty good. They won the RAF tennis doubles in 1920 and, in 1926, they made it into the first round of doubles at Wimbledon, where they were resoundingly thrashed. Bertie was left-handed and a bright spark in the crowd shouted 'Try the other hand, sir'. He found the whole thing so humiliating that he never played tennis in public again.

In 1920, when he was 24, Bertie attended a ball at the Ritz where he met Lady Elizabeth Angela Marguerite Bowes-Lyon, the ninth child of Claude Bowes-Lyon, from an old aristocratic Scottish family. Not being very confident around women and lacking the experience of his womanising older brother, Bertie decided to keep things simple and propose to the first woman who took any interest in him. Elizabeth was a classic no-stuff-and-nonsense, stomping-around-on-the-Scottish-moors-in-stout-shoes-and-unflattering-cloche-hat type. She was quite a sturdy woman and the sharp-tongued Wallis Simpson called her 'Cookie' because, as far as she was concerned, Elizabeth looked like a lumpen Scottish cook who rather enjoyed her own pies.

Knowing that she'd have to give up a lot of the things that she enjoyed in life if she were to marry a royal prince (and actually preferring his equerry), Elizabeth turned Bertie down. But Bertie persevered and proposed again, only for Elizabeth to turn him down again. In fact, it took him three attempts before she eventually gave in, after a long walk yomping through the countryside together. Resistance was futile; Bertie obviously had very strong feelings for her.

Elizabeth turned out to be a very good choice. She became a well-loved queen. Most people today will remember her as the Queen Mum and will only have known her as an eccentric old lady. She had a good long life and lived to 101, by which time she'd become something of a comic figure: a gin-swilling, fag-smoking, soap opera-watching old dear with yellow teeth who liked to have a flutter on the gee-gees. But during George's reign, she was his stalwart partner and support. He relied on having someone tough to help him overcome his shyness and lack of confidence.

Elizabeth and Bertie returned from an imperial tour in 1925 in time for him to give the closing speech at a big British Empire Exhibition at the new Wembley Stadium. Bertie had been dreading it but he did his duty and went ahead. It was as much of an ordeal for him as for the audience, who had to stand there listening to him stuttering and searching for his words, unable to say some of them. Rumours started going round that he was mentally deficient and not fit for public office, and, in 1926, having tried several treatments before without much success, he approached an Australian speech therapist called Lionel Logue to help him deal with his stammer.

Logue's technique wasn't really based on any established scientific underpinnings, but it worked very well for Bertie and the two of them became lifelong friends. Logue had enough initial success with Bertie to provide the future king with the confidence to travel to Australia and New Zealand and give several speeches in 1927, which all went off without any comment.

That same year, Bertie and Elizabeth moved into a house in Piccadilly, using the Royal Lodge in Windsor Great Park as their place in the country, and, by the end of 1930, they had two girls, Elizabeth and Margaret. Their life was casual and informal, and the family could often be seen cycling together in Windsor Park where they would obligingly stop for photographs. Bertie always wanted to make himself accessible to the public and was happy to meet them, chat to them and, as I say, give the appearance of being one of them.

He was interested in labour relations and the lot of the working man and was happy to talk to trade unionists (although he wasn't very happy when Buckingham Palace staff tried to form a union). In fact, he got so involved in industrial relations that he became known by the family as 'The Foreman'. He even set up a scheme to bring working-class and public-school boys together at the Duke of York's Camps, a series of summer camps where there were games and competitions and discussions around the campfire. Bertie would turn up as 'The Great Chief' and lead singalongs of 'Underneath the Spreading Chestnut Tree', complete with all the gestures.

His life remained placid until the constitutional crisis of 1936. Other than advising Edward not to go through with his threatened abdication, he tried to stay out of it and the two brothers didn't meet in person. The two of them had never really been close and their relationship now soured completely. Bertie was shocked and disgusted when Edward quit.

Bertie was crowned as King George VI at Westminster Abbey on 12 May 1937, the date that had been planned for Edward's own coronation. The ceremony was broadcast by BBC radio and parts of it were filmed by the newly formed BBC Television Service – although cameras weren't allowed into the abbey itself. The footage was sent round the world as a Pathé newsreel and Bertie's radio broadcast to the empire that evening was delivered pretty much faultlessly.

All of the ugly rumours that his stammer had worsened, that he suffered epileptic fits, that he would barely be able to undertake his royal duties were forgotten and the nation had confidence in him to do his job properly and serve as king. It was going to be tough, though; his older brother may have been blasé about Hitler, but his threat was now all too obvious. The prime minister, Neville Chamberlain, visited the Führer in Munich in September 1938 and returned with a promise that there would be no war. George was so pleased with Chamberlain that he invited him onto the balcony at Buckingham Palace to share his joy and relief with the crowds. In many ways, it wasn't done to have a monarch so openly supporting a prime minister, but these were exceptional circumstances. The memories of the First World War were still vivid in people's minds and nobody was eager for a repeat of that apocalyptic conflict. Ninety-two per cent of the population didn't want a war with Germany and Winston Churchill was one of the few politicians who opposed the idea of trying to be nice to Hitler.

Chamberlain's appeasement policy is still controversial. Many historians believe it bought Britain more time to prepare for war, while others argue that Britain was already well-prepared (the country was the leading armaments exporter in the first half of the 1930s) and that, if we'd confronted Hitler sooner, we might have stopped him. We'll never know.

Whatever the case, Britain had an extra year to secure stockpiles of raw materials around the empire, to build more aeroplanes, tanks, ships and artillery, and manufacture ammunition. In 1939, King George was the first reigning monarch to visit the United States where he made sure he reinforced his relationship with President Franklin D. Roosevelt. In fact, George probably did more to bolster Anglo–American relations than the government. He had been nervous about the visit because his suave and self-assured brother had been such a hit in the US, where he'd been treated like a movie star. But George's old-school, upper-class British charm and reserve went down very well. He and Elizabeth were equally well-received in Canada. If war broke out, Canada was going to be absolutely crucial. There's an idea that 'Plucky Little Britain' held out during the Second World War completely alone, while the rest of Europe fell, that this tiny cluster of islands managed to stand up to the might of Hitler. Well, yes, but those tiny islands were at the heart of a worldwide empire that included Australia, Canada and India. As long as Britain could ensure that convoys and flights could get through, it had massive support, plus reserves of raw materials, food and manpower to call on. So, it was very important for George to visit places like Canada to get assurances and strengthen relationships.

In September 1939, he had to give the speech of his lifetime when he announced that Britain was at war. If you listen to his radio address, you can sense him concentrating to work around his stammer, but his slight hesitation could equally well be because he was struggling to keep his emotions in check.

In his Christmas speech, three months later, he included some lines of poetry by Minnie Louise Haskins that he'd seen in *The Times*: 'I said to the man who stood at the gate of the year/Give me a light that I may tread safely into the unknown.' The well-chosen words cemented the idea that George was going to be there for his people, that he was going to help them through this war. They would walk side by side through the darkness.

Six years later, over 50 million people were dead, including 357,500 British citizens and another 466,000 from the Commonwealth.

At the outbreak of war, Neville Chamberlain was old and sick. Bertie wanted him to carry on, but, after a military disaster in Norway, Chamberlain threw in the towel and a national government, made up of politicians from all parties, was formed. King George wanted Lord Halifax to lead it, but he felt that Winston Churchill would be a more capable wartime leader and stood aside.

So, more by chance than design, the UK ended up having the right people in place to lead the country through the war: King George VI and Winston Churchill. At first, Bertie disliked Winston, who'd been a big supporter of Edward, but after a few meetings, the king realised that he and Churchill made a very good partnership. Churchill gave extraordinary, rousing and fiery speeches, and his tough, no-bullshit attitude in parliament went down very well when balanced with George's quieter, more measured and reassuring approach. The two of them started to have lunch together every Tuesday and they ended up having about 200 of these get-togethers. No one else was allowed to be in attendance. No bigwigs from the palace, no members of parliament or the civil service. These were informal, private conversations, in which both participants could say exactly what they wanted and they found it enormously useful.

When Germany started bombing England – and London in particular – there were discussions about evacuating George and his family to Canada, but Queen Elizabeth said that the children wouldn't go without her, she wouldn't go without George, and George just wouldn't go. So that was that.

At the height of the Blitz, London was being bombed almost every night and, from the start, George and Elizabeth went out and about in London to show their presence and support. George would appear impromptu, knowing that if he announced a visit in advance, the unwieldy and expensive royal apparatus and cumbersome security detail would lumber into action and make it an ordeal. It wasn't long before Buckingham Palace itself was bombed. Queen Elizabeth was glad, saying that, now, 'we can look the East End in the face.'

In all, Buckingham Palace was bombed nine times during the war. The royal princesses were moved to Windsor – where they would often sleep in the dungeons. The king and queen stayed for the most part in Buckingham Palace attending to business, but visited their daughters as often as they could, and themselves slept at Windsor during times of very heavy bombing. The royal family also joined every other family in the country in accepting rationing of both food and clothing. Of course, being the royal family, they got more coupons than the average household, but they did stick with it and, by the middle of the war, when George appeared in the newsreels, people would stand and applaud.

George was able to visit frontline troops on a few occasions. In 1943, he travelled to north Africa after the defeat of the Axis Powers there and, on the way home, he put in at Malta, the strategic island in the middle of the Mediterranean that had been part of the British Empire since 1814. Malta had held out against repeated German attacks and was crucial to the British Navy and shipping. He awarded the whole island the George Cross, the medal he'd created to honour civilians who'd helped in the war effort.

In 1945, he gave a well-received speech in parliament to members of both houses and broke down at the end when he talked about the death of one of his younger brothers, Prince George, Duke of Kent, who'd been killed on active service in 1942 when a seaplane carrying him and several officials crashed in Scotland near Dunbeath.

Once again, King George had put himself on the same level as his subjects. So many families had lost husbands, sons, fathers and brothers, as well as mothers, sisters and daughters. Some 70,000 civilians were killed in the war.

By the end of the war, there had been no general election for 10 years and people were asking what they'd been fighting for. They wanted change, they wanted a fairer country that cared for all its people. Churchill was voted out and a Labour government elected under Clement Attlee. Attlee was a modest man – 'with much to be modest about,' according to Churchill – but he did make significant changes. His government overhauled the welfare state and the school system, nationalised the railways and many industries, and established a free National Health Service. King George supported many of the Labour government's reforms and understood that Britain could no longer justify ruling a quarter of the planet. He played an important part in the development of the Commonwealth, a system whereby countries who wanted independence could still keep their connections to Britain and the benefits it brought them. In 1947, only two years after the war, India won its independence, spelling the end of the British Empire.

By now, George was quite ill with chest, heart and throat problems that his doctors tried to downplay even to George himself. There's a tradition whereby the royal household don't let the general public know how ill a monarch is until it's all too late. Announcements are often made along the lines of 'The king is slightly unwell. Oh, and by the way, he's just died.'

George's illness was kept secret from everyone, but it was obvious something was wrong when, in 1951, he had a lung removed. The following year, against his doctor's advice, he went to the airport to see his daughter Elizabeth off on a royal tour. While she was away, George died. He was only 56. Just like his father, George V, and his grandfather, Edward VII, he'd been a heavy smoker all his life and it was eventually lung cancer, not Hitler's bombs, that finished him off.

41

THEN LIZZIE 2

ELIZABETH II – 1926–2022
Lilibet/Brenda
Reigned 1952–2022
Lived for 96 years. Reigned for 70 years.
Died of old age.
Remembered for: being the UK's longest-lived
and longest-reigning monarch.

Elizabeth is the first monarch in this book that I actually met in person. In June 2006, she threw a garden party at Buckingham Palace for her 80th birthday, themed around British children's literature. I was invited, along with just about every British children's author you could think of, and we were all presented to her. She went down the line saying hello and had a very clever technique for getting through these things. As she reached out to shake your hand, she simultaneously pushed you away, so that she could move swiftly on to the next person. Prince Philip came along behind her mopping up, full of bonhomie and cracking jokes, and then it was over.

There was a barbecue in the evening for the authors, with a few minor royals in attendance. A lady-in-waiting told me that the queen would have really liked to be there and was probably watching from one of the palace windows, but had had to make the decision a couple of years ago about whether she'd join in. She couldn't change her mind now because it would have meant a different level of security. It confirmed my suspicions that it wasn't a great life being the queen, when she couldn't even go to her own barbecue. That was why she liked escaping to Balmoral, because the estate was big enough and private enough that she could behave as close to a normal person as possible. What a change she saw in her lifetime, from happily cycling round Windsor Great Park as a child to being a prisoner in her own palace as an old woman.

She lived her whole life in public, in a world of ever-increasing media scrutiny. Every aspect of her reign has been picked over and she was one of the most photographed people in history.* And yet, she somehow remained very private. It's impossible to separate her from her 'role' and, despite all that exposure, did we really know her at all? In the end, she was 'The Queen' – an entity, not a person. Her success largely stemmed from the fact that she embodied the idea of 'royalty' very well and, essentially, while all those around her struggled, squabbled, made a lot of noise and made a lot of history, she, herself, did nothing.

Because she lived for so long, she saw huge changes during her reign. When she came to the throne, homosexual acts were still criminal; by the time she died, gay weddings were legal. She lived through the invention of the birth-control pill and the sexual revolution, rock 'n' roll, the Beatles, psychedelia, heavy metal, prog rock, glam, disco, punk, ska, electronica, rap, hip hop, drum and bass, rave and Glastonbury, vinyl, cassettes, CDs, streaming … She saw the death penalty abolished. She saw men walk on the moon. She saw the eruption of the Troubles in Northern Ireland in the late 1960s and an agreement being finally reached in 1998. She saw computers become everyday items that transformed the world of work and leisure, and she saw the birth of the internet, a wonderful invention that opens a window into the universe and all human knowledge – but also into every level of hell.

Queen Elizabeth had such a thoroughly documented life that I can't do it justice in one short chapter so, instead, I'm going to simply present 45 facts about her.

1. Elizabeth was the longest-reigning *female* monarch in history. King Louis XIV beat her to the position of longest-reigning monarch of all time (at 72 years and 110 days). He was only four

---

* Although with the ubiquitousness of the smartphone, your cousin Rita's adorable, new, little baby Bruno has probably already had more photographs taken of him than the late queen.

when he came to the throne, though, which gave him an immediate advantage over the 25-year-old Elizabeth.

2. My meeting the queen was no big deal. She carried out 21,000 royal engagements during her reign and hosted more than 50,000 guests at Buckingham Palace *every year*. It's believed that 31 per cent of the British population either met the queen in person or saw her at one of her public appearances.

3. The lives of 007 and Queen Elizabeth were intertwined. *Casino Royale*, the first James Bond book, was published in 1953, the same year that Elizabeth was crowned, and the two of them became probably the most famous male and female representatives of Britain. Elizabeth attended the premieres of three James Bond films. The 11th Bond book was called *On Her Majesty's Secret Service* and, famously, Elizabeth and Bond appeared together in a short film for the opening of the 2012 London Olympics, where the two of them 'parachuted' into the Olympic Stadium together. In the end, Daniel Craig's James Bond died the year before the queen.

4. Queen Elizabeth was born just six weeks before Marilyn Monroe, making them pretty much the same age. But the queen (like Victoria) is remembered as an old lady, whereas Marilyn died at 36, so her image is forever youthful.

5. Paul McCartney famously said that when he was a teenager, he thought the Queen was a babe. He was 10 when he watched her coronation on the TV – and here was this glamorous young woman with a radiant smile. Both Churchill and Attlee announced the dawn of a new Elizabethan age and there was a feeling that Elizabeth was a different type of monarch for changing times.

6. The Queen was a shape-shifting lizard. At least according to the former goalkeeper, TV sports presenter and conspiracy theorist David Icke.

7. Fifteen prime ministers served under her. The first was Winston Churchill – a monumental presence in British history. Her last was Liz Truss, a footnote to history and a figure of fun. Whatever you may think of Churchill, it was very much a case of going

from the sublime to the ridiculous. Along the way, she dealt with the likes of Harold Wilson, Edward Heath, Margaret Thatcher, Tony Blair and Boris Johnson – an interesting line-up. Six ex-PMs, and Truss, attended her funeral, the number being so high because towards the end, the Conservatives were getting through a prime minister nearly every week.

8. Elizabeth was also queen to 170 prime ministers of Commonwealth and Dominion countries and, as the most travelled of all British monarchs, she made sure she met them all. Crucially, she also knew who they all were. After one state visit to Canada, the premier said that Elizabeth knew more about what was going on in his country than any of the foreign politicians he'd had dealings with.

9. She only had one sibling, Princess Margaret, who was born in 1930 – a fascinatingly flawed, and quite tiny, character who never got over being second fiddle to her big sister. Elizabeth was very serious, dedicated and dutiful, always on her best behaviour. Margaret was the complete opposite.

10. Elizabeth and Margaret were educated at home under the supervision of their mother, and their governess, Marion Crawford. 'Crawfie' was very close to the girls and, when she retired, she was granted a grace-and-favour house in the grounds of Kensington Palace. But when she wrote a very innocuous and sweet little book called *The Little Princesses*, against the advice of the palace, she was completely ostracised. Neither the Queen nor any member of the royal family ever spoke to her again and she was kicked out of her house.

11. Elizabeth's parents tried to give her as normal an upbringing as possible. In 1937, a special Girl Guides group, the 1st Buckingham Palace Company, was formed so that she and her sister could socialise with girls of their own age. The group was made up of children of the aristocracy, the royal household and estate workers, and they did things like make camps in the Palace gardens.

12. During the eight months of the Blitz, when it was too dangerous for the family to sleep at Buckingham Palace and they decamped to Windsor every night, the princesses kept up morale by putting

on shows and staging pantomimes to raise money for the war effort.

13. In 1940, near the start of the war, Elizabeth made her first radio broadcast at the age of 14, which went out during the BBC's *Children's Hour*. The speech is on YouTube and sounds like a ridiculously plummy parody of a young Queen Elizabeth, using a style of pronunciation that has completely disappeared. Even at that age, Elizabeth wanted to reassure every child listening that she was doing her duty and serving her country. 'We are trying, too, to bear our own share of the danger and sadness of war.'

14. Elizabeth's speech of 1940 was echoed in her speech of 2020 during the COVID pandemic: 'We will succeed. And that success will belong to every one of us. We should take comfort that while we may have more still to endure, better days will return. We will be with our friends again. We will be with our families again. We will meet again …'

15. The image of her sitting, masked and alone, at the funeral of Prince Philp is a very a poignant reminder of the miseries of the COVID pandemic. About the same number of UK civilians died of COVID in 2020 as were killed during the whole of the Second World War.

16. Elizabeth was famous for using the royal 'We'. It was her and her subjects as a single entity, all in it together.

17. Elizabeth's catchphrase was 'My husband and I'. She used it perhaps once too often in her annual Christmas broadcast and her many speeches, and, by the 1960s, it had been picked up on and satirised so much that she stopped using the phrase. In a speech she gave at the Guildhall on her 25th wedding anniversary in 1972, she said 'I think that everybody really will concede that on this, of all days, I should begin my speech with the words "My husband and I".'

18. Another phrase that she regularly used was 'Have you come far?'. She was introduced to so many people over the years and had no time for any kind of meaningful conversation with them (particularly as it was not done to ask her a personal question) that she used the phrase as an all-purpose ice-breaker.

19. Towards the end of the war, in 1945, Princess Elizabeth joined up. She was made a second subaltern in the Auxiliary Territorial Service, where she trained as a driver and a mechanic. She was photographed fixing army vehicles and the image stuck. She was often to be seen driving her beaten-up old Land Rover across rough terrain in Balmoral and gave the impression that if it broke down, she'd jump out and fix it herself.

20. At the end of the war, on VE Day, Elizabeth and Margaret left Buckingham Palace and went out onto the streets of London, incognito, to mix with the celebrating crowds. 'We asked my parents if we could go out and see for ourselves. I remember we were terrified of being recognised ... I remember lines of unknown people linking arms and walking down Whitehall, all of us just swept along on a tide of happiness and relief.'

21. Elizabeth got to know Prince Philip of Greece and Denmark during the 1930s. They were distantly related (as all the royal families of Europe are) and could both trace their ancestry back to Queen Victoria. In the 1940s, Elizabeth decided that this was the man she wanted to marry. The establishment were a bit sceptical about him, as he didn't have any money of his own. The Greek royal family, having been abolished in the 1920s and restored in 1935, was a little shaky. Some advisers didn't think that Philip was good enough for Elizabeth, but in November 1947, they married. He was never King Philip, though, and he had to renounce all his other titles. When he and the queen had children, they were given the surname Windsor. 'I'm just a bloody amoeba,' said Philip. 'I'm the only man in the country not allowed to give his name to his own children.'

22. Austerity and rationing were still in place in 1947 and Elizabeth made a big show of using her clothing coupons to make her wedding dress.

23. Elizabeth's coronation in 1953 was the first to be filmed and broadcast live to the general public, which led to a huge boost in television sales and was a real leg-up for the BBC. Despite the inevitable opposition from the stuffier members of parliament

(most notably Churchill) and the palace, it was a major PR coup for the queen both at home and abroad.

24. The coronation was a global broadcast, connecting to the rest of Europe via the newly built Eurovision Transmission Network and proving that you could successfully broadcast live to the whole of Europe. It was the catalyst for the Eurovision Song Contest.

25. Shortly before the coronation, Princess Margaret told Elizabeth that she wanted to marry Peter Townsend, a divorcee. Margaret could have had a civil wedding, but would have had to renounce her right of succession. Elizabeth took the blame for banning the marriage, putting royal protocol before family but, in the end, Margaret liked being a royal princess and it was as much her decision to call the wedding off.

26. Elizabeth was the first reigning monarch to visit Australia and New Zealand, and the crowds that came out to meet and greet her were staggering. About three quarters of the population of Australia saw her.

27. Unlike her father and her grandfather, Elizabeth never had to lead the country through anything as cataclysmic as a world war, but there were some minor wars, in Suez, the Falklands, Iraq and Afghanistan, not to mention the Cod Wars (disputes, really, rather than *actual* wars, over fishing rights in the North Atlantic).

28. There was also the Cold War. In 1951, it came out that a group of men at the heart of the British Secret Service were communist double agents working for the Soviet Union. The first of the 'Cambridge Spy Ring' to be uncovered were Donald Maclean and Guy Burgess, who managed to escape to the Soviet Union. Their co-conspirator, Kim Philby, escaped 10 years later in 1963, after which the British intelligence services dug deeper and discovered two more members of the ring, Anthony Blunt and John Cairncross, neither of whom was publicly exposed until much later. The wider scandal was originally kept under wraps, but it came out that Anthony Blunt had worked for the Queen as surveyor of the royal paintings while known to be a spy.

29. The next major scandal was in 1956 when the Egyptian president, Gamal Abdel Nasser, decided that he would take over running

the Suez Canal, as it, basically, went through his country. The British prime minister, Anthony Eden, wanted to send in the army to secure it for the West, but he couldn't convince the US to come on board. Instead, he made a coalition with France and Israel and went ahead with his plan anyway. The military campaign was successful, but politically it was a disaster, and seen as bullying by a fading imperial power, desperate to regain status and influence. Worldwide condemnation (particularly from America) forced Eden into a humiliating withdrawal.

30. There were two final stages in the death throes of empire during Elizabeth's reign. Margaret Thatcher's attempt to re-establish the UK as an imperial nation by engaging in the Falklands War in 1982, was one. The return of Hong Kong to the Chinese, in 1997, was the other.

31. The queen had a notoriously pronounced 'resting bitch face'. She often appeared to have a face like thunder during royal appearances but claimed that was just how she looked in repose.

32. Elizabeth lived in a private wing of Buckingham Palace, in a slightly homely style, and kept her breakfast cereal in a Tupperware box.

33. When Prince Andrew was born in 1960, it was the first birth to a reigning monarch for 100 years. Charles had been born in 1948 and Anne in 1950, with Elizabeth's fourth child, Edward, arriving in 1964.

34. In 1966, a mountain of waste from the local coalmine in Aberfan in south Wales slipped during heavy rain and engulfed part of the village, including, most tragically, the school, killing 116 children and 28 adults. The Queen didn't want to be a distraction and a diversion, and thought that a royal visit would get in the way of the emergency services, so she initially stayed away. The general public viewed this as cold, distant and uncaring. Eventually, after eight days of vocal criticism, a visit was organised. When Elizabeth arrived, she made an effort to talk to local people and was obviously very concerned and upset by what had happened, as was every other mother in the country, so she was forgiven.

35. In 1969, Elizabeth, reminded of how successful the broadcast of her coronation had been, reluctantly allowed the BBC and ITV to make a joint TV documentary about her everyday life. *Royal Family* was watched by something like 37 million viewers in the UK and 350 million worldwide. But Elizabeth considered it a big mistake and promptly had it withdrawn. God knows why – it's dull rather than intrusive.

36. The 1970s were a difficult time for everyone. There was an energy crisis, crippling industrial action, the introduction of the three-day working week to try to save energy, people leaving the country in droves and 'Long Haired Lover from Liverpool' by Little Jimmy Osmond was a number-one hit single.

37. In 1977, Johnny Rotten sneered 'God save the queen/She ain't no human being', but while a few punk rockers jumped up and down and professed to be anarchists (me included), the majority of the population celebrated the Queen's silver jubilee with street parties and patriotic Union Jack bunting, drinking tea out of mugs with her face on them. It was a celebration of Britishness, a big event to bring the whole country together with Elizabeth as the figurehead. Johnny Rotten later went full Tory and said he thought the Queen was actually better than the Sex Pistols.

38. The Queen liked horses, corgis (she had 30 of them over the years) and Paddington Bear.

39. In 1979, two things shook Elizabeth. First, Anthony Blunt was finally exposed as a member of the Cambridge Spy Ring, and then the IRA blew up Lord Mountbatten and members of his family on a fishing boat in Ireland. Mountbatten was the embodiment of the British Empire. He'd been Prince Philip's uncle and mentor, a close adviser to the Queen and the last Governor-General of India who'd overseen independence and partition.

40. The Queen herself was the target of some fairly half-hearted assassination attempts. In 1981, during the Trooping of the Colour, a 17-year-old teenager called Marcus Sarjeant fired six blanks at her. A typical lone crank. The Queen stayed calm and skilfully controlled her horse, making her popularity rating soar.

QE II AND HER CORGIS

In the same year, on a visit to New Zealand, another young
crank, Christopher John Lewis, fired at her with a .22 rifle but
missed. He was only charged with unlawful possession and
discharge of a firearm.

41. In 1982, Michael Fagan twice broke into Buckingham Palace, and
on the second occasion managed to make his way to the Queen's
bedroom. She quickly scarpered and went to get help, but it was
a long time in coming and security at the palace was exposed as
being pretty shoddy. The idea that she and Fagan had a good old
chat is sadly a myth.

42. In the 1980s, the tabloid newspapers dropped any sense of
deference and went overboard on royal coverage. Kelvin
MacKenzie, the editor of the *Sun*, basically told his staff that he
wanted stories about the royal family every week. Apparently he
didn't care if it was all made up as there was little the royal family
could do about it, and it sold a shitload of papers. Tabloid
exploitation of the royal family persists to this day.

43. The lowest point for the Queen was 1992. She described it as her
annus horribilis. There had been a rise in republicanism and bad
press following the publication of details about just how wealthy
the royal family were. The marriages of all her children, except
Edward, were falling apart. Someone threw eggs at her on a state
visit to Germany and, to top it all off, there was a devastating fire
at Windsor Castle. With her speech, the Queen was once again
saying, 'I'm just like you. I can have bad years, too', with an
implied request for a bit of privacy.

44. In 1997, Princess Diana was killed in a car accident in Paris and,
just as after the Aberfan disaster, Elizabeth was accused of not
caring as she showed no *public* grief. People screamed that the
Queen hadn't flown the Buckingham Palace flag at half-mast,
despite the fact that she wasn't at Buckingham Palace (she was at
Balmoral), so they weren't allowed to fly a flag at all. But then, of
course, people asked why she was hiding up at Balmoral. The
PM, Tony Blair, eventually persuaded her to make an 'emotional'
speech to the nation where she stressed that she greatly admired
Diana and felt her loss, particularly as a grandmother to the two

princes. It worked and Elizabeth was reinvented as the beloved granny of the nation.

45. After that, she stayed in public favour, so much so that when she died of 'old age' (possibly bone marrow cancer) in 2022, more than a quarter of a million people queued to see her coffin, lying in state in William II's Westminster Hall (another 33,000 had queued to see her lying in state in Edinburgh). Nobody could believe that she'd gone. It was the passing of a second Elizabethan era and the dawn of a new age of uncertainty.

42
WITH CHARLIE NEXT TO SEE US THROUGH

CHARLES III – 1948–
Reigned 2022–

That's it. We've reached the end of the rhyme with 'Charlie next to see us through'. How could I have known when I learned it in the 1960s that I'd have to wait so long for Charlie to become king? Elizabeth was our longest-reigning monarch and Charles was our longest-serving Prince of Wales, the oldest heir to ever come to the throne.

I'm not going to say much about Charles. His reign is still ongoing as I write this and we probably won't make sense of it until 10, 20, 50, 100 years' time, when future historians will look back and be able to see clearly what happened, what was important and what was a distraction. Who knows what future events will come tearing out of the blue and cause history to jump the rails. What will be the future versions of the Twin Towers attack, the crash of 2008, Brexit, COVID, Putin's invasion of Ukraine, Donald Trump …?

I can't quite believe that this story, which started with William the Conqueror crossing the Channel with a load of men dressed in chainmail, has ended with driverless cars, Netflix-and-chill and the *Voyager* space probes hurtling through space, transmitting information back to us from more than 15 billion miles away. We've covered nearly 1,000 years of history, from the Normans through the Plantagenets, the Crusades, the Wars of the Roses, the Renaissance, the Reformation, the Tudors, the Stuarts, the Interregnum, the Restoration, the slave trade, the growth of empire, the mad Hanoverians, the Industrial Revolution, the growth of parliament and civil rights, two world wars, and here we are with Charles. And he can follow that same story, the big difference being that all the kings and queens we've covered are, one way or another, all his ancestors.*

And how will Charles's story end? So far, he hasn't had a chance to do very much and his health problems have kept him away from the public eye more than he would have wanted. When he went in for a routine prostate operation at the start of 2024, his doctors discovered cancer and the secretive nature of the royal court means that we have no way of knowing how serious this is.

Charles seems to be a fundamentally decent bloke – self-conscious, occasionally petulant and, like many of his generation, emotionally cautious and reserved. The writing was on the wall for his marriage to Diana when, on the day she and Charles announced their engagement, the couple were asked by a reporter if they were in love. 'Of course we are,' replied Diana. 'Whatever "in love" means,' added Charles. As a relic of an older, more emotionally undemonstrative generation myself, suspicious of love heart emojis and gushing senti-mentality, I know what he meant. Diana, though, was clearly traumatised.

That being said, Charles is no royal gammon. If he'd been king in the Middle Ages, he would have failed. He's not warlike, he's not a ruthless alpha male. He's quiet and thoughtful, he's set up numerous charities to help the less well-placed in society, he reads books and he writes books (the best known of which is his children's book *The Old Man of Lochnagar*). He's almost as famous for his biscuits, sold through his 'Duchy Originals' organic food business, as he is for being king. He was interested in nature, conservation and protecting the environment long before it was fashionable. He talks to his plants. He's definitely more Henry VI than Henry V.

For someone of my age, Charles's story is very well known. I've grown up with him as a constant presence. I vividly remember watching his investiture as the Prince of Wales when I was an 10-year-old schoolboy in 1969. Here was this slightly awkward young man, uncom-

---

* If you were willing to put in the time and effort, you could probably trace a family line back to William I as well, but that wouldn't make you a monarch.

fortable in his crown and robes, and he's been on our television screens ever since.*

The facts of his life are too well known to go into here in any detail. He grew up with a love of the radio comedy series *The Goon Show* and has displayed a sense of humour uncommon among British monarchs. He was the first heir to the throne not to be educated at home and had a pretty miserable time at school. He did a history degree at Cambridge and then served in both the Royal Air Force and the Royal Navy. He was deeply affected by the death of his great-uncle, Lord Mountbatten, who'd been an alternative father figure for him. His marriage to Diana was a mistake. The two were ill-suited: Charles was nearly 13 years older, serious, introverted, emotionally cautious, intellectual. Diana was none of those things; she was a straightforward, outgoing, kind, emotional and caring young woman who preferred Billy Joel and Duran Duran to Bach and Haydn. They both had well-publicised affairs and fought their corners via competing biographies. Diana won and became an international superstar, Charles became a bit of a laughing stock.

He was dogged by a run of controversies, rumours, scandals, disasters – Squidgygate, Tampongate, Jimmy Savile, the Black Spider Memos, the death of Diana in a car crash, the Carbuncle Controversy, Poundbury, homeopathy, Harry and, of course, the behaviour of his younger brother, Prince Andrew, the Duke of York.†

In his younger days, when he still looked dashing in his uniform, Andrew was known as Randy Andy, an epithet that hasn't aged well. It's interesting that both he and Harry are 'spares', neither of them ever being first in line to the throne. If you've been paying attention through this book, you'll have noticed that spares have often caused trouble for the monarch. As I said in the introduction, Harry jumping ship – saying he no longer wants to be an active member of the royal family and retreating to the US with his American wife, Meghan – has been presented by many as a major scandal that could bring down the

---

* He still doesn't know how to rock a crown, though, and always looks daft in royal regalia.

† If you're not familiar with all of these, look them up!

monarchy. But I think you'll agree that compared to some of the behaviour that I've written about in these pages, it's very minor indeed.

Charles was eventually able to marry the woman he'd always loved, Camilla Parker Bowles, in a quiet civil ceremony in 2005. And, as the memory of the all-but-sanctified Diana recedes, Camilla, who was originally painted as a wicked witch who destroyed Diana's marriage, has been rehabilitated with the public. She has proved herself to be a capable and personable woman, well suited to the role of queen, and she and Charles are obviously very happy together.

There's a slight feeling that Charles, having come to the throne as an old man, is perhaps just keeping it warm for the very popular Prince William. There were anti-monarchy protests at Charles's coronation, but the republican movement in the UK isn't particularly strong. My feeling is that when William comes to the throne with, god willing, Kate at his side, it will be a big PR boost for the royal family.

I started this book by saying I was neither a monarchist nor a republican but, having told their story, I find that I'm fatally drawn to the royals. Their lives, their stories, their portraits, their castles and their palaces connect us Brits to our history and provide a colourful but twisted thread to follow through it.

I've come to the conclusion that being a monarch is a thankless task, though. Most of the kings and queens in this book ended their lives in misery. But at least British monarchs are trained from birth in diplomacy, statesmanship, shaking hands, surviving tedious dinners and the art of not picking political sides, so they're ideally suited to being heads of state. In a world of rabble-rousing, populist demagogues intent on tearing down everything around them in return for clicks and likes, I think an elected head of state would be a complete disaster.

You may well have a very different view and are already polishing your guillotine, but I hope you've enjoyed this story.

ACKNOWLEDGEMENTS

I've always been a bit suspicious of endless acknowledgements at the ends of books, but I've realised now that if you're writing a history book, you do need a hell of a lot of help (particularly if, like me, you're not really a historian to start with).

First of all, I'd like to thank Joel Simons, my commissioning editor at Mudlark, who approached me out of the blue and asked if I thought Willie Willie Harry Stee would make a good book, and, as that had been my dream from the beginning, I thought *This is the man for me*. His advice and editing suggestions have all made this a much better book than I ever hoped to achieve. Gaurika Kumar was also a huge help on the editing front. As was Nige Tassell, who had the unenviable task of copy-editing my efforts, and then the amazingly patient Daniel Watkins who had to fact-check more than 1,000 years of history, written by someone who never had the rigorous academic training of a proper historian and who made up a lot of stuff off the top of his head. If any mistakes *do* remain, they are my own, not Daniel's. Sometimes, in my efforts to tell a good story, I've had to sneak some dubious 'facts' past him.

Huge thanks to Jim Moir for the illustrations. Thanks to the rest of the team at HarperCollins: Sarah Hammond, Orlando Mowbray, Christopher Kwok, Hetty Touquet, Tom Dunstan, Dom Brendon, Ben Hurd, El Slater, Claire Ward and Alan Cracknell.

Over the course of making the *Willie Willie Harry Stee* podcast, I've had more than 60 different historians on as guests. These guys are the real experts and I've learned so much from talking to them. They were all chosen because they'd either written books about the monarch I was looking at, or about the wider history of the time. A special thanks to Tom Holland for being my first-ever guest and giving me the historical stamp of approval.

If you want to read in more detail about any of the monarchs in this book, or get alternative takes on their stories, then I can recommend all of the books mentioned below. All but a handful of these writers have been my guests and I take this opportunity to thank them heartily for giving up their time and their expertise to an amateur like me.

OTHER HISTORIES OF THE MONARCHY

Various authors – *The Penguin Monarchs* series. These are very good short books about individual monarchs. Where I've mentioned specific ones below, it's because the author was a guest on the podcast.

Stephen Bates – *The Shortest History of the Crown*. The *Shortest History* series is excellent.

Tracey Borman – *Crown and Sceptre*. An expert on the royals, particularly the Tudors.

Suzie Edge – *Mortal Monarchs*. An entertaining look, from a medical point of view, at how every monarch died.

David Mitchell – *Unruly*. Damn, he got there before me! (But he only goes up to Elizabeth I.)

The Ladybird History Books – Short and beautifully illustrated. I grew up reading these and they instilled in me a love of history. They even did a two-volume *Kings and Queens of England* (you could have saved yourself a lot of time and just read that instead).

GENERAL BRITISH HISTORY

James Hawes – *The Shortest History of England*. The best book on English history ever written!

James Hawes (again) – *Brilliant Isles: Art That Made Us*. A look at British history through carefully chosen cultural artefacts.

Robert Lacey – *Great Tales From English History*. Really fun and accessible. The inspiration for my podcast.

Marc Morris – *The Anglo-Saxons*. A look at what happened before the Normans arrived.

Simon Jenkins – *A Short History of England*. A very thorough, well-told history.

Matthew Lewis – *History Hit Guide to Medieval England*. Matt really knows his stuff. Fun and accessible.

Ian Mortimer – *Time Traveller's Guides to Medieval/Elizabethan/Restoration/Regency England*. What was life like for ordinary people in these periods? From fashion to food, to housing, to illness, to religion …

Suzannah Lipscomb – *A Visitor's Companion to Tudor England*.

Helen Castor – *She-Wolves: The Women Who Ruled England Before Elizabeth*. A great book about key women of the Middle Ages.

THE MONARCHS

WILLIAM I & WILLIAM II

Marc Morris – *The Norman Conquest*

Tracey Borman – *Matilda: Wife of the Conqueror, First Queen of England*

Judith A. Green – *The Normans: Power, Conquest and Culture in 11th-Century Europe*

HENRY I

Charles Spencer – *The White Ship*

STEPHEN & MATILDA

Catherine Hanley – *Matilda: Empress, Queen, Warrior*

Matthew Lewis – *Stephen and Matilda's Civil War: Cousins of Anarchy*

HENRY II

Matthew Lewis – *Henry II and Eleanor of Aquitaine: Founding an Empire*

John Guy – *Thomas Becket: Warrior, Priest, Rebel, Victim*

RICHARD I

Dan Jones – *The Plantagenets: The Kings Who Made England*

Dan Jones – *Crusaders: An Epic History of the Wars for the Holy Lands*

KING JOHN

Nicholas Vincent – *John: An Evil King?* (Penguin Monarchs series)

Nicholas Vincent – *Magna Carta: A Very Short Introduction*

Marc Morris – *King John: Treachery, Tyranny and the Road to Magna Carta*

HENRY III

Sophie Therese Ambler – *The Song of Simon de Montfort: England's First Revolutionary*

Thomas Asbridge – *The Greatest Knight: The Remarkable Life of William Marshall, the Power Behind Five English Thrones*

EDWARD I
Marc Morris – *A Great and Terrible King*

EDWARD II
Helen Carr – *Sceptred Isle: A New History of the Fourteenth Century*

EDWARD III
Ian Mortimer – *The Perfect King: The Life of Edward III*
Helen Carr – *The Red Prince: The Life of John of Gaunt, the Duke of Lancaster*

RICHARD II & HENRY IV
Helen Castor – *The Eagle and the Hart: The Tragedy of Richard II and Henry IV*

HENRY V
Dan Jones – *Henry V: The Astonishing Rise of England's Greatest Warrior King*
Juliet Barker – *Agincourt: The King, the Campaign, the Battle*

HENRY VI
Amy Licence – *Henry VI & Margaret of Anjou: A Marriage of Unequals*
Joanna Arman – *Margaret of Anjou: She-Wolf of France, Twice Queen of England*

EDWARD IV
Amy Licence – *Edward IV & Elizabeth Woodville: A True Romance*

EDWARD V
Matthew Lewis – *The Survival of the Princes in the Tower: Murder, Mystery and Myth*

RICHARD III
Alison Weir – *Richard III and the Princes in the Tower*
Matthew Lewis – *Richard III: Loyalty Binds Me*

HENRY VII
Nathen Amin – *Son of Prophecy: The Rise of Henry Tudor*
Nathen Amin – *The House of Beaufort*
Nathen Amin – *Henry VII and the Tudor Pretenders*

HENRY VIII

John Guy & Julia Fox – *Hunting the Falcon: Henry VIII, Anne Boleyn and the Marriage That Shook Europe*

John Guy – *Henry VIII* (Penguin Monarchs series)

Tracey Borman – *Thomas Cromwell: The Untold Story of Henry VIII's Most Faithful Servant*

EDWARD VI

Stephen Alford – *Edward VI* (Penguin Monarchs series)

MARY I

Anna Whitelock – *Mary Tudor: England's First Queen*

ELIZABETH I

Tracey Borman – *Elizabeth's Women: The Hidden Story of the Virgin Queen*

John Guy – *My Heart is My Own: The Life of Mary Queen of Scots*

Stephen Alford – *The Watchers: A Secret History of the Reign of Elizabeth I*

JAMES I (& VI)

Anna Whitelock – *The Sun Rising: James I and the Dawn of a Global Britain*

Clare Jackson – *The Mirror of Great Britain: A Life of James VI & I*

Alexander Courtney – *James VI: Britannic Prince*

CHARLES I

Leanda de Lisle – *White King: Charles I, Traitor, Murderer, Martyr*

Leanda de Lisle – *Henrietta Maria: Conspirator, Warrior, Phoenix Queen*

OLIVER CROMWELL

Jonathan Healey – *The Blazing World: A New History of Revolutionary England*

CHARLES II AND JAMES II

Charles Spencer – *To Catch a King: Charles II's Great Escape*

Charles Spencer – *Killers of the King: The Men Who Dared to Execute Charles I*

Clare Jackson – *Charles II* (Penguin Monarchs series)

Rebecca Rideal – *1666: Plague, War, Hellfire*

WILLIAM AND MARY
Ophelia Field – *The Kit-Cat Club: Friends Who Imagined a Nation*

QUEEN ANNE
Ophelia Field – *The Favourite: The Life of Sarah Churchill*
Jane Ridley – *Queen Anne* (Penguin Monarchs series)

GEORGE I, II, III AND IV
Catherine Curzon – *Kings of Georgian Britain*
Catherine Curzon – *The Real Queen Charlotte: Inside the Real Bridgerton Court*
Catherine Curzon – *The Elder Sons of George III*
Alice Loxton – *Uproar!* (a look at the Georgian printmakers and satirists)

WILLIAM IV
Roger Knight – *William IV* (Penguin Monarchs series)

QUEEN VICTORIA
Jane Ridley – *Victoria* (Penguin Monarchs series)

EDWARD VII
Jane Ridley – *Bertie: A Life of Edward VII*

GEORGE V
Jane Ridley – *George V: Never a Dull Moment*
Alexandra Churchill – *In the Eye of the Storm: George V and the Great War*
Alexandra Churchill and Nicolai Eberholst – *Ring of Fire: A New Global History of the Outbreak of the First World War*

EDWARD VIII
Alexander Larman – *The Crown in Crisis: Countdown to the Abdication*

GEORGE VI
Alexander Larman – *The Windsors at War: The Nazi Threat to the Crown*
James Holland has written many excellent books on the Second World War – too many to list here. Check them out for yourself.
Sally Bedell Smith – *George VI and Elizabeth: The Marriage That Shaped the Monarchy*

ELIZABETH II & CHARLES III
Craig Brown – *A Voyage Around the Queen*
Alexander Larman – *Power and Glory: Elizabeth II and the Rebirth of Royalty*
There are also several great books by Dominic Sandbrook about this period.

Willie, Willie, Harry, Stee,
Harry, Dick, John, Harry three,
One-two-three Neds, Richard two,
Henrys four, five, six – then who?
Edwards four-five, Dick the bad,
Harrys twain and Ned the lad,
Mary, Bessie, James the vain,
Charlie, Charlie, James again,
William & Mary, Anna Gloria,
Four Georges, William and Victoria,
Edward, George, then Ned the eighth
quickly goes and abdicat'th,
leaving George six, then Lizzie two,
with Charlie next to see us through...
That's the way our monarchs lie
since Harold got it in the eye!
PS. Sorry, Lady Jane Grey –
you got the 'chop!